DATE DUE

BRODART   Cat. No. 23-221

Taming the
Great
South
Land

Taming the Great South Land

A History of the Conquest of Nature in Australia

WILLIAM J. LINES

UNIVERSITY OF CALIFORNIA PRESS

Berkeley and Los Angeles

To the memory of my
grandmother
Mary McRae (1888–1988)
an Australian pioneer

and for
Earth First!

First published in 1991
Allen & Unwin Pty Ltd

First published in the USA in 1991 by
University of California Press
Berkeley and Los Angeles

ISBN 0 520 07830 6

Library of Congress Cataloguing-in-
Publication Data has been applied for

Set in 11/11.5 Bembo by Adtype Graphics, NSW
Printed by Kim Hup Lee Printing Co Pte Limited, Singapore

FOREWORD

MY GRANDPARENTS were driven out of Japan by poverty at the beginning of this century. They came to Canada to seek their fortune. They had no intention of staying in what they considered a 'primitive' and backward country, all they wanted was some of its wealth to take back home. My grandparents were aliens in an unfamiliar landscape with which they had no historical or cultural link, let alone a sense of reverence for its sanctity. Instead, Canada to them represented an 'opportunity', the land was a 'commodity' full of 'resources' to exploit. My grandparents became a part of a massive assault on the New World begun after Columbus' arrival and causing vast ecological and human catastrophe.

Following the Second World War, my family moved to Ontario, the industrial heartland of Canada and the most populous province in the country. First in Leamington, then London, I grew up in a land named after the homeland of the original European settlers. There were few reminders that this area had long been occupied by people with proud histories, people who had been mistakenly labelled 'Indians' by the newcomers. But lumped together as red Indians were dozens of Nations including Algonquins, Mohawks, Cree and Ojibway. Today, the aboriginal peoples of Canada are invisible, sequestered on reserves or extinguished through forced assimilation.

In London, we lived on the northwest edge of town next to the railway tracks along whose banks I would pick asparagus in the spring and hunt for insects. One summer I worked on a vegetable farm only a mile or so down the railway line. A few blocks east of our house was the Thames River which was full of catfish, carp, bass and sunfish which I would catch for my family to eat. The first softshell turtle I ever saw was in the Thames. In the spring, spawning striped bass, pickerel and pike would jam the river.

Bicycling west on Oxford Street, I would quickly run out of pavement and hit the gravel road. In about 20 minutes, I'd be at my grandparents' 10 acre farm at the end of Proudfoot Lane. But first I'd always stop at the large swamp beside the road to look for frogs, snakes and damselflies. Many times I returned home with boots full of mud and bottles with frogs' eggs and dragonfly larvae. The woods surrounding the swamp always beckoned with the promise of a glimpse of a fox, skunk, raccoon or owl.

My grandparents' farm was a child's paradise. Besides large vegetable and berry patches to be raided, there were several hundred chickens to be fed, eggs to be gathered and fences mended. At the end of the fields, a creek ran year round. That was where I dipped for darters, discovered freshwater clams and hunted snails. In the fields, pheasants tooted like trains, groundhogs sunbathed in front of their burrows while hawks skimmed above the ground in search of rodents.

In the thirty-five years since my boyhood, the Thames River has been saturated with industrial effluent and agricultural runoff accumulating along its length. The river was too convenient for dumping garbage and chemical wastes. Now there are few clams, crayfish or minnows to be seen. Londoners today recoil at any suggestion of eating fish from the Thames or asparagus from the tracks.

When I arrived in London in 1950, its population was just over 90 000. Five years later, we were proud when the city passed 100 000. By 1960, it had almost doubled to over 185 000, and reached a quarter of a million 10 years after that. Today, London boasts 300 000 people. This spectacular rate of growth was accompanied by a booming economy and a sense of civic pride. But at what cost?

The road to my grandparents' farm is now a wide highway with the city extending all the way to the village of Byron. My grandparents' farm is occupied by a cluster of highrise apartments while the creek runs through culverts. My beloved swamp is covered by an immense shopping mall and parking lot while the woods beside it have given way to a huge housing complex. Along the Thames River and all around the city, once productive agricultural land has been converted to housing subdivisions.

Within my lifetime, the ecological devastation has been massive. But when my grandparents emigrated to North America, the real holocaust had already occurred. Only two hundred years ago, Ontario was covered by a dense, ancient forest, the plains of the midwest echoed to the hooves of 60 million bison while the skies were darkened for days on end by billions of passenger pigeons. By the beginning of this century, they were all gone, yet we have learned little from that unprecedented ecological annihilation and continue our destructive rampage so that we can see the destruction before our eyes.

In the topsy turvy world of economics, farmland, swamps, woods, rivers and ponds adjacent to expanding cities acquire value that makes them irresistible for development. So the animals and plants disappear while increasingly, our children grow up in a sterile human-created environment. But with diminished opportunities to experience nature, our future generations become even more estranged from the systems that support their lives.

My hometown of London is a microcosm of what has been happening around the planet, but particularly in the New World and especially since the Second World War. Seen from a plane above Canada today, the land is crisscrossed by geometric straight lines of highways and rectangles of clearcuts and agricultural fields. Everywhere the imprint of human beings has been stamped on the land in mathematical precision that pays no attention to geographic and biological realities. We act as if our political subdivisions of the land are meaningful and fail to observe the realities of 'bioregions', ecosystems and watersheds to which living things conform.

Our alienation from the land is so great that we have no sense that it is sacred so that our ability to exploit it is a great privilege accompanied by responsibility. Impelled by our faith in our technological prowess and scientific knowledge, we assault the planet as if it is limitless and endlessly self-renewing. Like an exotic species introduced to a new environment, we feel no natural restraints, only the deadly belief that all of nature is there for us to use as a resource in any way we wish. The great Chief of the Nishga Nation, the late James Gosnell, lived his early life in British Columbia as a nomadic hunter-gatherer as his people had done since the beginning of time. He told me about the first time he had come across an area of the forest that had been clearcut by loggers. He said he couldn't breathe and his chest ached as he tried to comprehend how anyone could treat a forest in such a terrible way.

Why spend so much time on Canada in a preface to Bill Lines' book, *Taming the Great South Land: A History of the Conquest of Nature in Australia*? Because the story Lines tells was not unique to Australia, it was repeated over and over in different parts of the world. Driven by a profound disconnection from the land, newcomers to the New World sought to tame it and its human and nonhuman occupants. The combined technology and the western attitude of rightful dominion over Nature, were unstoppable. That has been the legacy passed on to the present time.

Lines' magnificent book puts the lie to the myth of the heroic history of modern Australia and reveals it as the sordid tragedy it really was. Seen from a perspective of respect for the unique flora and fauna of the continent and the indigenous people whose cultures were so exquisitely evolved to live in rich harmony with the land, technological and economic optimism of the British invaders becomes a policy of greed, shortsightedness and arrogance.

It can be argued that one of the great tragedies that led to the current crisis in wilderness destruction was the attempt by colonising peoples to re-create their familiar European surroundings in alien lands. In Australia, forests, grassy plains and swamps, were forced to become like bits of home. And the introduction of species like sparrows, foxes and rabbits was an ecological catastrophe.

It's all there in Lines' story which should be required reading for anyone who wants to understand the roots of today's global ecocrisis. In this heartbreaking story is the hope that we may recognise that deliberate decisions and conscious choice often altered the course of history. That being true, then if we recognise the folly of our current path, we can act to change directions. The history of Australia says we must act quickly.

DAVID SUZUKI, 1991

CONTENTS

Note on

MEASUREMENT

Where possible this book employs contemporary units of measurement. Equivalent measures and conversion to metric units are given below.

	currency	
12d (12 pence)	1s (1 shilling)	
20s (20 shillings)	£1 (1 pound)	$2
	weight	
	1 pound	.453 kilograms
2240 pounds	1 ton	1.02 tonnes
	length	
	1 inch	25.4 millimetres
12 inches	1 foot	
3 feet	1 yard	
1760 yards	1 mile	1.61 kilometres
	area	
4840 square yards	1 acre	.405 hectares
640 acres	1 square mile	
	capacity	
	1 pint	.568 litres
8 pints	1 gallon	
8 gallons	1 bushel	

ACKNOWLEDGEMENTS

MOST ACKNOWLEDGEMENTS begin or end with an admission that without the help and presence of certain individuals and/or institutions the author would not have written the book in question. Not so with *Taming the Great South Land*. During the two years I spent on this book I worked entirely alone, without corporate, state, institutional or collegiate encouragement. This book would have been written come what may. It was made necessary and possible by all those who made Australia's history and whose deeds are recorded on the landscape and in libraries. I am indebted to the existence of both.

Under the philistine and remorseless imperative of the bottom line, Australian governments appear intent on privatising libraries, if not outright then through stealth, by means of budget cuts and insidious 'user pays' fees. During their evolution into profit centres, libraries offer users shorter opening hours, overburdened staff and restricted access.

Fortunately I did not require extended assistance from the under-financed and under-provisioned libraries of Australia. I found almost all the information I needed at the library of the University of California at Berkeley. With preference towards none and equal treatment for all, the staff there extended unfailing courtesy and assistance to an unknown, unaccredited individual. I record here my gratitude.

The alacrity which characterises public institutions in the United States is not, unfortunately, duplicated in the private sector, particularly among publishers. Publishers in Australia, however, still accept and read unsolicited manuscripts; for their initiative, enthusiasm and counsel, I thank my editors at Allen & Unwin, Mark Tredinnick and Bernadette Foley.

The advice of two friends made the work better. The timely and stringent intervention of Peter Vintila saved me from many potentially embarrassing lapses of logic and clarity. The persevering, resolute and loyal scrutiny of my sweetheart Carol Hartland challenged my complacency and rendered intelligible much otherwise obscure and remote writing. To Peter and Carol, my thanks.

As at the beginning, so at the end—final responsibility for the book rests with me.

WILLIAM J. LINES
Sydney, March 1991

INTRODUCTION

*CIVILISATION DID NOT BEGIN IN AUSTRA-
LIA UNTIL THE LAST QUARTER OF THE
EIGHTEENTH CENTURY.*

Manning Clark, A History of Australia,
1962

*WE ARE INDEED A CIVILISING RACE ...
WHEN WE CAME HERE, THE ABORIGINES
COVERED THESE WIDE PLAINS IN THOU-
SANDS. WHERE ARE THEY TODAY? WE HAVE
'CIVILISED' THEM—THEY ARE DEAD.*

Donald MacDonald, Gum Boughs and
Wattle Bloom, *1887*

NINETY KILOMETRES above earth's surface, America's first manned orbiting satellite streaked over the dark, undifferentiated Indian Ocean and passed over the Australian continent. The apogee of technological civilisation, the precisely calculated launch of John Glenn's spacecraft from Cape Canaveral in February 1962, finally liberated the spirit of conquest from any purpose beyond itself. Ever since the Enlightenment, the most influential men in western civilisation had convinced others that progress in science and technology and the extension of human dominion over the planet would abolish need, and that moral progress, based on the absence of need, would abolish evil and secure freedom. *Friendship 7*'s unerringly accurate and programmed orbits, however, aimed not to free people from toil, drudgery and disease but committed humankind to a new frontier, a new conquest—mastery of the cosmos—and the development of a new technology, monumentally irrelevant to building freedom and equality here on earth.

Over the western edge of Australia Glenn reported to the world a solitary glow of earthbound light: illumination sprung from the city of Perth. On the evening of 20 February, the capital and largest city in the 2.5 million-square kilometre state of Western Australia turned on public and private lights as a promotional exercise for the mutual benefit of the United States' space programme and the city. East of Perth Glenn saw only the same opaque uniformity as before: the vast interior of Australia is virtually uninhabited by Europeans, except for the graves of dehydrated nineteenth-century explorers.

Before going to bed that night I checked to ensure our outside light remained on. Although my family lived on the outskirts of

Perth, I hoped our 75 watts of veranda power would combine with the collective luminescence to provide a beacon for Glenn. Only ten years old, I believed the influential men of the city who said Glenn's brief acknowledgement of the 'City of Light' would somehow 'put Perth on the map'. People in Perth in those days craved cartographic recognition.

There were other reasons for gratefully accepting Glenn's endorsement. Australians felt with Americans a commonality, an affinity, based on the knowledge that both peoples were engaged in subduing a continent. Glenn's flight confirmed mastery and reassured Australians of their membership in the western industrial empire centred in the United States of America.

Yet, to me, in isolated, provincial Perth, industrial civilisation's ascendancy seemed tenuous and remote. I read maps well enough to see that Perth occupied but a tiny portion of the extreme west coast of an unimaginably vast continent, mostly roadless, even trackless, unprogressive and unresponsive to the imperatives of industry and the economically rational, subject only to the timeless cycles of an organic other world, of birth and death, decay and renewal. Another decade passed before a single, continuous paved road spanned the continent, linking east and west. And just ten years before Glenn's orbit, my parents had trekked down a sandy track between the citrus orchards and the bush in the town of Gosnells to build a frame house on 1.2 hectares of mostly swamp land.

Winter floods brought to the swamp migrating birds, herons, waterfowl, frogs, rodents and snakes. The rising water, the growth of reeds and algae, the hatching of tadpoles, the nesting of birds, the flight of ducks, the appearance of gilgies and freshwater tortoises, and then the drying up during the long summer filled my mind with one kind of nature: intuited nature, the experienced nature of everyday life, and a conviction that nature is real and love of nature a part of that reality. But I also lived another kind of reality, socialised and educated to understand another kind of nature: the abstract, universal, mathematised nature of western science, a world view introduced into Western Australia only 133 years before John Glenn saw the light generated by power-house dynamos.

Outside school I learned about and grew to love the Australian bush but I remained entirely ignorant of Australia's original inhabitants. Australian schoolbooks said almost nothing about the Australian Aborigines except to refer to them as savages of the most primitive kind and to their country as a wilderness. Most Australians preferred to believe that the Aborigines had melted away, not because European society had destroyed them but because their own ferocity and intractable indolence made it impossible for them to exist in civilisation's presence. Unlike the Americans who made the destruction of Indian society a commodity of Hollywood and commercial culture, most European Australians, after conquering the continent and its inhabitants, proceeded to forget about their existence. Only much later did I realise that Aborigines had once camped around our swamp to live off the winter abundance of life—the birds, freshwater crustaceans, frogs and tortoises. Until I acquired this knowledge I knew little of past relations with Aborigines except for glimpses at harrowing photographs of recalcitrants roped and chained by the neck under the watchful eye of their European masters. Not that such treatment was confined to the distant past. As late as 1958, police at Halls Creek, in the north of Western Australia, kept Aboriginal prisoners on neckchains. The State Police Commissioner defended the practice by claiming that Aboriginal prisoners preferred chaining to being locked up.

Celebrated by the felling of a tree, British civilisation began in Western Australia in June 1829 and commenced to steadily force back wild nature. Meanwhile, the first conquest of nature in Australia had actually begun 40 years before when unwilling settlers founded a colony at Sydney, 4260 kilometres east of Perth. The founding, in 1788, coincided with the Industrial Revolution in Britain, which meant for Australia no history of living with the land before industrialisation, no consciousness of making the land a home before the invention of technological civilisation. Instead, Australians grew accustomed to a highly contrived, dynamic habitat of expanding settlement and relentless invasion of the bush.

Yet in 1962, only one kilometre from my Gosnells back door, the bush stood virtually untouched. Although circumscribed by deed and bound by grid lines in survey charts, pockets—and, in places, large unbroken regions—remained physically unchanged from before the coming of Europeans. Two kilometres away a river flowed unimpeded, along a course channeled by the floods of tens of thousands of years. I felt a thrill knowing, and being repeatedly warned, I could get lost out there, in the bush.

The history of Western Australia during the 1950s and 1960s, the generalised record, open to relatively dispassionate inspection, reveals change, transformation and economic growth. The record documents a 'State on the move'—a slogan employed by the state government of the day to advertise its commitment to unlimited economic expansion. All Australia in the 1960s became subject to the post-war dominance of the politics of development, wherein governments sponsored a frenzy of destruction: razing forests, damming rivers and mounting massive mining assaults on the reefs, beaches, ranges and interior plains of Australia. During the first ten years of my life, the natural cover of one million hectares of land in Western Australia alone had been bulldozed to grow wheat. During the following decade, hundreds of thousands of hectares of forest and woodland fell each year, and by the time Neil Armstrong took a giant leap for mankind on the moon, Western Australians had obliterated another 1.2 million hectares of bushland. Trips through the countryside under assault revealed massed piles of stumps and logs, broken and splintered timber, ready for burning. Bonfires raged for weeks, leaving the broken ground scattered with ash and charcoal.

The bush outside my back door, however, belonged not to the empire under construction, but to a time antedating and possibly superseding human time, and the remembered past, the background to my own life, is static and eternal. I remember living on the edge of a continent where the grey-green jarrah forests of the western escarpment ceded the coastal plain to gum trees and banksia scrub. I remember a world of long dry summers, a land scorched by the glare of an overarching sun, of temporary relief in a waterhole from the ferociously hot easterly winds blowing dust and heat from the interior, primeval red-dirt deserts, of short, wet winters when the air burst alive, pungent with the smell of the season's first rain mingling with summer's dust, when wildflowers bloomed and grass briefly turned green. The bush, the wilderness of Australia, was then a given. Australia's droughts, floods, deserts, forests, coastline and assemblage of insects, marsupials and birds loomed much larger than my social world. Australia's limits stretched beyond where I had ever been. Civilisation's productions seemed insignificant in comparison, for the bush made no concessions to the frenzied activities of humans. Events in the bush were not those of the moment but were measured in the endless, imperceptible suspirations of a life that only casually included people. Human secondariness, however, did not worry me. On the contrary, the fact of a huge, powerful, living continent afforded a vague, yet exciting, affirmation of existence. In splendid indifference to whatever I did, the sun continued to generate energy and animals and plants lived out their own immutable cycles, as ancient as the earth. But experience overturned this possibly imagined world.

My parents were among the first to live along the sand track that became Fremantle Road, a major transportation artery linking the metropolis with the suburbs. What I later came to sense as loss, to regard as tragic—the subjugation and obliteration of the bush—they experienced only as life and necessity. Most people labour in the service of immediate interests and needs. Later generations, with the benefit of hindsight, easily spurn the significance of their predecessors' activities and lament the consequences. For my parents and for the several million people among previous generations of Australians, however, progress—the subjection of crude nature—promised opportunity, a new independence and freedom from want.

Australians since first founding had felt free to appropriate anything on or below the surface of the continent for their own use. They justified their rapacious behaviour with reference to the Enlightenment promise of a future free from decay, a promise which spoke also of confidence in human reason and of what human beings might achieve through an understanding of nature and mastery of the physical world. Nevertheless, those expectations remained largely unfulfilled; the satisfaction of material wants and the establishment of social tranquility can never be obtained through the conquest of nature. The quest for knowledge represented by the launching of space rockets from giant steel ramparts in Florida obscures the real unknown: the existence of life on earth.

While technicians at NASA made preparations for Project Apollo and the exploration of the moon, I witnessed, in Perth, successive encroachments on the bush and the swamp. Developers and land speculators built houses and constructed roads, which encouraged more houses. New neighbours complained of the pestilential presence of the swamp. And so the local authorities put down a ditch which drained the winter floods; ducks and waterfowl no longer appeared, the aestivating crustaceans and tortoises died in their burrows, frogs ceased to spawn, and the thicket of brush and water-loving trees clustered in the centre stopped flowering. And when, in the interests of suburban expansion, the town laid a pipe in the ditch and buried the swamp, the land became another sub-division. Although my parents regretted the absence of the ducks, given the necessary inevitability of progress, growth and expansion, they regarded protest as pointless.

Few among our previously scattered neighbours considered the changes an improvement. Most viewed the development as a diminishment of their surroundings. And as the vacant land filled up, as houses and new roads replaced the fields and bush, and Fremantle Road carried more and more traffic, our original neighbours sold out and left, to build anew in more open, less developed environs. We too moved to a new house in a tranquil bushland setting in the hills. Eventually, of course, suburbanisation caught up with all the movers.

Water for the thirsty new suburbs flowed from several dams in the Darling Range, the dissected edge of a plateau which covers the interior of Western Australia and terminates at the coastal plain on which Perth lies. The city, immensely proud of these engineering marvels, regularly bussed school children on educational outings to see and admire these earth and concrete monuments. Adults guided out-of-town visitors to the dam sites, which accommodated them with landscaped parking and picnic tables. The attraction probably lay in the refusal to admit a great dam holds back only water or produces nothing but electricity. People do not believe so much effort produces only material results. The dams were, in effect, icons to a rational and technical order under construction in Australia. Few of the supplicants before the smooth grey walls of concrete would have conceded the possibility of a different existence, regulated by a consciousness of living on a continent shaped only by natural processes, surrounded by oceans, where the wild creatures of the open spaces, the vast spinifex plains, and the dense forests of eucalyptus embody a human longing no less civilised for being primitive, no less real for being felt rather than thought.

After I left Perth and travelled through Asia, Europe and the Americas, I never lost the memory of that expansive sense of place which seemed possible in wild Australia. But during my peregrinations, technology and human population growth encroached on the earth's biological integrity. Never before have means of destruction been so powerfully, so efficiently mobilised against life. Wilderness is no longer the natural state of the world, stretching for hundreds of unbroken kilometres around settlements of artificial light on continental shores. The great surging, restless, avaricious megatropolis of humankind now encircles outposts of wilderness. In Australia, the bush exists only at the discretion of Australians. Australian children no longer grow up in astonishment at the greatness and vastness of the natural world, for they now truly are lords of the earth—free to destroy.

1

A CONTINENT ADRIFT

ROCK STAYS,
EARTH STAYS.
I DIE AND PUT MY BONES IN CAVE OR EARTH.
SOON MY BONES BECOME EARTH...
ALL THE SAME.
MY SPIRIT HAS GONE BACK TO MY COUNTRY...
MY MOTHER.

> *Bill Neidjie,* Kakadu Man

THE EVENTS which created Australia's unique community of plants and animals began 200 million years ago when Pangaea, the supercontinent which bound all the world's continents, started to split apart. Continental drift vitally influenced the history of life on earth, of the ancestors of every organism alive today. Pangaea had provided all creatures with a single arena for biological competition and only one set of winners in the struggle for survival and reproduction. For 200 million years, reptiles, including the dinosaurs, dominated all land animals in Pangaea and the two massive daughter continents—Laurasia in the north and Gondwana in the south—which formed after 20 million years of drift. Yet, during all this time, reptiles diversified into only 20 orders. In comparison, the Age of Mammals, which coincides with the final breakup of the continents and covers only the last 65 million years, gave rise to 30 mammalian orders. Greater numbers of mammalian forms evolved because the isolation of more and more lands, consequent upon continued continental drifting, restricted competition.[1]

Soon after the rift with Pangaea, Gondwana itself started breaking up. India broke free to begin rafting across the ocean to eventually join the Asian mainland and uplift the Himalayas. A rift formed between Africa–South America and Antarctica–Australia, but not yet enough to become an effective barrier to the movement of land animals. During early to middle Cretaceous times—beginning 135 million years ago—similar animal groups spread to all corners of the habitable world. But as the continents drifted further apart, animal populations became isolated and conditions of quarantine became decisive for the evolution of the mammals inhabiting the daughter continents of Gondwana.

The Age of Reptiles, the separation of Pangaea, and the formation and subsequent breakup of Gondwana cover vast reaches of time, yet life predates even Pangaea. Every organism alive on earth today represents the product of an uninterrupted series of organisms extending to the very beginning of life—2000 million years ago or more—an event that almost certainly occurred only once. Living beings exist because ancestral forms have reproduced with desperate eagerness ever since. Because each living form necessarily derives from another living form, and not from spontaneous generation, all life descends from a single, common ancestor. Every animal, every plant, every microbe, forms a link in an indissoluble chain of reproduction. Living systems either reproduce or disappear. Some forms have succeeded each other through a vast number of generations without changing. Some annual plants, for example, have remained unchanged for millions of years, and therefore through at least as many successive cycles.

The struggle for survival arises from a contest for progeny—an endless competition recommencing with each generation. Only one criterion governs this eternal conflict—fecundity. Through the interplay between populations and environment, the most prolific automatically survive. Although reproduction almost always leads to the formation of an identical organism, sometimes something different is born. This narrow margin of chance is sufficient to ensure the variations needed for evolution. Evolution has given rise to perhaps 500 million animal species since life began. Today, the survivors number a few million, yet every single extant organism represents the last link of a chain of life on planet earth uninterrupted over some 2000 million years. This pattern of evolution reveals no intention; no concerted action by environment on heredity can direct variation into predetermined paths. The contingency of history alone determined the outcome of the struggle to survive. There is no *a priori* necessity for the existence of the living world. Yet we exist.[2]

Each day throughout the natural history of the land that became Australia, creatures mated, gave birth, lived and died, the sun rose every morning, storms rolled across the land, rain fell, and bushfires burned forests and grasslands. Around Sydney, filled-in Triassic (230 to 180 million years ago) lakes and swamps record life's daily rhythms. Networks of fossilised sun cracks caused by the shrinking of drying mud appear on the surface of shales; pitmarked rocks reveal the impress of raindrops in soft mud; fossilised stone preserves ripple marks made by waves in shallow water and even the tracks and burrows of worms squeezing through the Triassic mud.

While still attached to Gondwana, swamps and huge lakes lay across Australia's interior. Lake Walloon, in the east, covered an area of over 770 000 square kilometres and constituted one of the largest bodies of fresh water in the history of the world. During the lake's several million years of existence, inflowing rivers deposited nearly 1500 metres of shale and sandstone sediment. Erosion of mountains provided much of the alluvium which filled Lake Walloon but the great flood of the Cretaceous, 110 million years ago, finally buried the lake and much of the rest of Australia. Although the immersion of Australia was shallow, inundation was extensive and disastrously narrowed the living space for whatever flora and fauna existed at the time.

By the end of the Cretaceous and the beginning of the Cenozoic, or the Age of Mammals, 65 million years ago, Africa and South America separated from Gondwana and afterwards, 49 million years ago, Australia rifted from Antarctica and drifted northward to its present position. The final severing of all land connections and isolation from the rest of the world meant that henceforth Australian plants and animals—the survivors of the Cretaceous flood—developed singular characteristics.

After the great flood's retreat, tropical forests spread into Australia. The modern Australian tropical rainforests, confined now to the north-east coast, survive as remnants of the original Cretaceous forest, not much different from other tropical rainforests. Some species and even genera, however, developed that were peculiar to Australia and typical of present-day open forests and woodlands: Eucalyptus, Casuarinae, Banksia, Lomatia and Persoonia.

Three main and distinct types of vertebrates evolved under Australian isolation: the Ratites (large, flightless birds like the emu) and two classes of mammals, Monotremata (egg laying mammals such as the echidna and the platypus) and Marsupials (pouched mammals), which were sub-divided into two orders—the Peramelidae (comprising several bandicoot genera) and the Diprotodontia (containing kangaroos, wombats, phalangers and a number of extinct forms).

On other continents, mammals increased their genetic efficiency by developing into placentals, in which the embryo, fed by an umbilical cord or placenta, grows within the mother's womb and is born relatively well developed. Marsupial embryos, by contrast, remain inside the mother's body for no more than a few weeks and are born, when hardly bigger than ants, to grope blindly through belly fur, tumble into the marsupial pouch and stretch their lips over one of the teats inside. There they hang until mature enough to get around on their own.

The approximately 310 extant species of native mammals in Australia include 125 species of Australian marsupials. These range in size from the tiny planigales (pygmy marsupial mice), less than 50 millimetres long, to the red kangaroos, males of which may weigh 90 kilograms and measure two metres in height. Most of the mammals now limited to Australia probably originated there, a product of scenarios never duplicated and comprising a unique assemblage of animals as specialised in the general balance of life as any that evolved elsewhere.

Of all the drifting Noah's arks of mammalian evolution only two—Antarctica and Australia—persist in isolation to this day. The unknown mammals of Antarctica perished under the ice that engulfed their world. Australia therefore became the only continent possessed of a pristine mammalian fauna. Until much later, Australia, after splitting from Antarctica, remained closed to further ingress of invertebrates.

The earliest evidence of mammalian life in Australia dates from 22 million years ago, the Miocene epoch. Reptiles, however, existed much earlier and their Australian descendants include crocodiles, tortoises, turtles, lizards and snakes—a group similar in composition to the tropical Asian reptiles. Seven-hundred-and-twenty species of reptiles live in Australia, including two species of crocodiles, 110 land snake species and 190 species of frogs. Of the world's 25 species of goanna lizards, 20 are indigenous to Australia.

While oceans constitute insurmountable barriers to most vertebrates, birds can fly. Consequently, most of the world's bird families find representation in Australia, except for vultures, woodpeckers, true finches and buntings. About one-half of Australia's 700 resident bird species are endemic and breed nowhere else. These birds provide the characteristically Australian part of the avifauna usually associated with and adapted to the climate and unique vegetation of Australia.

During the Pleistocene epoch, which began two million years ago and ended at the conclusion of the last great Ice Age, central Australia was a lush country. The climate was generally cool, and although interspersed with warmer periods, adequate rain always fell. Permanent rivers and lakes intersected the rich plains. Food grew in abundance and the green interior teemed with life. At the conclusion of the last Ice Age, 10 000 years ago, the climate became warmer and drier. The winds no longer brought masses of rain-laden clouds across the country, precipitation declined, the large rivers ran intermittently and many dried up altogether. The interior lakes became smaller and smaller, their content of salt and gypsum higher and higher, until the muddy and mineralised waters became unfit for most animal life. Many of the larger species became extinct, leaving the distinctive forms of today.

Long before the Pleistocene, since the end of the Cretaceous, the agents of erosion had shaped the Australian landscape. Warping of the earth's crust created changing patterns of low- and high-lying areas. Water and wind attacked the raised areas and gravity brought the detritus down to fill the lakes and swamps formed in the depressions. Eventually, erosion reduced vast areas of the continent to an unending peneplain, a land so worn and lowered and the fall of drainage so slight, that water no longer ran in rivers nor carried away the soil. Not since the dawn of geological history had the country been so featureless.

Eons of continental drift and erosion created Australia's present appearance and geography. The Australian continent extends 3700 kilometres south to north, from 39° south latitude to 9° south, and a maximum 4400 kilometres east to west, extending 154° to 113°

longitude, comprising an area of nearly 7750 million square kilometres. A land of plateaux and plain, only a few peaks in the south-east exceed 1500 metres, and only 7 percent of the land lies above 600 metres, less than in any other continent. Two-thirds of the land plateaux, however, average between 300 and 600 metres. Considering Australia's size, extremes of temperature are not so great as in some other lands. Parts of Australia lie well within the tropics but the greater proportion of the continent, as well as Tasmania, enjoys an essentially temperate climate. Except for a few coastal areas, however, precipitation is extremely variable, especially in the summer, and evaporation intense. Annual evaporation from an open tank exceeds annual rainfall everywhere on the mainland except in the eastern highlands. One-third of the country receives less than 250 millimetres of rain per annum and even this is very erratic. Drought is the normal condition of the inland, alternated with brief periods of heavy rains. Yet, in the whole of this immense region, only a few limited areas are absolute desert, entirely deficient in animal and plant life. Most of the country supported, until recently, a remarkable, stable mantle of plants.

Xerophytes (dry living), plants which developed means of conserving moisture, thrive under this general aridity and they dominate Australia. To cope with dry conditions, xerophytes developed tough and thick or long needle-like leaves, with stony cells and minute breathing pores, or thick bark full of insoluble resin to protect the precious sap within. Xerophytes grow large root systems which penetrate deeply to reach the merest trace of water far below the surface. Fruits are hard, woody and slowly maturing, and bear seeds capable of retaining their fertility after lying for long periods on the scorched earth until a favourable conjunction of rain and sun germinates them. Annual floras, in contrast, mature and seed so quickly that the occasionally good rains are sufficient to maintain an adequate seed supply to ensure the survival of the species.

Xerophytes belong to four main orders: Acacia, an order worldwide in extent, consisting of 800 species, of which about 500 are indigenous to Australia; Proteaceae, an order nearly confined to Australia, to which belong banksias, waratahs and hakeas;

Casuarinaceae, a family peculiar to Australia;[3] and Myrtaceae, to which belong all eucalypts and tea trees.

Eucalypts provide one-third of all the species of the family Myrtaceae and predominate in the landscape of Australia. Over 600 species of Eucalyptus grow in Australia, practically confining the genus to that continent. They span the country from the tropics to the cool temperate zone, from rainforest to desert to tree line, wherever trees will grow. The ubiquity of eucalypts unifies Australia, although the trees are far from uniform. Enormous diversity characterises the genus. Even within species, eucalypts maintain a remarkable individuality on account of their opportunistic growth form: casually shedding leaves and bark, dropping branches when too long, sprouting new growth when half-devoured by insects, incinerated by bush fires or hacked about by humans—lesions that would prove fatal to almost any other tree.

The genus reached its greatest magnificence in southern Australia. The giants here belonged among the tallest trees in the world, comparing in height, if not in girth, with the Sequoias of California. In south-western Australia the karri's (*Eucalyptus diversicolor*) smooth white trunks rose, with little taper, to 60 metres before reaching the first branch. In Tasmania grew the giant gum (*E. delegatensis*), the mountain ash (*E. regnans*) and the giant stringybark (*E. obliqua*), and across Bass Strait, in Victoria's Gippsland, grew other great forests of the same species. Eucalyptus forest and woodland continued up the eastern third of Australia, filling the plains, climbing the sides of gullies, covering the summits of the tablelands and spilling over the divide into the hinterland. Forests of eucalyptus spread far into the interior western plains, where belts of Murray River gum, water gum and coolabah lined the banks of the rivers or followed the dry watercourses, which ran only after occasional rains. Few areas, even in the heart of the continent, are without a patch or two of gum trees. While eucalyptus dominate Australian vegetation in bulk and extent, they nevertheless coexist with an astonishing variety of flora. Between 10 000 and 11 000 Australian flowering plants alone have been named.[4]

Several tens of thousands of years before the modern period of aridity the first large placental mammal arrived in Australia. Humans probably crossed onto the continent some 60 000 years ago, thousands of years before the first migrants from Asia reached the Americas.[5]

Homo sapiens found a hunter's paradise in Australia. Giant emus and marsupials lived in the Pleistocene lushness. A species of rat kangaroo grew as large as the present grey kangaroo and the largest kangaroos—about three metres high, short-faced, cumbersome creatures—towered over the first Australians. But the diprotodon, for example, a rhinoceros-sized wombat, was not aggressive, and, like most other large Australian mammals, lived exclusively on grasses and bushes. The country was full of toothsome herbivores utterly inexperienced in defending themselves against human aggressors, and they provided the newcomers with seemingly inexhaustible quantities of protein and fat. About one-third of the giant mammals that existed 50 000 years ago were extinct by 15 000 years ago. Although their demise corresponds with the arrival of the Aborigines, no clear evidence links humans to their extinction. The drying of the continent at the end of the Pleistocene was probably more decisive. Australia's megafauna had a gigantic thirst and as the lakes and waterholes dried up, they became doomed to extinction. While paleo-Aboriginal hunters may have pushed some animals over the brink to which changes in climate and forage had driven them, they possessed neither the numbers nor the weaponry to eradicate them. The passing of the large marsupials did not, however, go unnoticed. The giant creatures were remembered in the stories told from generation to generation by the descendants of those who hunted them.

Diprotodon bones are common around the mostly dry salt Lake Eyre in central Australia. According to the Dieri people who lived in the area, the deserts of central Australia were once fertile, well-watered plains. A vault of clouds covered the earth and huge gum trees formed pillars to support the sky. The trunks upheld a canopy of vegetation that protected the country beneath from the drying rays of the sun. In this roof of vegetation lived the giant Kadimakara, which often grazed in the pastures below. One day, while many Kadimakara revelled in the rich foods of the lower world, the gum trees died and toppled over. Thereafter the Kadimakara had to roam on earth and they wallowed in the marshes of Katitanda (Lake Eyre). There they died, and to this day their bones lie where they fell. After the destruction of the gum trees the small holes in the forest-roof increased in number and size until they touched one another and all the sky became one continuous hole, wherefore the sky is called Puri Wilpanina, which means Great Hole.[6]

The first Australians most impacted their environment through the use of fire. Aborigines regularly and systematically burned large areas of the country—for signalling, to open up the bush for travelling, to drive animals into traps and for longer-term hunting strategies. When rain fell after a fire, lush grass grew, which encouraged game and increased hunting prospects. Regular, low-intensity fires, which consumed the litter of leaves and branches but did not burn down the trees, were the pattern all over Australia. Many abundant species of Australian flora, in addition to being drought resistant, tolerate fire, and their proliferation must be at least partly attributed to the conflagrations which became more frequent after Aborigines arrived.

Aborigines also practised river control and on northern rivers built dams to enlarge the areas of lagoons available for fish, plant and bird life. In south-western Victoria Aborigines built dykes, races, canals, traps and stone walls to create marshlands for fish, eels and birds. Aborigines planted yams, used fire to encourage the growth of *Macrozamia*, a species of cycad, the nuts of which provided highly nutritious food, and reintroduced young animals into areas after droughts to replenish stocks.

The second large placental mammal arrived in Australia 4000 to 6000 years ago. Probably introduced from the Indian sub-continent by Asian visitors, the dingo (*Canis familiaris dingo*) competed with the other main Australian carnivores, the thylacine (*Thylacinus cynocephalus*) and the Tasmanian devil (*Sacrophilus cynocephalus*). These native carnivores survived only on Tasmania, which the dingo never reached. As a result of habitat destruction and hunting, the thylacine became extinct early this century.

The Aborigines lived in all parts of Tasmania and mainland Australia. Before the British invasion they probably numbered from 750 000 to 900 000 people, but densities varied.[7] Only about 18 000 people inhabited the 650 000 square kilometres of the arid interior of South and Western Australia, while in coastal or riverine regions and in favoured areas of northern Australia, densities probably reached as high as three persons per square kilometre. All over Australia Aborigines regularly and ingeniously manipulated their environment, not only to increase food supply, but also to increase the regularity and reliability of food resources. Nevertheless, 60 000 years of Aboriginal occupation only lightly touched the environment and did not fundamentally alter the natural fecundity of the land, nor greatly disturb relationships within the community of plants and animals living in Australia.

The natural history of the earth is a series of catastrophes, a cascade of transformations spread out over long periods. The surface of the earth cooled down, the planet's crust folded and bulged, continents emerged and mountains reared up, and as certain lands subsided, new seas surged forth. Over the millennia Australia underwent great climatic changes involving both temperature and precipitation, but the changes were never so drastic as to entirely obliterate life. Some wildlife always reoccupied the changed environment and new patterns of biological community emerged.

During the last 10 000 years gardening and livestock rearing spread over much of the world but the Australian landscape remained unaffected. Elsewhere, land cultivation and animal husbandry challenged nomadic life and brought about the domestication of men and women, bound by the demands of crops and flocks to one pocket of ground; the Australian Aborigines remained wanderers, living on what they could catch, dig up and gather.

Aborigines lived in a society with roots in the Pleistocene, the longest continuous cultural history in the world. In the Dreamtime their Spirit Ancestors roamed over the earth and created all the features and life upon the land; the task accomplished, they themselves became rocks, hills, watercourses and animals. Australia is criss-crossed with the tracks of the great creative beings. Thus were the Aborigines related to the very contours and life of the land, an essential constant which made their plan and code of life intelligible. The bands in which they lived and the tribes with which they associated did not exist as self-sufficient entities but were interdependent across the continent. Through marriage, economy, trade, friendship, ceremonial intercourse and even patterned conflict, the Aborigines built an interconnected culture across Australia. Their forms of speech, songs, poetry, religion and ceremonies expressed their total vision of life, and embodied a unique Aboriginal response to the problems generated by their own peculiar world—a response as authentic and ultimately incommensurable with that of later, more enlightened ages to their own problems. Over much of the world, agriculture permitted people to accumulate surplus and led, on the basis of the command over the surplus, to stratification, classes, permanent differences of status, and civilisation. Australia was the last of all the continents, save Antarctica, to come within the domesticating influence of civilisation.

But the changes initiated by 200 years of European occupation utterly confounded the integrity of the continent's natural cycles, evolved over 200 million years of evolution and a further 60 000 years of Aboriginal presence. Enlightened civilisation introduced a level of biological instability unmatched in the world. Since the first British settlement, Europeans have destroyed over 70 percent of Australia's original woodland and forest. Agricultural and pastoral activities have degraded two-thirds of all arable land and one-half of all grazing land. Land deterioration already costs hundreds of millions of dollars each year in lost agricultural output and imperils future production. Of Australia's 7750 million square kilometres only the unused desert areas of Western Australia contain no degraded land.

Extinction threatens one-third of Australia's mammals, most of them unique to the continent, and over 2200 native plant species, 10 percent of the total, including nearly one-quarter of all eucalyptus species. In 200 years European technology, warfare, culture and political economy have swept across the Australian landscape as an expression of manifest destiny, changing forever the face of the land. Nowhere else on earth have so few people pauperised such a large proportion of the world's surface in such a brief period of time. In under 200 years, a natural world millions of years in the making, and an Aboriginal culture of 60 000 years duration, vanished before the voracious, insatiable demands of a foreign invasion. The events, which destroyed the Aboriginal way of life and sundered a living community contrived by eons of evolution, began in Europe a few hundred years ago.

2

TERRA INCOGNITA

WHAT THE IMMENSE TRACT OF INLAND
COUNTREY [OF THE GREAT SOUTH LAND]
MAY PRODUCE IS TO US TOTALY
UNKNOWN: WE MAY HAVE LIBERTY TO
CONJECTURE HOWEVER THAT THEY ARE
TOTALY UNINHABITED . . .

Joseph Banks, 1770

ROUND 150 AD Ptolemy made an ambitious effort to map the entire known and unknown world. Because Greek standards of symmetry demanded land in the far south to balance that known in the northern hemisphere, Ptolemy invented a vast continent south of the equator. Belief in the necessary existence of a southern land mass persisted for many hundreds of years. During the sixteenth and seventeenth centuries Renaissance cartographers drew the land boundaries for a continent in the south temperate zone and affixed the name *Terra Australis Incognita*—the unknown south land. In 1597 the Dutch historian Wytfliet described the fabled continent:

> The *Australis Terra* is the most southern of all islands and is separated from New Guinea by a narrow strait ... [it] begins at two or three degrees from the equator and is maintained by some to be so great an extent that, if it were thoroughly explored it would be regarded as a fifth part of the world.[1]

European certainty of the existence of *Terra Australis* points to the durability of prejudice and myth, while the provisional *Incognita* reveals an ethnocentric arrogance towards the non-European world. Countries remained unknown only until European discovery and possession ripped away their concealing masks.

The breakup of Gondwana had, however, placed a land mass approximately where Wytfliet, with such trifling excuse, expected one, and over the next 200 years European mariners landed at many points on the continent's coast. For then-existing life on the island continent, the great south land remained incognita to those who charted the coast, named prominent features, classified the natural productions and eventually, in the late eighteenth century, took possession. Indigenous life in the great south land remained anonymous still to those who explored the landscape and settled the land, perhaps concealed forever from minds shaped by the Age of Reason. Australia's entire history since the first British settlement, in 1788, lies within the modern world. Unlike the Americas, where settlement began much earlier, European civilisation in Australia cannot claim any historical tradition or influence predating the Enlightenment.

During the Middle Ages the commands of God and fear of damnation determined individual practical decisions. People believed in a geocentric cosmos, fixed and hierarchic, where supernatural forces could, and regularly did, influence the workings of the natural order. The material severity of life, and vulnerability to the caprices of nature, to famines, epidemics and disease, compounded the repressive quality of the social order. But the new findings and habits of mind resulting from scientific inquiry during the seventeenth century and the eighteenth century Enlightenment, especially in astronomy, physics and biology, marked a major turning point in human history. A new, rational outlook undermined the medieval world view. Scientific advances promoted a method of inquiry into nature which permitted explanation of natural phenomena far superior to prior interpretation. The many scientific breakthroughs of the age convinced most educated people that a decisive break with the past had occurred. New habits of thought liberated humans from superstitious belief in evil forces, in demons and fairies.

The possibilities of improving life on earth never looked better. Commercial and industrial activity directly altering the earth—mining, drainage and deforestation—increased economic wealth and provided conditions for a world of greater justice. Shipping, metallurgy, textiles, glass, soap and paper making made unprecedented demands on the earth's resources, on a scale unknown in European history. The new demands required a new view of nature. And the scientific revolution provided one. Progressive thought promoted the notion of nature as a mechanism—a system of dead, inert particles moved by external forces, a set of objects, meaningless and valueless in themselves except insofar as they could be made to serve human interests.

The founders of modern science constructed a mechanistic model of nature which yielded context-free, value-free knowledge of the external world. They foresaw a science and technology[2] possessed of sufficient power to transform man's[3] relation to nature. Francis Bacon (1561–1626) provided the new science with the language and metaphors of conquest. Bacon saw science not just as a method of inquiry but as a project, a collective undertaking aimed at mastery of nature. *Organised* scientific research must penetrate and subdue the natural order; the knowledge acquired must serve the purposes of power—dominion over things.[4]

The harnessing and control of nature, of wind and water and fire and the earth, expanded opportunities for greater exploitation of other people. The class of men which owned and administered the scientific and technical apparatus responsible for augmenting human productivity obtained disproportionate superiority to the rest of the population. By the nineteenth century they were able to organise men, women and children to labour in factories and this gave rise to new forms of domination. For those controlling the new science and technology, power over nature turned out to be power over fellow humans. Profit could be far more effectively extracted from the many and channelled to the few. Knowledge equalled power and this formidable equation knew no obstacles. What some people wanted to learn through science about the world was how to employ nature more usefully to dominate it and other people.

The leaders of the Enlightenment, the popularisers of science, conducted war against ignorance and obscurantism, against brutality, stupidity, suppression of the truth, cynicism and disregard of human rights. They believed that just as a science of the behaviour of things explained the material world, so a science of the behaviour of men would decipher the human world. Anyone who grasped and applied the principles of this latter science could realise all the goals towards which humanity was striving. All reality, all branches of knowledge, whatever mere appearances may have indicated to the contrary, formed a rational, harmonious whole, predicated on the ultimate unity of human ends.[5]

The Scottish philosopher Adam Smith (1723–1790) provided the perfect political and economic complement to science's presupposition of a wholly rational, harmonious universe. In his *Wealth of Nations* (1776), Smith claimed to have found a grand architecture underlying the chaos of daily life; where others found discord and confusion, he found order and moral purpose. Smith had discovered the laws of the market—the invisible hand—which guided the private interests and pursuits of men and which yielded perfect harmony for the whole society. In Smith's market economy the drive of individual self-interest resulted in competition—competition which ensured the provision of those goods that society wanted. The forces of supply and demand guaranteed a supply of goods precisely in the quantities society desired and at precisely the prices society was prepared to pay. Thus the interaction of selfish men gave rise to the most unexpected of results: social harmony.

The social implications of Adam Smith's political economy provided enormous comfort to the rising class of factory owners, merchants and entrepreneurs. The *Wealth of Nations* justified the creation of a new class of human beings—the working class—competing with each other to sell a new commodity—human labour—at prices permitting previously undreamed of levels of profit. This arrangement, the division of labour between a class of capitalists (owning the means of production and buying labour) and a class of labourers (selling themselves to the capitalists) formed, according to Smith, the basis of the natural order and brooked no interference.

In the pursuit of enlightened self-interest and profit, capitalists introduced new scientific schemes for the management of labour: mechanisation, division of labour, systematic routing of the production process, and new disciplines of industrial work such as punch clocks, bells, rules and fines. During the last quarter of the eighteenth century, Josiah Wedgwood, for example, rationalised factory organisation in England. He designed a new system of pottery production based on strict division of labour, then trained workers to conform. Wedgwood aimed, through unremitting supervision and obedience to written rules and regulations covering every detail of factory work, to 'make such machines of men as cannot err'. To ensure prompt and regular attendance he introduced bells to summon workers at precisely specified times. He fostered competition and used rewards and fines to encourage punctuality and prevent loss of working time. Older workers objected to Wedgwood's regime of punctuality, constant attendance, fixed hours and drinking bans. These strictures violated centuries of traditional labour practices where workers enjoyed independence of employment and worked as hard or as easy as they pleased. But Wedgwood persisted. In common with other employers, he found a solution to the problem of labour discipline: by paying the worker so little, he or she would have to work steadily through the whole week in order to make a minimum subsistence income. Additionally, Wedgwood decided to educate workers in the new disciplines from youth. He responded to the challenge with enthusiasm. 'It is hard, but then it is glorious to conquer so great an Empire with raw, undisciplined recruits,' he wrote. Scientific attention to detail and the introduction of a supervisory foreman class enabled Wedgwood to impose new forms of oppression and control: the regimentation of human nature in the interests of production and profit. An authoritarian moral improver, Wedgwood believed that disciplining his workers was for their own good. In common with other liberal reformers of the day, he assumed his charges lacked the ability to make their own decisions.[6]

The project to master nature required a new role for reason. Originally, reason meant the activity of understanding and assimilating the eternal ideas which served as goals for humankind. The seventeenth century reinterpreted reason as a useful and even necessary tool for handling human affairs. The eighteenth-century Enlightenment, however, considered reason not merely necessary but even sufficient for the solution of *all* problems. Reason became a tool, adapted to finding means for goals chosen at any particular time. The rational became that which is serviceable and reason became the judge of life. Science transformed what counted as an end, and ends became engulfed by the very means summoned to their attainment, rendering the traditional means–ends distinction problematic.[7]

When the Swedish systematist Carolus Linnaeus (1707–1778) proposed a classification to impose rank and relationship on the multitudinous diversity and interplay of the living world, the language of means and ends became totally inappropriate. Linnaeus' comprehensive system, based on the reproductive organs of plants, introduced order and reason where incomprehensible chaos previously reigned. Development of the system represented a triumph of empiricism. Classification derived not from *a priori* theory, but from a minute and objective observation of thousands of plant species. A botanist simply counted the number of stamens and pistils in a blossom and noted their position to determine where the plant belonged in the overall scheme of things. The system encouraged the habit of thinking of organisms, and of other natural objects, as falling into well-differentiated classes, rather than as members of a qualitative continuum.

Francis Bacon had advocated that scientists join together to organise science so as to create more opportunities for discovery. The knowledge thus accumulated would bring a mastery over nature hitherto undreamed of. Accordingly, Linnaeus' European contemporaries formed and joined scientific societies to organise and relate scientific discovery on a scale never before attempted. These fraternities adopted an ideology asserting a utilitarian aim for science: domination over nature allied to the national interest. The changes wrought by science in the relation of western man to the world around him reflected a general transformation associated with the political conquest of the globe as men completely renewed their geographical and mental maps of the world. The time was approaching when no territory in the world lay beyond the reach of those in western European government and business who might find advantage in occupying or appropriating. Among the most aggressive fraternities which sought to further the coextensive interests of science, capital and the state was the Royal Society of London (founded 1662). The Royal Society sponsored Captain

James Cook's first voyage to the South Seas (1768–1771), during which he claimed the east coast of Australia for Britain.

The Society designed the voyage so the expedition's astronomer could observe, from Tahiti, the transit of Venus across the face of the sun. The data obtained would enable a calculation of the distance between the earth and the sun—which distance would serve as a unit for the measurement of the universe itself. Additionally, Cook's Admiralty instructions concerned the so far undiscovered southern continent, the unknown south land:

> Whereas the making Discoverys of Countries hitherto unknown, and the Attaining a Knowledge of distant Parts which though formerly discover'd have yet been but imperfectly explored, will redound greatly to the Honour of this Nation as a Maritime Power, as well as to the Dignity of the Crown of Great Britain, and may tend greatly to the advancement of the Trade and Navigation thereof; and whereas there is reason to imagine that a Continent or Land of great extent, may be found to the Southward [on leaving Tahiti] You are to proceed to the southward in order to make discovery of the Continent above-mentioned . . .[8]

The Society appealed to all aboard to observe carefully, record accurately, and to experiment. Few on board the *Endeavour* arrived in Australia better equipped to execute those instructions than botanist Joseph Banks. Animated by the scientific spirit, Banks wanted to know the details of the natural world—he had little time for metaphysical speculation—and his economical, arranging mind put Linnaeus' system of taxonomy to unprecedented use. Banks excelled at botanising and he appropriated flora at every opportunity. At Madeira he collected 18 fish species and listed 230 plant species as wild, naturalised or cultivated, 25 of them hitherto unnamed; at Rio de Janeiro, even without going ashore, Banks managed to obtain material on 316 plants; at Tierra del Fuego he found 104 species of flowering plants, six ferns, a *Lycopodium* and 34 mosses and lichens. In the Society Islands, although he remained close to the coast at all times, Banks gathered some 255 species, and in New Zealand, again confined to the coast, he found some 400 species.

Banks' diary records the first sighting of the Australian mainland on the morning of 19 April 1770. Apparently unexcited, he dismissed the coast as sandy and retired below until an afternoon report of water spouts induced him above decks. On the 22nd he wrote, because of the absence of smoke from fires, which elsewhere indicated cultivation, 'we thence concluded not much in favor of our future friends'.[9] Banks' chance of intercourse with the country's occupants came six days later when, after the *Endeavour* put in at what Cook later named Botany Bay, he boarded a boat to the shore. A man and a boy fiercely contested the Englishmen's attempts to land, and repeatedly threw spears, despite gunfire from the crew in the boat. The opponents—from the Gamaraigal tribe—withdrew only after being several times wounded by musket shot. Later, Banks discovered some children huddling together in a hut, into which he 'threw some beads, ribbands, cloth, &c, as presents', and confiscated some 40 to 50 spears.[10] Besides dispensing largesse, Banks collected so many plants at Botany Bay their preservation became a problem. Of the country's inhabitants Cook observed, 'all they seem'd to want was for us to be gone'.[11]

On the sixth of May the *Endeavour* left Botany Bay. In the far north the ship struck a coral reef and with the crew engaged in repairs, Banks gathered about 300 more species of plants. But after a while he became bored and impatient to leave; by then Linnaeus' technique had served its purpose and nothing more about Australia remained unknown. On July 28 Banks confessed: 'Botanizing with no kind of success. The Plants were now entirely compleated and nothing new to be found, so that sailing is all we wish for if the wind would but allow us.'[12]

In three months of exploration Cook charted 3700 kilometres of Australia's east coast and named the most prominent landmarks. Although he examined the country at Botany Bay and at Endeavour River, in the north, he kept brief his landings at six other places and the explorers did not venture far from the shore. Banks, however, became acquainted (in a Linnaean fashion) with over 400 species of Australian flowering plants.

Cook's instructions contained orders to take possession of the *Terra Australis* if he found it unoccupied or, if occupied, with the consent of the indigenes. Cook did not find the country unoccupied, nor did he seek the consent of the occupiers when, on 21 August 1770, on Possession Island off the northern-most part of Australia, he carried out a final act of annexation and declared:

> ... the Eastern Coast from the latitude South down to this place I am confident was never seen or visited by any European before us, and Notwithstanding I had in the Name of His Majesty taken possession of several places upon this coast, I now once more hoisted English Colours and in the Name of His Majesty King George the Third took possession of that whole Eastern Coast from the above Latitude [38° South] down to this place by the name of *New South Wales*, together with all the Bays, Harbours, Rivers and Islands Situate upon the said coast ...[13]

Britain's new possession, however, did not impress Banks and he wrote disparagingly:

> For the whole lengh of coast which we saild along there was a sameness to be observed in the face of the countrey very uncommon ... A Soil so barren and at the same time intirely void of the helps dervd from cultivation would not be supposed to yeild much to the support of man.[14]

Of the inhabitants, because they did not practice agriculture, he conjectured, 'their reason must be supposd to hold a rank little superior to that of monkies'.[15] Such a superficial acquaintance with and indifference towards the land and its people did not, however, deter Banks from proposing Botany Bay to a 1779 Committee of the British House of Commons appointed to make recommendations regarding the transportation of felons. Banks viewed the prior Aboriginal presence as insignificant and told the committee the natives at Botany Bay were unlikely to mount any opposition to British colonisation. He ventured not more than 50 lived in the whole neighbourhood and, while treacherous and armed with lances, were extremely cowardly.

Although in possession of no new information regarding the east coast, and notwithstanding the contrary opinion expressed in his *Endeavour* journal, Banks testified again before the committee in 1786 and suggested the soil of parts of New South Wales between latitudes 30° and 40° south was sufficiently fertile to support a considerable number of Europeans.

Banks appeared before an audience predisposed to suggestions of overseas settlement. The politicians of the time instinctively linked colonial activity with wealth and position. The British, French, Spanish and other European powers believed in the value and necessity of colonies for supplying the home country with raw materials and providing a market for manufactures. Accordingly, imperial powers maintained colonies wherever they could obtain them in the fertile parts of the Americas, Africa and the east. Rivalry and conflict accompanied their mercantilist expansion.

As one of a series of responses to the French threat to India, the British government in the 1780s decided to use convicts to build a new base to increase Britain's capacity to protect its Eastern Empire. Convinced of the need for a naval base in the Pacific, Prime Minister Pitt's government decided to settle Botany Bay—to preclude the French from settling there, to provide a strategic outlier to India and South America and to supply naval materials to India. Banks' artful insistence on the mercantile value of a colony 'larger than the whole of Europe' appealed to a ministry still smarting from the cession of a continent to the victorious and newly independent Americans. The need to remove unwanted convicts from the realm neatly complemented imperial motives. The proposed naval station was so remote and so lacking in commercial attractions that free labour would not have gone there voluntarily, whereas convicts would be transported under guard and could forcibly be prevented from leaving.[16]

But use of convicts to found a new colony came under immediate attack. Eighteenth century prison reformers regarded transportation as an ineffective punishment and totally incompatible with colonisation. They proposed more rational means of punishment and rehabilitation. Men of learning and scientific vision believed in the efficacy of total discipline to recast the character of the deviant. Enlightened reformers considered just, reasonable and humane the lengthy confinement of prisoners to solitary cells, clothing them in uniforms, regimenting their day to the cadence of the clock, and correcting their minds with dosages of scripture and hard labour.[17] The utilitarian philosopher Jeremy Bentham (1748–1832), for example, opposed transportation to New South Wales all his life. In his view only assuredness of punishment deterred the criminal classes. The uncertainty of transportation—it might inflict considerable pain or very little—obviated its deterrent value. A penal colony in New South Wales, composed largely of criminals, could not attend to moral improvement; there would be too few decent people to supervise and establish order and discipline. But, worst of all, transportation was expensive.[18]

No one in the debate over transportation pondered the effect on the Aborigines of transferring European civilisation to a vast south land. For the British, the wilderness of Australia required redeeming and the land lay open for the taking. Australia constituted a *terra nullius*, a 'no person's land'. The land belonged to no one and could be occupied on the basis of first discovery. There would be no purchase from (or other recognition of) the original inhabitants. Cook's voyage and formal act of possession, the first recorded by a European, gave Britain the first right among its neighbours to settle there.

Unable to devise a civilian administrative and judicial structure for the new penal colony of New South Wales, the Pitt ministry launched the colony as a land-borne naval vessel, with a naval commander, jurisdiction by Court Martial, and provisioning out of stores. On most other matters they deferred to Joseph Banks, who organised the young colony's scientific life and further exploration and virtually appointed all the colony's governors up to, and including, Captain William Bligh in 1806. Banks advocated the colonisation of New South Wales for the benefit of science, for his nation and for his private satisfaction. In Banks' imperial view, science served and furthered mercantilist interests. 'I see the future prospect of empires and dominions which cannot now be disappointed', he wrote to the New South Wales governor, Captain John Hunter, in 1797. 'Who knows but that England may revive in New South Wales what it is sunk in Europe'.[19] Banks was then president of the Royal Society. His prescience proved remarkable, for the decision to settle Australia led, in time, to a vast expansion of the British Empire in the east. The augmentation of that empire depended on control over nature.

Banks' protégés, the sons of the Enlightenment—practical men, rational men—ruled and settled Australia. The new moral science of the Age of Reason prepared them for the coming struggle with the wilderness. Australian settlement advanced under the guidance of a modern outlook, a uniform way of thinking devoted to the simplification of life and thought and to the formulation of efficacious techniques for the conquest of nature. Reason and violence built, on Australian soil, a new empire.

3

No Eden

THEY [THE AUSTRALIAN ABORIGINES] ARE
THE ONLY SAVAGES IN THE WORLD WHO
CANNOT FEEL OR 'KNOW THAT THEY ARE
NAKED'; AND WE ARE TAUGHT IN THE
SCRIPTURES THAT THE EYES OF MAN
CANNOT BE OPENED TO WHAT WE CALL A
CIVILIZED OR ARTIFICIAL LIFE, KNOWING
GOOD AND EVIL, TILL HE ACQUIRES A
SENSE OF SHAME.

Barron Field, New South Wales Chief Justice,
1825

BANKS' TESTIMONY and Cook's observations comprised the whole body of knowledge of New South Wales when the first reluctant settlers—just over 1000 people, including over 700, mostly male, convicts—sailed from England in May 1787. The assumption of *terra nullius* provided the justification for the new colony, and imperial ambition supplied the motive.

On 20 January 1788 the First Fleet cast anchor at Botany Bay. Within a few days, however, the colony's governor, Captain Arthur Phillip, declared the area unfit for settlement and moved the convicts to Port Jackson, the future Sydney, fifteen kilometres north. Upon landing, Phillip's secretary, David Collins, rhapsodised over the arrival of rational order in the wilderness. He described the spot chosen for disembarkation as

> at the head of the Cove near a run of fresh water, which stole silently through a very thick wood, the stillness of which had then, for the first time since the creation, been interrupted by the rude sound of the labourer's axe, and the downfall of its ancient inhabitants . . . Parties of people were every where heard and seen variously employed; some clearing ground for the different encampments; others in pitching tents, or bringing up stores as were more immediately wanted; and the spot which had so lately been the abode of silence and tranquility was now changed to that of noise, clamour and confusion: but after a time, order gradually prevailed. As the woods were opened and the ground cleared, the various encampments were extended, and all wore the appearance of regularity and decorum.[1]

Appearances of order and mastery notwithstanding, the newcomers were unfit to survive in the new land. Crop failures, shortages of provisions, and theft from the stores reduced Australia's first European settlement to near starvation in the midst of what seemed natural abundance to the original inhabitants. Nevertheless, privations did not still the spirit of private enterprise. The invaders quickly turned their attention to exploiting the colony's most accessible natural resources.

In July 1790 the settlers spotted a sperm whale in Sydney harbour and some boats, armed with harpoons, gave chase. But the whale turned on its pursuers, rammed and upset the boat, and three men drowned. Proof of the presence of whales excited the imagination of the colony's influential men and in December 1791, Governor Phillip wrote to Banks about the vast numbers of whales to be seen about the coast; he predicted prosperity for a future whaling industry. The first English whalemen intending plunder arrived in the ships of the Third Convict Fleet in 1791. The convoy's master reported shoals of sperm whales off the coast of New South Wales, from noon to sunset, as far around the horizon as could be seen from the mast. After disposing of its human cargo the Third Fleet immediately returned to sea. One ship killed seven whales in less than two hours but foul weather forced the abandonment of the hunt. In any case the pressing needs of a barely functioning, starving settlement postponed a more systematic exploitation of the colony's marine fauna. The delay exasperated those who could afford the luxury of a discriminating mercantile instinct. In October 1793, a visiting American sea captain expressed surprise to find the inhabitants unable or unwilling to send small craft after the seals, of which he had observed a plentiful harvest along the coast.[2]

Mariners in the southern seas in those days sailed through an abundance of marine life unimaginable to Australians today. Indeed, the southern oceans then served as a vast undisturbed sanctuary for the sperm whale (*Physeter macrocephalus*) and the right (or southern black) whale (*Balaena australis*). Every season, in their tens of thousands, right whales swam north from Antarctica to mate and calve in the bays and estuaries along the coasts of New Zealand, Van Diemen's Land and southern Australia. In addition, every beach of the Tasman Sea, each rocky promontory of Bass Strait and all the islands off the southern coast of Australia teemed with rookeries of elephant seals (or southern walrus) and fur seals. Most lived unmolested and knew nothing of humans apart from the occasional

Aboriginal hunter. But to the global economy then in genesis, dead seals meant profit. Elephant seals yielded oil and hides for shoe leather, and fur seals provided exquisite skins for sale in England and China. News of the living bounty in the 'southern fisheries' reached the northern hemisphere at a time—the late eighteenth century—of diminishing catches of whales and seals. Revivified fleets set sail at once from Le Havre in France, Hull in England and from New Bedford and Nantucket in America, for the new southerly riches. Likely profits more than compensated for the long voyages.

American ships took tens of thousands of seals from the Falklands in the 1790s. In 1794 one ship returned to New Bedford with a load of 16 000 seal skins. But the slaughter had only begun. After extinguishing the seals of the Falklands, American sealers rounded Cape Horn and in five months during the penultimate year of the eighteenth century, killed 33 400 seals on Mas Afuera Island in the South Pacific. Over the next few years they reached Australia.[3]

The British, however, initiated the seal killing business in the antipodes when the ship *Britannia*, owned by the whaling concern, Enderby & Son, arrived in Sydney in mid-1792 under the command of William Raven. Raven sailed for New Zealand and left a dozen men in Dusky Sound where in ten months they killed 45 000 seals. The expedition proved not only the presence of seals but also the ease with which they could be killed.

In February 1798, Matthew Flinders sailed to Bass Strait and observed that among the Furneaux Islands 'the number of seals exceeded anything we had, any of us, before witnessed.'[4] This information was rapidly communicated to the rest of the world. In June, while in Canton disposing of a cargo of sea-otter pelts obtained during an expedition to the north-west coast of America, ex-Royal Navy gunner Charles Bishop learnt that in Bass Strait 'the Islands thereabout abounds with fur seals.'[5] He immediately sailed for Sydney Cove and late in the year accompanied Flinders back to Bass Strait and saw for himself the immense amount of wildlife among islands thickly populated with brush kangaroos, wallabies, wombats, swans, ducks and seabirds. Flinders reported that his surgeon, George Bass, at Albatross Island, off Cape Barren Island, 'was obliged to fight his way up the cliffs of the island with the seals and when he reached the top, to make a way with his club amongst the albatross'.[6] On Cape Barren Island itself, Bishop found 'fur seal of the best quality in such numbers that we could average 200 skins a day'.[7] There Bishop left a gang of fourteen men and two months later the crew had skinned 9000 seals and boiled oil from about 125 elephant seals. Sealing companies from Britain and Sydney quickly emulated Bishop's pioneering achievements.

Sealing provided opportunities for the colony's budding capitalists who sought a local commodity, saleable overseas. The enterprise required only a small initial investment, as a longboat and a crew sufficed for the hunt on the islands off the southern coast. Seals were ridiculously easy to kill. Hunters simply beat to death, with metal studded clubs, the young seals and lanced the older ones. Despatching the large bull elephant seals, however, required a different technique. The sealer, armed with a musket loaded with a brace of balls, advanced to within a few paces of an animal rising on its forelegs or flippers, mouth wide open in a roar of protest. At that moment the sealer fired through the roof of the creature's upper jaw, blowing out the brain. As the animal fell forward, the sealer completed his destruction with a lance. When the hunters came upon colonies of sleeping seals they simply pressed the musket to an animal's head and discharged the shot directly into the brain. The loudest noise would not awaken seals and the sealer often shot one without awakening those alongside and in this way proceeded through the whole rookery, shooting and lancing as many as were wanted.

To avoid offending the East India Company's monopoly on southern ocean trading, the British government forbade the colonists from building boats. British authorities also feared colonial vessels might provide convicts with a means of escape. Governors John Hunter (1795–1800) and Philip Gidley King (1800–1806), however, ignored the prohibition. In 1802 Governor King admitted to the colonial secretary that the vessels engaged in Bass Strait sealing belonged to the colonists; moreover, he added, 'I . . . shall encourage that pursuit as much as possible to those who may be of industrious and enterprising dispositions'.[8] By the turn of the century, sealing gangs, through the agency of colonial-built boats, occupied all the islands of the Furneaux Group, the Kent Group, as well as King Island, and all the rocks of Bass Strait. To further assist the trade, King established a colony closer to the killing waters.

Exploration and the activities of sealers had confirmed the existence of a strait separating Van Diemen's Land from New South Wales. To foreclose possible French and American claims and to consolidate British sovereignty, Governor King decided to settle the newly revealed island and in 1803 he sent ships and convicts to establish a colony there. The new settlement provided a home and headquarters for Bass Strait sealing parties.

King's initiatives greatly assisted colonial sealing and sea elephanting concerns, particularly the partnership formed in mid-1800 by emancipists (freed convicts) Henry Kable and James Underwood. Between March 1803 and June 1804 two Kable & Underwood vessels brought in 28 282 seal skins and oil from over 1000 sea elephants. By October 1805, Kable & Underwood, and another Sydney emancipist-merchant, Simeon Lord, employed 216 men in sealing. In 1805 Lord sent a sealing gang to Antipodes Island, off the South Island of New Zealand, where they killed 59 000 seals. Four-and-a-half thousand kilometres west, on Kangaroo Island, the crew of the American ship *Union* gathered 12 000 skins.

Sealing was a brutal and brutalising occupation. François August Peron, zoologist to Captain Nicholas Baudin's voyage of discovery in the Pacific between 1800 and 1804, visited the sealers on King Island in Bass Strait. He was appalled at the slaughter and remarked:

> Seeing a cruel sailor, armed with a heavy stick, run sometimes for fun through the midst of these marine herds, killing as many seals as he hits, and soon surrounding himself with their corpses, one cannot help bemoaning the kind of lack of foresight or the cruelty of nature which seems only to have created such strong, gentle and such unfortunate beings in order to deliver them, like an unnatural mother, to all the blows of their enemies.[9]

Despite pleas for conservation as early as 1803—when officials called for age limits and the sparing of females with young—the killing continued. To fill a ship of several hundred tons required a very large catch, which took months of butchering, curing and boiling down. Sealers worked year round, even during mating and pupping time, killing pregnant seals in myriads and leaving young pups, milkless, on the rocks to starve. The sealers took only the skins and left hills of carcasses behind. The rookeries became bogs of putrefaction; the seals abandoned their haunts and stopped breeding.[10] By 1806 Bass Strait sealers had killed well in excess of 100 000 seals and by 1810 the nearer Bass Strait sealing grounds were exhausted.[11] Small gangs of runaway convicts, who kidnapped Aboriginal women and pressed them to hunt the few remaining seals, now took over the islands. After 1810 the commercial hunt moved to distant Macquarie Island but the fur skin rush lasted only another four or five years. At the peak of the killing over 100 000 seals a season had been taken at Macquarie but by 1815 several gangs on the island managed to find and kill only 6000 seals between them. By 1820 southern seals had been hunted to near extinction.

Sealing, initially highly profitable, became less so as the large number of skins on the market depressed prices. Although they continued killing, the Sydney traders gained very little from the extinction of the vast rookeries on Campbell and Macquarie Islands. Nevertheless, trading in seal skins and oil gave many traders a start in general business and helped establish an indigenous Australian capitalism. Few of the actual hunters, however, gained at all from the slaughter.

Although sealers were entitled to 'lays'—a percentage of the profit—the company store practices of their employers, who sold rum and other goods at inflated prices on credit against future wages, frequently reduced sealers to debt at the end of the voyage. Inadequately provisioned, remote sealing gangs invariably exhausted their rations long before relief came and existed for months on seal flesh, seal oil, seaweed and whatever they could scrounge on the barren, windswept rocks of the killing grounds.

Soon after reports of the extravagance of life in the oceans to the south of Australia reached Britain, whaling firms began to pressure the government to lift the pre-emptive rights of the British East India Company over all the produce and trade in the southern hemisphere. Besides Governor King, who consistently sought a lifting of the restrictions on whaling (which prohibited Australian-based traders from exporting whale or seal products direct to London), the whaling companies found an ally in Joseph Banks. In 1806 Banks wrote to Lord Liverpool protesting the East India monopoly and added: 'the Americans will most Certainly catch the Seals in Van Diemen's Land if the Colonists do not & there cannot be any Reason why they should not also Catch the Whales in their own Seas.'[12]

As early as 1801, despite the legal monopoly of the East India Company, independent whalemen began to frequent New Zealand waters, where the seas abounded in sperm whales. The first regular visits of Europeans to New Zealand, in fact, were entirely due to those islands' lavish biological display: whales spouted in the bays, seals basked on the shores and fine timber grew in the forests. Forty years of untrammelled and unsupervised private exploitation followed, until the British government formally annexed New Zealand in 1840.

In New South Wales whalers enjoyed official patronage. In 1803 the British whaler *Albion* sailed from Sydney in the company of the Van Diemen's Land founding party and on the way caught three sperm whales. During the first winter and spring, the Derwent estuary, the site of the new settlement of Hobart, swarmed with right whales, mostly pregnant females seeking refuge in the sheltered waters to give birth. Sometimes 50 or 60 might be seen in the shallow parts of the river. Day after day the diary of the Reverend Robert Knopwood records whales. On 1 July 1804, 'At 1/2-past 10 Lt Johnston and self went to Risdon, by order of Lt.-Governor Collins, and performed divine service there. We passed so many whales that it was dangerous for the boat to go up the river, unless you kept near the shore.'[13]

The whales did not enjoy their tranquility for much longer; the Van Diemen's Land invaders quickly realised the commercial possibilities of their congregation. Later in the month of Knopwood's diary entry, Lieutenant-Governor Collins wrote enthusiastically to

Banks about whaling and noted that in the Derwent 'Three or four ships might have lain at anchor and with ease filled all their casks'.[14] But the first Van Diemen's Land whalers did not even need ships; they simply set up a shore factory in a bay where the animals were known to gather and attacked them from small boats. Although the new colony suffered terribly from starvation—by the end of 1805 the convicts were rationed to 1.2 kilograms of salt pork and 1.8 kilograms of bread a week, normally a two-day ration—the whalers were not distracted, nor the whales ignored. In 1806, mobile whalers began frequenting the Derwent, filling their ships with the oil procured from whales in the river and adjacent bays, and William Collins (no relation to the Lieutenant-Governor) established what was probably the first Van Diemen's Land bay whaling station, at Ralph Bay, on the east side of the Derwent. Bay whaling stations quickly spread to other suitable coastal indentations.

Ships from America, Britain, France and Sydney joined the slaughter, set up shore stations and made temporary land bases in safe inlets everywhere along the southern coasts. In the first two decades of the nineteenth century American whalers took over 150 000 southern right whales just from South Australian waters.[15] The opportunity had to be quickly seized. By 1841 there were 35 bay whaling stations on Van Diemen's Land alone but decline set in rapidly. After 1845 the right whale ceased to come to the slaughter. The species never recovered. A 1978 Australian government inquiry into whales and whaling concluded the numbers of right whales left were so few and their prospects so uncertain that counting was not possible.[16]

From the time the American fleets invaded the southern Pacific at the close of the eighteenth century, the business of sperm whaling fluctuated according to political events in the northern hemisphere. At first the Napoleonic Wars depressed European interest, then the British–American war of 1812–14, and subsequent trade embargoes effectively closed all British ports to American vessels until 1830. In any case, Australian ports were ill-equipped to service the whalers, and no more than half a dozen American whalers called at Sydney in the three years before 1812. Scores of American and other ships, however, hunted whales in the surrounding seas. The ubiquitous presence of foreign whalers prompted one local patriot in 1827 to deplore the failure of the colonials to take advantage of 'the lucrative prospect [of] the whale-fisheries ... We see the London and American ships congregating at our doors, as it were, by dozens, and carrying off yearly thousands upon thousands of the rich harvest which the bounty of Providence had placed within our grasp.'[17]

Not all the colonials felt inhibited, however, and some of those who had profited from sealing invested in the new business of deep sea whaling. Sydney merchants sent two ships after sperm whales in 1823, and employed 26 in the business by 1830. The next year, Archibald Mosman, a merchant and shipowner, erected wharves in a cove of Sydney harbour for the equipment of vessels occupied in the whale fishery. By the early 1830s, with the Americans back in port, both Sydney and Hobart offered whaleships a full range of repair and supply facilities; for a brief while Hobart became one of the great whaling ports of the world. American whalers preferred to operate in the northern Pacific or along the equator, but with falling catches they sought new killing grounds and soon established a regular commerce with Australian ports. While welcome, their presence continued to remind the colonials of their own inadequacies.

In 1837 the first recorded American whaler appeared off the south-west coast of Australia and the *Perth Gazetteer and Western Australian Journal* editorialised: 'We welcome any and every stranger on our coasts, but it is painful for us to see strangers sweeping from us one of our richest harvests—the whale fishery—while we are indolent spectators.'[18] The possibility of profit induced two local companies to commence whaling operations out of Swan River in 1837–38. In their first year they exported oil and whalebone to the value of £3000. Competing American ships, however, secured oil and whalebone ten times in value. Three years later a visitor to Perth counted thirteen American whalers at anchor in the harbour and he regretted the colonists' abandonment of this department of industry.[19] South of Perth, at Port Leschenault, the government resident reported visits from 24 whaling ships, most of them from

New England, in the first three months of 1841.[20]

They probably found few whales, for the Australian catch was in decline and most whalers had moved their operations to New Zealand. In 1831 Sydney merchant Robert Campbell established the first successful bay whaling station in the South Island. But the number of years which sufficed to break up the great schools of whales visiting the New Zealand coast was small. In 1836, 186 whaling ships visited the Bay of Islands, in the North Island, and the peak of bay whaling in New Zealand waters occurred two years later. The catch thereafter fell into spectacular decline and only deep sea whaling offered any return.

By 1846 the American whaling fleet comprised a navy of over 900 vessels, most of them engaged in the Pacific, and the hunting of sperm whales reached its height and then rapidly declined. In a little more than 50 years—1790s to late 1840s—when every creature within reach of the clubs, guns, lances and harpoons was regarded as prey, the whalers and sealers had combed the vast southern oceans so thoroughly that large marine animals were no longer to be easily found there.

With the demise of sealing and decline of whaling, colonial capitalists looked to the South Seas for another easily exploitable natural resource. The huge colonial consumption of Chinese tea (convicts received 100 grams of tea in their weekly rations from 1820 on) required New South Wales to find a means to pay for the imports with a commodity the Chinese wanted. The South Sea traders had discovered an abundance of sandalwood (*Santalum album*) in the late 1830s—an intensely fragrant timber used by the Chinese for incense, perfumery and furniture making—only ten to twenty-one days' sailing from Sydney, among the islands of New Caledonia, the Loyalties and the New Hebrides. By 1842 colonial merchants had taken more than 2000 tonnes of sandalwood from the small Isle of Pines alone, and between 1841 and 1851 dispatched several hundred expeditions to strip the islands bare of sandalwood till not a stick remained.[21]

Although imperially tenacious and commercially aggressive, the

British established, with respect to managing the local environment, only a precarious hold on the Australian continent. Declining yields from crops grown in continuously cultivated soil pointed to early environmental failure. In March 1796, secretary Collins explained that the reason for the season's poor harvest lay in the exhaustion of the soil: '. . . the ground being overwrought, from a greediness to make it produce golden harvests every season, without allowing it time to recruit itself from crop to crop, or being able to afford it manure.'[22] Meanwhile, on Norfolk Island, which contained the greatest area of cultivated land at the time, rains washed the earth from steep hills cleared of timber and subjected to four or five years' cultivation. Eroded soil filled the valleys.[23]

In the beginning, colonial authorities tried to grow food on government farms, but after 1793 the Governor provided grants of land to officers, emancipists and free settlers. Within three decades practically all the usable land in the Sydney region passed into private hands. About 80 men owned 60 percent of all alienated (transferred to private ownership) land in New South Wales by 1821.

In the fields of Europe, by the turn of the century, horses and oxen supplemented human labour. In Australia, however, human muscle power performed almost all the farm work. Men working together, not the labour of individuals working separately, accounted for much of the early economic growth and development of Australia. On one occasion 500 men cleared and burned 300 acres in 30 days. Besides clearing and hoeing the ground, convicts and ex-convicts made roads, built and kept houses, raised children, lumped casks off ships and walked after the first generations of sheep. The authorities assigned convicts to private masters or to government service according to their abilities and in the expectation that a period of hard and regular work would lead towards reformation. Employers maintained labour discipline through the exercise of penal authority: floggings, extension of sentences and imprisonment in chain gangs.

Despite the spectre of coercion, which extracted more labour from convicts than they would have provided voluntarily, many decades passed before the colony became self-sufficient in food. In

1809, floods, aggravated by riverbank clearing, destroyed almost the whole of the grain crop and rendered the colony, once again, dependent on food imports. Ten years later an infestation of caterpillars denuded crops and pastures, threatening food supplies and forcing reduced rations. Over half a century after first settlement, a drought in 1839 precipitated a reintroduction of rationing. Nevertheless, in 1838 Governor Bourke could still truthfully declare: 'In New South Wales, by the aid of convict labour, the industrious and skillful settlers, have, within a period of fifty years, converted a wilderness into a fine and flourishing colony . . .'[24]

While monopoly and land speculation afforded profitable opportunities for those with large capital, farming did not appeal to emancipists and free settlers of small means. But the nature of Australia offered other, more easily exploitable assets.

Red cedar (*Toona australis*), one of Australia's few deciduous trees and the only long-lived tree, once grew from Ulladulla, south of Sydney, along the coast to Queensland's north. The tree attracted early attention because it cuts easily, floats easily, warps very little, is naturally durable and versatile and grows with a straight bole up to 45 metres high. Today, not even a stump remains. The colony exported the first cedar logs to India in 1795 and by 1802 logging had grown to such ferocious dimensions on the Hawkesbury River, north of Sydney, that Governor King, who otherwise encouraged the plunder of natural resources, issued a special order prohibiting cutting without his permission. But the cedar getters ignored his restrictions and the hunt spread along the coast; sawyers reached Port Macquarie in the early 1820s and moved on to the Manning River by 1828.

Alexander Harris, who arrived in New South Wales as a free settler in 1825, joined the cedar getters at the Hawkesbury, where

the cedar grew in such quantities, [there] was a forest so dense overhead that there must have been miles where no sunbeam had penetrated for ages ... The underwood and vines, matted together, rendered it impossible to travel without first making an opening with the axe ... There were plenty of stumps ten feet in diameter, and trees lying felled ready for cutting down into logs, of seventy and ninety feet barrel without a limb, and so symmetrical that they might have been imagined columns preparing for some gigantic temple. Many of them were of such large diameter that the logs had to be halved by splitting before they could be sawed with the whipsaw.[25]

Some of the giants felled during this unrelenting attack on the ancient forest exceeded 1000 years in age.

Harris described a feverish scene of men felling and sawing the cedar, working ten, twelve, fourteen hours a day, exhausting a stand and restlessly moving on to unexploited groves further up river or the coast. He found the result of all this labour pleasing:

> Countless, and motionless, and gigantic stood the forest army, up and down all the hill sides around us; in strong contrast to this, stood the great piles of plank, squared with mathematical exactness, which spoke of *men and labour*.[26]

In the early 1830s cedar getters moved on to the Clarence and Macleay rivers and in ten years cut out all the accessible timber from the Macleay. In twenty years they felled and burnt down all the cedar brushes on the Clarence. By 1842 cedar getters had hacked their way to the Richmond River in the far north of New South Wales and a few years later invaded the Tweed River area. Cedar parties then attacked the timber along the rivers and creeks of south Queensland and by 1847 had cut out all accessible cedar near Moreton Bay.

In the 1840s, in a preview of the tactics if not the motives of modern-day eco-activists, pitsawyers drove metal spikes into logs on the way to the mills. Although damaging to saw blades, the sabotage failed to persuade millers to abandon the use of power-driven machinery. Men and machines then united to clear out all accessible stands of cedar, from the entire east coast of Australia. A comment by a journalist, who visited the still luxuriant cedar stand at the Tweed River in 1869, proved prescient:

> There are few places in the colony where [cedar] is now to be found in such profusion. The devastating axe of the timber getter has made dire havoc amongst the cedar brushes and where a few years ago immense quantities of the wood were to be found, there is not now a single tree worth cutting. The sawyers are a wasteful set of men. They destroy

more timber than they use. They cut and square only the best parts of a tree, leaving great masses of cedar . . . to rot unheeded in the brushes. They destroy young trees too, with most culpable carelessness, and wishing only to seize the present advantages, care not a button how many young trees they destroy in cutting down an old one. In about twenty years such a thing as a cedar tree will not be found in the country.[27]

The colonists, of course, did not confine their tree-felling to cedar. The early settlers lived in a world made of wood, and cut down forests for housing, fuel, fences, boats, ship masts and the means of moving on—axe handles, wagon hubs and drays. In order for civilisation to advance, the trees had to go. According to Harris, the whole bush around Sydney in the 1820s and 1830s

> thronged . . . with men who get their living by various kinds of bush work; some felling and squaring whole trees with the squaring axe for girders . . . to use in the colony or export, some splitting posts, rails, paling, for fences; some sawing the various sorts of building stuff, and some cutting and splitting firewood for domestic purposes at Sydney or for the use of the various steam-engines that were already in operation on water and on land.[28]

Later, after the bush workers moved on, Harris travelled through the north shore of Sydney harbour where he 'could not but take notice of the immense numbers of tree stumps. Each one of these had supplied its barrell to the splitter or sawyer or squarer: and altogether the number seemed countless.'[29] The stump, a symbol of nature subdued, became an enduring image in Australian history. The bush, like the wildlife and Aborigines sheltering within, stood in the way, not only of order and light, but of progress. The stump represented victory.

At no time during the European settlement of Australia did the dispossession of the Aborigines disturb the conscience of the dispossers. On the contrary, the British believed their invasion could only benefit the Aborigines; civilisation was the antidote to their natural savagery.

The British camp at Sydney Cove in 1788 occupied the best hunting grounds of the Gamaraigal people. In fact, as a courtesy, the Gamaraigal had originally led Phillip to the run of fresh water which Collins had found so picturesque. Now displaced, and deprived of access to game, the Aborigines starved during the following winter, and pestilence—possibly deliberately introduced—followed. In April 1789 the chroniclers of the British invasion recorded an outbreak of smallpox among the Aborigines. The epidemic killed half of all the Port Jackson Aborigines and spread throughout south-eastern Australia, as far west as the future South Australia and as far north as the future Brisbane. As an exterminating agent, smallpox proved highly effective and must have carried away in excess of 125 000 people, freeing enormous new resources for European exploitation.[30]

The next year, to avenge the spearing of a convict servant, M'Entire, Phillip ordered into the bush a punitive expedition to collect ten Aboriginal heads, any heads, and two live captives whom he planned to publicly hang to serve as an example. Armed with decapitation axes and bags to hold the heads, the punitive party twice set out, but each time failed to find any Aborigines.

The British combined aggressive intent with the Enlightenment hope that the natives were not beyond the claims of civilisation. Collins wrote of the Aborigines in 1796: 'that they are ignorant savages cannot be disputed [but] it is hoped that they do not ... appear [in his account] to be wholly incapable of becoming one day civilised and useful members of society.'[31] The Aborigines, however, did not care to be useful. They were ill-disposed to be the servants of others, even for an hour. They preferred independence of action, followed their own values and refused to adopt those of the invaders. They remained unconvinced—with the sight of men chained together in gangs, working under armed guard, floggings and public hangings—of the superiority of the invaders' civilisation. That the Aborigines might freely choose life in the bush to the savagery of penal society appeared beyond Collins' understanding. He and his fellow officers found incomprehensible the behaviour of Aboriginal children who, brought up by Europeans, nevertheless absconded to join their Aboriginal parents.[32] The enlightened masters found equally extraordinary the several cases of convict escapees and emancipists who sought the company of the

Aborigines in the bush. In 1797 the rulers of New South Wales found rumours of a convict woman cohabitating with Aborigines on the north shore threatening and disturbing. Search parties were immediately sent to rescue her from the embrace of her native husband, but all returned unsuccessful. The lady's plight shocked Sydney society because her fall represented civilisation's failure to fully possess and domesticate the wild people and their wilderness.

The British did not succeed in dispossessing the Aborigines without a struggle. In their defence Sydney Aborigines began a guerrilla war—raiding isolated farms, destroying crops and stock and spearing stragglers. But British organisation, numbers and guns eventually prevailed. During the resistance the British beheaded one of the leading rebels, Pemulwuy, and sent his pickled head to Sir Joseph Banks. By 1817 only a dwindling remnant of Sydney Aborigines, forced into mendicancy and parasitism, remained. Two years later the colony's leading churchman, the Reverend Samuel Marsden, concluded, 'They are the most degraded of the human race, and never seem to wish to alter their habits and manner of life.'[33] The British invasion, however, had just begun and civilisation found other chances to alter Aboriginal habits. In Van Diemen's Land, the British succeeded in entirely effacing the way of life of the indigenous people by means of genocide.

At the time of first contact probably some 4000 to 5000 Aborigines lived on Van Diemen's Land. The slaughter began a few months after the first settlement on the Derwent estuary. On 3 May 1804 a group of some 300 to 400 Aboriginal men, women and children drove a mob of kangaroos out of the bush towards the water where they intended to corner and feast upon them. A convict, watching the hunt, summoned a troop of soldiers who fired point-blank into the group, blasting them with shot. Forty or more Aborigines were killed, but nobody counted the exact number.[34] That evening, the Reverend Knopwood received an invitation from his friend, the colony's surgeon, Jacob Mountgarret, for dinner and to inspect 'a fine native boy' of about two, whose parents were killed in the massacre. Mountgarret also had the body of one of the dead and he further invited Knopwood to be present at the dissection. But prior commitments prevented the Reverend's attendance.[35]

Conflict continued as colonists—suffering the starvation which invariably accompanied most new settlements in Australia—competed with the Aborigines for the available game. Kangaroo became the major source of fresh meat for the invaders. Although the Van Diemen's Land species of kangaroo survived the slaughter, the emu shortly became extinct. Hunters shot Aborigines as freely as kangaroos and emus. On one occasion:

> A *respectable* young gentleman, who was out kangaroo hunting, in jumping over a dead tree, observed a black native crouched by the stem, as if to hide himself. The huntsman observing the white of the eye of the native, was induced to examine the prostrate being, and finding it only to be a native, he placed the muzzle of his piece to his breast and shot him dead on the spot.[36]

Others shot Aborigines to feed their dogs, while men like 'Abyssinian Tom'—posing as public benefactors—notched the butts of their muskets for each Aborigine shot. In the degraded society of the penal colony life counted for little. One escaped convict abducted an Aboriginal woman, killed her husband, cut off his head and forced her to wear it slung around her neck.[37] Near Hobart Town, convict stock keepers kept Aboriginal women as sexual slaves, secured to their huts by bullock chains.[38] Two other stock keepers, cohabitating for some time with an Aboriginal woman, then tiring of her, strung her up by her heels and left her to perish.[39] Another time, stock keepers chased an Aboriginal woman up a tree where they commenced firing at her. Every time a bullet hit she pulled leaves off the tree and thrust them into her wounds, till at last she fell lifeless to the ground. Other stock keepers would capture the men, cut off their penises and testicles, then watch them run as they bled to death.[40] In Bass Strait sealers prosecuted their slaughter of seals with the slave labour of kidnapped Aboriginal women. When one woman tried to run away the sealers cut off her ears and made her eat the flesh cut from her thigh. Sealers burnt women alive, regularly flogged them and forced them to perform all kinds of drudgery.[41]

1 Aboriginal occupation of the Great South Land: not a wilderness but an inhabited wild place.

Marysville, Victoria, c. 1880–84: a new settlement in the Australian bush. In centre view the British flag proclaims Imperial allegiance and sovereignty over the broken bush.

Mount Laura, Camperdown, Victoria. Fences divide the newly subjugated land into a deedable commodity, excluding the original inhabitants who now gather as fringe dwellers among stumps and broken trunks.

Concordia Gold Mine, Victoria, 1850s. Rumours of gold sent thousands of miners rushing from one prospect to the next, descending upon and abandoning one place after another. They left behind a torn up and devastated landscape.

A contemporary cartoonist's view of the 1880s Melbourne land boom.

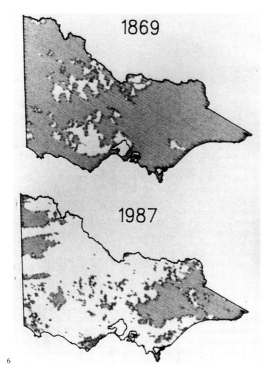

1869

1987

Forest cover changes in Victoria. Like the rest of Australia, Victoria suffered profound forest destruction over the course of European settlement. Most of the loss occurred during the last 100 years, following Land Acts which apportioned the earth into private property and transformed land into a commodity.

6

7

A mallee roller at rest. In mallee rolling, a heavy roller, often a converted boiler, pulled through the scrub by a team of horses or oxen, knocked down the slender, brittle mallee trunks. A fire set at the end of summer consumed the destroyed trees.

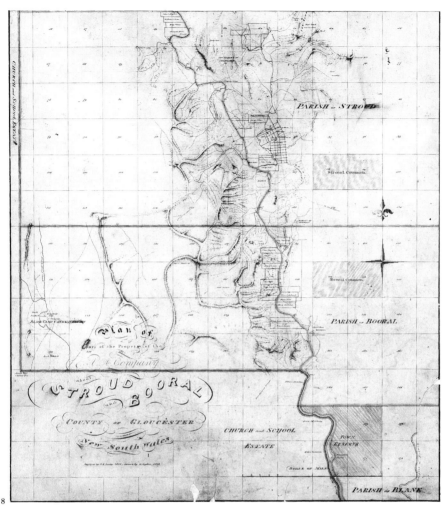

8

Colonial maps, by imposing grids and straight lines onto the living and unruly Australian landscape, facilitated expropriation.

Crushing the Scrub

Burning off

The Mallee Country

Ploughing with Stump Jumping Plough

Under Cultivation

Reclaiming the mallee. Nineteenth century pictorial celebration of the transformation of the mallee, which once stretched 'like a blue and level sea to the horizon', into wheat fields. Denuded, eroded and sand-blown deserts followed the cropping of the wheat.

10

Bridge over Sea Elephant River. Once a killing ground for seals and sea elephants, King Island in Bass Strait suffered catastrophic loss of forest, due to clearing and ringbarking, in the first decade of the twentieth century.

11

Land clearance in Gippsland's Strzelecki Ranges, c. 1900. The collective result of individual Gippsland selectors' efforts was the effacement of an entire temperate eucalyptus rainforest. The photograph reveals the devastation of the fire which followed ringbarking and felling.

12

Two men in neck chains being brought to jail for cattle spearing, Northern Territory, c. 1928. One man borrowed a shirt from his captor's 'camel boy' to prevent the chains from chafing his neck. In 1930 the Minister ordered an end to the widespread practice of chaining Aboriginal prisoners and witnesses. Police disregarded the directive.

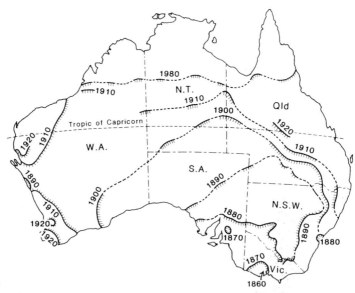

13

The rate of spread of the rabbit in Australia exceeded that of any other introduced mammal anywhere in the world. European settlement and accompanying disruption of the land through pastoralism, which promoted herbage favoured by rabbits, clearing, which provided habitat, and eradication of predators and other native wildlife, which opened an ecological niche, greatly assisted the rabbits' destructive colonisation.

Adaminaby Dam Site, Snowy Mountains Scheme, December, 1956. Men and machines engaged in the 'great art of geographical engineering, to reshape the earth'.

14

15

Bulldozers greatly increased the efficiency of the quintessential Australian activity of clearing the land. In Rocky Gully, WA, in 1953, contractors employed the new 'Hi-Ball' method. Two bulldozers dragged a 16-millimetre-thick reinforced steel ball, 2.5 metres in diameter and weighing five tonnes, through the bush. A third bulldozer followed to add its weight against particularly tough trees. In light timbered country the Hi-Ball cleared 40 hectares a day; in heavier timber, 25.

After the Great War Australia's leading men decided to develop Australia under the slogan 'Men, Money and Markets'. To fulfil these goals, the country needed, above all else, vast numbers of British immigrants.

The arcadian 'land of tomorrow' portrayed in this immigration poster bore no resemblance to the actual land of Australia.

The main railway systems of Australia by mid-twentieth century. From 1860 onwards, iron rails spread across Australia like cracks in glass. The railways tethered the bush to the world and symbolised the conquest of nature.

19

Bulldozing a road to the Guthega Bridge site, Snowy Mountains Scheme, November, 1951. The lesson of World War II, the efficacy of heavy power, was quickly applied to an attack on the topography of the Snowy Mountains.

20

Dead forest in salty marshland in south-west WA, 1982. No other comparably sized area in the world has suffered as much destruction of natural vegetation as the WA wheatbelt. What took nature geological eons to achieve, the leaching of salts from the root zone of plants, the land clearer and agriculturalist reversed in a matter of decades. Downstream of cleared areas, salt reaches deadly concentrations.

21

Prime Minister Robert Menzies at the Tumut Pond opening ceremony in 1958 surveying the empire under construction by the 'big men' of the Snowy Mountains Scheme.

22

By 1967, just twenty years after the development of Greenwich Park, near Goulburn, NSW, into a grazing property, erosion scoured the land. The property's manager stands in one of the eroded gullies which cut through the once extensively timbered country.

23

The Minister for National Development, W. H. Spooner, inspecting bauxite samples at Weipa, c. 1957. In the interests of turning Australia into a world quarry the Queensland and Commonwealth governments granted a foreign-owned consortium mining rights over 5800 square kilometres of Aboriginal land on Cape York Peninsula.

24

Denuded mountains surrounding the copper mining town of Queenstown, Tasmania, 1972. Sulphur, from smelting, which began at the turn of the century, killed virtually all the vegetation, fires consumed the dead forests, and heavy rain washed away the topsoil; only bedrock remained.

British nuclear tests in Australia, 1952–57: an alliance of politics and science. Of these experiments in new and more efficient means of destruction, Prime Minister

13 October 1952

14 October 1953

19 June 1956

27 September 1956

22 October 1956

14 September 1957

Robert Menzies claimed, 'No conceivable injury to life, limb or property could emerge from the test[s] . . . conducted in the vast spaces in the centre of Australia.'

26 October 1953

16 May 1956

4 October 1956

11 October 1956

25 September 1957

9 October 1957

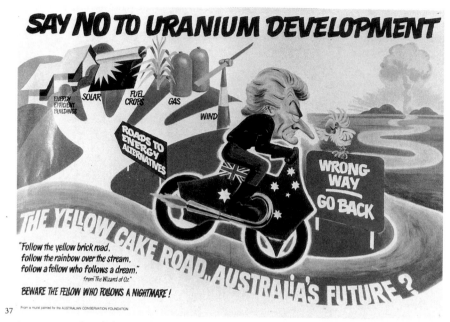

A poster produced during the anti-uranium campaign of the 1980s. Despite the best efforts of opponents, the influential men of Australia, led by Prime Minister Bob Hawke, remained grimly determined to commit the country, and the world, to a nuclear future.

The Federation Tree 100 years on. Planted by Sir Henry Parkes in 1890, in the gardens of Parliament House, Melbourne to commemorate the first federation conference, this English oak symbolised Empire solidarity and 'the crimson thread of kinship [which] runs through us all'.

By 1818 the Aboriginal population in Van Dieman's Land had fallen below 2000, while the European population had increased to 3114. But until 1820 agricultural settlers used only small areas of land and did not interfere with the Aborigines' traditional patterns of migration about the island. The semblance of mutual co-existence broke down when, during the following decade, settlers occupied every available block of grazing land. By the late 1820s the face of Van Diemen's Land revealed a picture of a wilderness in retreat—incised by rough but serviceable roads, fastened down by thriving townships, emasculated by settlement. Stockwhips cracked in the hills as mustered herds broke from isolated yards; sheep flocks spread out to feed along river flats, fenced off from cultivated clearings; and acres of blackened stumps marked the line of the forest's retreat. In 1826, over half a million sheep browsed among the forests and grasslands; in 1828 more sheep grazed Van Diemen's Land than on the whole of the mainland; three years later the island supported over a million of them. Quadrupeds replaced kangaroos and other game and ate the shrubs and plants the Aborigines depended on for edible roots and fruits.

Other assaults were more direct. Stock keepers abducted Aboriginal women and settlers kidnapped children, ostensibly to save them from starvation and barbarism, but in actuality using them as cheap labour. In retaliation for the appropriation of their land and the seizure of their kin, the Aborigines raided huts, burned hayricks, harassed stockmen, and speared and drove away cattle and sheep. When the Aborigines raided the property of Isaac Sherwin in 1828 they called out to him, 'Go away, you white buggers! What business have you here?'[42] The Aborigines rarely attacked *en masse* against the concentrated firepower of the settlers. Instead, they set fire to thatched roofs to drive the invaders into the open; they lured isolated stockmen into the bush where they could more easily be killed, and then plundered and burned the undefended hut. After a raid the Aborigines disappeared into the hills, successfully eluding their pursuers. In any case, the settlers were reluctant to confront the Aborigines in their own element and so devised other means of offense. They set up decoy huts containing arsenic-laced flour and sugar and, in bags of flour, buried powerful steel traps to sever hands and arms.

In 1830, Colonel George Arthur, Lieutenant-Governor of Van Diemen's Land, offered rewards of £5 for the capture of every Aboriginal adult and £2 for every child. In addition he convened a committee to inquire into the causes of Aboriginal hostility. The committee confirmed the existence of an Aboriginal strategy of resistance and the chairman concluded:

> a systematic plan of attacking the settlers and their possessions has been but too completely verified by the events of the last two years . . . It is manifest that they have lost the sense of the superiority of white men, and the dread of the effect of fire-arms.[43]

Although the government believed the settlers faced about 2000 hostile natives, by 1830 only about 100 Aborigines were actively continuing the resistance. But the settlers became hysterical in their calls for concerted military action and late in 1830 Arthur formed the Black Line. He mustered 2200 men, armed with 1000 muskets, 30 000 rounds of ammunition and 300 pairs of handcuffs, into a line stretching across two-thirds of the island. Advancing simultaneously they aimed to drive all encircled Aborigines onto the Tasman Peninsula, to the south, where they could be kept imprisoned forever. All but two Aborigines—one man and one boy—slipped through the cordon. Accidents killed five people in the line.

In the meantime Arthur engaged the services of George Augustus Robinson, a Christian man driven by a philanthropic mission to replace Aboriginal culture with a theocentric subsistence agriculture. Accompanied by a party of convicts and four Aboriginal men and three Aboriginal women, Robinson began, in 1830, the first of six expeditions into the interior, where he made contact, by the end of 1834, with every group of Aborigines remaining. He won them over with food, presents and false promises and persuaded nearly 200 members of remnant bands to join him and settle on Flinders Island in Bass Strait. At the end of each trip Robinson collected a reward from Arthur.

The Chief Justice of Van Diemen's Land, John Lewes Pedder, opposed sending the Aborigines to an island and preferred a treaty whereby the Aborigines might retain some part of the Van Diemen's Land mainland and live much as they had always done. On an island, he argued, they would soon pine away

> when they found their situation one of hopeless imprisonment, within bounds so narrow as necessarily to deprive them of those habits and customs which are the charms of their savage life ... their known love of change of place, their periodical distant migrations, their expeditions in search of game, and that unbounded liberty of which they had hitherto been in the enjoyment.[44]

Robinson rejected Pedder's suggestion. He believed the Aborigines would respond to Christianity only after they had been stripped of their land and culture. On Flinders Island he proposed to give them clothes, new names, Bibles and elementary schooling and to show them how to buy and sell things so they might acquire reverence for property. Governor Arthur supported Robinson. He preferred that the Aborigines despair and decline quietly and unnoticed on some remote island than die as heroes in front of British guns.

In October 1832, the itinerant Quaker preacher James Backhouse visited the settlement at Flinders Island, wrote glowingly of Robinson's community and commented on the miracle of clothing:

> Naked human beings, when in a lean condition, are forlorn looking creatures; but many of these people have become plump, and are partially clothed, and these circumstances have removed much of what was forbidding to a civilised eye.[45]

Backhouse visited the community again the following year and noted that the more complete adoption by the Aborigines of decent clothing showed 'decided marks of advancing civilisation'. He held a religious meeting, and confided in his diary:

> There was something peculiarly moving, in seeing nearly the whole of the remaining Aborigines of Van Diemen's Land, now a mere handful of people, seated on the ground, listening with much attention to the truths of the gospel, however little they might be able to understand what was said, and conducting themselves with equal gravity in the times of silence.[46]

Despite feeling moved, Backhouse evinced no consciousness of bearing witness to the policy of genocide by the British Empire.

Attracted by more remunerative employment as Protector of Aborigines on the mainland, Robinson shortly abandoned his captive Aborigines on Flinders Island. His scheme resulted only in death. The Van Diemen's Land Aborigines never accepted the superiority of European civilisation, or the market economy, nor believed the story of gentle Jesus. By 1843, 54 remained alive. The survivors continued to die, of broken hearts, soaked with rum and riddled with pulmonary diseases. In 1855, only three men, two boys and eleven women remained. The men died first and the last woman, Trucanini, died in 1876.

When the last man, William Lanney, 34, died in 1869, rival groups of scientists fought over his bones. They beheaded the body, stole the head and replaced it with one from a European corpse. According to contemporary scientific dogma, Lanney represented the missing link between apes and man, and his remains constituted inestimable scientific value. Afraid her body would suffer similar ignominy upon her death, Trucanini begged that her remains be scattered in D'Entrecasteaux Channel, near the home of her ancestors. But when she died, scientists sloughed the flesh off her bones and later put the skeleton on display at the Tasmanian Museum, where it hung until removed to the basement in 1947. In 1976 public protest forced officials to cremate Trucanini's remains and scatter the ashes in D'Entrecasteaux Channel, according to her wishes—100 years after her death.

The sweep of European technology, warfare, culture, and political economy across Van Diemen's Land prefigured the ruthless conquest of nature on the Australian mainland. In contrast to European preconceptions of North America, no antipodean invader ever entertained a sentimental vision of Australia as nature's garden, a prelapsarian Eden—quite the opposite. To the British, Australia stood in need of redemption. For the influential men of the colony, civilising Australia constituted an imperial mission, a long journey of Biblical proportions through a dark wood to a transfigured landscape. After days of travelling through the bush in 1821, the Judge-Advocate of New South Wales, Barron Field, came upon a settled district and wrote of his unbounded delight:

> I could hardly believe I was travelling in New Holland this day; so
> different—so English—is the character of the scenery—downs, mead-
> ows and streams in the flat—no side-scenes of eucalyptus ... Stock-
> men, cattle and sheep occasionally form your horizon, as in Old
> Holland—a Paul Potter or Cuyp effect rare in New Holland. At sunset
> we saw wooded hills, distant enough to display that golden blue or
> purple which landscape-painters love ... These things may seem trif-
> ling to an English reader; but by an American or Australian, accus-
> tomed to travel through the eternal valley of the shadow of
> monotonous woods, the charm of emerging into any thing like Euro-
> pean scenery will be duly appreciated.[47]

The unreal and contrary nature of Australia—its seeming
sameness, trees which shed bark rather than leaves, droughts, floods
and insect plagues—lacked 'all the dearest allegories of human
life',[48] and belonged to an order of unreason which rejected the
Enlightenment project of reducing the world to uniformity. The
Australian landscape appeared implausible because it did not resem-
ble anything in the settler's previous experience. The imposition of
civilisation, however, rendered antipodean nature more agreeable
and intelligible. The newcomer understood domesticated nature
because he helped to create it. Once those features associated with
European activity—downs, meadows, stockmen, smoke rising from
chimneys—appeared on the Australian landscape, the country
became imaginatively possessed. Early Australian explorers supplied
those preconceptions, the mental maps, necessary for settled occupation. Explorers inaugurated the process of appropriating the land
from the wilderness and the Aborigines.

The facts of existence in an alien, incomprehensible land
favoured a utilitarian cast of mind, and explorers, throughout the
period of Australia's early history, noted only those geographical
features likely to yield a profit. Explorers' journals contain few
descriptions of wildlife, or speculations on the natural history of
the land. Beauty appears in their calculations only in relation to the
land's possible use. The discovered country, for example, might
constitute 'a very beautiful and extensive cattle range',[49] or be easily
envisaged as 'favourably adapted to sheep-pasture'. The explorer

always bore in mind the convenience of the land's future possessors. One explorer celebrated the discovery of a pass through the mountains because, 'not only my horses, but the cattle and sheep of the farmer, might pass without danger, to those extensive pastures situate on their northern side'.[50]

Those tracts of open country, deceptively uninhabited, and so appealing to Europeans, were, in fact, contrived landscapes, almost artefacts of Aboriginal culture. The Aborigines had, for thousands of years, used fire to thin the woods, promote pasture and encourage game. They did not build fences between themselves and an untamed wilderness and knew of no boundary between wild and civilised. Their home was the entire habitat. But for the British in Australia, home was restricted to the farm, the house, or even to far away England—mostly to what was legally and personally owned.

The early explorers and settlers perpetuated the myth, first promulgated by Joseph Banks, of an empty continent, an unpeopled wilderness. The invaders chose to see only a country waiting for their occupation. The Aboriginal presence was merely temporary, for as Judge Field pointed out:

> The Australians [Aborigines] will never be civilised ... We have now lived among [them] for more than thirty years; and the most persevering attempts have always been made, and are still making to induce them to settle and avail themselves of the arts of life; but they cannot be fixed ... [I predict] decay or extermination [for] the simple race of Australia.[51]

Aboriginal landscape-making activities notwithstanding, the colonists determined to improve the nature of Australia. Of British descent, they believed themselves, alone among the peoples of the earth, possessed of the rational habits of mind—belief in reason and theory—necessary for enlightened settlement.[52] They had inherited the power bequeathed by science which would be employed toward the exploitative acquisition of Australia. In an 1822 address before the Philosophical Society of Australia, Alexander Berry, a large landowner, proposed:

> As this country is so peculiar, and has so many apparent disadvantages in the midst of some seeming advantages, it becomes our duty to

improve the latter and to obviate the former. It is therefore perhaps happy that its colonisation has been deferred until the present time, when the sum of human knowledge, both moral and physical, is so extended, that these attempts may be made upon just and rational principles, the result of which may be expected to be very different from such as originate in mere expedient or (what is still worse) from such as are the offspring of a false theory.[53]

The application of correct theory would overcome those aspects of Australian nature which defied logic—at least the logic of British minds. Barron Field accused one New South Wales river of 'spending the rains in flooding a barren country, instead of improving its own channel ... as a river should'.[54] The fact that many of Australia's newly discovered rivers flowed inland, dissipating their waters in remote swamps, proved frustrating to settlers accustomed to European drainage patterns. Proper rivers, running linearly, from their source in the mountains to their final issue in the sea, carried with them the prospect of arrival and ending, and supplied directions desired by commerce. Australian rivers upset these calculations.[55]

The British government, in order to facilitate efficient appropriation of the empty country, carefully instructed the early governors on the disposition of land. A proper land survey should precede settlement, which imperial authority intended should proceed block by rectangular block, according to a grid of straight lines on a map. Intersecting at exactly 90° angles, grid lines represent rationalised landscape—an abstract conception projected upon the living earth. Modelled after the American system, and esteemed by colonial governments for its speed, cheapness and simplicity, the rectangular land survey expedited rural settlement and became the basis of modern Australia's rectilinear landscape.

But until the early 1820s, settlement, more often than not, preceded survey, as farmers took up uncharted land. The understaffed Surveyor-General's Department could only map 145 farms a year, insufficient to meet the growing colony's needs. Demand for land came from the increasing number of free immigrants and the rising population of emancipists who could no longer profitably farm the deteriorating Cumberland Plains, the area immediately around

Sydney. In their virgin state the Plains appeared luxuriant and productive, but overstocking soon killed off the most valuable native grasses, locust plagues destroyed pasture, and crop yields fell. Farmers moved on to new ground.

Between 1822 and 1826 settlers appropriated nearly 150 000 hectares in the Hunter River Valley to the north of Sydney, the first major area settled outside the Cumberland Plains. Many of the new settlers, knowledgeable and experienced agriculturalists and stock breeders, brought with them the new implements and methods of the British agrarian revolution: superior bloodstock and new varieties of grain and grass seed for pasture improvement. The arrival in 1825 of a representative of the Australian Agricultural Company—formed by Australian and English investors for the purposes of agriculture generally, but more particularly for the rearing of sheep of the finest breed—signalled the beginning of interest by English capitalists in the colonies as fields of enterprise.

As settlement spread, the colonial authorities faced the need to impose conceptual order on the wild and unruly Australian landscape, to turn the vast, unbroken surface of Australia into a commodity appropriate to capitalist production. In 1828 the British government appointed a new Surveyor-General, a man equal to the task of charting and girding the Australian vastness, the energetic Thomas Livingston Mitchell. As an army surveyor, Mitchell had accompanied the British forces during the Peninsula War. In 1826, based on his war experience, Mitchell published *Outline of a System of Surveying for Geographical and Military Purposes*. He thus arrived in Australia equipped with a method to lay the groundwork necessary for the peopling of an uninhabited country by 'civilised inhabitants'. As Surveyor-General of New South Wales, he wasted no time in putting the system of his *Outline* into practice and led four expeditions of exploration into the interior. Mitchell regarded land survey as a strategy for translating the raw space of Australia into an apprehensible object, delineated by mind and deed. Through unceasing labour he laid out the colony's principal roads (still in use), apportioned the whole settlement into counties and parishes, and in 1831 produced the first map of the colony made from trigonometrical survey. During his explorations through Australia's eastern third, Mitchell gave form, differentiation and denomination to the previously anonymous landscape. He brought space into the realm of civilised discourse; his maps opened the land to invasion, enabled the history of conquest to begin, and transformed the amorphous face of Australia into an imperial possession.[56]

4

A CAMPING GROUND FOR PROFIT

THE MOUNTAINS SAW THEM MARCHING BY:
THEY FACED THE ALL-CONSUMING DROUGHT,
THEY COULD NOT REST IN SETTLED LAND:
BUT, TAKING EACH HIS LIFE IN HAND,
THEIR FACES EVER WESTWARD BENT
BEYOND THE FURTHEST SETTLEMENT,
RESPONDING TO THE CHALLENGE CRY
OF 'BETTER COUNTRY FURTHER OUT'.

A. B. Paterson, 'Song of the Future'

DURING THE YEARS 1780–1840 industrialisation transformed the face of England. The application of new inventions to mineral extraction, manufacturing and transportation brought about the most profound reshaping of the physical appearance of England since the Ice Age. The reorganisation of production also overturned traditional ways of life and uprooted rural populations. People crowded into towns seeking work in the new mills and factories, where an escalation in the intensity of human labour generated extensive poverty and dissatisfaction. People attached to more irregular, pre-capitalist rhythms of work rebelled against the notion of week after week of structured labour. And despite opprobrium from the churches and employers who complained of the profligacy, improvidence and thriftlessness of labour, urban workers and rural labourers resisted enslavement in the emergent industrial order. Apologists for the new regime counselled acceptance and urged people to look beneath the surface ugliness of the industrial landscape in order to exult the triumph of man over nature, the awesome precision and power that factories represented.[1]

Throughout Europe British working people became known for their protests against the hegemony of the property-owning classes. Riot and direct action—occasioned by high bread prices, turnpikes and tolls, impositions of new machinery, enclosures, press gangs and scores of other grievances—accompanied the Industrial Revolution. Through individualistic criminal acts and sporadic insurrectionary actions, protestors defied the laws of the propertied. The demonstrations of working people—pitmen, clothdressers, cutlers, weavers and labourers—in villages and towns over the whole country, claiming rights for themselves, panicked the propertied classes.[2]

The British government, fearful of riot and revolution, found a palliative in transportation, which aimed, not at punishing individual crimes, but at banishing an enemy class from British society. Those convicted and sent to Australia did not belong to a British criminal class. As a cross-section of the English and Irish working class, they possessed the skills needed to build Australia, and were suited to the tasks of performing the hard physical labour required to conquer a new country.[3]

Transportees included not only men and women convicted of crimes against property but also political agitators. Between 1790 and 1850 representatives of nearly every protest movement known to the authorities arrived in Australia as convicts. In the 1790s the government shipped to New South Wales the 'Scottish Martyrs', including the lawyer, Thomas Muir, convicted of lending out political tracts, among them Thomas Paine's *Rights of Man*—which the prosecution described as 'a most wicked and seditious publication'. The government intended the sentence as an example to professional men foolish enough to cooperate with plebeian reformers. Prime Minister William Pitt, who authorised the colony at Botany Bay, applauded Muir's sentence as effecting the suppression of 'doctrines so dangerous to the country'.[4] A few years later the British shipped out Irish Dissenters, and between 1815 and 1840, with the Irish countryside in a state of insurrection, the British transported over 1000 land-and-tithe protestors. From England, frame-breaking Luddites were sent out in 1812–13, and food rioters from East Anglia in 1820. Members of the Cato Street Conspiracy were also sent in 1820. Radical weavers came from Scotland in the same year and from Yorkshire in 1821. Over a third of those convicted during the Swing riots and machine-breaking of 1830, when thousands of farm labourers demonstrated for a minimum living wage and an end to rural unemployment, were transported to Australia. Rioters from Bristol followed in 1831 and from Wales in 1835. For the insolence of forming a trade union, the Tolpuddle Martyrs were removed to Australia in 1834, followed by more than 100 Chartists between 1839 and 1848.[5] Although a small minority of the total number of people transported, the presence of dissenters disclosed the political nature of convict transportation to Australia.

The scale and intensity of workers' organisation and demonstrations for political change in England unnerved the propertied classes, many of whom, during the economic depression after the Napoleonic Wars, experienced falling incomes. Fearful of change and anxious to preserve stratified social relations, some seized the chance, which came at the end of the 1820s, to restore their wealth and to recreate a paternal, feudal order in a new land.

In 1829, the British government claimed the west coast of New Holland to forestall the French and the Americans. On 2 May 1829, at Swan River, Captain Charles Howe Fremantle took possession, on behalf of the Crown, of the whole of New Holland not already included in the territory of New South Wales: one-third of the continent, 2.5 million square kilometres of land and 7900 kilometres of coastline. Under international law the whole of the Great South Land now belonged exclusively to Britain.

Captain James Stirling proposed to establish a province for Britain's gentry, solely underwritten by private capital and enterprise at the Swan River. He formed an association to obtain, from the British government, power to grant land to persons of capital and to those who guaranteed the passage of workers. On the basis of a rowboat journey of a few days' duration up the Swan River in 1827, Stirling predicted a glorious future for the colony. Although his own ship was nearly grounded at least three times, he claimed the river offered safe passage and anticipated that Fremantle would become a busy port of call for ships sailing from Europe to places as far apart as Canton and Sydney. Shipbuilders, using native timbers, would establish shipyards, the fertile and well-watered soils would support a productive agriculture, and the healing climate would enable Swan River to become a convalescent home. Stirling's artful promotion and the offer of Swan River land (at the rate of one acre for every 1s 6d invested in the colony—the most generous terms available in the world at the time) stimulated what contemporaries labelled 'Swan River Mania'. Because of the extreme distance and isolation and consequent high risks, prospective migrants needed to be highly motivated or highly gullible. Those who embarked with

Stirling in February 1829 looked forward to the life of rural gentry, believing they could recreate, in the Australian wilderness, an English village, complete with squire, parson, tenant farmers and agricultural labourers. Refugees from an industrialising England, they carried with them an Arcadian image of their future: a vision of nature as both passive and manageable.

The circumstances at the colony, however, cruelly frustrated their dreams. The Swan River Association granted land so recklessly to absentees and speculators, few actual settlers could obtain any. By July 1830, nearly 0.5 million hectares had been alienated but only 64 hectares were in cultivation. Land hunger gripped all classes: Stirling claimed huge areas for himself, labourers deserted employers and looked for their own land, and all ignored actual land use. The colony consisted of speculators who owned land, officials who schemed for land, farmers who wanted land and traders who profited from those clamouring for land.

Thomas Peel, the colony's principal investor, had planned to grow cotton, tobacco, sugar and flax, to rear horses for the East India trade and to raise large herds of cattle and swine for supplying His Majesty's and other shipping with provisions. He had looked fervently to the time when he would be Peel of Swan River, owner of a vast estate, whose tenants would look to him as their patron and lord.[6] But soon after landing, his servants deserted and he 'was obliged to make his own bed and to fetch water for himself, and to light his own fire'.[7] Servants everywhere assumed a status of equality, a usurpation masters found most annoying and among the greatest drawbacks to their comfort.[8] Although a nightmarish situation for landowners, working people prospered. One labourer wrote home in 1832:

> We bless the day we left England . . . I am at work brick-making . . . we work eight hours . . . we have no rent to pay, no wood to buy. We just go out of doors and cut it down . . . It is not here as in England, if you don't like it you may leave it: [here it is] pray do stop, I will raise your wages.[9]

Contrary to Stirling's optimistic assessment, the first settlers found the coastal plain composed mostly of very sandy soils, which offered sparse natural grazing for horses, cattle and sheep. The land supported trees and hard-leaved shrubs, but produced very poor crops when cleared. Because English axes proved unsuitable against the country's hardwoods, settlers resorted to fire as the major clearing weapon. A thick smoke haze covered the coastal plain throughout the summer months and bushfires became endemic and destructive. European weeds, mixed with the seeds sown for the first crops, spread rapidly. Weeds and trees from South Africa—doublegee (*Emes australis*) and Cape tulips (*Homeria breyniana* and *H. miniata*)—also took root. Because of the summer drought, and the environmental unsuitability of European seed types, colonists abandoned agriculture and moved sheep onto inland pastures. Exotic weeds followed in their tracks and quickly replaced the native grasses.[10] But by 1834, poison weed, poor husbandry and Aboriginal spears had reduced sheep numbers to half that of four years before.

As fewer ships and labourers came to the colony some settlers began to look on the Aborigines as a future indigenous servant class—the shepherds, bottle-washers, kitchen boys, stable hands and ploughboys of British civilisation. Most, however, decided the Aborigines were not human beings, but monkeys of grossly offensive habits. Settler John Morgan described the Aborigines as 'a miserable race of animals—moving upon two legs—They are considered human beings, but I repeat to say that the link which connects them with the brute, is at all times—very painfully perceptible.'[11]

The original inhabitants of the south-west of Australia, the Nyungar, lived, hunted and foraged over a land among the most bountiful of Australian tribal areas. Kangaroo roamed in herds of 500 or more, flocks of cockatoos, parakeets and pigeons darkened the sky. Ducks appeared in great numbers on swamps and pools and the rivers teemed with fish and crustacea and the rich marine life of salt water estuaries supported enormous numbers of teal, brown ducks, swans and pelicans. Edible roots, nuts and seeds grew in abundance along watercourses and in the bush.

Initial contacts with the British did not bring conflict. During the early days of exploration and settlement the Nyungar welcomed the strangers, shared food and showed them to sources of fresh water. The Aborigines soon saw, however, that the settlers' avaricious intentions meant disruption of the landscape, disturbance and death of native animals and a hostility and indifference that they keenly resented. In retaliation they began spearing stock, burning down buildings and attacking isolated settlers. The new settlers interpreted Aboriginal resistance as unprovoked depredations by treacherous, thieving savages. The problem, they agreed, was native ingratitude. Like European invaders elsewhere, the Swan River colonists formed their views of the indigenous inhabitants in accordance with their own purposes. Those who came for quick profit and speculation saw deceit and malignancy on every side—a mirror image of their own intent.

In 1833, upon the capture of one of the leaders of the resistance, Midgegooroo, vengeful crowds gathered and called for his death. At the urging of the mob, troops dragged the struggling Aborigine from his cell, lashed him to the gaol door, blindfolded him and shot him dead. Two months later, two colonial boys, after taking Midgegooroo's son, Yagan, into their trust, shot him at point-blank range. A settler then cut off Yagan's head, which he smoked and cured, and decorated with a head band and feathers for exhibition in English sideshows. Nyungar resistance continued. In the York district Aboriginal raids provoked violent reprisals from the military and settlers, who nailed the skulls of their victims above their doorways and strung the ears of slaughtered Aborigines above kitchen hearths.

Although they ultimately achieved superiority in the use of force, the security of their huge land-grab worried the colony's 1800 Europeans; they wondered how they might hold their half million hectares against determined Aboriginal opposition. In 1834 Stirling wrote that the settlers had found the Aborigines very formidable enemies, and, 'If they [the Nyungar] had the inclination and the power to combine their efforts, it would be useless to attempt to maintain our conquest with our present numbers.' [12]

Stirling held ambitious development plans for the inland area which depended on establishing regular commerce with Albany on the south coast. The Murray River tribe, whose territory embraced the road south and who frequently camped on the site Stirling desired for his first military post, stood in the way of these plans. To convince the Aborigines of the foolishness of opposing civilisation's advance, Stirling, in October 1834, mounted a punitive expedition with an armed and mounted party of 25 men. They scoured the countryside and early in the morning of 28 October 1834, at Pinjarra, they rushed an Aboriginal camp of approximately 80 men, women and children. In less than an hour and a half Stirling's men completed their carnage and left twenty or more Aborigines dead.[13]

Despite the effectual securing of British property against Aboriginal reappropriation, however, settlers continued to leave the depressed colony. In 1835, Perth, the colony's capital, shrank to a meagre township of 600 persons. In the countryside, large areas of deeded land remained idle without the labour to work them and scarcely a property remained free of mortgage. All attempts to encourage immigration failed.

In 1839–40 the directors of the London-based Western Australia Company issued a prospectus, showing the plan of a beautifully laid out city, Australind, south of Perth, and offered sub-divisions for sale. When the promoters learned that the colonial government might resume the land they quickly reimposed the Australind map onto country 550 kilometres north of Perth. Since they regarded land as entirely fungible—one piece exactly like another—they could imagine no objection to the transfer. The actual location of their city made no real difference; the rationality and perfect order of the plan itself constituted the most important part of the scheme. But many investors took fright at the change and withdrew their money. The directors, insensitive to the imperatives of geography, of the need to physically locate the scheme and to ensure a sense of place, transferred the location back to the south of Perth; the intervening uncertainty created by all the changes, however, undermined the scheme.

Many newly arrived Swan River colonists found the excessive heat, the pervasive sand, the ubiquitous flies and the monopoly in freehold disagreeable. A few returned to their ships for the cooler, unsettled regions along the southern coast. Georgiana Molloy and

her husband, Captain John Molloy, joined the exodus.[14] In April/
May 1830 they sailed around the surging seas of Cape Leeuwin,
where the Indian and Southern Oceans meet, and dropped anchor
in Flinders Bay. A few days later, while a servant held an umbrella
over a bed in a leaky tent, Molloy gave birth. The baby survived
only a few days. Some time later Molloy wrote of her loss to a
friend who had just lost her own child:

> I could truly sympathize with you, for language refuses to utter what I
> experienced when mine died in my arms in this dreary land ... I
> thought I might have had one little bright object left me to solace all
> the hardships and privations I endured and have still to go through.[15]

Molloy turned to religion for solace against Australian hardships
and sought refuge in the knowledge of a future world and in the
memory of one she had left behind. As she tended her English
garden of orange nasturtiums and peach trees, planted at the edge
of unbounded wild Australia, she thought of violets and primroses
and from the safety of her sanctuary she wrote with qualified alarm
of the cultural darkness of the bush:

> This is certainly a very beautiful place—but were it not for domestic
> charms the eye of the emigrant would soon weary of the unbounded
> limits of thickly clothed dark green forests where nothing can be
> descried to feast the imagination and where you can only say there must
> be some tribes of natives in those woods and they are the most
> degraded of humanity.[16]

Georgiana Molloy lived on the edge of an unconquerable forest.
An English axe made no impression against the huge trees. Half a
dozen men worked two or three days to fell, dig up and cut up a
single tree. The work of pioneering, of building a new home and
founding the settlement of Augusta, reduced her to 'skin and bone'.
Her life demanded constant energy and by the end of her first year
in Augusta she expressed the wish that she had never come out to
Australia.

Molloy gave birth to a second child in November 1831 and when
wildflowers bloomed the following spring she began taking a per-
ceptive interest in her Australian surroundings. She wrote
admiringly of the bush birds and especially of the effusion of

flowers. In December 1836, by which time she had given birth to two more children, she received, unsolicited, a box of seeds from a Captain James Mangles, an amateur English horticulturalist. His request, to return the box filled with samples of Australian flora, marked a turning point in Georgiana Molloy's life. When, a few months later, her nineteen-month-old son drowned in a well, she did not seek solace in the Bible. Instead, she turned to the beauty of the living world. Plant collecting became an all-consuming passion. With her children 'running like butterflies from flower to flower' she mounted almost daily expeditions into the bush to investigate and to collect. She botanised for love of the beauty of the world, not for the use which might be made of her discoveries; she found splendour, not utility, in the bush. Collecting inspired her with 'ardour and interest' and she thanked Mangles

> for being the cause of my more immediate acquaintance with the nature and variety of [Australian plants] ... but for your request, I should never have bestowed on the flowers of this Wilderness any other idea than that of admiration.[17]

In the year after the seed box arrived Molloy spent more time in the bush than in her entire previous seven years' residence at Augusta. She abandoned her Old World religious preoccupations, the generalised abstractions of her Christian heritage, in exchange for the vivid freshness of immediate experience. She began to feel at home in a familiar world and no longer found the bush lonely—a theme which dominated European Australian attitudes toward the bush until it ceased to exist to any significant extent. Molloy entered fervently into an exploration of the natural world and found that 'being in the Bush is ... one of the most delightful states of existence, free from every household care'.[18] But the birth of her seventh child in December 1842 left her weakened and Georgiana Molloy never again ventured into her beloved Australian bush. Bedridden, she suffered through the heat of the summer and died in April 1843, aged 38.

Meanwhile, in post-Napoleonic Wars Britain, continuing protests by English working people against endemic poverty terrified the ruling classes. A revolt by farm labourers, who burned hay ricks and smashed farm machines, in the autumn of 1830, alarmed the owners of property already apprehensive at the spectre of democracy. By the 1830s the working class presence was the most significant factor in British political life. The ruling class looked for a means to mitigate working class revolt, preferably one that simultaneously augmented the wealth of the British empire. In 1829 Edward Gibbon Wakefield proposed 'systematic colonisation', a scheme directly opposed to the speculative fiasco perpetrated by venture capitalists at the Swan River settlement. Wakefield reacted with horror at the bankruptcy there of members of illustrious English families and their degradation to a life indistinguishable from barbarism, where masters made their own beds and fetched their own water. Wakefield understood that the occupation of land by every man subverted the division of labour, upon which the modern economy depended. To restore proper social relationships, governments had to sell Australian land at a fixed price, calculated to prevent labourers from becoming landowners 'too soon', but sufficiently low to attract men of capital. The proceeds from land sales would be used to finance the emigration of young workers of both sexes for employment by the landowning class. Wakefield aimed to unite, in profitable association, surplus English capital, the unoccupied land of Australia, and the redundant population of the British Isles.

Systematic colonisation aspired to reproduce, on the other side of the world, those class relations prevailing in Britain—an intent clarified by a younger contemporary of Wakefield:

> E. G. Wakefield ... discovered ... in the colonies the truth as to the conditions of capitalist production in the mother country ... [His] colonisation theory ... attempted to effect the manufacture of wage-workers in the Colonies ... Wakefield discovered that in the Colonies, property in money, means of subsistence, machines and other means of production, does not as yet stamp a man as a capitalist if there be wanting the correlative—the wage-worker, the other man who is compelled to sell himself of his own free-will. He discovered that capital is not a thing, but a social relation between persons, established by the instrumentality of things.[19]

Under Wakefield's patronage, a group of influential men, including Sir William Molesworth, John Stuart Mill and Jeremy Bentham, established a National Colonisation Society to promote a 'general system of colonisation, founded on the main principles of selection, concentration and the sale of waste land for purpose of emigration'.[20] All the members hoped to profit from any future colony they helped found, and southern, central Australia became the focus of their propagandising.

In 1834 the British Parliament established the Colonisation Commission of South Australia, with authority to sell land, raise loans on the land fund thereby established, and select migrants of sober, frugal and industrious habits. With the hyperbole common to realtors, the Commissioners described South Australia as furnishing a vast extent of land in one of the finest climates in the world, abounding with gulfs, bays, lakes, peninsulas and islands and adapted to almost every pursuit of agriculture, fishing and commerce.[21] In 1835, John Morphett, one of several wealthy individuals attracted by the huge profits likely from colonial land speculation, wrote:

> The purchase of land in new colonies experience has shown to be one of the most profitable modes of employing capital which commercial enterprise or speculation has ever discovered; and of course those who lay out their money on the first formation of a colony make their capital most productive.[22]

In 1836 the Commissioners instructed Colonel William Light to survey 2800 kilometres of the South Australian coast, select the best sites, survey a principal town, divide 388 square kilometres into farming sections and make reservations for secondary towns. But with the first settlers only three months behind, Light lacked time to survey the whole coast. Instead, he chose for settlement the eastern shore of Gulf Saint Vincent because there the coast already bore a capitalist appearance. The country, he observed, 'looked more like land already in the possessions of persons of property than that left to the course of nature alone'.[23]

Although not occupied by 'persons of property', in the sense understood by Light, the land he surveyed was inhabited. And, on the night in December 1836 when the first colonists disembarked at Holdfast Bay, near the future city of Adelaide, the original residents set fire to the bush. The newcomers took the flames as a sign of welcome by the primitive people and not the gesture of those without more effective means of expressing opposition to the invaders. The message became more explicit later the next year after an Aboriginal woman acquired sufficient knowledge of the colonists' language to tell them, 'You go to England, that your country; this our country'.[24] But when words failed to persuade, the Aborigines adopted more direct methods to repel the invaders: spearing and scattering stock and ambushing shepherds. The invaders immediately claimed the right of revenge because, as a colonist reminded his compatriots, they did not come to usurp or thieve Aboriginal property but rather to settle South Australia on the basis of a great law of nature. The earth and the fullness of its produce belonged in common to all mankind until the labour of industrious agriculturalists created that advance from communal to private property, which signified progress from barbarism to civilisation. Defiance of this new order equalled rebellion against the creator of the universe. Thus, the colonists reasoned, they were fully justified in hanging and punishing Aborigines for transgressions against the laws of nature and property.

Such a marvellously self-serving doctrine easily classified land as vacant or virgin when actually inhabited. Under English law, land that had never been made property was vacant in fact. And so with a vast domain available for speculation, the colony prospered. By the end of 1839 absentees held more than two-thirds of all the province's alienated land and the buying and selling of town and country lots for immediate gain became the colony's chief business. But the colony actually produced nothing and after four years of speculation the settlement fell into economic depression, relieved only by the discovery, to the north of Adelaide, of exportable copper in the early 1840s.

Meanwhile the colonists had established commercial ties with the older colonies. In April 1838, the first cattle driven overland from the east reached Adelaide. An observer later described the event as 'one of the early and essential instruments in the successful conversion of a vast wilderness into a fruitful garden'.[25] While the

European invaders justified their usurpation by law, the society they introduced was, in fact, lawless. Most of the overlanders who arrived in Adelaide, driving sheep and cattle, boasted of the brutalities they committed against the Aborigines on the way. The diary of Alexander Buchanan, who drove sheep from New South Wales, along the Murray River, to South Australia, records the stunning casualness with which the overlanders treated Aboriginal lives:

> 15 November 1839
> . . . we from the opposite bank fired upon them also and killed the old chief, when they all took to the Murray and we kept firing as long as they were within shot. There were five or six killed and a good many wounded. We then broke up their canoes and took all their nets and burnt them.
> 22 November 1839
> As we were putting the sheep in camp for the night a black was seen in some reeds and the carter fired upon him and killed him.
> 7 December 1839
> Halted and fed the sheep. Saw a good many blacks opposite bank of the river, fired upon them and killed one, the rest made off immediately.[26]

The overlanders reported favourably on the fertile hill country through which they passed and stockholders quickly spread into the area. The expansion led, as one colonist reported, to 'the necessary slaughter of blacks'.[27] In 1841, for example, a large punitive expedition, under the command of the South Australian Protector of Aborigines, murdered more than 30 members of the Rufus River tribe.

By 1842, six years after founding, South Australia's British population reached almost 15 000. Notwithstanding declining yields on the exhausted soil cultivated around Adelaide, the country appeared subjugated. J. F. Bennett, who visited South Australia in 1838 and again in 1843, observed:

> I have seen the plains and forests around Adelaide changed from their original desolation into a continuous mass of farms—some thousands of acres bearing their crops of wheat, maize and barley—while in the more distant parts in which no track or trace of human being could be found when I first rode through them I ultimately saw spotted with sheep and cattle stations with an occasional field of corn . . . I could

scarcely imagine a more interesting scene than to observe a country in the course of being rescued from a state of nature.[28]

The forests of tall stringybark (*Eucalyptus obliqua* and *E. baxteri*), within reach of Adelaide, fell rapidly to the shingle and paling cutter; axemen hewed construction and fencing material out of red and blue gum (*E. camaldulensis* and *E. leucoxylon*), and chopped mining props and firewood from whatever was available. The sound of the chief tool of deliverance, the axe, became like music to the ears of the colonists. George Angas travelled through the Mount Lofty Ranges, above Adelaide, in 1847 and described where

> occasionally in some deep glen in the mountain forest there is suddenly revealed a group of busy workmen, with their gypsy-like encampment around them scattered with felled timber and planks on all sides, while the sharp sound of the axe rings echoing through the solitude, proclaiming the dawn of civilization and industry.[29]

Because Wakefield so directly addressed the problem of how to construct a bourgeois society in the new world, of how to transplant a class society, his influence extended beyond South Australia. Prior to 1830 colonial governors in New South Wales, Van Diemen's Land and Western Australia made land grants on the basis of ill-defined and freely interpreted regulations. For capitalism to flourish, however, the land, the soil, had to be worked by profit-pursuing private enterprise and turned into a commodity, possessed by private owners and freely purchasable and saleable by them. And, as the whale and seal fisheries declined, land became the principal productive asset in the colonies. In recognition of this new economic fact the British government ordered an end to all land grants in January 1831. Henceforth, land could be alienated only by sale and auction, and the proceeds used to finance the emigration of unemployed English workers. The instructions placed the colonies on a firm capitalist foundation and put in practice principles celebrated by Adam Smith. The rules would enable, Secretary of State for Colonies Viscount Goderich explained to New South Wales Governor Ralph Darling, 'the Agriculturalist to apply the great principle of the division of labour'.[30]

By their schemes the systematic colonisers attempted to

regularise capitalism, to remove chance, lessen uncertainty, and build a balanced society, an economy in equilibrium between labour, capital and land. Systematic colonisation, however, never succeeded according to the prescriptions outlined in Wakefield's *A Letter to Sydney* (1829) and *England and America* (1833). Each colony gave rise to conditions not foreseen in theory, and colonists, gathered indiscriminately from buyers of shares, could not be depended upon to engage in farming and to refrain from land speculation. Nevertheless, several Wakefieldian principles became established. In particular, authorities accepted the need to tame the wilderness in an organised manner. Wakefield believed too quick a spread of persons over the land, too sudden a contact with primeval nature, produced ruder habits of life, and asserted, 'CONCENTRATION [of settlement] would produce what never did and never can exist without it—CIVILIZATION.'[31]

From their earliest days in the New World of North America, the English had evinced a similar fear of the wilderness and had sought to keep the colonists together while holding the natives and the unknown wilderness at a safe distance. In Virginia, Massachusetts and Connecticut, the authorities prescribed penalties for those who moved ahead of the line of settlement and lived surrounded by only woods, animals and Indians.[32] Similarly, in Australia, as Goderich explained to Darling:

> Nothing could be more unfortunate than the formation of a race of men, wandering with their cattle over the extensive regions of the interior, and losing, like the descendants of the Spaniards in the Pampas of South America, almost all traces of their civilization.[33]

Accordingly, New South Wales surveyors mapped out nineteen counties—a total of two million hectares —which, the government claimed, provided sufficient land for the 70 000 people in the colony in the late 1820s. Settlement outside the boundaries was forbidden. Commercial imperatives soon rendered the boundaries irrelevant, however.

In New South Wales the demands of the British woollen industry prevailed over the fears of decadence in the wilderness. Colonial wool—longer, silkier and more resilient than any but the very best

Saxon—served ideally for the upper-grade fabrics then in demand. New South Wales sheep, however, required more extensive pastures than those contained within the boundaries of location. British capital, alert to the profits possible from antipodean wool growing, found many colonists willing to drive stock to the idle and open lands beyond the boundaries. A man with sheep or cattle could go anywhere, regardless of government stricture and, even before the posting of boundaries, flocks and men marched across the limits.

With astonishing rapidity the squatting movement, which spread from the south-east corner of the continent, laid claim to most of habitable Australia. By 1835 sheep flocks were already 550 kilometres from Sydney in two directions, grazing the unsanctioned wilderness. Wool exports soared. In 1831 Australian wool represented 8 percent of British imports; less than 20 years later Australia supplied over half of all British raw wool needs, relieving British dependence on foreign supplies. As sheep numbers increased and flockmasters sought new pastures, British policy yielded to Australia's spectacular pastoral suitability. The Secretary of State, Lord Glenelg, acknowledged Australia's imperial value in 1836:

> The whole surface of the country exhibits a range of sheep walks which ... are ... of almost unrivaled value for the production of the finest description of wool ... The motives which are urging mankind to break through the restraints [prohibitions on settlement outside the boundaries] are too strong to be encountered with effect by ordinary means. All that remains for the Government in such circumstances is to assume the guidance and direction of enterprise which, though it cannot prevent or retard, it may yet conduct to happy result.[34]

The colonial government quickly moved to legitimise and regulate that which it could not prevent, and in 1836 required pastoralists beyond the boundaries to obtain, for ten pounds, a license which certified the holder as fit to live beyond police supervision. To facilitate pastoral development, Governor Richard Bourke sent the Surveyor-General, Thomas Mitchell, out to investigate the suitability of the land between the mouth of the Murray, over 1000 kilometres distant, and the Australian Alps. Mitchell left in March 1836 and when he returned, in November, he reported effusively on the land he had seen. On the future Western District of Victoria, to which he gave the name Australia Felix, he wrote:

> We had at length discovered a country ready for the immediate recep-
> tion of civilized man; and destined perhaps to become eventually a
> portion of a great empire. Unencumbered by too much wood, it yet
> possessed enough for all purposes; its soil was exuberant, and its climate
> temperate . . . it was traversed by mighty rivers, and watered by streams
> innumerable . . . Every day we passed over land, which, for natural
> fertility and beauty, could scarcely be surpassed; over streams of unfail-
> ing abundance, and plains covered with the richest pasturage.[35]

Mitchell employed at least three permanent Aboriginal guides on
his expedition and, wherever he could, obtained local guides with
whom he hoped to pass from tribe to tribe. They brought him to
water, showed him the best routes of travel and advised him on
what lay ahead. Without their assistance, he and his party of 25
would probably have perished, for Mitchell, like virtually all Australian explorers, was vitally dependent on Aboriginal knowledge.
Although his diary records almost daily encounters with different
Aborigines—on occasion upwards of 200 people—Mitchell nevertheless claimed to have discovered an unpeopled wilderness: 'a
country which is yet in the same state as it was when formed by its
Maker . . . A land so inviting, and still without inhabitants!'[36]
Mitchell made this claim, despite the contrary evidence of his own
observations and those of his predecessor, Charles Sturt, who in
1829–30 journeyed down the Murray and covered some of the
same ground Mitchell later crossed. Before his own trip, Mitchell
read Sturt's journal, which, although it included evidence of recent
massive depopulation, reported a still formidable Aboriginal presence:

> from the number and size of the paths that led from the river, in various
> directions across the plain, I [concluded] . . . we were passing through a
> very populous district. What the actual number of inhabitants was it is
> impossible to say, but we seldom communicated with fewer than 200
> daily.[37]

A month before Mitchell's return, the new Governor, Sir George
Gipps, arrived in Sydney to find stock rolling north, and already on
the fringes of the future Queensland. Mitchell's glowing tales of

open forest vales, grassy hills, glades and verdant vales, now fell
with irresistible allure upon the minds of men confined within the
boundaries. By year's end, squatters, mustering flocks for 'the
Major's Line'—tracks left by Mitchell's drays—headed for the heart
of Australia Felix. Others had already arrived.

In 1835, John Batman had sailed from Van Diemen's Land to
Port Phillip Bay, and the mouth of the Yarra River—now
Melbourne. Batman possessed a practical mind—a mind ignorant
of beauty unrelated to use—and an eye for sheep pasture. After a
brief exploration around Port Phillip, he described the land as:

> beautiful and all good sheep country . . . The land excellent and very
> rich, covered with kangaroo grass two feet high, and as thick as it
> could stand. Trees not more than six to the acre, and those small sheoak
> and wattle. I never saw anything to equal the land in my life.

Keen to prosper, Australian-born Batman had, a few years previously, hunted Tasmanian Aborigines in the hopes of obtaining a
land grant. He murdered two wounded men, captured several
women, and won his grant.[38] Now he turned his talents to concil-
iating the Port Phillip Aborigines. In exchange for 50 pairs of
blankets, 50 pairs of scissors, 50 tomahawks, 20 suits of slop clothing and other unsaleable goods, he secured several straggling marks
on an already-prepared treaty, purporting to represent the commitment of the Darebin Aborigines:

> [We] do, for ourselves, our heirs and successors, give, grant, and con-
> firm unto the said John Batman, his heirs and assigns, all that tract of
> country situate and being in Port Phillip, running from the branch of
> the river at the top of the Port, about seven miles from the mouth of
> the river, forty miles N.E., and from thence S.S.W. across Vilumanata
> to Geelong harbour at the head of the same, and containing about
> 500 000 acres more or less.

Batman concluded a similarly worded treaty for another 100 000
acres but actually claimed a total of 680 000 acres, which he
divided into seventeen allotments, one each for the members of the
Port Phillip Association, including the sheriff of Hobart, the deputy
sheriff of Launceston, the Postmaster-General, the Collector of
Customs and the manager of the Derwent Bank at Hobart. Batman

and his associates now ranked among the largest landowners in the world. Back in Van Diemen's Land Batman spoke of the finest basin of water, the most extensive plains he had ever seen, of the rich black soil and the waist-high kangaroo grass, the considerable river at the head of the port and of the friendly natives who so readily agreed to divest themselves of their land. His purchase caused a sensation, exciting land hunger on an island beginning to seem overcrowded. On a tour of the colony in 1835, the Reverend John Dunmore Lang reported on the commotion:

> [I] found almost every respectable person I met with preparing, either individually, or in the person of some near relation or confidential agent, to occupy the Australian El Dorado . . . as the southern coast of New Holland was a waste country in the occupation of no European power . . . it was free to be taken possession of by the first comers, or by those who could make the best bargain with the aborigines.[39]

In the first six months of 1836 at least eleven ships plied Bass Strait, between Van Diemen's Land and Port Phillip, and in 48 crossings brought in 20 000 sheep. The colonists sailed through a fantastic seabird sanctuary, where black cormorants sat on dead branches, ·

> projecting from the water [and flocks of] Pelicans . . . their long pink beaks and snowy plumage reflected in the glistening waves [while] large flocks of ducks wheeled backwards and forwards through the air or chased each other in wild gambols through the water.[40]

But the settlers saw beauty only in sheep; more than 300 000 grazed in the district by 1837.

Although they were outside the boundaries of location, Governor Bourke permitted the occupiers and their sheep to remain. But he voided Batman's purchase, as well as a later, and even more audacious, engrossment of 20 million acres of the South Island of New Zealand by wealthy Sydney landowner William Wentworth. These contracts, Bourke argued, pre-empted the prerogative of the imperial government: until uncivilised inhabitants of any country establish a settled form of government and subjugate the ground by cultivation, they exert but a qualified dominion and right of occupancy, and therefore cannot grant or transfer land they do not fully possess. If a civilised power should make a settlement, Bourke continued, the right of pre-emption of the soil, the right of extinguishing the native title, lies exclusively in the government of that power. Individual Englishmen, therefore, cannot form separate colonies in Australia without the consent of the British Crown.[41] Bourke found ample precedent for his views in the history of European colonisation. In 1629, the governor of Massachusetts Bay, John Winthrop, had ruled that most land in America fell under the legal rubric of *vacuum domicilium*. Because the Indians had failed to subdue the land, they, therefore, could claim only a *natural* and not a *civil* right of possession.[42]

Lord Glenelg confirmed Bourke's judgement of Batman as a trespasser on Crown land and added:

> I yet believe that we should consult very ill for the real welfare of that helpless and unfortunate Race by recognising in them any right to alienate to private adventurers the Land of the Colony. It is indeed enough to observe that such a concession would subvert the foundation on which all Proprietary rights in New South Wales at present rest . . .[43]

Glenelg did not argue against Batman's claims on legal grounds. Instead, he ignored the question of the Crown's title to Port Phillip or any other land in Australia and simply asserted that right. Recognition of Batman's treaty would be tantamount to admitting Governor Phillip's settlement at Port Jackson was illegal.

During 1838, despite drought, sheep runs crept over the unbroken forest country between Port Phillip and Sydney and squatters moved onto unoccupied land in the west. By 1839 squatters had moved forward 550 kilometres. The only boundaries they recognised were impassable ranges or deserts; as long as the hope of better land further out beckoned, they pushed on. In five years unauthorised settlers made the 'southern district of New South Wales', later Victoria, into a settled colony and depastured 750 000 sheep there. By the end of 1840, a little more than 700 men with 6000 servants and dependents watched over 1.3 million sheep and 400 000 cattle on lands outside the old boundaries.

The pioneering of the sheep runs was usually done by proxy. While the financiers remained on their Crown-granted principalities, within the narrow confines of old New South Wales, employees led the squatting infiltration north, south and south-west. Henry Dangar, of Neotsfield in the Hunter Valley, for example, had, by 1842, taken out licenses for the Gostwyck run of 19 300 hectares, Paradise Creek of 12 900 hectares, Bald Hills of 7750 hectares, Moonbi of 10 100 hectares, Bulleroi of 25 800 hectares, Karee of 25 800 hectares and Myall Creek for 19 400 hectares —each managed by an overseer and worked by teams of assigned servants, ticket-of-leave holders, emancipists and the odd free worker.[44]

Most of the free men who drove sheep into the interior regarded squatting as an expedient. Farmers, gentry, retired officers, lawyers' sons, all reasoned that with a little capital investment they could make a fortune in Australia and then return home—as most colonists referred to Britain. Their common purpose was to exploit rather than to settle; residency was merely a means of increasing the efficiency of exploitation. Squatter George Leslie summed up the prevailing attitude in a letter to his aunt at home:

> Australia, is a very nice agreeable country for a person to stay a few years in, but to settle in ultimately would never enter my head . . . a little money is yet to be made and accordingly I mean to try and then spend it in old Scotland.[45]

And huge profits were possible, at least for absentees. The Clyde Company partners of Edinburgh began sheep raising at Port Phillip in 1836. Over the next 21 years their capital outlay amounted to less than £16 000. Upon liquidation of the partnership in 1857–58, the parvenu landlords realised, including dividends, a total of £250 000, a return of over 1500 percent! But George Russell, their manager in Australia, concluded:

> [I] would have been better off if I had not been connected with it, that if I had bestowed the same care and attention on a station of my own I would have come off better in the end; and that I would have had more satisfaction in working on my own account than I had in working for men who were residing in Scotland, who had no colonial experience in country matters, and who did not have any desire to form a permanent establishment in the Colony but looked solely to getting as great a return for the money they had invested as possible.[46]

75

With the price of wool rising throughout the 1830s and land available for nothing, the prospect of quick gain constantly excited the colonists' roving propensities. Animated by restlessness, forever tormented by the possibility of 'better country further out', and easily deluded by the vaguest rumours of passing travellers, the squatter, while securing one run by discovery or negotiation, would range the neighbouring country for better sites. Firstcomers generally claimed as much territory as they could persuade later arrivals to accept as legitimate. The first squatter on the Canning Downs, in southern Queensland, proclaimed a principality of some hundreds of thousands of hectares, 'from the bottom of Toolburra to the head of the Condamine'.[47] The squatters who drove the first seven flocks across the Goulburn River, in northern Victoria, settled themselves over lands separated by hundreds of kilometres.[48] Pioneers deeply resented newcomers, although, for a while at least, accommodating new settlers, wedging them in, served the interests of all, since a reasonable occupation strengthened everybody's position. But the accumulation of vast estates had less to do with rationality than with unconstrained self-interest. As one early settler noted: 'the jealousy with which we heard of the arrival of any one in our neighbourhood, notwithstanding the vast tracts of land we each laid claim to, was one of the remarkable features of our early settlement.'[49]

Squatters obtained their chief profit from the natural increase of their flocks. Sheep multiplied so fast, a flock of 500 could become 900 in a year. Under the best of conditions the value of wool might cover annual expenses, but sales of surplus stock to new squatters pushing further out yielded returns of over 20 percent in normal years. Profits thus depended on the perpetual multiplication of sheep flocks and occupation of new land.

Whenever, during his expeditions, Mitchell encountered hostile natives, he ascribed their enmity to a savage disposition, natural to the race.[50] Like all invaders of new lands, Mitchell, and the squatters who followed his tracks, assumed an innate and absolute superiority over the indigenous inhabitants; that the Aborigines intended defending their land escaped European understanding. Nevertheless, although initially hospitable towards the invaders, as the number of sheep multiplied and British land claims escalated, the Aborigines of Port Phillip and elsewhere began fiercely resisting further encroachment. The invaded made use of their skills of camouflage and bushcraft and their intimate knowledge of the land to attack pastoral enterprises at their most vulnerable points—the stores, the shepherds and the stock. The resistance became pervasive. As John Walpole Willis, puisne judge at Port Phillip, admitted in 1841: 'the frequent conflicts between settlers and blacks made it ... sufficiently clear that the Aboriginal tribes are neither a conquered people nor have they tacitly acquiesced in the supremacy of the settlers.'[51]

Although they mostly confined their resistance to guerrilla warfare, the Aborigines sometimes mounted mass attacks, driving away squatters and dispersing sheep flocks. In May 1838, a combined force of 300 Pangerang Aborigines ambushed and killed seven members of George Faithful's party travelling to a station near the Goulburn River in north-east Victoria. Although Faithful left the area, the attack slowed the squatting advance only momentarily; within six months another squatter took possession of Faithful's abandoned run. Faithful himself soon took his revenge and on one punitive expedition shot dead dozens of Aborigines. He reported: 'We were slow to fire, which prolonged the battle, and 60 rounds were fired, and I trust and believe that many of the bravest of the savage warriors bit the dust.'[52]

A handful of squatters acknowledged their role as aggressors and usurpers, but they largely confined their opinions to their diaries. Few bothered to get to know any Aborigines. But for those who did, acquaintance led to some surprising discoveries. Squatter Edward Curr wrote of the Aborigines:

> their sympathies, likes and dislikes were very much what ours would have been if similarly situated ... This fact only gradually dawned on me, as I had somehow started with the idea that I should find the Blacks as different from the white men in mind as they are in colour.[53]

Most squatters abhorred the Aborigines. They resented their 'wandering propensities', their independence, their pride and their unwillingness to accept the hierarchical authority Europeans equated with enlightenment. For 50 years Aborigines had rejected the civilisation Europeans sought to impose on Australia. Their inclination towards independence of action and refusal to accept the values of the invaders greatly exasperated the British. Their disdain for European habits marked them as barbarians and supplied the Europeans with an antithesis—civilisation versus barbarism—highly useful as a rationalisation for aggression. To counter Aboriginal resistance the squatters appealed to the government to clear the land. When the colonial authorities equivocated, the squatters adopted their own solutions.

At Myall Creek, 650 kilometres north of Sydney, shortly before sundown one day in June 1838, a group of mounted stockmen, armed with muskets, swords and pistols, rounded up 30 or 40 Aborigines encamped at a sheep station. The horsemen roped the men, women and most of the children together and forced them to march four kilometres into the bush. The untied children, crying, followed their mothers, who carried those too young to walk. One of the stockmen snatched up an untied boy about seven (a favourite of his), placed him behind a tree and told him to remain there till later. The child, however, ran back, crying, 'No, I will go with my mammie'. He was then fastened with rope to the adults. A few days later the station manager became curious as to the whereabouts of the Aborigines previously camped in the area. The hovering of eagles, hawks and other birds of prey directed him to a spot where he discovered the mangled and half-burnt remains of at least 28 people. For the most part, heads were separated from bodies, and fire marks appeared on the disjointed limbs. Charcoal and burnt logs indicated an attempt to efface all evidence. The manager, however, recognised ten to twelve small heads he took to be those of children, and a large body which he believed belonged to 'Daddy', an Aborigine known for his remarkably large frame.[54]

When the government laid murder charges against the men responsible, squatters and the press screamed in outrage at the absurdity of indicting civilised men for the death of creatures on the lowest rung of creation. Few of those associated with squatting had not killed Aborigines and they continued to declare their right to clear the land of an inferior race. One squatter boasted he 'would shoot a black fellow wherever he met him as he would a mad dog'.[55] The jury returned a verdict of not guilty. One juror explained:

> I look on the blacks as a set of monkeys and I think the earlier they are exterminated the better. I know well [the accused] are guilty of murder, but I, for one, would never consent to see a white man suffer for shooting a black one![56]

The government eventually obtained a conviction at a second trial. Before their execution, the seven condemned men acknowledged their guilt but stated in their defence 'that in destroying the aborigines they were not aware they had violated the law, or that it could take cognizance of their having done so, as it had been so frequently done in the Colony before.'[57]

The Myall Creek massacre became notorious, not because of the murder of the Aborigines, but because of the conviction and punishment of the murderers. It was only the second and the last time in Australian history Europeans were executed for the murder of Aborigines.[58] Henceforth squatters acted with impunity; the Myall Creek trial only encouraged them to be more secretive and thorough. One recommended that, where firearms failed or became too obvious, poison in the form of strychnine or arsenic mixed with flour be given to the Aborigines.[59]

Squatters believed that their ten pound licence fee entitled them to the exclusive use of their runs—a right which justified the violent expulsion of the original residents. In February 1840 the Whyte brothers took up their Konong-wootong run in the Western District. A month later they hunted down an Aboriginal group, suspected of stealing 127 sheep, and killed between 20 and 30 of them. Although the Whytes admitted the killings, the government failed to prosecute and a month later the brothers pursued and killed members of another group of Aborigines.[60] In 1841 a party of seven settlers shot dead 51 Aborigines on the banks of the Glenelg River near the South Australia-Victoria border, for abducting 50 sheep. Long after, according to a local squatter, 'the bones of the men and sheep lay mingled together bleaching in the sun at the Fighting Hills'.[61]

Throughout the 1830s the price of wool increased, English capital poured in, land beckoned, and new settlements sprang up along the southern coast. Boom times seemed eternal. In Port Phillip, land changed hands over and over. Blocks in the city increased a hundred-fold in price in a few months and colonists paid huge sums of money for land they did not want but had to buy to forestall competing speculators. In February 1839, 1002 acres of suburban land at Port Phillip sold for £7.11s an acre and subsequently resold for £44 to £46 an acre. Country land purchased from the government in the Port Phillip district in 1841 at an average of £9.3s.6d an acre realised between £40 and £60 two months later. Two new English banks, besides three existing banks and three new loan companies, supplied credit to the speculators and provided an inflated amount of credit for a population of only 150 000. One censorious observer described the land boom years 'as marked by prudence in no quarter, unbounded credit and extravagant speculation everywhere'.[62]

Colonial profits from wool had depended on continuing geographical spread but by the 1840s the best grazing lands were already taken. Given existing squatting techniques, the effects of drought and a growing shortage of labour, further growth offered little prospect of profit and the speculative boom collapsed. Falling land prices coincided with a decline in the price of wool. Unable to sell their principal product, squatters found sheep meat equally worthless and bones nearly so. But the carcass of a sheep, even in moderate condition, could realise, when boiled down, from twelve to fifteen pounds of tallow (used in candle making and the manufacture of glycerine for explosives), then selling for £2 to £31 a hundredweight in London. Nearly 200 000 sheep were slaughtered and boiled down before the end of 1844. More than 750 000 sheep went into the vats in 1845 and by 1850 over two-and-a-half million sheep a year, in addition to 260 000 cattle, were being boiled down. Ingenious tallow men built huge boilers to hold 300 sheep at once.

Despite low wool prices, sheep continued to breed and squatters took over still more land. At the end of 1839 they were encamped 800 kilometres north of Sydney and approaching the penal settlement at Moreton Bay, the future Brisbane. In March 1840, the Leslie brothers occupied the Darling Downs, in south Queensland. Within four years, 25 other stations surrounded them. By 1844 squatters occupied both banks of the lower Murray and reached Mount Gambier in the far south of South Australia. During the following year squatters filled up the remote parts of the Murrumbidgee and took over the Riverina Plains in southern New South Wales. Two years after Mitchell explored the interior of Queensland in 1845–46, squatters followed his tracks onto the Western Plains. At the end of the 1840s sheep runs covered three-quarters of Victoria and, during the following decade, the interior saltbush plains of New South Wales. In Queensland, squatters marched to the mouth of the Flinders River, in the north, and to the Barcoo and Isis Downs in the west. By the early 1860s squatters grazed over 20 million sheep and over 4 million cattle, and occupied almost all the land in eastern Australia that would ever be settled for economic use.

A decade before the squatting advance reached its limit, the Aboriginal tribes in south-eastern Australia had been decimated by disease and massacre and overwhelmed by the never-ending flow of British immigrants. Those who survived were exhausted by years of guerilla war. The living and the dead now became subject to an unprecedented level of literary vilification. The world's written record hardly contains an equivalent to the malicious, unrelenting and unanimous reprobation visited upon the Australian Aborigines. Few national histories contain such odious rationalisation of ugly deeds. Nineteenth-century Australian writers expressed violent and profound loathing for Aborigines, an attitude which remained respectable until late into the twentieth century.[63] Most writers believed the Aborigines were a freak of nature which civilisation would speedily erase from the face of the earth. Judge Therry, who assisted in the Myall Creek prosecution, shared the common view as to the imminent extinction of the Aborigines—a prospect he viewed with equanimity: 'If in the arrangement of an All-wise Providence, at whose disposal all things are, this poor inferior race of people should become altogether extinct, their disappearance could not well be regarded as a calamity.'[64]

Doomed race theories formed part of the language of colonisation and served to mask the real impulses of empire building and conquest. Colonisation generates profit only on the basis of the successful exploitation of the people and the resources of the subject country. In Australia, prior Aboriginal occupation barred the way of capitalist enterprise. In contrast to the invaders, Aborigines had successfully managed the Australian environment for tens of thousands of years. Europeans, however, had developed superior techniques for managing other people. Incapable of conquering true wilderness, they were highly competent at opportunistic exploitation. Squatters avoided the heavy labour of clearing woods whenever possible, bending their chief efforts to acquiring land already cleared by the Aborigines. The collapse of Aboriginal resistance and mass death freed enormous new resources for British use. The fecundity of water and land awed the early explorers and squatters on their advance through south-eastern Australia: lavish fish catches, great masses of shell-fish, yabbies and eels, vast flocks of waterfowl and other birds, substantial numbers of emus and large populations of kangaroos, wallabies, possums, bandicoots and wombats, an abundance of yams and huge stretches of reaped grassfields.

Private property triumphed over this landscape, not only because of the Aborigines' military defeat, but also because the business of sheep raising changed the very nature of the country. It subverted the environment, destroyed the material basis of an aboriginal culture inextricably bound to topography, flora and fauna, and delivered the land into the hands of the pastoral pioneer. The squatters and their flocks drove away the game, and the sheep ate the plants and killed the roots upon which the Aborigines lived. But the transformation did not stop there. The grazing of sheep first opens then kills forests, first converts grasslands to wealth then reduces them to indigence. In fact, by the time of Australia's first European settlement, sheep and goats had nearly extinguished the soil and pauperised the biota of much of the Mediterranean world. Generations of humans succeeded one another on such lands, unaware of the destruction of once richer surroundings. A comparable process of biological impoverishment now began in Australia.

Many temperate pasture species, the seeds of which arrived in every ship bringing settlers and livestock to Australia, became established in the earliest years of settlement. Partly through natural spread, partly assisted by settlers, perennial ryegrass (*Lolium perene*), cocksfoot (*Dactylis glomerata*), and white clover (*Trifolium repens*), became common in favourable habitats. Tasmania, especially, was quickly colonised by these temperate exotics. In 1854 one visitor wrote:

> In the glades, in the woods, and even in the cultivated fields I observed enormous thickets of sweetbriar, covering in some places whole acres of land. The sweetbriar, the furze and the thistle . . . have propagated in this climate to such an extent that [they] are beginning to be regarded as a real nuisance.[65]

The ingress of temperate European species was insignificant, however, compared to the massive biological invasion of southern Australia by the annual grasses, legumes and forbs of Mediterranean regions. The concentration of stock over eastern Australia opened the ground to infestation by these aggressive annuals. Undisturbed native grasslands showed some capacity to resist, but sheep and cattle distorted the balance between indigenous vegetation, nomadic people and soft-footed marsupials. Native animals hopped and walked on padded feet instead of hooves—rubber soles instead of hobnails. Once ungulates regularly trod and nibbled a piece of ground, it did not revert to its original condition, even if spelled for a period. On disturbed, climatically suitable sites, the free-seeding, fast-growing, opportunistic annuals of the Mediterranean multiplied. Sheep ate the sweeter grasses, leaving the tougher, less nutritious and more deeply rooted botanical communities, and native perennials, unadapted to close or regular defoliation or to treading by hoofed animals, died out. After thirteen years of grazing by sheep and cattle, Western District squatter John Robertson noticed how

> herbaceous plants and grasses give way for the silk-grass and the little annuals [which] die in our deep clay soil with a few hot days in spring, and nothing returns to supply their place until later in the winter following. The consequence is that the long deep-rooted grasses that

held our strong clay hill together have died out; the ground is now exposed to the sun, and it has cracked in all directions, and the clay hills are slipping in all directions; also the sides of precipitous creeks— long slips, taking trees and all with them. When I first came here, I knew of but two landslips, both of which I went to see; now there are hundreds found within the last three years.[66]

Charges of monopoly accompanied the squatting advance. By the end of the 1840s landless immigrants began questioning the right of the squatters to maintain their exclusive occupancy. James Walker of Willerowang, New South Wales, for example, held, by virtue of a single ten pound licence, 27 stations, totalling 2.02 million hectares in 1845. Advocates of 'unlocking the land', however, faced formidable obstacles. By 1849, 1019 squatters held nearly 17.7 million hectares in eastern Australia, and squatting interests dominated the colonial governments until the discovery of gold in the 1850s hugely increased the numbers and influence of the landless.

In the meantime squatters petitioned in favour of the continued transportation of convicts. Even during the early 1840s, despite widespread urban and rural unemployment, employers sought to inundate the colonies with convict and indentured workers. Accustomed to appropriating the convict's toil for nothing, they resisted paying for a free man and opposed free immigration. Because Australian rural society lacked the foundations of authority of the Old World—the traditions of church, class and property relations— Australian employers faced the problem of finding a sanction over the free as effective as the lash and other punishments which tyrannised the bound. Only convicts could be compelled to tend sheep in the loathsome, remote wilderness. Few free persons would tolerate the irksome monotony and loneliness of the shepherd's life; constant contact with sheep, day after day, for months, repelled most men. Convict labour was also needed for building the roads, bridges and other public works necessary for the advance of settlement into the interior. 'The domination of man', declared Thomas Mitchell, 'cannot indeed be extended well over nature there, without [compulsory penal] Labour. The prisoners should be worked in gangs, and guarded and coerced according to some well organized system'.[67]

During periods of labour shortage, squatters imported coolies from India, who, they argued, accustomed to labour in indigo factories up to their waist in water, could probably put up with the cold of New South Wales. The Indian shepherds received ten shillings a month, a few clothes, a blanket and a lascars cap. Their rations—a little rice, some dahl and ghee and a pinch of salt—cost only sixpence a day and saved the squatter 4 1/2d on every pound of wool.

Official opinion, however, objected to the permanent introduction of an inferior and servile element into the population and banned the importation of coloured labour. Conditions of life beyond the boundaries, the authorities believed, already augured a reversion to barbarism.

Men lived in the bush in concubinage with Aboriginal women, dwelt in shelters of slab and bark, and slept on rough bedsteads of sheepskins or possum rugs. A bark table or sea chest served every other purpose. Smoke from a stone fireplace vented through a hole cut in the slabs, and wool-packs hung from the door. Shepherds ate mutton at every meal accompanied by damper (flour and water baked in the fire or fried). A discarded pannikin, filled with clay and topped by mutton fat, upon which floated a wick, gave light at night. Bush life reeked of mutton fat and smoke. Even a prosperous squatter contented himself to live in a collection of slab hovels, with hurdles for the sheep, moving from place to place as each became filthy with heaps of sheep dung and sheep bones. A few British women lived in the bush and there their children grew up. Yet few clergy were available to minister to the growing flock of souls, and no churches or schools existed to instruct the colony's future citizens.

Throughout the 1840s members of the British House of Commons voiced horror over the religious destitution in the colonies, the spread of bush barbarism and the growing deviation from middle-class standards. At the time, on the assumption that divine providence, science and industry had combined to present the earth to them on a platter, the British middle class possessed a ferocious and dynamic self-confidence. Middle-class groups dominated the commercial enterprises, bureaucratic agencies and philanthropic organisations essential to the dissemination of the ideas and institutions of industrialising imperial Britain. They supported a civilising mission directed at transforming individual behaviour and consciousness by providing the prerequisites for civilised life: marriage, families and education. The English gentlewoman, Caroline Chisholm, carried this mission to Australia.

In the late 1830s, in the company of her husband and three native servants from India, Chisholm toured eastern Australia, where the barbarism of bush life and the small numbers of women—as low as one convict woman for every seventeen convict men—appalled her. She became convinced that the men of the colony needed the moral policing only women could provide. In Sydney she established a temporary home for immigrant women and took them out to the country where their civilising presence would have the greatest effect. Returning to England she founded the Colonisation Loan Society to arrange for the emigration of selected young women—those deemed suitable as female servants, instructed in housekeeping and the habits of duty. She believed this class most suitable for marriage and recommended her female charges and their offspring to prospective employers as of 'sober, industrious, and frugal habits, a most valuable description of labourers'.[68] '[To] break up the bachelor stations [is] my aim; happy homes my reward,' she wrote, 'to introduce married families into the interior is to make squatters' stations fit abodes for Christian men.'[69] Chisholm enlisted the support of Charles Dickens, who recommended marriage as a suitable estate for those about to subdue the wilderness. A contemporary, in evaluating Chisholm's work, wrote 'she showed how closely the extension of national power was connected with the social and domestic virtues inseparable from family colonisation.'[70]

Chisholm and Dickens belonged to a crusade, prosecuted by parsons, priests and schoolmasters. The crusaders aimed to evoke the weight of divine authority to enforce the bourgeois virtues of industry, frugality, humility, and the obedience of servants to masters, and wives to their husbands. Colonial governments naturally shared these aims and hoped social reformation would follow changing material conditions. Like all pioneering, politicians argued, squatting life would naturally and eventually give way to a closer, more wholesome settlement of the land. They looked forward to a future when, 'The loaf bread and the chinaware finally defeated the damper and the pannikin'.[71] Already, the industry of civilised man had transformed the former trackless, inhospitable country of Van Diemen's Land into a park. By the late 1830s rich green English grasses carpeted the land, and fenced fields and solid stone buildings bespoke of beauty and bourgeois orderliness. Colonial governments sought to impose a similar capitalist order on the mainland landscape. The discovery of gold supplied the capital and population necessary for such empire building.

In 1851 Edward Hargraves notified the New South Wales government of a gold discovery. A few months later richer discoveries were made in Victoria. In April 1852 six ships reached England carrying the first eight tons of Australian gold. Tens of thousands of people immediately sought passage to the new goldfields. Lord Ashley recorded in his diary that the discovery in Australia was undoubtedly, 'God's chosen way to force the world to fulfill his commandment and "replenish the earth" '.[72]

5

DARK **D**EEDS IN A SUNNY **L**AND

WHEN A RACE OF MEN IS EXTERMINATED
SOMEBODY OUGHT TO BEAR THE BLAME,
AND THE EASIEST WAY IS TO LAY THE
FAULT AT THE DOOR OF THE DEAD: THEY
NEVER REPLY.

George Dunderdale, The Book of the Bush,
1870

BUT GOLDEN DAYS ARE VANISHED,
AND ALTERED IS THE SCENE;
THE DIGGINGS ARE DESERTED,
THE CAMPING-GROUNDS ARE GREEN;
THE FLAUNTING FLAG OF PROGRESS
IS IN THE WEST UNFURLED,
THE MIGHTY BUSH WITH IRON RAILS
IS TETHERED TO THE WORLD.

Henry Lawson, 'The Roaring Days', *1889*

CONVICTS IN AUSTRALIA hated work. Their refusal to labour willingly for their masters disturbed respectable observers. Opponents of transportation believed the problem lay with the government's assignment of convicts to farmers and squatters of dubious character. The abolitionist Alexander Harris wondered whether convicts would work better under more liberal conditions. He asked those he met, 'Do you think you would do any better for a good master than for a bad one; better if well treated than if kept, as you call it, with your "nose to the grindstone?" '[1] To Harris' eternal bafflement his subjects refused to take him seriously; they laughed at him, and ridiculed the notion of good or bad masters. Convicts did not want to work for *any* masters, good or bad. They objected to the very idea of subordination, and never accepted their roles as servants to colonial lords. In fact, most working people, convict and non-convict, resented servitude and looked to escape. The opportunity came in 1851.

The news of the gold discoveries in New South Wales and Victoria fell with irresistible allure on the minds of those enchained in a dull routine of incessant and unrequited labour. Digging for gold and the chance of wealth promised freedom and independence. At first hundreds, then thousands, of men and women left their jobs for the goldfields.

Moral improvers, squatters and the urban bourgeoisie accused artisans and labourers of rushing after the banner of Mammon and warned of the futility of laying up treasures on earth. But their sermons masked more immediate fears. The rush for gold might subvert law and industry. What would happen if shepherds left their flocks or farmers abandoned their ploughs? What would happen if seamen deserted their ships, schoolmasters absconded from schools, policemen vacated their beats and jailers escaped from their prisoners? And so the list of derelicts might grow. But the rush could not be prevented. It was as hazardous, concluded New South Wales Governor Charles Fitzroy, to stop the waves of the sea, as the rush to the diggings.[2]

Nevertheless, governments could, and did, regulate and control people on the diggings. An onerous licence fee of thirty shillings a month heavily taxed those who found gold in New South Wales and discouraged thousands of others from seeking gold. The Victorian government followed a similar expedient a few months later when the news of gold sent the whole town of Geelong into 'hysterics, gentlemen foaming at the mouth, ladies fainting, children throwing somersets, and all on account of the extraordinary news from Buninyong'.[3]

For a while at least, fortune favoured those most used to physical exertion—artisans and common labourers. The search required great physical effort: displacing rocks, digging through river gravel and sinking shafts. The work and independence, however, suited many. Five station hands who left their employment on a Riverina squatting run to go digging at Kiandra, in the Snowy Mountains, wrote back in April 1860 to report that despite snow and rain they were staying: 'We get on the average about thirty shillings per man each day . . . we prefer being our own masters'.[4]

Goldseekers came first from the adjacent colonies—Van Diemen's Land, South Australia and Western Australia—then from India and the Cape, and at length from Britain and Europe: Germans, Scandinavians and Dutch. Australia's population soared. In the ten years after 1851 half a million people from the British Isles alone, or about one person in every fifty, sailed for Australia. Most immigrants disembarked at Melbourne, where William Howitt, who arrived in September 1852, described

> the reality of the rapidly running torrent of immigration. Here is a new settlement in all its newness. The houses are some of them complete, others just erecting. A balder and more unattractive scene cannot meet the eye of man. Every single tree has been levelled to the ground; it is one hard bare expanse, bare of all nature's attractions, a wilderness of

wooden huts of Lilliputian dimensions; and everywhere around and amongst them, timber and rubbish.[5]

Out of the squalor of Melbourne the diggers marched upcountry to the diggings and, casually and indifferently, shot all the wildlife they met. Their favourite targets were possums and giant tree-lizards, which they erroneously believed were venomous. At the goldfields they attacked the wooded hills, ranges and valleys, tearing up the earth in quest of gold. They cut down the trees for fuel and for timber to line shafts and reinforce tunnels. 'The diggers seem to have two especial propensities', observed Howitt:

> those of firing guns and felling trees. It is amazing what a number of trees they fell. No sooner have they done their day's work, than they commence felling trees, which you hear falling continually with a crash on one side of you or the other.[6]

The removal of trees laid bare the ground, and the savage gully erosion, which still scars wide areas of the old diggings, followed. The use of water under pressure to clear away the topsoil undercut hillsides and stream banks, and muddied and polluted creeks and rivers. Diggers dumped huge amounts of overburden into the rivers and streams. Vast quantities of sludge moved down the valleys, blocking natural watercourses and inundating agricultural and pastoral land. A similar combination of benefits (wealth) and costs (environmental devastation) accompanied the extraction of minerals in all the Australian colonies at one time or another.

In South Australia copper mining and processing began in the 1840s. Smelters required huge amounts of timber. In 1851 the three Apoinga smelters consumed daily about 150 tonnes of firewood, while at Kapunda, 78 kilometres north of Adelaide, smelters required 120 or so tonnes a day. Gangs of timber-getters scoured the countryside and illegally removed trees from private and Crown land. One observer in Burra, 160 kilometres north of Adelaide, described how in 1851 'drays loaded with wood were arriving every instant . . . to replenish the forest of cut logs and wood piled up, circling the whole area of the works and filling every available space'.[7]

Unlike the early years of goldmining, copper extraction did not depend on individual, independent diggers. Copper mines were intensely capitalistic enterprises and, according to Anthony Trollope, who visited the mines in the 1870s, they afforded 'a more wholesome class of labour'—by which he meant wage labour. Like the colonial bourgeois, Trollope despised digger independence on the goldfields, which he contrasted unfavourably with the 'parsimonious', 'sober' and 'industrious' habits of the committed copper miner.[8]

Mining utterly confounded the natural systems about diggings. Accompanying increases in population and wealth, however, generated political and economic changes of more subversive consequence. The gold rushes altered the economic and demographic foundations of Australia. Colonial gold, coupled with California's, created an international market. Australia became more completely integrated into that market. In addition, nearly three-quarters of a million people arrived in Australia in the ten years after 1851, increasing the European population from 403 000 to 1 142 000 by the end of 1860. Seventy years after first settlement, Australia's European population finally exceeded the population the Aborigines alone had maintained prior to invasion.

On the way to this demographic watershed, New South Wales came close to recreating the social order of the mother country. The influential classes who controlled the growing wool industry, most of the banks and leading firms of importers, had constructed almost a plantation society, a land of large freeholds allied to larger leaseholds. In the settled part of the colony, an English-style landed gentry owned large estates which they leased out to tenant farmers, who hired labourers to work the land. In the pastoral regions, men of substance controlled large areas of land on long leases and the rest of the population worked for them. One independent squatter described the situation as one which

> suit[s] pretty well the highest class . . . but . . nobody else . . . They entirely prevent persons of small property from becoming landholders and agriculturalists; by which again they coercively construct an immensely larger labouring class than otherwise would exist in the colony.[9]

Convicts had formed the bulk of the labouring class, but anti-transportation agitators prevailed upon the British government to terminate transportation to New South Wales in 1840. The squatters continued to insist on convict labour, however, and persuaded the British to reverse the decision. The prospect of convicts outraged Sydney's smaller merchants and professionals, committed to a colony of free people only. These men, who favoured colonial self-government and called themselves liberals, formed a Constitutional Association in 1848 to oppose the reintroduction of transportation. Huge protests forced the local Legislative Council, which otherwise favoured the squatting interest, to vote against the importation of convicts in 1850.

In the same year the British Parliament passed The Australian Colonies Government Bill, which gave the Legislative Council power to draw up a local constitution. Nearly all those who had advocated self-government assumed that the constitution of the new country must be modelled on that of the old, with strict limits on popular power. Like their English counterparts, the colonial squatocracy considered themselves civilised but were unsure about the lower orders—especially with respect to such attributes as foresight and discipline, and the new attitudes toward time, work and nature, essential to civilised life. Accordingly, the large landholders and their wealthy Sydney allies, who controlled the Council, made plans for a two-chamber parliament—an arrangement they regarded as a legitimation of the inequality which marked a British society. The colonial ruling class were also antagonistic to universal manhood suffrage, which meant, according to Supreme Court Justice Roger Therry, that in theory at least 'a wild black fresh from the Bush, with whose intelligence a gorilla well might vie . . . has an equal right to vote with the wealthiest and most intelligent.'[10]

Colonial liberals opposed the new constitution. Although, like the conservatives, they did not believe in democracy, some liberals doubted the wisdom of restricting the vote. Liberal champion Robert Lowe, who after making his fortune in the colony returned to England and a seat in the House of Lords, persuaded his fellow Lords that a wider franchise in the colony meant admitting more respectable men to the rolls. A larger base of voters would lessen the convict influence and prevent them and their tainted descendants from acquiring absolute power. Because Lowe convinced enough influential men to declare in favour of extending the franchise, the colony adopted nearly universal manhood suffrage. Most importantly, the self-governing colonies now controlled the disposition of Crown land.[11]

Following the decline in availability of alluvial gold and, as highly capitalised operations took over the goldfields, displaced diggers, eager to maintain their independence, clamoured for land and the breakup of the huge squatting runs. Petition after petition demanding the opening of Crown lands to freehold settlement continued to reach the legislatures, and demonstrators held protest meetings in Sydney and Melbourne. The squatter, the reformers argued, was inefficient and incapable of altering his environment for the better. Pastoralism failed to fully utilise the soil; only closer settlement and cultivation would domesticate the landscape and ensure full occupation of the land: 'Pastoral autocrats with acres by the hundreds of thousands . . . cannot fill up the country. They are the precursors of population, and, as the population comes, should make way for it.'[12]

As long as the country remained one huge sheep walk and unreclaimed forest, the reformers believed, the colonists could not claim domination over nature. Moreover, common and scientific knowledge demanded the clearance of forests. Learned people during the nineteenth century believed disease arose spontaneously out of the dank, dark reaches of 'miasmic' forests. Standing forests were thus unhygienic; only open country was healthy:

> The immense quantity of vegetable matter rotting on the surface of the earth, and still more of that rotting in the waters . . . cannot be very healthy. The choked up valleys, dense with scrub and rank grass and weeds and the equally rank vegetation of swamps, cannot tend to health. All these evils, the axe and the plough and the fire of settlers, will gradually and eventually remove.[13]

In the 1860 elections, the liberals appealed to the people to uphold the principle of 'free selection', which provided, not free land, but for the right of any person to claim, settle and pay for land anywhere. The supporters of free selection promised that once the people, and not the squatters, worked the land, the wilderness would be turned into a garden and that the conquest of the soil would bring freedom and happiness. The liberals won the elections and in 1860 and 1861 Victoria and New South Wales passed legislation to open land to freehold settlement. Both Land Acts sought the breakup of large leaseholds into smaller freehold selections so as to make land, like every other commodity in a capitalist society, freely transferable.[14] The legislation proved remarkably ineffective in settling farmers, and remarkably effective in giving squatters the land they wanted. A month after passage of the Victorian legislation one squatter pronounced the law a dead letter. 'The Land Act has entirely failed in its object, almost all the land selected under it had been by and for the previous occupiers.'[15]

Squatters contrived these results by several means. The most extensively employed procedure was 'peacocking'—picking the eye out of the land. Because squatters retained pre-emptive rights to buy portions of their leasehold, they selected areas surrounding waterholes, thus closing the run to effective agricultural settlement. In another common ruse Aborigines on the stations gained new value as 'dummies', wherein squatters employed proxies to fill residency requirements on newly acquired land.

The Land Acts, and a mania for freehold, encouraged people to take up land with insufficient capital. Squatters borrowed heavily to finance their purchases. Banks, money-lenders and merchants provided the necessary funds, often at exorbitant rates of interest (25 to 50 percent). One lender defended the practice, claiming, 'The fact is, I can give a man accommodation [for his expenses] and pay his rent, but I cannot give him brains. If he is not sharp enough to see he is slated [cheated] that is his business.'[16] Small selectors defaulted on mortgages and left the land while solvent squatters and those with good credit increased their holdings. Everywhere in eastern Australia legislation to break up the squatters' monopoly produced the same result: concentrated ownership and the transfer of enormous public assets to private hands. By 1880, 2100 companies or individuals in the colonies of South Australia, New Zealand, New South Wales and Victoria owned 17.3 million hectares.[17] The monopoly in leasehold was even greater. In 1865, 9200 leases in

New South Wales covered 49.2 million hectares but by 1883, less than half that number of leaseholders, 4300, held an even larger area.[18] In Victoria by the mid-1880s more than 100 000 selections had been made under an 1869 Land Act and its amendments. But the actual number of working farms—35 000—indicates the number of failures, reselections and absorptions of selections which had taken place.[19]

To meet debt payments, pastoralists increased their flocks, and through overstocking, degraded the land. In Monaro, New South Wales, one squatter reported on the consequences:

> Before the passing of the Land Act ... The Matong Creek ... was a succession of deep waterholes, there being no high banks, and grass grew to the water's edge. Hundreds of wild ducks could be seen along these waterholes, and platypus and divers were plentiful. Five years after the passing of the Act the whole length, instead of being a line of deep waterholes, became a bed of sand, owing to soil erosion caused by sheep. The water only came to the surface in flood time, when it spread the sand over the flats.[20]

With telling consistency colonial governments repeatedly failed to frame land acts which favoured individual settlers over speculators and monopolists. This outcome surprised only the critics, who failed to appreciate that the colonial governments were themselves manifestations of a capitalist culture committed to speculation and monopoly. The critics of land monopoly—urban liberals, populists and visiting English literati—insisted on the superior merits of small farms and evoked the image of an old ideal: the small, freehold farm of the sturdy, independent yeoman, worked by the family, producing from the field, garden, orchard, woodlot and from livestock, and yielding a modest surplus from a variety of crops carefully tended and planted. But the Australian farmer and pastoralist worked within an entirely different context. They were part of the immense nineteenth century effort to establish human dominion over the earth. Australian pioneers felt no emotional ties to the land. No heritage or tradition bound them to this new and strange country. They did not inherit their land; they purchased it. Sub-divided Australia was a commodity: an investment rather than a legacy. Land represented potential wealth, and wheat and wool were the proven means of realising that potential. These products were destined not for the family, neighbours and village, but for the new world market.[21]

Many of the legislative enactments and institutional arrangements necessary to transform the Australian landscape into a commodity suitable for capitalist production were pioneered in South Australia. Until the early 1860s progress followed Wakefieldian lines and settlement advanced through the efforts of farmers on 32 hectare sections. Energetic and successful, individual settlers cleared nearly 30 000 hectares in the seven years to 1867.[22] But by the late 1860s the pressure of growing wheat for worldwide competitive markets demanded a reappraisal of land use, tenure and development.

In 1865 the Surveyor-General, G. W. Goyder, set out 'to determine and lay down on a map, as nearly as practicable, the line of demarcation between that portion of the country where the rainfall has extended and that where the drought prevails'.[23] Goyder's Line soon began to be regarded as separating lands suitable for agricultural use from those fit only for pastoral use. To develop the former, Goyder recommended more liberal conditions of tenure, a scheme, he said, 'that if carried out will change the face of large areas of the country from hopeless scrub to smiling fertility'.[24] The Waste Land Acts which followed provided for freehold selection on generous terms of credit. Selectors easily exploited the provisions. The down payment became only a modest fee for the right to hold a block for several years and the interest payments served as a moderate rental. These arrangements encouraged farmers to seek quick profits through harvesting a succession of crops without spelling or fertilising the land. When final payment came due on the selection, the selector turned the now degraded land back to the government and obtained another block. Successive legislative alteration to the Waste Land Act reduced the selection fees, lengthened the schedule of their payment and magnified the speculative possibilities.[25]

A succession of good years in the early 1870s and the rapid occupation of the demarcated agricultural land soon made Goyder's Line an indefensible barrier; farmers demanded and obtained the opening of new land beyond the Line. The good seasons culminated in 1878, when tremendous rains spread over the lands east of the Flinders Ranges and far out to the north and west. Creeks flooded and vast areas of waving grass covered all the ground yet unbroken by the plough. The green face of the once sun-scorched land seemed proof of the popular and convenient idea that 'rain follows the plough'. Indeed, in South Australia, climatic change appeared to be actually running ahead of the plough. A similar succession of good seasons over the same decade in the American west had also brought comfort to developers, speculators and farmers and resulted in the founding of a new school of optimistic meteorology.[26]

In both countries plenty of scientists came forward to explain the beneficial climatic change. Although exact explanations varied, all agreed civilised settlement improved the environment and that the consequence of settlement 'is nearly always more grass and more water—the pasture thickens, dry creeks fill, and swamps become standing lagoons'.[27] When droughts came and forced cultivation back within Goyder's Line, people viewed the setback as temporary: in time, with more cultivation, some definite amelioration of aridity would surely occur.[28] Farmers continued to believe in the superior ability of ploughed land over virgin land to absorb and conserve rain. Moreover, the slower evaporation from cultivated soil induced more rain. The notion that ploughing attracted rain probably enticed more farmers onto marginal land and did more to expand settlement than any single invention in farm machinery.

From the beginning, the colonists of South Australia demonstrated remarkable determination to overcome the problems of imposing an efficient capitalist order on the land. Wherever the needs of subduing the land were paramount, South Australia provided a model. South Australian efforts to promote rationality in the design of human life achieved conspicuous success with town planning. The colony's founders believed township design was basic to colonisation, and the elements of Adelaide's design—a central core of rectangular blocks designated for shops, an encircling belt of parklands reserved for public use and a perimeter of suburban residential blocks sub-divided by a radial pattern of straight roads leading from the central district—provided a model for over 200 South Australian townships. Colonel Light's grid division of Adelaide into rational, equal, purchasable blocks of land formed an essential precondition of capitalist settlement; the plan neatly parcelled land into saleable real estate.

But two decades of speculation and private sub-division had made such chaos of South Australian land titles that mortgaging became insecure and conveyancing costly. Over the determined opposition of the legal profession, the government introduced the Torrens System of land registration in 1858, providing for a central register of all property transactions and the issue of certificates of title. A sale merely required the cancellation of the old and the registering of a new certificate. The old system could never provide the buyer of real property (land) a guarantee of purchase. The new system increased security of land tenure and found application all over the world, wherever private, transferable property was the basis of the economy. The Wall Street Journal championed the Torrens System for the United States, cited the example of South Australia and described the law as 'the ploughshare of modern economic life . . . the creation of a business man for business purposes'.[29]

To provide a further field for speculation and settlement, South Australian pastoralists demanded the colony extend its borders northward, all the way to the Arafura Sea. In 1863 the British government granted their request and annexed the Northern Territory to South Australia, doubling the colony's area. The government immediately arranged for sale of Territory land without survey and quickly sold most of the first 100 000 hectares. But none of the buyers, more interested in speculation than actual settlement, took up land. The sale had been more than sufficient to satisfy initial demand and the purchased land quickly fell in value. Some buyers sold out at a loss, others successfully sued the government for the return of invested sums. Six years later, G. W. Goyder made the first real survey party to the Northern Territory, and in 1869 founded Port Darwin.

In 1870 South Australia undertook to build a telegraph line spanning the whole continent, from Port Augusta to Port Darwin, there to connect with an undersea cable joining Australia to England. The telegraph and some minor gold discoveries led to the permanent European occupation of the Territory. Cattle moved in from Queensland and by the end of 1882, pastoralists had applied for 1.2 million hectares of the Northern Territory. Many abandoned their claims during the droughts and economic depression of the 1890s but the appropriated land did not revert to the dispossessed Aborigines. By now the British were totally unequivocal about their claims to the continent. As the Territory administrator, J. L. Parsons, explained in 1890, 'the intrusion of the white man is a declaration of war and the result is simply the survival of the fittest'.[30] The fittest wielded superior weapons. In 1884, the leader of one extermination party against Aborigines, Corporal George Montagu, concluded, 'One result of this expedition had been to convince me of the superiority of the Martini-Henry rifle, both for the accuracy of aim and quickness of action.' The *Northern Territory Times* thought Montagu's exploits jolly fun, and versified:

> These white men with their loaded guns
> Make black men scarce as married nuns.[31]

Meanwhile the wheat farmers of South Australia were busy removing another impediment to their occupation of the land. The mallee—a scrub forest of dwarf eucalyptus (chiefly *Eucalyptus dumosa*, *E. uncinata* and *E. incrassata*) which branch from a thick, shallow root into an umbrella-like cluster of stems and canopy, and which vary in height from 1.5 to 8 metres and in density from a near thicket to an open scattering—once covered more than 70 percent of the present settled regions of South Australia. To the early settlers the mallee stretched 'almost like a blue and level sea towards the horizon'[32] and proved vigorously resistant to normal methods of clearing. The technique which finally succeeded in erasing the mallee became known as mullenising, after farmer Mullens, the alleged inventor.

A heavy roller, pulled through the scrub by horses or oxen, knocked down the slender, brittle mallee trunks. A fire set at the end of summer consumed the dry branches and trunks. To till the ground containing the stubborn stumps, South Australians invented the stump-jump plough. Mould-boards mounted on hinged beams allowed the ploughshares to rise gently out of the ground on meeting an obstruction. Weights fixed to the beam extensions pressured the share back into the ground after the plough cleared the obstacle. After harvest another fire burned the stubble and killed the new mallee shoots. Successive cropping and burning eventually killed the mallee and left a clean surface.

Mullenising spread rapidly throughout South Australia during the 1870s, 1880s and 1890s. On Yorke Peninsula mullenising and the stump-jump plough led to the occupation of 278 000 hectares in the four years to 1884 and a further half million hectares in the following ten years. Clearing reached such a frenzy by 1881 that a local newspaper described the view up and down the Peninsula as consisting of 'Smoke! smoke! smoke! anywhere, everywhere, nothing but smoke'.[33] But, as in the Amazon today, clearing produced more than smoke. The farming practices followed in South Australia—deep ploughing and frequent cultivation, up to twelve times a year—caused destruction of soil structure, loss of nitrogen, depletion of fertility, and exposure to erosive winds. The soil became powdery and subject to drift. Under average climatic and soil conditions each hectare lost about half a tonne of organic matter per fallowing. If the farmer left the fallow uncultivated, the surface became hard and impenetrable to water and the increase in run-off led to sheet and gully erosion. Continuous cropping quickly exhausted the light, sandy soil and average wheat yields plunged from 1.8 or 2.7 cubic metres per hectare, obtained at the beginning of agriculture, to a colony-wide average of just 0.15 cubic metres per hectare in 1896–97.

In Victoria the mallee mantled one-fifth of the colony, or 4.4 million hectares. The first squatters reached the edge of the mallee before the end of 1845 and began their invasion the following year. By 1849 all the best of the open mallee was under leasehold; what remained was unworkable since all water supplies had been claimed. In 1853 over 150 000 sheep and 5500 cattle grazed in the mallee country. Eight years later nearly a quarter of a million sheep and nearly 9000 cattle depastured there. By 1864 practically the entire Victorian mallee had been parcelled out in runs, though much was held speculatively and was not stocked. As the sheep multiplied, the Aborigines declined. According to one of the earliest settlers, hundreds of Aborigines lived around Lake Corong, in the middle of the mallee, when he first arrived in 1845. Seventeen years later one boy remained alive.[34]

A few years later, driven from their own colony by declining yields from exhausted soil, South Australian mallee farmers began crossing the border with their mullenising machines to clear and farm the Victorian mallee. By 1890 there were 500 farmers growing wheat in the western and southern mallee. In 1910 Victorian mallee farmers sowed over 400 000 hectares.[35]

In all parts of Australia, average wheat yields declined between 1856 and 1896, while the area under wheat expanded. Because continuous cropping brought down the yield to an unprofitable level, farmers had to give land a rest and bring alternative areas under the plough. And because farmers believed virgin soil gave the highest yield, they continuously brought new land under the plough, while abandoning used land. As wheat became the sole crop in some areas, diseases—rust and take-all—became more common and more severe. Thus, paradoxically, the expansion in the area under wheat, combined with the cropping of inferior land and the adoption of slovenly farming practices, caused the decline in yield. Advances in technique, particularly in farm machinery, which increased the profitability of large areas and reduced labour costs, enabled farmers to offset and ignore the decline in yield. In Victoria alone, in the 24 years after 1866, the number of mowing, reaping, and winnowing machines and strippers increased nearly tenfold, from 3046 to 29 669.[36]

Gold put an end to convict transportation to the eastern colonies of Australia. The discoveries made Australia a desirable destination and with a fair portion of the population of Britain clamouring for tickets to the southern El Dorado, malefactors no longer looked upon transportation as such a terrible punishment. As Van Diemen's Land Governor-General Fitzroy explained to the British Secretary of State in 1851, 'few English criminals ... would not regard a free passage to the goldfields via Hobart town as a great boon.'[37] In 1852 the last convict ship left for Van Diemen's Land. In the west, however, transportation was just beginning.

Throughout the 1840s, while the eastern colonies prospered, Western Australia languished. After two decades of settlement, the colony's European population in the south-west remained under 6000—less than the number of Aborigines who lived off the same tract of country before the British invasion. An acute need for labour and capital induced the impoverished colonists to petition the Home Office 'to make and declare their Colony a Penal Settlement Upon an Extensive Scale.'[38] The first convict ship arrived in 1850, 21 years after Western Australia's foundation as a free colony. Over the next eighteen years nearly 10 000 convicts arrived in the west, to labour on roads, bridges, mines and public buildings. They stimulated trade, provided a market for the colony's produce, increased the demand for timber, expanded the area under cultivation, introduced Imperial capital (£100 000 a year) and augmented the settlers' labour supply. The Governor reported back to England that convicts made a major contribution to the progress of the colony 'from a most lamentable state of stagnation and despair to one of rapidly increasing prosperity'.[39] When transportation ceased, in 1868—because of protests from the other Australian colonies—Western Australia again fell into economic dormancy. Exploring and pastoral expansion continued, however, particularly in the north.

In 1861 explorer F. T. Gregory reported the country between the Ashburton and Oakover Rivers as prime pastoral, and in the next few years settlers took up parcels of 40 000 hectares each, free of rent for the first four years and with low rental for the next eight years. By the end of 1864 flockmasters held nearly 1.2 million hectares under lease. The pastoralists pressed the dispossessed Aborigines into service as shepherds, shearers, shed hands, house-cleaners and concubines. Once assigned they became the effective property of the lessee. Absconders had their feet burnt as punishment, others were branded with the master's initials. Those who continued to resist enslavement were placed in chains and transported to the Aboriginal penal colony on Rottnest Island, a thousand kilometres to the south.[40] A single European objected to the system of slavery.

In 1885 the Western Australian Anglican church appointed the Reverend J. B. Gribble as priest to the Aboriginal mission reserves at the Vasse, Murchison, Roebourne and the Gascoyne, in the north-west. In common with his Christian contemporaries Gribble believed it was the white man's task to missionise Aborigines in order to redeem himself as well as the unfortunate heathens. He also believed that Aborigines occupied the bottom of the human scale. Unlike his peers, however, Gribble found the system of ownership of native peoples repugnant and protested the methods of punishment meted out to Aborigines who refused to labour for their conquerors. He objected to the chaining of prisoners by the neck and the almost universal practice of concubinage. Gribble, alone among Europeans, sensed that incarceration, torture and banishment were no more pleasant for flesh in black skins than in white. He returned to Perth to lay his charges before the church authorities. The Anglican bishop, unwilling to alienate pastoralists contributing money for the construction of a new cathedral, refused to listen. Gribble's protests also antagonised the press, which began a campaign of ridicule and denigration. The *West Australian* called him 'lying, canting humbug.' Angry settlers drew up two petitions denouncing Gribble's interference with the native labour system and seeking the revocation of his appointment. Undeterred, Gribble returned to the north-west, where townspeople boycotted him and stores refused him supplies. He continued his investigations of a regional economy where European industry depended on the enslavement of thousands of men, women and children, and published his accusations in a pamphlet entitled *Dark Deeds in a Sunny Land* (1887).

In addition to exploitation in the pastoral industry, Gribble exposed the practice by the operators of pearling luggers of employing the police to round up Aboriginal labour. Marooned in groups on off-shore islands and in near-starvation conditions, they provided the crews for the boats. None of Gribble's protests led to any amelioration of the situation in the north-west or elsewhere in the colony and his lone struggle had little effect on the further northward expansion of pastoralism and continued dispossession of Aborigines.[41]

In 1879 Alexander Forrest explored the Kimberleys, in the far north of Western Australia, and recommended the area for pastoral development. The first sheep arrived later in the same year and by July 1883, eight stations held leases totalling nearly 20 million hectares. Absentee investors and speculators, mostly from the eastern colonies, grabbed huge selections. James Munro, a Victorian financier and politician, speculated on half a million hectares of Kimberley leasehold, while the Victorian Squatting Company took up two million hectares on Cambridge Gulf, primarily as a speculation.

Until denuded beyond recognition by the erosion caused by the hard-hoofed stock of the invaders, the grassed plains of the Kimberley river valleys—reminiscent of the African savannah—supported abundant wildlife. Henry Taunton, who accompanied one of the first Kimberley settlers, described the stunning prodigality of the region's wildlife:

> ... on all sides one could hear the rustling of wings, and could trace the dark plumage of the wild pheasants as they flew noisily from tree to tree; or one could see the grey, uncanny looking frilled lizards scrambling up the trunks or along the branches on either hand, as we disturbed them by our passage. Small red kangaroos would bound across the path, wombats and other small game starting up almost under our horses' feet ... whilst all around us overhead, immense flocks of multi-coloured cockatoos shrieked discordantly as we rode beneath.[42]

Elsewhere Taunton came upon thousands and thousands of flying foxes and huge flocks of ducks and waterfowl. Their dominion, however, was shortly to end.

Cattle, driven overland from Queensland, reached the east Kimberleys in the early 1880s. Twenty-two thousand sheep grazed the Kimberleys in 1883, and despite foot-rot, scab, dingoes and poison plants, numbers increased to over 100 000 by 1890. A flood in 1894 drowned 30 000 sheep but still they increased, and by the turn of the century the Kimberleys grazed a quarter of a million sheep. But absentee owners cared less about flock and pasture management than immediate profit, and pushed sheep numbers beyond carrying capacity. By 1910, when the eroded river frontages and denuded plains could support no more sheep, numbers peaked at around 320 000. Floods, vermin and continued erosion reduced sheep numbers thereafter and by 1924 only 124 000 sheep grazed the Kimberleys. Sheep had a similarly devastating impact in Queensland.

Following self-government in 1859, Queensland politicians immediately turned their attention to developing the land. To promote rapid occupation of the colony's vast domain, Parliament in 1860 offered pastoralists fourteen-year leases. Southern investors began an immediate rush north and the area claimed by squatters doubled by 1866. Queensland's Governor, Sir George Ferguson Bowen, beheld

> something almost sublime in the steady, silent flow of pastoral occupation over north-eastern Australia. It resembles the rise of the tide of some other operation of nature, rather than a work of man. Although it is difficult to ascertain exactly what progress may have been made at the end of each week and month, still, at the close of every year, we find that the margin of Christianity and civilisation has been pushed forward by some 200 miles.[43]

Heavy stocking and the practice of annual burning off led to a rapid deterioration of pasture. Stock ate the country bare, leaving the exposed soil vulnerable to erosion. Only the hardy, poorer type of vegetation survived. One observer commented, 'The luxurious tropical vegetation is only to be witnessed in all its beauty before the advent of the white man and his flocks and herds'.[44] Those who came in the 1860s land rush took up run after run, worked feverishly for quick returns, and abandoned each degraded pasture for virgin land further out.

In 1864 Biddulh Henning, already ensconced on a huge property in central Queensland, drove 7000 sheep up to the Gulf country. By depasturing them along 90 kilometres of the Flinders River, he laid claim to 500 square kilometres of northern Queensland. With no intention of settling there himself, he planned to hold the land till occupation of surrounding country pushed up the value of the property, then sell out. A year later he sold a half share of the property for £5000.[45] Henning sold just in time. A bank crash and a drop in wool prices halted the expansion after 1866. But price stability, an influx of Victorian speculative capital and the Queensland Land Act of 1868, which permitted free selection over large areas, stimulated a new era of expansion in the 1870s, based mostly on monopoly. Fraudulent selections enabled speculators to grasp larger blocks of land than the law allowed. Combinations by members of a family gathered into one hand tens of thousands of hectares in coveted districts.

The squatters who moved into Queensland carried with them the experiences of the southern squatting expansion; they expected to have to fight for the land. Because they were prepared to destroy without mercy, the Queensland squatters prevailed against a particularly militant Aboriginal resistance. In the months after Aborigines raided the Fraser family station and killed nine people in 1857, armed gangs of Europeans scoured the countryside, rounded Aborigines up like cattle, roped or handcuffed them and shot them. One hundred and fifty to 300 Aborigines were killed. One of the avenging squatters, George Pearce Serocold, a man of firm Anglican upbringing, explained the typical method of retribution during one incident:

> It was necessary to make a severe example of the leaders of the tribe and about a dozen of them were taken into the open country and shot. They were complete savages and never wore any clothes, and were so much alike that no evidence could ever be produced to enable them to be tried by our laws. These men were allowed to run and they were shot at about thirty or forty yards distant.[46]

The New South Wales Colonial Secretary, Charles Cowper, objected to the shooting of women in the back but he found acceptable execution without proof and without trial. A parliamentary inquiry regretted the slaughter but recognised the need for severe chastisement of the Aborigines. The conquest of Queensland by force had to continue.[47]

Battle is only one way to destroy an antagonist's will to resist; in Queensland, massacre achieved the same end with less risk. Europeans obtained their victory with the aid of the Native Police, an institution, common in British colonies, calculated to enlist the traditional animosities of the indigenous people to the invader's account. Colonial officers recruited members from among young Aboriginal males whose world was collapsing and who felt no particular loyalty to unrelated Aborigines. Generally small, Native Police detachments comprised a senior European officer, a camp sergeant and usually between four and six, or ten, Aboriginal troopers. The force effectively combined the advantages of European technology—arms, horses, equipment—with the hunting skills and topographical knowledge of the Aborigines.

The Port Phillip administrator, Charles La Trobe, assembled the first Australian Native Police unit in 1841. La Trobe saw their function as simply one of terror. Confronted by the Native Police, he explained, 'The Native soon saw that in yielding to his natural aggressive impulses he would be opposed to those who were not only his equals in savage cunning and endowment, but his superiors by alliance with the Europeans.'[48]

During the standard method of extermination, the police and numerous enthusiastic, well-armed volunteers spread themselves out in a line and scoured the country. Every Aboriginal man, woman or child within sight was shot or driven forward within the cordon and butchered in cold blood. Officers and troopers regularly shot prisoners, kidnapped and raped Aboriginal women and indiscriminately shot unresisting Aborigines. Squatter Harold Finch-Hatton found the ruthless character of the force rather jovial:

> Whenever the wild Blacks in the neighbourhood become troublesome, and take to spearing cattle, or otherwise misbehave themselves, it is [the business of the Native Police officer] to sally out with his mounted troops, and 'disperse' them, the meaning of which word is well known all through the colony.[49]

The invaders found other means besides guns to disperse Aborigines. Finch-Hatton reports how a neighbour decided to give 'the niggers . . . something really startling to keep them quiet', and fed them rations which

> contained about as much strychnine as anything else, and not one of the mob escaped. When they awoke in the morning they were all dead

corpses. More than a hundred Blacks were stretched out by this ruse of the owner of the Long Lagoon.[50]

In a more serious mood Finch-Hatton could opine:

> Whether the Blacks deserve any mercy at the hands of the pioneering squatters is an open question, but that they get none is certain. They are a doomed race, and before many years they will be completely wiped out of the land.[51]

Human slaughter thus liberated the country for sheep. In 1859 Queensland grazed 3 500 000 sheep; 21 700 000 depastured there in 1893. At least 200 000 Aborigines lived in Queensland in 1840; no more than 15 000 remained alive by the turn of the century.

After the gold rushes and the Land Acts of the 1860s, colonial governments assumed responsibility for providing the infrastructure, particularly railways, necessary to consolidate the permanent European occupation of rural Australia. Without government guarantee, private capital spurned the initiative to open unsettled or sparsely settled country. To the Australian ruling classes, government existed to afford all possible assistance to private capital—that is, to themselves. Decisions where to locate a particular railway line vitally interested local landowners, real estate agents and other businessmen. Moreover, the assumption by the state of the risks of railway development—the guarantee of dividends on government railway bonds—appealed to British investors. Unprecedented millions of pounds of capital poured into Australia in the several decades following the gold rushes to finance railway construction and the farms, mines and sheep stations the railways made profitable.

Iron rails spread across Australia like cracks in glass. Between 1875 and 1891 the railways grew from 3000 kilometres to more than 18 500 kilometres. They opened many millions of hectares of low rainfall inland to wheat growers, new districts to dairying, and forests to timber millers. Railways brought the commerce of the world to the bush and the products of the bush to the world. They incorporated the most essential features of the emerging industrial order: the substitution of metal for wood construction, mechanised motive power, vastly enlarged geographical scale, speed, rationality, impersonality and an unprecedented emphasis on precise timing. The astonishing advance in communications sanctioned a belief, or at least a new degree of confidence in, the perfectibility of civilised man. No other invention revealed the power and speed of the new age as much as the railroad, which became the most pervasive and compelling image of the age. The iron road, racing across Australia, was the very symbol of man's triumph, through technology, over nature.

Politicians quickly grasped the railroads' civilising significance, their ability to conquer time, shrink space and master nature. Everywhere the rails arrived, local dignitaries welcomed them for their great contribution to material progress and political unity. The railways would do for commerce, the celebratory crowds were told, what the printing press had done for learning and literature.

Railways facilitated the transfer of a vast domain into private hands. By 1892, with a population of 3 984 000 (excluding Aborigines), the area in Australia alienated or in the process of alienation amounted to 5 025 000 hectares. This land was not distributed according to the average of 1.26 hectares per head, however; huge monopolies controlled the bulk of the estate. Sidney Kidman, for example, acquired his first station in central Australia in 1886. By the time of the Great War he controlled station country considerably greater in area than England or Tasmania and nearly as large as Victoria. There was no country in the world with a similar population in which individuals held such immense areas. Nowhere else in the world have so few people been in a position to reshape the face of so much of the earth's surface.

Australians exercised their ascendancy in an age—the last 50 years of the Victorian era—driven by an unusually fierce determination to make the civilising process permanent. Rapid industrialisation in Britain had made the notion of progress palpable, improvements became obvious to everyone, and the idea that man, specifically Anglo-Saxon man, was lord of creation and of all nature, assumed popular assent. Writers urged the youth of Europe to migrate, in the name of progress and civilisation, to the interior regions of Africa and Australia and make the resources there available to Europeans, who alone possessed the scientific knowledge and technical skills necessary to put them to productive use.

Civilisation depended on the vigorous conquest of nature by science. But civilisation also depended on a conquest in the social sphere. Relations between human beings—especially those between the weak and the strong or the poor and the rich—traditionally belonged in the province of moral rules and judgements. In the heyday of nineteenth century European colonial expansion these old-fashioned connections were eliminated. Relations between people became a neutral or amoral terrain inviting scientific rather than moral scrutiny. Struggle and competition appeared as natural phenomena; their outcomes—survival of the fittest or victory of the strong over the weak—accepted as the inevitable consequence of natural processes. Struggle and competition became celebrated as the driving forces of progress and expanding civilisation. In a curious reversal, this amoral terrain became the source of new values: self-assertion and aggrandisement became an ethic superseding all other values.[52]

In the hundred years after first settlement, scientists in Australia shipped hundreds of thousands, possibly millions, of preserved specimens of animals and flowers, as well as rocks and Aboriginal skeletons, skulls and pickled heads to Europe. Early observers believed the new landscape supported some of the world's most primitive and grotesque forms of botanical and zoological life and offered unique insights into the nature of the world. Phillip Parker King, marine surveyor and naturalist, enthused in 1822: 'No country ever produced a more extraordinary assemblage of indigenous productions—no country has proved richer than Australia in every branch of natural history.'[53] The traffic in trophies from the scientific assault on nature in Australia excited imaginations at the centres of European research and contributed significantly to theoretical developments in evolutionary biology and geology. Material gathered in the Antipodes strengthened scientific knowledge, augmented the growing systematisation of biological data and consolidated the scientific picture of the physical world.[54]

The nineteenth century Victorians linked scientific elaboration and material achievement to a new sense of understanding of the meaning of civilisation. They discarded the earlier ideas of *civilité*—embodying elaborate etiquette and genteel manners—in favour of contrasting their laws, political institutions and material culture with those of others. Progress necessarily involved the downgrading of those others. Europeans more and more identified their scientific outlook and capacity for invention as the basic attributes which set them apart. Australians assimilated these attitudes as they reimported their exported specimens and data in the form of a consciousness of the uniqueness and superiority of western civilisation.

In all the new worlds to which they migrated during the nineteenth century, the British faced conflict. These experiences made such a strong impression that intellectuals raised the condition of struggle to the status of a permanent ecological law. The social Darwinist, Thomas Huxley, for example, believed civilisation depended on a constant battle to maintain and improve in opposition to the State of Nature. Civilisation and nature were considered to be deeply antithetical; there was no possibility of a state of being without tension, either within the self or between the self and environment. Huxley cited Tasmania as an example of how the State of Nature must give way before civilisation: a shipload of English colonists there put an end to the wilderness; they cleared away the native vegetation, extirpated or drove out the indigenous populations of animals and people, and took measures to defend themselves against the recovery or reimmigration of either. In their place they introduced English grain and fruit trees, English dogs, sheep, cattle and horses: English men settled amidst an English garden.[55]

For Huxley's contemporaries the garden of introduced flora and fauna epitomised civilised landscape and represented both a place of virtue and of material productivity—mutually reinforcing ends. William Howitt, the English author, visited Melbourne in the 1850s and after touring a gentleman's fine house and garden, commented:

> Thus is the Englishman converting the wild forests of the most distant regions of the earth into homes of beauty and taste and making them, as it were, a portion of the mother country. Everything receives so

completely the English stamp, that spite of the totally different vegetation, all looks like a piece of England.[56]

The English admired, above all, those qualities of mastery,
strength, pugnacity, toughness and determination which they
believed were intrinsic to themselves. Inspired by the sight of the
civilising transformation wrought by the English garden, Howitt
exclaimed, 'England reproduces herself in new lands; and how
feeble seem the native races against the sinewy, plucky, pushing,
predominating Englishman'.[57]

Nineteenth century achievements in science and industry convinced the British they had advanced far beyond all other peoples
and civilisations. Scientific and technological control over nature
proved that British modes of thought and social organisation corresponded more closely to the underlying realities of the universe
than did those of other people. And as belief in blood and race
strengthened, members of the master race became less patient with
those human beings unwilling to accommodate themselves to the
new regime of progress. Australian Aboriginal resistance to an alien
culture of work, written laws and stratified hierarchy was interpreted as an incapacity for civilisation as such. The Aborigines held
the naive view that they were entitled to rule themselves in their
own land; all Europeans agreed on the error of that belief. During
his travels in Victoria, Howitt came upon an encampment of Aborigines and could not help wondering

> on seeing this miserable spectacle of humanity, in the midst of a race
> full of activity and progress, whether such a race could be intended by
> Providence to ramble over, without possessing, much less improving,
> large regions of the earth? and I could not avoid admitting to myself
> that that which will not go onward in the world's progress, must go
> down.[58]

Howitt's observation reflected the general complacency and hard-
ness of contemporary bourgeois opinion. In Australia he found
evidence to question whether Aborigines were even fellow human
beings, much less the equals of Europeans. Their perceived inability
to control and master their environment—in contrast to the 'plucky

Englishman'—determined their rank on the scale of savagery and civilisation.

For reasons of their own, however, Aborigines did not necessarily want to join in the world's progress, especially since assimilation meant entry into European society at the very lowest level of the social hierarchy. 'They do not court a life of labour', wrote a Victorian Justice of the Peace of Aborigines in 1849:

> [The life] of our shepherds and hut-keepers—our splitters or bullock drivers—appears to them one of unmeaning toil, and they would by no means consent to exchange their free unhoused condition for the monotonous drudgery of such a dreary existence.[59]

But European efforts to change Aboriginal habits of life did not cease. In the last half of the century many Aboriginal survivors in southern and eastern Australia were living in hovels on the margins of civilisation and dying of pulmonary and venereal diseases. Here Christian missionaries saw opportunities for Christian enterprise, a chance to show the vanquished the path to heaven. In accordance with the church's traditional self-interest and collaboration in earthly human suffering, Presbyterians, Anglicans and Methodists established missions to instruct Aborigines on the Christian catechism and to bring them the good news that Christ died for their sins. God, the missionaries said, was colour-blind, and in the mansions of the Lord the black man would be as fair as the white.[60] Their efforts reflected age-old priorities. 'I would rather,' Bishop Augustus Short of Adelaide told a South Australian Committee of Enquiry in 1860, 'they [the Australian Aborigines] die as Christians than drag out a miserable existence as heathens. I believe that the race will disappear either way'.[61]

Indeed, by the middle of the century, the Aboriginal birthrate in settled and semi-settled areas began falling dramatically. Explained one Aborigine to an investigator for the 1858–59 Victorian Select Committee on Aborigines: 'Why me have lubra [wife]? Why me have picaninny [children]? You have all this place, no good have children, no good have lubra, me tumble down and die very soon now.'[62] But Aborigines did not entirely disappear. Along the major rivers of the Murray, the Murrumbidgee, the Darling, and their tributaries, and up and down the coast, wherever employment opportunities supplemented traditional food sources, Aborigines continued to survive. Those few Europeans who meditated on the Aboriginal problem and opposed mass slaughter concentrated on devising strategies of control directed towards making the survivors fit European society. Since instruction might make Aborigines useful to the Europeans, the missions tried, but failed, to interest the government in providing some Aboriginal education. In any case, to the Aborigines, education appeared an unreal and futile exercise, and to a people who had lived freely for tens of thousands of years in their own country according to their own fashion, useful equalled slavery. No one dared suggest the Aborigines decide for themselves. In any case, most settlers believed the natives constitutionally incapable of understanding the superiority of European civilisation, and did not want Aborigines civilised; their mere presence was deemed inconvenient. Anthony Trollope, who visited several Australian missions in the early 1870s, was shocked by the sight of healthy Aboriginal children and believed the missions seriously erred in their encouragement of Aboriginal procreation:

> An increasing race of aborigines in the land . . . would be a curse rather than a blessing . . . Their doom is to be exterminated; and the sooner their doom be accomplished . . . the better will it be for civilization.[63]

Unlike the case in Africa and the Pacific, no Australian mission ever produced communities which founded indigenous churches. Evangelical efforts failed. Aborigines used the missions for their own purposes. Missions all over Australia confronted a people who refused to display the gratitude expected for all the material and spiritual benefits lavished on them. Aborigines wanted refuge from marauding settlers, and, especially in times of drought, food; they did not want religious instruction or work.

Alexander Berry's 1822 exhortation[64] to apply rational theory to the conquest of nature in Australia found a formal response in the 1850s. To encourage scientific progress, learned men established the Victorian Institute for the Advancement of Science and The Philosophical Society, both in 1854. These utilitarian assemblies believed the exchange of scientific data would foster the development of the colony's resources. Members made prodigious data-collecting efforts to further this end. Botanist Baron Ferdinand Von Mueller, for example, had by 1868, after sixteen years botanising, assembled a personal collection of 350 000 specimens of Australian flora. Mueller, committed to turning the flora of the world to profitable use, favoured practical application of his discoveries. But while he believed in putting the land to use, he doubted that the kind of settlement then advancing across Australia necessarily improved the country. Compared with the unredeemed grandeur of the forests Mueller encountered on his botanising expeditions, he found the reclaimed landscape an uninspiring prospect, an aesthetic failure. In an 1871 lecture Mueller asked his audience to

> Contrast the magnificence of a dense forest, before the destructive hand of man defaced it, with the cheerless aspect of wide landscapes, devoid of wooded scenery—only open plains or treeless ridges bounding the horizon. The silent grandeur and solitude of a virgin forest inspires us almost with awe, much more so than even the broad expanse of the ocean . . . No settlement, however princely—no city, however great its splendour, brilliant its arts, or enchanting its pleasures—can arouse those sentiments of veneration which, among all the grand works of nature, an undisturbed noble forest-region is most apt to call forth.[65]

Mueller also believed in the economic value of Australian eucalypts but feared their value would never be realised if wholesale clearing continued. In vain he urged colonial governments to set aside a greater proportion of the country as forest preserves.

Another member of Melbourne's scientific community, Edward Wilson, vigorously advocated intervention in the processes of nature. While the phenomena of nature were profuse and varied, the distribution, he believed, was erratic, and he saw no reason why people should not correct the balance. Australia's indigenous animals were interesting, but, unfortunately, were practically useless, and provided only 'a little sport and an occasional meal'.[66] Dissatisfied with a 'country half supplied with the requirements of civilisation', Wilson championed the idea of acclimatisation—the introduction of exotic species into Australia.[67] Natural variety was an obstacle to man's dominion on earth—nature contained too many useless species. To increase Australian usefulness, Acclimatisation Societies introduced dozens of exotic plants and animals, including blackbirds, thrushes, starlings, sparrows, robins, pheasants, partridges, skylarks, Indian mynas and nightingales; trout, salmon and carp; blackberry and prickly pear; donkeys, alpacas, angora goats, llamas, ostriches, camels and zebu cattle. Most of the successful introductions proved disastrous for native wildlife. Anthony Trollope applauded the vigorous adaptations of the products of Europe to Australia:

> In some districts . . . the English rabbit is already an almost ineradicable pest; in others is the sparrow. The forests are becoming full of the European bee. Wild horses roam in mobs of thousands over the distant sheep and cattle stations.[68]

Trollope was right about the rabbits. The introduction of the British sub-species of the grey European rabbit (*Oryctolagus cuniculus*) proved the costliest and most destructive transfer ever of an animal from one country into another.[69]

Early Australian settlers kept large numbers of hutch-bred rabbits and many escaped into the bush. Sailors, sealers and whalers also left breeding pairs on islands and on the coast to provide a future food source. None of these escaped or released animals ever bred in significant numbers. Native predators—tiger-cats, hawks, eagles and packs of prowling dingoes—kept them in check. But the early settlers, enthusiastic eradicators, also baited and shot anything they thought troublesome—wombats, rat-kangaroos, wedge-tailed eagles, all hawk species, ravens, dingoes, native cats and lizards. Hunting and habitat destruction drove many animals in the eastern colonies to near extinction. The platypus, bustards and even emus and kangaroos were becoming rare in the Murray District by the late 1850s. In all settled districts where native predators were scarce, an ecological niche opened up.

In 1859 the squatter Thomas Austin of Barwon Park, near Geelong, imported English wild grey rabbits which he crossbred with hutch-bred rabbits to provide prey for recreational hunting. He gave breeding pairs to his friends, who carried them all over Victoria. The progeny acclimatised to the Australian environment with frightening fecundity. In 1865 Austin reported a tally of 20 000 rabbits killed on his property and estimated 10 000 remained alive.

In the late 1850s Victorian courts convicted and fined a man £10 under the poaching laws for having shot a rabbit on the property of John Robertson at Colac. But by 1868 rabbits had become a pest in the Western District and squatters began employing full-time trappers. In April 1869, William Robertson, John Robertson's son, estimated he had spent £9500 to clear his property of over two million rabbits.

In the 1860s Riverina squatters opened the back country (country away from the rivers) to their flocks, by sinking ground tanks and digging wells. When rabbits crossed the Murray in the late 1870s there was plenty of water throughout the district to sustain their destructive rampage. They felled pithy kurrajong saplings up to 175 millimetres in diameter and devoured the leaves, branches and trunks; they barked and killed the mallee, sandalwood, pine, belah, wild-lemon and leopard-trees; they stripped orange bush three metres from the ground and wiped out saltbush, cottonbush, bluebush and lignum.

Rabbits also invaded the Victorian mallee, where their voracious appetites destroyed the natural fodder, decreased sheep numbers by 75 percent, and forced the abandonment of 62 sheep runs. On eighteen other runs the wool clip fell by four-fifths. In 1878 the Lands Royal Commission described the mallee as an 'abomination of desolation', caused by rabbits, and in 1880, Charles Duffy, Minister of Lands, visited the area:

> we went over miles and miles of the country without seeing a solitary sheep or sign of life except for thousands of rabbits and so thoroughly had these devastated the district that there was not a blade of grass to be seen and the trees were stripped of their bark as high as the rabbits could reach.[70]

The colonies declared rabbits vermin. Poison baits were laid, bounties posted and competitions announced for finding effective means of eradication. In the meantime, the rabbits multiplied and spread. At the northward rate of 100 kilometres a year, they reached Queensland by 1886. New South Wales reported ten million rabbits destroyed in the first eight months of 1887, but all efforts to turn back the invasion failed. By 1890 New South Wales supported 62 million sheep and many, many millions more rabbits. One lessee, west of the Darling, spent £27 000 on rabbit destruction in one year, and calculated that at the end of that time he had twice as many rabbits as when he started.

In the good seasons of the late 1880s and early 1890s rabbits invaded the Cooper's Creek region of the South Australia–Queensland–New South Wales border area, and bred in countless millions. They burrowed under the canegrass which held the sandhills together, and when, in the dry seasons the sandhills began to drift, the sand choked the watercourses, filled the waterholes and covered the trees which lined the creeks. One pastoralist, who abandoned his run because of rabbits, recalled:

> They came in like water through a funnel, in a steady stream, ravaging all before them, rooting up the perennial grasses, destroying the edible bushes, and ringbarking all that they could not climb . . . I have seen their bodies six feet and more from the ground, when they had slipped and got hung by the neck in a fork in the branches . . . When in December the great heat set in, they died by thousands round the waterholes, and tainted the air so much that we could not keep the meat, no matter how carefully we salted it.[71]

The outer colonies, Queensland and Western Australia, tried fencing themselves off. Queensland built a fence from Haddon Corner, at the colony's south-west boundary to a point west of the Warrego, over 500 kilometres. As long as gates remained shut, fences were effective, at least in the short run. On the New South Wales side of the fence, thousands of dead rabbits piled up against the wire and carpeted the ground, starved to death on ground they had eaten bare, in sight of the untouched green on the other side. But the rabbits had, in any case, nearly reached the northern limit of their natural habitat and this constraint checked their invasion more than the fence. Climate, however, proved no barrier to their westward advance.

Western Australia hoped the Nullarbor Plain—a vast, treeless, waterless desert, straddling the South Australia border—would keep the rabbits out. But overlanders, who looked on rabbits as free meat, carried them from one patch of green to another and by this means rabbits reached Fowlers Bay, in the west of South Australia, by 1891. By 1896 they were beyond the border, and by 1901, all over the Coolgardie goldfields and south to Esperance. Between 1902 and 1907 the state government erected a rabbit-proof fence, from Starvation Harbour, west of Esperance, to the Eighty Mile Beach between Port Hedland and Broome: 2109 kilometres long, 106 centimetres high, of 17 guage, three centimetre mesh. In 1907 the Western Australian Department of Agriculture reported that there was 'not a blade of grass' to be seen on the eastern side of the fence.[72] But gold seekers and travellers took rabbits inside the fence before it was even completed and others left gates open. By the 1920s rabbits infested the south-west of Western Australia in plague proportions. As in Queensland, however, rabbits failed to establish themselves in the north of the state.

In 50 years rabbits took over every major pastoral and agricultural district in Australia south of the Capricorn. In competition with sheep for food, they probably halved the value of Australia's woolclip; their contribution to the biological pauperisation of Australia is incalculable. Rabbits ate out the palatable ephemerals and native grasses, and forced sheep and themselves to eat and finally destroy shrub and scrub throughout southern Australia. These two herbivores ensured that Australians will never again see the waving plains of Mitchell grass or the rich and diverse native herbage the Aborigines knew and worked.

While rabbits ate their way through Australian vegetation, acclimatised foxes wasted Australian wildlife. Foxes were first successfully released, for hunting purposes, in Victoria in the early 1870s. By 1880 they ranged over about 13 000 square kilometres of the colony and by 1893 had crossed the Murray. In 1903 foxes were declared vermin at Armidale, 900 kilometres north of the Murray. They had reached southern Queensland by 1911 and were west of Kalgoorlie, in Western Australia, by 1917.

Foxes ate birds, birds' eggs, mice, frogs, fish, lizards and bats and, in combination with faunal destruction by sheep and rabbits, contributed to the extinction or near extinction of numerous native rodents and small marsupials. Foxes preyed on the bilby (*Macrotis lagotis*), (once so common over half the continent, it supported a fur trade), left homeless through competition with rabbits for burrows and also a victim of poison baits and traps. Habitat destruction and predation by foxes were also responsible for the probable extinction of the barred bandicoot (*Parameles bouganville*), the once widespread pig-footed bandicoot (*Chaeropus ecaudatus*), the formerly abundant yallara (*Macrotis leucura*), another bandicoot species, and the drastic decline in numbers of the bridled nail-tailed wallaby (*Onychogalea fraenata*), once common in New South Wales and southern Queensland. Foxes also preyed on the now virtually extinct, but once abundant, brush-tailed rat kangaroo (*Bettongia penicillata*).[73]

When they had banished the indigenous people, made the native animals scarce, and secured their tenure, squatters began eradicating trees on a widespread scale to ensure clear grazing for their flocks. And where the Land Acts had succeeded in placing selectors on the land, the lucky farmers embarked on a war against the bush: ringbarking, grubbing (digging out stumps), fencing and ploughing. But possession of a selection did not guarantee economic independence and working conditions often approached 'absolute slavery'. One Wimmera farmer recalled: 'Day after day on poor food and bad water you had to walk behind the plough and harrows, and following the harrows on rough-ploughed land has to be experienced before one can give any idea as to what it is like.'[74] Porridge, bread and dripping (fat), and corned meat comprised the staple diet. Children were also pressed into labour. One boy recalled:

> ... we fed the fowls, gathered the eggs, chopped the kindling wood and when older and big enough to use the large axe, chopped the wood for the fires. In summer we also carted water from the dam 100 yards away—as many as 50 four gallon tins of it. This was put onto the vegetables and fruit trees. In between times we dug around the fruit trees, cut bathurst burrs, dug drains ... my brother and I considered ourselves lucky that Father was a sheep and wheat farmer, and not a 'Cow Cocky', as some of the neighbours were. [Their children] were indeed to be pitied. It meant, week in, week out, generally starting before dawn, milking then separating the cream just in time to get

ready for school, starting the milking not long after school was out, and it seemed to us that they went on till after dark. We thought it a life not worth living.[75]

Sheep suffered the ravages of scab, and cows, pleuro-pneumonia; grub and blight afflicted the crops; rust beset the wheat. Rabbits ate out the best grasses and left the weeds, devoured the crops, dug up the potatoes and ringbarked the fruit trees. But farmers persevered and gradually, everywhere over the settled crescent of eastern Australia, farms and pastoral runs were won from the forest, woodland and scrub. By 1870 some 1.2 million hectares had been cleared in Australia for agriculture; over the next 30 years a further 3.5 million hectares were similarly transformed. Land settlement virtually exterminated the native flora over hundreds of square kilometres. In their place exotics sprang up. In Victoria about five new weed species became established every year between 1870 and 1930.[76] When a property became degraded the selectors, like the squatters before them, simply moved on. Joseph Jenkins, a Welsh swagman, noted in 1871 that the 'Smeaton district, once considered the garden of Victoria, is now a ruinous area from continued exhaustion of the land. The farms are overrun by weeds. There are numerous deserted homesteads.'[77]

The first attempts to clear the 5000 square kilometre virgin forest of Victoria's Gippsland began in the mid-1870s. Most of Gippsland's big timber—dense stands of mountain ash, blue gum and messmate—was at least 45 metres high, and some enormous trees measured 22 metres round, 1.5 metres from the ground. On the forest floor through uprooted and decaying trunks, through a network of fallen branches, grew fern-trees (20 metres high in moist places), big shrubs, young trees and wattles, a jumble of life and death. In the soil, spongy with centuries of humus and a 1000 to 1400-millimetre annual rainfall, ferns flourished and insects— flies, mosquitoes, ants, caterpillars, tarantulas—abounded. Although Parson J. W. Eisdell felt 'overawed by the majestic grandeur of Nature' in the Gippsland he reasoned the forest existed only 'for man to come and claim [because there] the great Architect of the Universe had planned to provide for his sustenance and happiness'.[78]

Hewing a farm out of virgin Gippsland forest required prodigious labour. A settler needed muscle and an axe to clear a track, blaze the bounds of his block, roughhew a house from bush timber, and then commence years of clearing. Axemen first 'nicked' (partly cut through) the timber and the felling of one giant would bring down the rest. Cutting took place during the winter and spring, followed by the summer burn. Bishop James Moorhouse recalled the all consuming, unforgettable conflagrations and the restlessness which invariably accompanied conquest:

> When night came on we were surrounded by great red blazing trunks of trees. It reminded one of Pandemonium more than anything else . . . I have been frequently told by them, when smoking my pipe in their company at night by their fires, that it almost drags the heart out of a man to get the country clear. One man said to me, 'I have been ten years at it, and have not done it yet.' . . . It is a life work, but there is something at the end of it, and there is something also for that man's son and his son's sons . . . But . . . [w]hen a man begins to have too many neighbours there is sometimes a desire to get away. A man will say to himself, 'Ah, there is another fellow actually within a mile of me! I must be off'.[79]

The Land Acts had parcelled out Gippsland selections indiscriminately, without regard to creating preserves or green belts, and encouraged a proliferation of clearings. The cumulative effect of the many uncoordinated local acts produced a profound ecological and visual change over huge areas. Within a decade of the European conquest of the Gippsland, exotic thistles riddled the land, watercourses eroded to several times their original size and rivers, like the Avon, formerly navigable for sixteen kilometres from the mouth, became too shallow for any craft. Wildlife rapidly disappeared. Farmers and pastoralists regarded clearing as an unexceptional, normal farm operation. In combination, however, Gippsland's selectors effaced an entire temperate eucalyptus rainforest, to produce denuded downs. The result surprised the individual selector:

> As time went by we could hear what seemed to be thunder in the distance, but it was in reality the noise made by scrub falling as it was cut. One day when up the track, my husband saw what appeared to be

a break in the tops of the trees to the North; so, the following Sunday we climbed to the top of the hill, and, behold! there was a gap in the scrub. Someone was clearing, and each week the gap grew larger. Then, in other directions, the same thing would occur, and the following February or March, we would see clouds of smoke. Each year the clearings grew larger, and the smoke more intense, and as the years passed, the great walls of scrub were cut down, and bands of men could be seen chopping the logs up after the fire had passed over them.[80]

For decades the gaunt trunks and amputated limbs of ringbarked trees dominated the landscape and as they died, the gum trees provided food and shelter for innumerable grubs which ate the sapwood and lived under the dead bark. Huge flocks of black cockatoos, which in Australia fill the same ecological niche occupied by woodpeckers in other countries, preyed on the insects and tore the bark to shreds. To cynical townspeople the only visible result of the settler's labour was to provide food for shrieking cockatoos—often the only animals seen on the selection. Bush settlers became known derisively as 'cockatoo farmers', later simply 'cockies'. But while, in the short run at least, a blessing to cockatoos, the larger benefits of ringbarking proved ephemeral. The real consequence of ringbarking, bark-stripping, burning and felling trees was the disembowelment of a living community. Erosion scoured the cleared land and streams flooded. Rye grass, cocksfoot and clover grew luxuriantly in the Gippsland ashes, but summer grasshopper plagues swept away the pastures. Many selectors despaired of ever seeing the economic benefits of their work.

By 1890, two years after Australia's centennial, over 100 million sheep and nearly eight million cattle grazed over much of the continent. In the space of 100 years, the original Australian bush had given way to a landscape and environment created largely in the interests of flocks of sheep and herds of cattle. Later generations accepted, even celebrated, this diminished and impoverished scene as typical Australian landscape. Nineteenth century British-Australians, however, remained antagonistic towards both the original and the transformed landscape. Artists and writers remained confused about just exactly what distinguished Australia. Certainly

the bush, and the country's unique flora and fauna, would never
serve as suitable definition:

> The Australian mountain forests are funereal, secret, stern. Their soli-
> tude is desolation. They seem to stifle in their black gorges a story of
> sullen despair. No tender sentiment is nourished in their shade . . . From
> the melancholy gums, strips of white bark hang and rustle. The very
> animal life of these frowning hills is either grotesque or ghostly. Great
> grey kangaroos hop noiselessly over the coarse grass. Flights of white
> cockatoos stream out, shrieking like evil souls. The sun suddenly sinks,
> and the mopokes burst out into horrible peals of semi-human
> laughter.[81]

Most nineteenth century Australians, even native born, referred
to Britain as home and looked on their own country as real estate, a
camping ground for money-making purposes. But in the last
decades of the century, out of the barren fecundity of the interior,
there appeared, in prose and verse, an incipient sense of place and
love of the land, a vision of a life lived with gusto by manly Britons
in the outdoors under Australian skies. A few squatters and cattle
herders delighted in the outdoor life, and found profound satisfaction living in the open:

> And he sees the vision splendid of the sunlit plains extended,
> And at night the wondrous glory of the everlasting stars.[82]

Meanwhile, practical men focused their energies towards altering
the face of the land. The Victorian drought of 1877–81 exposed
the vulnerability of farming in dry areas. The colony, unwilling to
accept limits to man's domain, appointed a Royal Commission on
Water Supply in 1884 to investigate the possibilities of irrigation.
The Commission's president, the young Victorian politician Alfred
Deakin, travelled to America to report on achievements and progress there. In Los Angeles in 1885, he met George Chaffey and his
brother William, promoters of two irrigation colonies in the California desert, Etiwanda and Ontario. Deakin's party fell in thrall of
the Chaffeys' ambitious engineering and keen business acumen and
Deakin suggested the possibility of an irrigation colony on the
Murray River. With the brothers in mind Deakin later wrote:

> The alert, inquisitive, intelligent, restlessly-inventive and progressive

Americans multiplying their machines and devices every year, bringing to their aid all the resources of scientific discovery, and to the management the keenest commercial spirit are likely to be masters in this regard for a long time to come.[83]

The Chaffeys embodied 'efficiency' and 'expertise', the qualities most needed to establish human dominion over a hostile environment and to force the niggardly nature of Australia to yield to the claims of the new century.

6

To the Firing Line

A NATION IS NEVER A NATION
WORTHY OF PRIDE OR PLACE
TILL THE MOTHERS HAVE SENT THEIR FIRSTBORN
TO LOOK DEATH ON THE FIELD IN THE FACE.

A. B. Paterson, 'Australia—A Nation'

AUSTRALIA'S PROSPERITY to 1890 depended on the reckless exploitation of untouched natural wealth. The mining of huge deposits of gold, copper, coal, tin and silver-lead generated fortunes. Vast grasslands grazed tens of millions of sheep, virgin soils readily grew cereals, and unbroken forests provided building materials and fuel. Australia's natural heritage yielded to the demands of industrial civilisation for the first time between 1840 and 1890, when technical advance enabled an unprecedented use of the land. Fatter cattle, heavier fleeces, superior breeds of wheat and hundreds of labour-saving devices—post and rail fences, wire fences, corrugated iron and water tanks, artesian bores and windmills, new ploughs, strippers, mechanical harvesters and mobile steam threshing machines—provided relatively high incomes for most Australians and generous returns for British capitalists.[1]

Huge dividends from tin mining at Mt Biscoff in Tasmania in the 1880s, and the promise of even greater returns from mining Broken Hill in New South Wales (one of the world's largest deposits of silver, lead and zinc), attracted immense amounts of British capital, and by the late 1880s Australia had become the favourite foreign field for British investors. Capitalists called upon Australia to play the role of pastoral lease and quarry in their expanding world economy.

Much of the money flowed into Victoria. During the 1880s, Victorian governments, municipalities, banks, building societies and pastoral and mining companies borrowed over £50 000 000— more than for all the rest of Australia. Debt, and a wealth of natural accessible resources, underwrote the growth of 'marvelous

Melbourne'. The city's population nearly doubled, from 268 000 in 1881 to 473 000 in 1891, and Melbourne became the thirtieth city in the world in numbers and the seventh city in the Empire—larger than most European capitals.

Easy credit encouraged stock market and land speculation. The shares of Broken Hill Proprietary (BHP), registered in Melbourne in August 1885, had a nominal value of 19 pounds. The last sales for 1887 closed at 174 pounds, 10 shillings. In February 1888 they stood at 409 pounds. Other Broken Hill companies rose with the leader, and sharp operators floated new mining concerns for country 55 kilometres around Broken Hill—nearly all of it worthless. In March 1888, gambling in silver shares on Melbourne's exchange reached a million pounds a day. The excitement of share market speculation spread to land. During the same year, 150 new land and property companies were registered, and the city's surrounding orchards, market gardens and grazing paddocks became prime real estate. Land boomers founded new banks, issued shares, solicited deposits and promptly lent the capital and deposits to the directors and their friends, who bought and sub-divided blocks of farmland. 'The more risky and uncertain the speculation,' commented the *Age*, 'the bigger is the amount of nominal capital . . . in the expectation that the public will be attracted by nothing mean and small.'[2] Suburban land speculation marked the beginning of an Australian way of life centred around housing families in private homes built on sprawling estates which extinguished all signs of nature. The dispersed urban areas which overwhelm modern Australian cities originated in the speculative frenzy which consumed Melbourne in the 1880s.

The government borrowed money in Britain to build railway lines to the rapidly expanding suburbs, and Victorian politicians, possessed of remarkable foresight, bought land precisely in those suburbs to which the suburban railway network was to be extended. Members of Parliament used their influence to get stations built, at public expense, on land they owned and hoped to sub-divide. 'Railways have a habit of running into the properties of the millionaires,' commented one English visitor.[3] Prices of outer suburban land rose five, ten and in some cases twenty times in five years. Speculators made fortunes.

Rich and poor alike, however, disposed of their wastes the same way—through the back door. Without sewers, all the liquid refuse from kitchens, baths, laundries, factories, stables and public urinals, as well as much of the solid effluent, drained into the streets and eventually into the Yarra River. 'Marvelous Smelbourne' stank and the city's death rate from typhoid was five times worse than London's. According to sanitary reformers the reasons for Melbourne's atrociously unhealthy environment were because:

> We valued so highly our constitutional rights—the right of a man to pollute running water; the right of a man to spread contagious diseases descending even to the third generation; the right of a man in every possible way to poison the life of the members of the community—that many of us would oppose to the death any interference with these privileges . . . the vested right of every Englishman to carry death into his neighbour's household.[4]

Nevertheless, most residents no doubt preferred life in Melbourne to that in any contemporary western European city. They enjoyed comparatively high standards of living and lived in exciting times. For despite the typhoid, the smell and the existence of slums, the enormous energy released in the rush to be rich—the scramble of construction, the amplification of commerce and manufacture, the advent of powered trams, gas and electric light and the rise of extravagant mansions—promised a future without limits. Material prosperity justified optimism and millennial hopes of a heaven on earth. Humankind was entering the modern age. Australia had joined the modern world economy.

The 1880s boom occurred during a period of international downward pressure on prices. As worldwide agricultural and industrial expansion augmented the supplies of most commodities, their prices fell. Late in 1890 a revolution in Argentina precipitated the collapse of Baring's, one of London's leading financial houses. British investors stopped lending money, and over the next year the value of shares listed on the Stock Exchange of Melbourne declined on average by 40 percent. By the end of 1891 neither Australian banks, building societies, mortgage companies, nor Australian governments could any longer borrow in London, and work on public projects and private building ceased. The price of wool, Australia's leading export staple, fell by about a third during the quinquennium 1890–94. The distress spread to rural districts and unemployment soared. BHP, however, prospered throughout the depressed 1890s and twice declared million-pound dividends.

To compensate for low prices, pastoralists increased their flocks and herds. The excessive numbers of sheep and cattle denuded inland pastures and when, between 1895 and 1903, drought dried up the inland fertile crescent of eastern Australia—from Queensland, through New South Wales, Victoria and into South Australia—the land was devastated. East of the Darling, 90 percent of the original perennial saltbush disappeared. Grass also vanished from paddocks and topsoil began drifting and blowing away. Albermarle Station near Wilcannia, New South Wales, lost topsoil up to a depth of 30 centimetres from 40 500 hectares. The great drought culminated in huge dust storms and the largest, on 11–13 November 1902, covered areas of South Australia, Queensland, New South Wales and Victoria. In Victoria, lightning and balls of fire accompanied gales of dust which so darkened the sky that fowls roosted in the middle of the day and people used lanterns to get about. On November 14 and 15 Australian dust storms covered parts of both islands of New Zealand, over 2800 kilometres from the drought-affected area. On 28 March 1903, 'mud-rain' fell on Victoria and deposited 13.7 tonnes per square kilometre of mud for every 25 millimetres of rainfall over a large area.

At the beginning of the dry seasons, rabbits, used to ample water and green feed, began to swarm and migrate south in their millions. No obstacles barred their passage. Wire fences did not stop them: in the corners and angles, the dead and dying rabbits piled up until they reached the top and the remainder of the horde passed on. By day, starving rabbits crowded under trees and shrubs; they crawled under the dying, ringbarked saltbush; they lay beside fence posts, and lines of rabbits crowded every futile pencil of shade. By night they ran on. The outback stank with scattered carcasses. Ten thousand a night, 100 000 a night, sometimes 200 000 a night lay dead around poisoned, fenced-in ground water tanks. But, through-out the barren land, small colonies of superior rabbits survived, living on yams and mallee roots and waiting for the grass to revive to begin breeding.

When the droughts began, Australia had grazed 110 million sheep. Eight years later, 57 million sheep remained alive and pastoralists abandoned large tracts of sheep country. In 1891 the western division of New South Wales carried fifteen million sheep; less than half that number depasture there now. Sixty years after the great drought, the dead mulga still stood, and some plants, common before the drought, did not reappear until 50 years afterwards.[5]

Before the drought, the boom industries—pastoralism, mining and maritime transport—employed large groups of men at demanding, labour-intensive toil. Payment by piecework discouraged ties between owner and worker; in fact, the cash nexus forced capital and labour into adversity. As the 1890s depression began, pastoralists, mine owners and steamship owners fought to restore profitability by lowering labour costs. Workers resisted with strikes. The first big walkout occurred in 1890 when maritime officers, in solidarity with shearers opposed to non-union labour, refused to handle non-union wool. The owners relished the opportunity for a showdown. When coal miners denied fuel to ships working with non-union labour, mine owners closed the mines. All striking unions were defeated and further stoppages over the next few years—notably by the shearers in 1891 and 1894 and the Broken Hill miners in 1892—were also broken. The struggles in those years involved every colony and every key industry. Employers used the tactic of lock-out as often as workers struck. The state pretended no neutrality and in 1891, 1892 and again in 1894, colonial governments deployed armed police to break strikes, prevent picketing, and arrest and imprison strike leaders.

The beleaguered labour movement turned to politics and formed the Labor Party. Subsequent electoral success persuaded established governments to appoint tribunals to arbitrate industrial disputes—a vindication of the view that the solution to labour and capital antagonism lay, not in the reapportionment of power and the assumption by working people of control over their lives and livelihood, but in the improvement of working conditions and the stimulation of the industrial machine to prevent unemployment. Management, not political struggle, guaranteed maximum efficiency.

Governments introduced industrial arbitration during a period of heightened advocacy for the rational use of human and non-human resources. Reformers condemned the wasteful consequences of Australia's Land Acts. Criticism, in Australia's nascent scientific journals, however, remained faithful to the utilitarian ethos which dominated the country. Critics confined their concern to waste and the loss of commercial opportunity. They expressed no remorse for the loss of natural and indigenous life forms and landscapes. These possessed no inherent value.

In 'The Effects of Settlement and Pastoral Occupation in Australia upon the Indigenous Vegetation' (*Royal Society of South Australia*, 1891), the Reverend Samuel Dixon described how cultivation and clearing had destroyed native vegetation and encouraged the spread of exotic and injurious weeds. He regarded the reckless use of fire by 'The farmer, the squatter, the miner and the swagman' as 'insane', deplored 'The unwise system of permitting "free selection" within the boundaries of natural forests' which resulted in enormous destruction of valuable timber, and denounced the practice of ringbarking. 'Injury to the original vegetation by overstocking', he added, 'has assumed so great a magnitude as to entail a national loss.' William Woolls, who protested 'The Destruction of Eucalypts' (*The Victorian Naturalist*, 1891), also condemned ringbarking as a practice ruinous of commercially serviceable timber.[6]

Dixon urged government to set aside national parks and campaigned for 27 years to preserve the rugged unsettled end of Kangaroo Island, now the Flinders Chase National Park. Woolls belonged to the Field Naturalist's Club of Victoria, formed in 1880 to encourage the popular study of wildlife. Nature study became a popular activity among late Victorian gentlemen and ladies, and by 1891 each mainland colony supported naturalist clubs. These organisations adopted mildly conservationist stances but none challenged utilitarianism. Although they succeeded in persuading governments to declare reserves in some small areas, in each case, reserves were established not to preserve beauty and wilderness but to safeguard objects of scientific curiosity.

Coincidentally, in the United States, by contrast, John Muir had begun protesting the destruction of forest and wildlife from an aesthetic and ethical perspective, arguing for conservation based on the equality of all life, not solely to meet the needs of humankind. Muir rejected the assumption that humans are the only source of irreducible value in the universe, or that utility was the measure of all things. Indeed, human interference in the processes of nature did not necessarily improve the world but often resulted in an uglier, impoverished landscape. Muir visited Australia in December 1903, and although he stayed only 27 days, during which he spent time in Perth, Adelaide, Melbourne and Sydney, he made an effort to see as much of the bush as possible, a sight he had 'dreamed of for many years but hardly hoped to see.'[7] He gloried in the 'forest primeval' outside of Melbourne and Sydney, but also noted the sad consequences of ringbarking: 'the tens of 1000s of dead bleached tree ruins'.[8]

Few of Muir's Australian contemporaries spoke on behalf of nature in such unabashed, fiscally unprofitable terms; in Australia, where Benthamite, utilitarian views prevailed, nature served the economic interests of the country. Utilitarianism profitably understood humans as existing apart from nature. Non-human objects—including all animals, plants and their communities—counted for little in comparison with humans, and external nature need not be included in human calculation. The only question was how best to organise objects—resources, including human resources—to human ends. Australians looked abroad for examples of how this might be accomplished.

Victorian politician Alfred Deakin visited India in 1890–91 and wrote a series of articles for the Melbourne *Age* about British irrigation projects. He discovered an 'irrigation system—bold, comprehensive, and original—by which millions are fed, a monument to the sagacity, ability, and magnanimity of British rulers'.[9] In Britain,

Deakin noted, the British espoused Herbert Spencer's *laissez-faire* libertarianism but abroad they asserted the unbounded power of the state, which created a situation where 'White [settlers] and native alike are mere ciphers, or exercise only such illicit influence as is permitted to women in England and Australia.'[10] Despite the despotism which accompanied British engineering—the human use of human beings—Deakin unequivocally admired the technological expertise which state power made possible. He wanted similar monuments for Australia. Irrigated India, he concluded, could teach Australia much about the mastery of water. He did not ask whether one can rule nature without being ruled oneself. He approved of state power because he believed a combination of government and capitalist enterprise best facilitated development.

Deakin practised what he found so admirable. In 1886, less than a year after Deakin's Irrigation Commission visited the United States, the land developers George and William Chaffey arrived in Victoria, hoping to duplicate their profitable Californian irrigation ventures. At Etiwanda and Ontario, in southern California, the brothers had purchased large ranches, together with their water rights, sub-divided the property and sold off individual allotments. The Chaffeys now turned to Deakin who, as Minister of Water Supply, helped them obtain 200 000 hectares of Murray River land at Mildura, on the north-western edge of Victoria's mallee region. The premier of South Australia, John Downer, offered them another 100 000 hectares at Renmark, on the South Australian Murray. To develop their properties, the brothers launched a sales promotion campaign in Australia and Britain. By December 1890 they had settled 3300 people at Mildura and 1100 at Renmark. Over the next few years, however, seepage from the unlined irrigation channels, land spoilation and management disputes led to settler discontent. The flowing water in the irrigation ditches provided an irresistibly favourable environment for yabbies—small indigenous crustaceans (*Paracheraps bicarinatus*)—whose burrows drained away the water. Soil salinisation blighted trees and vines and killed vegetables. When the Melbourne land boom collapse dried up credit, the Chaffeys filed for bankruptcy. Despite the setbacks, settlers remained at Renmark and Mildura and their example stimulated other development schemes in northern Victoria, New South Wales and South Australia, all of which drew water from the Murray or Murray tributaries. Deakin, in any case, entertained no doubts about the efficacy of the American model:

> The Australian awakening has come in the first place from the United States, where the marvelous multiplication of irrigated orchards has proved what we can accomplish in our similar climate with a similar soil, being of the same race, paying the same wages and enjoying the same civilised life.[11]

Deakin's interest in irrigation reflected his empire-building political ambitions. In the last decade of the nineteenth century Deakin attended all the conferences which planned the political machinery necessary to establish a single nation-state for the entire continent of Australia.

In the 1840s and 1850s the Colonial Office had proposed a General Assembly for the Australian colonies to deal with matters of common Australian interest. But the colonies lacked any compelling reasons to unite and preferred separate self-government. In 1889 the Imperial government tried again, and appointed Major-General Bevan Edwards to inspect the defences of Australia. He recommended the establishment of a single central authority to weld the various colonial forces into one army. Australian politicians now agreed on the need for a united Australia: to prevent invasion by Chinese, promote development and preserve the power of propertied interests. The unifiers also shared a rudimentary patriotic and nationalist sentiment based on pride in material pioneering achievement—the extent to which they had subdued the wilderness.

On the eve of the first all-Australia conference to discuss federation, in February 1890, Sir Henry Parkes, conference chairman and Premier of New South Wales, reminded the participants that

> The crimson thread of kinship runs through us all. Even native-born Australians are Britons . . . We know the value of our British origin; we know that we represent a race, which for the purposes of settling new Colonies never had its equal on the face of the earth.[12]

Throughout the conference, speakers stressed their loyalty to the Queen and the Empire and insisted a united Australia could remain British and conservative. They did not envisage federation as a step towards independence or separation from Great Britain. On the contrary, just as the greatness of the United States lay in its sovereignty, the greatness of a federated Australia would be its enduring membership of the British Empire. At the end of the conference, Chairman Parkes commemorated Australia's first step towards federation by planting an English oak tree in the gardens of Parliament House, Melbourne.

Colonial representatives met again in Sydney in March 1891 to consider a federal constitution and in 1895 the premiers of the colonies met in Hobart. In the midst of industrial strife and class conflict, many federation advocates regarded Australian political unity as the only means of preventing one or other of the colonies from going over to socialism.[13] In 1897–98 delegates from each colony met to draft a constitution, protective of wealth, and rigidly resistant to amendment, for the new Commonwealth of Australia. Most Australians, however, remained indifferent to the changes being planned in their name. Although electors in each colony subsequently approved the federation proposal, less than 47 percent of those eligible actually voted. The federators next sought the assent of the British Parliament. The Colonial Secretary, Joseph Chamberlain, however, citing the opposition of banks and other institutions, insisted on amending the constitution to provide for the right of appeal from Australia's highest court to the Privy Council in London.[14] The Australian petitioners agreed to the amendment, which effectively permitted Britain veto power over Australian legislation; with the security of British investments assured, the Australian Commonwealth came into existence on 1 January 1901.

The new nation lacked authority to declare war, maintained no diplomatic relations with foreign countries and conducted external relations through London representatives. As the first Australian Prime Minister, Edmund Barton, explained in 1901, 'There could be no foreign policy of the Commonwealth. The foreign policy belonged to the Empire.'[15] And, he might have added, so did the lives and bodies of the Australian people.

Throughout the nineteenth century, industrialisation, urbanisation and the geographical mobility of labour undermined the real communities to which people once belonged—village and kin, parish, guild and confraternity. The destruction of traditional orders of social life (in which lives were deeply involved) by the centralised and bureaucratic rationalisation of industrial progress, deprived great numbers of people of social and emotional security. The old associations no longer encompassed the new contingencies of people's lives, and displaced members looked for new forms of affiliation in the abstract community of the nation-state and Empire. States did not hesitate to take advantage of the readiness of their people to identify themselves emotionally with *their* nation, and to mobilise them accordingly. Nationalism could be developed and used politically for purposes of industrialisation, modernisation, exploitation of resources, and war.[16] The British Empire's constant need for soldiers provided several opportunities for Australian nation-building.

The pervasive presence of British capital provided the material reasons for Australian sentiment about British institutions and loyalty to the throne. Ideas of race and stock, of blood and breed, further bound together the nationalism and imperialism of the age. So motivated, the colonised proved an invaluable resource for the coloniser's wars of conquest. The Australian colonies furnished troops to help dispossess the Maoris of New Zealand (1863), avenge Gordon in the Sudan (1885), quell the Boxer rebellion in China (1900) and fight the Boers in South Africa (1899–1902).

Boer War hostilities broke out in October 1899. Months before, Colonial Secretary Joseph Chamberlain instructed the governors of Canada, Victoria and New South Wales to ask their ministries to make apparently spontaneous offers of contingents for service in South Africa in the event of war. In the face of an indifferent, even hostile public, and reluctant ministers, the British authorities needed to manufacture enthusiasm for their imperial conquests. Accordingly, the Colonial Office and imperialist organisations in Britain and South Africa aided by colonial military officers—

motivated more by professional rather than patriotic concerns—attempted to manipulate Australian opinion in favour of a South African war. They succeeded in at least affecting the appearance of spontaneity. When war did break out, the Australian colonies, assured that Britain would meet the expense of their commitment, individually volunteered troops to the imperial cause.[17]

Critics continued to draw attention to the real interests at stake—ownership of the rich gold mines on the Rand and of the diamond mines at Kimberley—but most Australian politicians preferred ignorance. When a member of the Western Australian Parliament asked in 1899 about the justice or injustice of a war against the Boers, the Premier told him, 'We do not want to know.'[18] One could trust the Imperial government to make the right decisions. Indeed, Australians had no choice: the country depended utterly on the unchallenged supremacy of Britain, and on British capital, for development. Therefore, a threat to the integrity of the Empire constituted a threat to Australia's continued prosperity.

Those who volunteered believed the cause a noble one. Moreover, they believed their bush experience specially fitted them to fight in the Boer War. As one champion of the life of conquest proclaimed, 'It is doubtful whether there is any better shot in the world than the kangaroo-shooter.'[19] On 28 October 1899, the first colonial troops marched through the streets of Sydney in pouring rain. Over 200 000 people lined the route cheering wildly. A week later a second contingent left and the New South Wales Chief Justice, Sir Frederick Darley, told the troops, 'Whether you come back with your shields or on your shields, I know you will bring back the honour of the Colony.'[20] Most Australians agreed. When the first troops returned, the writer May Vivienne wrote, 'those who fell on the field of battle, giving up their lives for their beloved Queen and country, will live for all time in our hearts.'[21] The jingoism, to which Vivienne gave such clichéd expression, provided the Commonwealth, which not only made the nation but needed to *make* the nation, with a chance to nation-build. Immediately after federation the Commonwealth government assumed responsibility for the recruitment, despatch and control of the Australian troops in South Africa. On 12 February 1902 Australia, as a nation, sent the country's first troops overseas to war. Prime Minister Barton told the departing soldiers Australia stood, not for militarism, but for truth and justice.[22]

While Australian troops fought to uphold the Anglo-Saxon's destiny to rule, the government introduced national legislation designed to create a society based on the same kind of exclusiveness the Boers later constructed in South Africa. The census of 1901 revealed that Australia was more British than Britain itself—98 percent British descent—a purity the new, all-male Commonwealth Parliament determined to maintain. Members agreed on the vital national importance of ensuring a 'White Australia' through the prohibition of coloured immigration. Alfred Deakin, who believed the great prize of the Australian continent had been reserved for Anglo-Saxons only, spoke in favour of the Immigration Restriction Bill, the main law designed to give effect to the White Australia policy, and said of Asians:

> these people do differ from us in such essentials of race and character as to exclude the possibility of any advantageous admixture or intermarriage if we are to maintain the standards of civilisation to which we are accustomed.[23]

Most speakers were not so gracious. William Morris Hughes, like Deakin, a future prime minister, said of non-Europeans: 'We object to these people because of their vices, and of their immorality, and because of a hundred things which we can only hint at.'[24]

For economic reasons, some capitalists and their allies opposed White Australia. They favoured a plantation society where non-Europeans would perform all the arduous, menial and monotonous toil. Without indentured coloured labour they feared the tropical third of the country would remain forever unproductive. New South Wales parliamentarian John Mildred Creed argued for a 'Rational White Australia', whereby indentured coloured labourers in the north would willingly

> work at a less rate, and subsist on less expenditure for food and clothing than is either practicable or desirable for members of our own race ... Were black labour permitted, the white men would occupy positions with which they would be well able to cope as overseers, mechanics,

deep level miners, clerks, etc. They would be allowed also to employ black house-servants ... In this way the wife would be saved from all exhausting labour, yet be able to ensure to the husband, on his return from work, the comfort and food necessary for his health and efficiency. A white man ... requires a tepid bath, clean clothes, cooled or iced drinks, and well cooked and properly served meals. No white woman, or even women, could ensure this, so easily accomplished by black servants.[25]

In suggesting this recipe for apartheid, which would elevate unskilled European labourers to positions as overlords, capitalists hoped to enlist the support of the working class for the continued development of Queensland.

Sugar growing began in Queensland in the 1860s when the Queensland Acclimatisation Society imported large numbers of cane varieties for planting around Brisbane. In the 1870s planters moved north, crossed the Tropic of Capricorn into the coastal rainforest and in the ten years to 1880, increased sugar production more than five-fold. They colonised the coastal areas, which consisted of long tracts of infertile soil, bearing hardwood forest, and occasional patches of rich soil, originally covered by tropical rainforest, or 'scrub' as it was locally termed. Because sugar cane quickly exhausted the soil, the industry depended on 'constant reclamation of wild lands.'[26] Fortunately, early settlers discovered that rainforest, although denser than neighbouring eucalypt forest, was actually easier to clear; unlike eucalypts, rainforest trees did not sucker after burning. Settlers also benefited from the pioneering work of cedar cutters who, in clearing the richest stands of cedar, provided an effective guide and rough preparation for sugar growing.

Nevertheless, clearing remained a formidable task:

Sheer muscle and tools could not effect the work [alone]. But the forces of Nature are enlisted. The method of clearing 'vine scrub' is almost invariable. First the smaller shrubbery and creepers are prostrated with axe and billhooks, a time of the year when a few months of dry weather may be expected being chosen for the operation. When the stuff thus levelled is pretty thoroughly sun-dried, the trees of magnitude are now attacked with axe, and for the bulkiest, cross-cut saw ... When in their turn the large trees are ascertained to be well dried, a windy day is chosen and fire applied. If the season has been favourable for drying, the result is splendid. The denser the scrub has been, the more thorough is the consumption.[27]

As a single firing rarely consumed all the downed timber, clearing required constant labour. Many farmers, to get their cane in quickly, left trees standing in the fields and ploughed around them. Stumps proved intractable and unless laboriously grubbed out by hand, continued 'to obstruct cultivation for a score, or scores of years.'[28] For labourers, work never ceased:

> It was not sufficient to conquer the scrub, and by prodigious exertions plant a crop amidst stumps and logs which had resisted the burning. Even when a splendid growth had rewarded their initiatory efforts, there was exhausting labour in keeping down rank weeds, and freeing the growing canes from superfluous leafage.[29]

The colonists themselves undertook very little of this heavy labour. They believed that people with dark skin were more adapted to the unpleasant task of scrub clearing. 'It has been conclusively proved', declared one resident, 'that white men cannot and will not do the work done by niggers in the field.'[30] And so to clear their land and to work their fields, growers imported indentured workers from the nearby Pacific islands. The first labour vessel arrived in Brisbane in 1863 with about 80 conscripted Melanesians (known as kanakas) aboard, whom planters engaged for about two-thirds the cost of white labour. Despite the opposition of the southern colonies, the disapproval of the British government and the agitation of abolitionist leagues, the recruitment of Melanesian labour continued throughout the nineteenth century. By 1883 Queensland's Melanesian population numbered 11 443.

In the beginning, blackbirders (recruiters) employed crude methods of enlistment. While anchored offshore the recruiting grounds, ships' crews enticed islanders alongside in their canoes and then holed or upset the canoes by dropping pig-iron or heavy harpoons into them. The swamped islanders were then hauled aboard and imprisoned below decks; those who resisted were shot. But force and fraud could work only once or twice and blackbirders soon learned the advantages of exploiting the ambition and acquisitiveness of coastal chiefs who, in return for arms, ammunition and trade goods, cajoled and coerced young men to sign up as indentured labourers. By the early 1880s, however, the rapidly expanding sugar industry had exhausted the supply of labour from the western Pacific islands and growers looked to the unexploited people of New Guinea.

On the pretext of thwarting German occupation, Queensland, in the name of the Queen, annexed New Guinea in 1883. The British Prime Minister, William Gladstone, advised by Britain's High Commissioner for the western Pacific that the Empire had 'already black subjects enough', repudiated Queensland's annexation.[31] These imperial posturings, however, provoked the German government into taking possession of the north half of New Guinea. Britain then declared a protectorate of the southern coast of New Guinea. Queensland blackbirders immediately began recruiting, and by subterfuge and kidnapping, obtained almost 6000 labourers from the New Guinea region by the end of 1884; hundreds immediately died of dysentery.

The existence of coloured labour in Queensland violated the intent of White Australia and in 1901 the Commonwealth legislated to prohibit the introduction of Pacific islanders after March 1904, and provide for their repatriation by the end of 1906. To sweeten the proposal, Parliament passed the *Sugar Bounties Act (1903)*, which awarded compensation to planters who employed only white labour. But many Melanesians did not want to return; they were married, had settled down and owned freehold land. Others had been away from home so long they feared they would not be able to adjust to island society. On the wharf one deportee harangued a crowd of islanders: 'White fellow no more want black man, use him up altogether, chase him away, plenty Kanaka no money, go back poor.'[32]

Europeans eventually assumed the full scale of work in an industry founded upon the pioneering labour of Melanesians. For decades afterwards Australian empire builders hailed the success of European labour in Queensland as 'one of the most remarkable white achievements witnessed in the tropics.'[33] In the meantime, the islands of the western Pacific had provided a vast pool of labour for

European enterprise in Queensland and a number of Pacific island colonies. About 100 000 islanders went as indentured labourers to Queensland, Fiji, Samoa and New Caledonia, from the New Hebrides, Solomon Islands, New Guinea and surrounding islands between the years 1863 and 1914.[34]

White Australia secured the continent against coloured invasion, the Boer War affirmed national virility, and the six states which on federation replaced the six colonies, turned to their primary mission, development—to exploit the continent's resources and expand industry and agriculture. Politicians claimed broadly divergent approaches to development but few real differences actually separated conservatives and their Labor Party opponents. Development, after all, gave expression to the highest ideals of science and civilisation. In Australia, contending political factions accepted development absolutely. Both Labor and conservative saw development as a solution to the problems caused by industrialisation, and both Labor and conservative promoted state intervention in economic life, largely for the purpose of helping capitalist enterprise. Under the highly visible hand of the state, the ideology of development became an integral part of Australian nationhood, continuing, and ensuring for the future, an unvarying commitment to the conquest of nature.

The discovery in the early 1890s of fantastically rich deposits of gold at Coolgardie and Kalgoorlie abruptly ended Western Australia's decades-long economic stagnation. Population increased from 48 000 in December 1890 to nearly 294 000 in 1901. The accelerated economic activity astounded Western Australians and they viewed their own industry with incredulity:

> Today there are large townships, busy hives of industry, possessing electric light, railway facilities, and immense industrial undertakings, where but a few years ago even the blacks could scarcely live, and where the kangaroo and the emu made a very poor existence.[35]

Gold attracted the capital for most of this expansion, but not all.

Jarrah (*Eucalyptus marginata*) originally covered an area of 5.25 million hectares along the Darling Ranges in a more or less compact block 370 kilometres in length, and about 37 kilometres in width, and grew in almost pure stands—an unusual occurrence in Australia. The best jarrah, known as 'prime jarrah bush', covered 1.6 million hectares and was probably one of the finest hardwood stands of its kind in the world. In the late 1860s the Western Australian government provided entrepreneurs with forest concessions in return for investment. The first timber concession, at Jarrahdale, covered 100 000 hectares, for which the annual rent cost just 50 pounds. The government made a land grant of 800 hectares for every mill the concessionaire erected. This agreement inaugurated a pattern of selling off the country's resources which Australian governments continue to the present day. The inclusion of jarrah, and another exceptional Western Australian tree, karri (*Eucalyptus diversicolor*), by Lloyds of London (in 1871 and 1873 respectively) among the A class of ship building timbers, brought these hardwoods more prominently before overseas buyers, and exports rose. But most jarrah and karri did not go towards ship-building. Millers cut the trees to satisfy British imperial ambitions of railway and telegraph line building in India and Africa. In one scheme, thousands and thousands of Australian railway ties went towards Cecil Rhodes' imperious and ultimately futile dream of a Cape to Cairo railway. A single tree, cut near Dwellingup, Western Australia, yielded 200 ties for Rhodes' African conquest. Problems of handling and transporting the large, heavy logs from the forest to the mill, and the heavy timber from mill to port, at first handicapped exploitation of the forests. But in 1893 the colonial government extended 390 kilometres of railway into the south-west to open up to exploitation the best jarrah country in the colony. Mills sprung up along the line and in the hills behind the line. English capitalists then bought into south-west sawmills to supply English demand for jarrah and karri as road-paving blocks. In the karri country around Denmark, fellers and sawyers worked day and night in relays cutting down and sawing the timber. Huge bonfires of bark and branches and logs up to 36 metres long burned continuously. During the decade to 1900 the value of timber exports increased more than five times and was second in value only to gold.[36]

Gold, however, remained the chief focus of economic activity and of psychological exaltation. Before the gold discoveries, Western Australia's political leaders had feared that the state would remain undeveloped for all time—left behind in the great wave of civilisation emanating at first from Europe, later from America. But Western Australian gold added to the markets of the world and the golden stream rafted the state onto the ocean of the international economy. Goldmining bestowed wealth and succour and the war against the earth accorded a scene of compelling seduction. May Vivienne described how

> the rumble and stamping of the batteries, the hum of the mighty machines, the beautiful bright engines that seem to work with perpetual motion, the enormous furnaces, the magnificent cyanide plant, with its wonderful machinery for extracting gold, the electricity that seems to fill the air and almost takes one's breath away, are all so vast and wonderful that a sense of something like awe came over me.[37]

Mine machinery needed a constant supply of water—a commodity in short supply on the arid goldfields. But without water, capitalists would not invest. To ensure continued gold production the Western Australian government undertook to build a pipeline from a weir in the Darling Ranges, to Kalgoorlie, over 550 kilometres away. 'Providence had designed (for His own purposes, no doubt)', conceded Premier John Forrest, 'that the principal goldfields of the Australian continent should be placed in a district where water was scarce'.[38] Forrest, a political conservative, believed that, whatever their political sympathies, all Australians shared a common purpose in overcoming nature in Australia. In undertaking the construction of the dam and pipeline, he explained, 'the object . . . was to subdue the wilderness, overcome the obstacles which Nature had placed in [our] way, and run a river of water into the [arid] districts'.[39] The first reticulated water reached Kalgoorlie in January 1903, a product of the then largest water diversion scheme in the world. The successful piping of water to the arid inland inspired an Australian mania for hydraulic engineering. The decisive influence of the state engineer, C. Y. O'Connor, who designed and built the scheme, inaugurated the dominant influence engineers and controllers of technology would exert over future Western Australian governments.

Despite a guaranteed water supply, gold production declined after 1900 as alluvial gold and the easily worked deposits were exhausted. Diggers left the goldfields as production came to depend on highly capitalised deep mines.

To provide employment for redundant gold diggers and to ensure fulfillment of the state's economic and imperial destiny, the government began promoting the development of a wheatbelt between the south-west and the eastern goldfields. The idea, explained James Mitchell, Minister for Agriculture, was to 'bring together idle land and idle people.'[40] For those willing to subjugate a barbarous country and render it fit for the purposes and requirements of civilised man, the government offered virtually free land, practical advice and financial assistance. The state warned intending settlers, however, that Western Australia offered little to the clerk, or the scholar or even the tradesman. The country needed, above all else, 'men of muscle and sinew'.[41] But success in the Western Australian wheatbelt—the clearing of bush, digging of wells and dams, stringing of fences, the erection of dwellings and outbuildings, planting and harvesting pasture and crop, and the care of animals—required more than insensate brawn. Besides skillful and intelligent labour, success depended crucially upon the support of the state. Although each farm operated as an individual or family enterprise, collectively the wheatbelt represented a political commitment by the state, an imperial quest to remake the landscape.

To encourage agricultural expansion the state instituted a large-scale rural credit programme. The State Agriculture Bank, which financed most wheatbelt settlers, recommended ringbarking and fire as the cheapest and speediest ways of reducing forest to sheep paddock and wheat field.[42] In the wetter districts, settlers confronted a land mantled with a community of banksia, tuart (*Eucalyptus gomphocephala*), jarrah and marri (*E. calophylla*). In drier districts settlers engaged scrub heath and woodlands of York gum (*E. loxophleba*), salmon gum (*E. salmonophloia*) and wandoo (*E. wandoo*). By 1910, reported the Agriculture Bank, farmers had cleared and ringbarked about 600 000 hectares. Deforestation continued another 60 years, until less than a quarter of the original forest and woodland remained. An enormous domain fell into private hands but individual settlers achieved little independence. Many of the 10 000 or so farms eventually established, most on rectangular, standardised 404 hectare blocks, were heavily dependent on loans and advice from government and agricultural advisers. Only a minority of pioneer families enjoyed any social life and most battled against loneliness as well as the bush. Unendurable conditions resulted in a high turnover in wheat properties.

The great expansion in Western Australian wheat farming coincided with the Australia-wide introduction of new, scientifically bred varieties of wheat, resistant to disease and suited to the continent's dry climate. Rust, a parasitic fungus, caused great losses in Australian wheat crops during the last years of the nineteenth century; in 1890 Australia had to import wheat, and William Farrer of New South Wales began experimental cross-breeding of wheat. Farrer aimed to obtain an early maturing, and hence rust-avoiding, high-yielding grain. His most famous variety, Federation, was released in 1901 and dominated Australian wheat growing until the end of the 1920s. No other wheat changed the Australian landscape so much. Federation's dark brown heads took the place of the pale golden colour of most of the redundant varieties; the golden yellow colour of the Australian wheat fields changed into a bronze brown. Federation thrived in the drier inland districts and encouraged wheat growing in marginal areas.

Between 1896 and 1930, the area under wheat in Australia more than quadrupled, from 1.6 million to 7.3 million hectares. Two-thirds of the crop was exported. During the expansion, all wheat-growing states established government demonstration farms, promoted experiments in wheat breeding and cultivation, and published agricultural journals to foster system and management in farming; all encouraged the application of science to extend human control over nature. The new wheat varieties and improved technique—the application of superphosphate and the fallowing of land—reversed the nineteenth-century trend to declining yields. Paradoxically, the factors which increased the yield in the short run, decreased it in the long run; new wheat varieties permitted expansion into drier areas of naturally lower return; fallowing led to soil erosion and soil exhaustion; and heavier crops removed more and more plant nutrient from the soil.

The problems nineteenth century Australians faced with drought, unpredictable and misunderstood climate, the poor nature of most Australian soils and the unsuitability of native plants and animals for commercial purposes, led to greater determination to change the environment, to remake nature, to unlock the land. In the new century scientists and educated people began promoting 'national efficiency,' based on the principles of conservation and resource management, and lobbying politicians to introduce 'expertise' and 'system' into the working of public policy. These ideas were derived from Britain. In the aftermath of the military's incompetence and blundering during the Boer War, critics called for restructuring the machinery of government. National life should be conducted along competent business lines. National efficiency became the political catchcry of the period. Contemporaneously, in the United States, scientists from a variety of fields, including hydrology, forestry and geology—beholden to a vision of a world in dire need of management—began expounding a new doctrine of conservation. They urged preservation and husbandry of the earth's resources to ensure sustainable use. Conservationists in those years planned to reorganize the natural world to serve the economic interests of the country. As defined by forester Gifford Pinchot, conservation was progressive, a conscious and purposeful control over nature for the benefit of humankind, an intervention, moreover, which subordinated the aesthetic to the utilitarian. Only the test of utility, argued the engineers of efficiency, guaranteed the perpetuation of civilisation; the preservation of natural scenery—of wilderness, of wildlife—counted for little against the goal of increasing national production. Concern over the unregulated use of natural resources blended harmoniously with the wider goal of efficiency in every phase of human life.[43]

Prompted by the imperatives of conservation and efficiency, Victoria passed a Water Act in 1905 providing for a single, centralised commission to oversee water use. In 1907 the American irrigation engineer and progressivist, Elwood Mead, became commission director. Mead was an optimist who believed science and technology, applied to irrigation, would open up unlimited opportunities for human achievement. Mead claimed irrigation would multiply the population of the state from ten to 100 times, give a corresponding increase to the value of products, and lead to a veritable cornucopia:

> With irrigation two farm crops can be grown in the year . . . four to six cuttings of lucerne can be harvested . . . and the dairyman can have green feed through the summer months and a continuous milking season . . . an irrigation district is freed from the vicissitudes and losses that come with recurring years of drought, and a densely peopled area has better good home conditions and more attractive social life . . .[44]

Mead saw the state as the paternalistic coordinator of industry, commerce and agriculture, its power directed at imposing an efficient order on nature and an organised mind on the farmer. He believed in the complementarity of irrigation engineering and social engineering and persuaded the Victorian government to buy large estates, sub-divide them into small farms, clear and grade the land, equip with fences, furnish with stock and provide low-interest, long-term loans and cash advances. As director he oversaw the reclamation of 32 irrigation projects and, by 1913, the settlement of over 1200 small irrigation farms. In the farmers he sought to instill 'the spirit of an army' intent upon conquest.[45] The straight lines and the neat hierarchy of holding sizes reflected the application of the military metaphor and Mead's confidence in rationality in human design. During his tenure Mead discovered that irrigation farmers required constant direction and supervision, and his Water Commission reserved the right to veto all decisions to protect settlers from their own folly. District inspectors made frequent visits to the holdings and recorded the operations of each farm. Mead did not confine his empire building to Victoria. In 1911 he advised the New South Wales government on the Murrumbidgee Irrigation Areas and returned again in 1923 and in 1927 to advise on irrigation development for the whole state. In

1914 he advised the Western Australian government on the development of the Harvey Irrigation Scheme.

Australian engineers and experts shared Mead's technocratic conviction that the life of a modern nation depended upon a prosperous, land-owning population exercising rational control over nature. In 1915 the Victorian hydraulic engineer, A. S. Kenyon, visited the former Chaffey enterprise at Mildura. Here he found civilisation's ideal, a technological utopia

> of gradually evolving respectability and suburban dullness ... Life there is lived under the most favorable conditions. Air tingling with life and sunshine; groves laden with fruit and greenness; social surroundings of the finest, barring slight incursions in the picking period; and a copious supply of money in all seasons, make it probably the most desirable part of Victoria.[46]

Kenyon's observation reflected the optimism of a technocrat who looked forward to an age where humans possessed unlimited power over nature, a power which would banish want, poverty and illness. Kenyon never asked who would exercise that power, and in whose interest.

But if Kenyon evinced little interest in the question of power the newly federated Australian states demonstrated no such reticence. By the early years of the century, state governments began acquiring the formal power to control those among the Australian population they perceived stood in the way of progress.

In 1850 at Pooindie on the Eyre Peninsula, the government of South Australia had granted land to Aborigines for a mission; similarly, in 1863, the Victorian government had bequeathed 930 hectares of farming land at Coranderrk, where a group of 120 Aborigines cleared the land, planted crops and reared animals. But in 1895, jealous European neighbours in both colonies demanded and obtained the eviction of the Aborigines and the resumption of their land. The resumptions marked the end of efforts to assimilate the Aborigines into the European way of life. Henceforth state governments eviscerated all attempts at Aboriginal self-determination. National efficiency mandated their removal from European society and their segregation, under strict supervision, on government reserves. Most states passed legislation forbidding

Aborigines to marry, consume alcohol, accept employment, manage their own assets or even leave the reserve without the permission of government officials. In the pastoral areas of Queensland, Western Australia, and South Australia, the reserves functioned as cinctures in which Aboriginal families produced labour for the stations and on which they were discarded when no longer needed.

And in the same way that land had been simply expropriated from Aboriginal tribes for the European's economic benefit, so too were Aboriginal women seized to serve his sexual needs. In Queensland armed parties of men went scouring districts for Aboriginal women to make sexual slaves. In 1900 Ardock Station held nine Aboriginal women behind rabbit-proof fencing for the use of station hands.[47]

Queensland pioneered Australian legal segregation. An 1897 legislative act placed all Aborigines and persons of part Aboriginal descent under the legal charge of protectors, prohibited them from drinking, and confined them to reserves unless employed in an approved job. The policy of exclusion and exploitation reflected the thinking of the majority of European Australians who expected (and hoped for) the Aborigines' eventual extinction. In 1892 a member of the Western Australian Assembly told his colleagues 'it will be a happy day for Western Australia and Australia at large when natives and the kangaroos disappear'.[48]

But Aborigines refused to disappear. In the newly settled Kimberleys region of Western Australia leasehold agreements provided for Aborigines to continue to hunt on pastoral runs. Lessees ignored these obligations, stationed stock around all water, destroyed game and killed Aboriginal hunting dogs. In response, Aborigines maintained an active resistance in the region through the late 1890s and into the early twentieth century. Several outlaws, familiar with the ways of the invaders, coordinated the insurgency, adopted guerrilla tactics and some of the technology of Europe: guns, wire, glass and iron. By 1905, however, Europeans occupied most of the land accessible for stocking and had crushed most of the overt forms of resistance. State Parliament then passed legislation to provide for Aboriginal segregation, and for the removal from their parents and the institutionalisation of part-Aboriginal children. The idea, the government explained, was to prevent those 'children, whose blood is half British, to grow up as vagrants and outcasts, as their mothers now are.' While 'it may be a cruel thing to tear an aborigine child from its mother,' conceded one Member of Parliament, 'it is necessary in some cases to be cruel to be kind.'[49]

The Chief Protector of the Aborigines, H. C. Prinsep, author of the legislation, wanted authority to break up Aboriginal families. He had previously complained that 'the natural affections of the mothers . . . stood much in [his] way.'[50] The Act removed all legal obstacles to unprecedented government interference in the lives of Aboriginal people. Prinsep, and successive Chief Protectors, acquired legal guardianship over every Aboriginal or part-Aboriginal child up to the age of sixteen; they controlled all property belonging to an Aborigine or part-Aborigine, and they could order the removal of any unemployed Aborigine to a reserve and declare specific areas out of bounds to Aborigines. The Act made careful provision to ensure the continued availability of Aboriginal labour, particularly in the north where pastoralists looked on and used Aborigines almost as free goods of nature. Indeed, the government recommended Aborigines to pastoralists, for, 'on the whole, [they] make very excellent station hands, and their labour is practically obtained for nothing'.[51]

At the turn of the century the south-western Aboriginal survivors of dispossession, disease and massacre remained relatively economically independent, hunted in the bush and lived on station land or on their own small farming blocks. They enjoyed elements of traditional life, some privacy and non-interference from the state. The government's commitment to agriculture and the wheatbelt in the south-west, and the settlement of vast tracts of previously unalienated land, however, finally sundered the vestiges of independence. A few Aborigines found work clearing— destroying the bush once their home. But development, progress and prosecution of the provisions of the 1905 Act, left most poverty stricken and homeless by the beginning of the Great War.[52]

Following the lead of Queensland and Western Australia, South

Australia legislated in 1911 for a Chief Protector to become the legal guardian of every Aboriginal or part-Aboriginal child, able to overrule parental authority until the child reached 21 years of age. As in Western Australia, the protector could assume the property of any Aborigine or part-Aborigine.

After federation, informed Australians began to view the Empire and Australia as a trust and resource. Science became a metaphor for Empire itself, a symbolic expression of what the Empire might become. Scientific knowledge would aid the construction of a free market, improve transportation and communication and ensure progress. The new Commonwealth, argued influential politicians, must exercise control over Australia's human and physical resources by enlisting the methods, strategies and ethos of science. In 1907 Prime Minister Deakin revealed the political implications of national efficiency to an audience at the British Science Guild—a group of scientists dedicated to maximising the social utility of science. The urgent task of the Empire, he told them, was 'the scientific conquest of its physical, and shall we not be bold to say, ultimately its political problems.'[53] One crucial problem lay in the defence of the Empire. The Anglo-German arms race had emphasised the necessity of strengthening the scientific basis of British society and administration and of increasing the Empire's readiness for war. The Australian state prepared to volunteer bodies.

The Australian Labor Party did not resist or challenge the preparations for war. Indeed, lacking a social democratic heritage, Labor adopted aggressive defence and foreign policy positions hardly distinguishable from those of the nation's conservatives. Devoid of ideas of social democracy—the right of individuals to decide the conditions under which they live and work and the type of society which will enable all human beings to live more abundant lives— Labor believed in the transcendent purposefulness of militarism. Universal military training, party leaders argued, inculcated morality and respectability and improved the morale, physique and tone of the nation. War and death uplifted a nation; on the battlefield a man acquired moral virtues; through blood sacrifice men gained an insight into the meaning of life. Exhilarated by notions of youth and sacrifice, and fearful of Japanese and other Asian reaction to the White Australia policy, the national Labor government introduced compulsory military training in 1909. The first English-speaking country in modern times to compel peacetime military service, Australia did not wait long before real war put the notions of immolation and Empire solidarity to the test.

The Great War in Europe erupted in August 1914, during an Australian election campaign. The Labor Party leader, Andrew Fisher, immediately pledged Australia to 'stand beside our own to help and defend her to our last man and our last shilling.' His conservative opponent, retiring Prime Minister Joseph Cook, concurred; when the Empire was at war, Australia was at war; the cause of England was the cause of civilisation. Radicals dissented; they understood that the advocacy of death in a good cause really meant that the death of some men is useful to other men. The Industrial Workers of the World (IWW) denounced the war from the outset: 'If the politicians of Australia want war, let them take their own carcasses to the firing line to be targets for modern machine-guns and food for cholera . . . If they want blood, let them cut their own throats.'[54]

Pro-war propaganda stressed German perfidy in invading Belgium, the noble acceptance by Britain and France of their treaty obligations, and the beastliness of the Hun. Propagandists depicted the war as a struggle between civilisation and barbarism, a dichotomy Australians cherished, and initial enthusiasm for the war ran high. Men of all ages crowded the recruiting offices. By December 1914, 52 561 had enlisted. Women too, joined in the patriotic fervour and organised themselves into charitable voluntary groups to raise money for the victims of war and to provide comforts for the boys at the front.[55]

The war's immediate impact was the reduction of living standards. Trade in metallic ores, previously exported to Germany, ceased. Stock exchanges closed for weeks. Local manufacturers, unsure of the domestic market, laid off workers. Uncertainty prevailed everywhere and unemployment soared; many men enlisted out of necessity. Prices and rents rose and working people began harbouring grudges that the burdens of the war were being unfairly unloaded upon them.

Before the outbreak of war, 70 percent of the lead-silver concentrates from Broken Hill were exported to Europe, mainly through German agencies. Prohibitions on trading with the enemy did not, however, reduce profits. On the contrary, for the owners of Australia's vast mineral wealth, war equalled even greater prosperity. To compensate for the loss of the German market, the Labor government assisted a new group of British and Melbourne capitalists to obtain control over the base-metal trade and enter into extremely profitable contracts with the British government. Capitalists appreciated the strong leadership of Labor Prime Minister W. M. Hughes. The war also benefited the directors and shareholders of BHP, which began, under government protection and war-induced shortages, an Australian iron and steel industry. Other commercial men also welcomed the war. The chairman of the Cascade Brewery in Tasmania, G. P. Fitzgerald, like the owners of BHP, looked forward to greater profits. The mainland states, he reasoned, no longer able to import beer from England, would be forced to drink Cascade.

As the slaughter and destruction mounted, patriots of Empire developed a semi-mystical interpretation of the meaning of war. Churchmen, in particular, welcomed the war for providing the means by which God might work His redemptive operations: only through the purifying effect of sacrifice would the nation be saved. The Church of England synods, the Assemblies of the Presbyterian Church and the Conference of the Methodist Church passed resolutions in favour of winning the war. The Sydney Anglican bishop, Stone-Wigg, wrote that not until the war had dealt Australians 'a shattering, sledgehammer blow' would the people awaken to war's 'cleansing . . . spiritual revelation.' God would not permit waste and destruction without producing a positive effect.[56]

People, however, gradually turned away from the fearful loss of life, and fewer and fewer young men came forward to offer themselves to the carnage. From January to July 1915 over 13 000 Australians a month volunteered, but by July of the following year fewer than 6000 came forward. Voluntary enlistment scarcely kept pace with battlefield losses. In 1916, for example, during a single charge between trenches on the Western Front, 2339 men of the Australian 4th Brigade were either killed, wounded or captured. 'The supply of heroes must be maintained at all costs,' declared an English Lord.

Prime Minister Hughes, concerned lest the fall in recruitment threaten Australia's imperial role, journeyed to London to discuss how more Australians might be persuaded to give their lives for King, Country and Empire. In the Imperial capital he enumerated war's virtues: the war, he told his hosts, had 'saved us from degeneration and decay. We were in danger of losing our greatness and becoming flabby.'[57] He insisted on a greater war effort; the defeat of the enemy demanded sterner resolution and the complete mobilisation of manpower and productive capacity.

Australian conservatives were overjoyed with Hughes' embrace of the Empire, his call to sacrifice and his praise of war as the ultimate good. With the support of the press and leaders of commerce, manufacturing and finance, Hughes introduced a referendum to permit the use of military conscripts overseas. The ensuing referendum campaign divided the nation: the rich and respectable generally supported conscription, while the poor were generally opposed. Authority urged a yes vote. The nation's daily newspapers, pulpits, business councils and most politicians spoke in favour. Most trade-union journals and the pamphlets of radical groups, such as the IWW, argued against conscription. The pro-conscriptionists invoked all those traditions—religion, philosophy and aesthetics—which reinforce patriotism and which regard abnegation of self—death—as the highest good. Dr Alexander Leeper moved in the Anglican Synod in Melbourne:

> That this Synod is so convinced that the forces of the Allies are being used to vindicate the rights of the weak and to maintain the moral order of the world that it gives its strong support to the principle of universal service.[58]

As the war progressed, however, working people realised it was they who bore the brunt of the war; their members did most of the fighting and most of the paying. By a narrow margin the Australian people rejected conscription. Voluntary recruitment fell even further—despite a revivified and manipulative recruiting campaign during which women were asked to pledge their favours only to men who had served their country: 'If there are not enough soldiers to go round I will cheerfully die an old maid.'[59] Prime Minister Hughes said Australia needed to provide 16 500 recruits each month, but by early 1917 no more than 5000 volunteers a month ever offered themselves for service; in the second half of the year less than 2500 came forward each month. There were insufficient volunteers even to replace the Australian dead and wounded of the Third Battle of Ypres. Of fifteen weeks' duration, Ypres cost both sides over half a million casualties—among them 38 000 Australians—and advanced the British line by five or six miles. Determined for more sacrifice, Hughes introduced a second conscription referendum.

When the Great War began, allied propaganda told Australians that this war would end war. But as casualties increased, more and more people realised that only peace, not war, could end war. In the second referendum, the working class, farmers and those closest to the actual fighting—the front line soldiers—voted against compulsion, and the majority against conscription increased. Hughes responded, 'It is not we [the Empire loyalists] who have failed, but the people of Australia.'[60] Although he pledged to resign if defeated over conscription, Hughes remained as Prime Minister, but not as leader of the Labor Party, which split over the issue. Australia became a deeply divided society during the Great War, but economic developments and the continued conquest of nature enforced a new conformity.

In 1892 an American metallurgist, Edward Peters, started the first roasting of copper ore from the Mt Lyell mines in the rugged mountains of western Tasmania. Peters built a makeshift pyre of layers of wood, ore, charcoal, silica and limestone. Soaked with kerosene, the fire burned for days and deep-yellow sulphur fumes rose into the low-lying clouds and withered nearby grass. The experiment proved that sulphur could be profitably roasted from the pyrite without the copper turning to powder. By 1900 the terrain around Mt Lyell was slashed and scarred by the mining boom. Railways criss-crossed the valleys and hillsides, and cut swathes through the forests. More than a thousand men worked every day cutting down the forest, sawing wood for bridges, houses, buildings, mining timbers and fetching firewood for the steam engines, concentrating mills and smelters. In 1902, another American metallurgist, Robert Carl Sticht, managed to fuel the smelters using the ore itself, which contained 48 percent sulphur, as fuel. Smelting became virtually self-fueling. But most of the sulphur escaped—50 to 60 percent according to Sticht—and in the mountains above the smelting centre of Queenstown, the pall of sulphurous smog from the chimneys of eleven furnaces choked the valley, thickened winter fogs, turned day into night and corroded iron telegraph poles. Sulphur killed virtually all the vegetation growing in the path of the smelter fumes, fires consumed the dead forests, and heavy rain washed away the topsoil; only bedrock remained. No new vegetation could grow within miles of the smelters.[61] Despite Sticht's self-fueling innovation, the smelters still required about 400 tonnes of fuel wood a day for over a quarter of a century. The cutting out of surrounding forest raised the cost of getting wood, and the exhaustion of one resource necessitated the exploitation of another.

In 1914 the Mt Lyell Mining Company opened a hydro-electric plant at nearby Lake Margaret. The power station generated 5000 horsepower of electricity as well as intense enthusiasm among Tasmanian politicians. Two years later the first government hydro-station opened at Waddamana. Dams, electricity and mastery over water impressed everybody. Politicians expounded the doctrine that the control of nature promised a future of unlimited abundance. Despite Great War divisions within Tasmanian society, the opposing parties offered the same pro-development policies in the first peacetime Tasmanian election. Both asserted the need for economy, promised extensive public works, and pledged to extend the hydro-electric scheme.

Victory for the technocratic vision, and for business' interpretation of the country's needs and goals, came only after the repression of fierce domestic conflict. Protest against the war's regimentation, against the domination by a few over the many, had not been confined to military conscription.

Working people all over Australia walked out on strike during the war, to protest compulsion, repression, limits to their freedom and reductions in wages. During 1916, 170 000 Australian workers were involved in over 500 industrial disputes for a total loss of 1.7 million working days—a reflection of the beginning of a loss of faith in the war. Over the next year protest increased. In June 1917 the New South Wales branch of the Labor Party blamed the war on capitalism and called for a negotiated peace. The Victorian, Queensland and South Australian branches followed, and in August one of Australia's largest-ever work disputes began.

In July, the New South Wales Chief Commissioner of Railways introduced, into the Randwick workshops, job time cards designed to record the exact time taken by each worker over each particular job. The Commissioner admired Henry Ford's factory system and enthused over Frederick Taylor's vision of scientific management. Under Taylor's influence the conception of human labour underwent a systematic devaluation in the early years of the twentieth century. Human labour became simply the product of the human machine. The qualities of teamwork, adaptability and use of intelligence and experience counted for little.

Workers at Randwick immediately objected that they, who were expected to work under the new system, had not been considered or consulted. The commissioner, obsessed with the notion of control, dismissed the protests; his objective—industrial efficiency— was too important to involve those expected to conform. On 2 August 1917, 5780 craftsmen employed as repair and maintenance men by the New South Wales Railways and Tramways walked out in protest. To the workers the cards meant the domination of the human being: 'a system of speeding up the workman to his utmost capacity; of pitting him against his fellows and against himself—a system which aims to . . . make him a machine'.[62]

The strike spread to other employees in the tram and railway service and workers in private industry. The strike's rapid extension demonstrated an accumulation of discontent with the war, with control and with compulsion. By early September, 68 000 workers were on strike and the total number of working days lost by the strikers alone amounted to roughly 2 570 000. The government, in cooperation with employers, devoted a huge amount of effort and resources to defeating the strikers, and commandeered all horses, lorries, carts and motor vehicles, recruited strike-breakers and doubled the police force. Scabs were guaranteed employment, the card system was retained and striking workmen lost their old jobs and seniority and were put on lower pay.[63]

Even without conscription Australia recruited for the war effort almost 10 percent of its entire population and nearly half of all males aged between 18 and 45. Of 416 809 enlisted men and women, 300 000 served overseas and two-thirds become casualties, including nearly 60 000 dead—the highest casualty rate of any Empire country. The war's successful sacrificial mobilisation of men and women opened up tremendous possibilities for capital. Through Commonwealth involvement in business—the establishment of BHP's steelworks at Newcastle and the reorganisation of the base metals industry involved massive state assistance—business acquired a much greater role in the affairs of the state. And, despite supporting the losing side over conscription, business actually gained in prestige during the war. The war showed how patriotism and development could be made themes in a conservative ideology; under the new corporatism, scientific management aimed to control the entire labour process in the interests of capital. At the close of the Great War business interests made clear their intention that the returning digger should be identified with the conservative business interests, that their sacrifices for Empire and civilisation had not been in vain.

The war had also afforded moral reformers the opportunity to advance their programme of state regulation of private life: people were to be made moral by law. Because they convinced enough people that drink detracted from a soldier's efficiency, temperance advocates succeeded in restricting the hours during which hotels could serve alcohol. New South Wales, Victoria, South Australia and Tasmania all helped to defeat the Hun by imposing six o'clock closing.

The state and private associations assumed a collective responsibility to reshape human relations so as to make society more orderly, efficient and united. By the end of the war, moral reformers preaching thrift, efficiency and sobriety combined with economic interests to impose a patriotic uniformity on Australia which stressed the paramount goal of development. The people had won the conscription referendums, but capitalism won the struggle for political power.

7

AN UNDEVELOPED ENTERPRISE

AUSTRALIA IS AN UNDEVELOPED ENTER-
PRISE THAT COULD, UNDER SKILLED MAN-
AGEMENT, ENRICH ITS SHAREHOLDERS.

Stanley Bruce, Prime Minister, 1923–29

WE AUSTRALIANS HAVE PLUNDERED THE
DELICATE BEAUTY OF OUR CONTINENT
AND DISFIGURED IT WITH A CARELESS TIN-
SHANTY SEMI-CIVILIZATION.

Frank Dalby Davison, 1934

DURING THE YEARS after the Great War an Australian professional middle class appeared prominently in public life for the first time. Educated, accredited experts assumed positions of command and authority. In industry, scientific managers oversaw a new routine and regularity in the conduct of work. New methods of organisation sought to educate workers to accept responsibility for increasing the efficiency of capitalist production and aimed to undermine the workplace as a source of working-class sedition. Economists from academe advised governments on ways to manage the economy in the interests of the powerful; anthropologists recommended new controls over Aborigines; forestry professionals endorsed the harmony of conservation and exploitation; eugenicists and demographers prescribed policies for population and immigration; and agricultural scientists planned new ways to increase rural output. All the advice, under the guise of progress and development, addressed the task of the conquest of nature in Australia.

For Australia's middle class, the Great War generated greater enthusiasm for the Empire and for Britain than ever. Most educated Australians identified more with the grandeur and sweep of British history, culture and Empire than with the crude newness of Australia. In Europe, four years of mechanised slaughter forced many people to question the conviction that they were the most rational of all creatures, in control of themselves and of all creation. But in Australia, the middle class did not doubt the virtues of their civilising mission. The Melbourne newspaper the *Argus* spoke for most in an editorial celebrating Armistice Day:

> Never before were there such tremendous moral issues submitted to the

arbitrament of the sword. Never before was there such tremendous destruction or such suffering and hardship inflicted upon so many millions of mankind. Never before was there such a cold-blooded exhibition of calculated brutality on the one side or such a heroic manifestation of high ideals on the other. Upon the result of the War hung the future of our Western civilisation . . .[1]

Western progress in science and technology fostered, during the Great War, a massive increase in destruction. Advances in metallurgy and machine-tooling made possible great increases in the size, range, accuracy and rate of fire of both artillery and hand weapons. Factory production and the development of interchangeable parts meant that millions of soldiers could be equipped with the new arms and supplied with the hundreds of thousands of shells necessary to feed the big guns that supported them on the field. For the University of Melbourne's Professor William Osborne, the Great War confirmed the central role of science in industrial progress. The war, the professor claimed, had generated

> a mighty awakening in England as to the value of science in all its aspects of citizenship—the effects on production, on defence, on health and on morality. If we [Australia] cannot be in the van of this great movement, let us not at least be found blundering in the rear.[2]

To avoid Australian retardation, Osborne organised fellow scientists to lobby for a federally funded scientific research organisation, for the sake of national and Empire development, and for the sake of science. In 1915 Prime Minister Hughes accepted Commonwealth responsibility for national scientific research. Science, he urged, must do its utmost to win the war and to develop a great continent when the war was over. The scientific method must be applied to all areas of production, to bring forth a new earth if not a new heaven:

> I have a profound belief in the destiny of this great country . . . In this Science can lend a most powerful aid. Science can make rural industries commercially profitable, making the desert bloom like a rose . . . Science can develop great mineral wealth . . . It can with its magic wand turn heaps of what is termed refuse into shining gold . . . Science will lead the manufacturer into green pastures by solving for him problems that seemed insoluble. It will open up a thousand new avenues for

capital and labour, and lastly science thus familiarized to the people will help them to clear thinking; to the rejection of shams; to healthier and better lives; to a saner and wider outlook on life.[3]

To realise this dream of bourgeois tranquility, of a society resigned to an easy life of production and consumption, Hughes appointed the first Council for Scientific Research (CSR). The Council's immediate aims were modest—to investigate solutions to some of the problems affecting rural Australia: sheep blowfly, cattle ticks, rabbits and prickly pear.

Prickly pear, a cactus plant of the order *Opuntia*, originally introduced as an ornamental scrub, throve in southern and central Queensland, and by 1916 had overgrown some eight million hectares of Queensland and one million hectares of New South Wales. The infestation, spreading at the rate of 400 000 hectares a year, caused widespread abandonment of properties, drove out native fauna and threatened to entirely overwhelm vast agricultural areas. By 1927 prickly pear covered 26 260 000 hectares. The CSR searched the world for a suitable insect enemy and in 1925 imported the moth *Cactoblastis cactorum*, which eventually brought prickly pear under control. Scientists hailed the moth's insatiable appetite as 'a triumph of science and technology and government involvement.'[4] This success paled beside the vaunting ambitions held for science.

After the Great War many Europeans questioned the belief that control over nature would bring universal happiness and well being. Reason no longer appeared in command; rational science had produced the ugliest of civilisations. In contrast, the power brokers, politicians, industrialists, and bankers—those most committed to technological civilisation—saw the problem differently: poor leadership and flawed methods of organisation, not industrial civilisation, were responsible for Europe's crisis. Australians, however, did not share this sense of crisis. They did not even acknowledge the debate.

Faith in the technocratic order remained unshaken. In Australia, in the year after the Armistice, technology won a great victory over distance and isolation. In quest of a Commonwealth government

£10 000 prize, offered to the first Australian aviators to fly from England to Australia in a British-made machine, Captain Ross Smith and three others left England in a British Vickers-Vimy aircraft on 12 November 1919. They landed at Darwin on 10 December. Prime Minister Hughes hailed the flight as a triumph of Empire. Smith's flight affirmed the country's faith in conquest, and demonstrated the unlimited potential of men, science and technology.

Over the next few years Australian politicians gave formal sanction to the creed of conquest by institutionalising the role of science in the progress of primary and secondary industry. The utilitarian imperative—to develop fully the economic potential of the continent—received official confirmation in 1926 when the national Parliament passed the Commonwealth Scientific and Industrial Research Bill (CSIR, later Commonwealth Scientific and Industrial Research Organization [CSIRO]), greatly expanding the funding and responsibility of federal science. The state charged CSIRO scientists with the task, previously undertaken by the nineteenth century acclimatisation societies, of remaking a land only half fit for civilisation.

Planning for the glorious future began before war's end. In 1917 the Imperial War Cabinet and Conference endorsed the principle of imperial self-sufficiency, based on the premise of a natural division of labour between Britain and the Empire. Manufactured products from the former would trade for the primary products of the latter. Empire development meant increasing production through research, and the emigration from Britain of people and capital. Of all the dominions, Australia was the most enthusiastic supporter of imperial self-sufficiency and the most enthusiastic recipient of British migrants and capital.

In 1922 Australia's Prime Minister, Stanley Bruce, proposed the slogan 'Men, Money and Markets,' to signify Australia's commitment to imperial self-sufficiency and to a destiny in land development. By men, Bruce meant families settling the land and helping to populate the country's great empty spaces; money meant the investment in the settlement process; markets meant the sale overseas of Australia's wool, wheat, frozen meat, dried fruits, dairy and other primary exports. But 'men' came first. Undeveloped Australia required, above all else, vast numbers of immigrants.

According to journalist E. J. Brady—in his monumental paean to Australian development, *Australia Unlimited* (1918)—increasing the country's population was Australia's most urgent task. Only through immigration could Australia 'advance the army of settlement against the last walls of nature'.[5] Brady accepted entirely the utilitarian assumption that more humans were necessarily better than fewer and that Australia ought to increase its human population up to maximum carrying capacity. Australia was a Golconda, from sea to sea one vast storehouse of undeveloped riches wanting only individual industry.[6] And, as the future centre of white settlement in a secure and revivified Empire, Australia would support a population of between 100 and 500 million:

> A sufficient population *must* be established in the Northern Territory, in South Australia, and in Western Australia to ensure permanent, effective occupation, and a realisation of the White Australia policy . . . [This is] not a question of either Labor or Liberal policy, of profits or wages; it is a question of preserving the integrity of the British Empire . . .[7]

Western Australia's Premier, James Mitchell, shared Brady's and Bruce's enthusiasm for land development. Mitchell believed good government consisted of raising finance on the London market to assist British migrants to farm the land. He believed Western Australia possessed unlimited land and unlimited agricultural potential.

For nearly 100 years the well-watered and heavily timbered south-west of Western Australia had resisted settlement. The region's unbroken forests, standing as a reproach to the state's development ideology, incited calls for their destruction. In 1920 Mitchell proposed conquering the area through Group Settlement, an idea derived from the Great War: 'the war had provided an object-lesson in the power of organised bodies of men to surmount physical obstacles before which, as individuals, they would have stood helpless.'[8] Against the forests Mitchell planned a mass attack, mounted by settlers deployed into units of 20 men under the command of a foreman for each 64-hectare homestead block. Groups received orders to clear an area of two hectares for intense cultivation and partly clear an additional eight hectares for pasture, as well as dig drains and dams, run out fences and build necessary outbuildings and dwellings. Ballots decided the right of ownership of any particular block. State strategists anticipated each group settler would take over a block at the end of two and a half years of preparatory work.

The first assault began near Manjimup in March 1921 and by December, 40 other groups had joined the attack. Mitchell, however, decided on reinforcements. In 1922 Britain passed the Empire Settlement Act, providing for subsidised emigration. Mitchell quickly signed an agreement to settle 75 000 new migrants (men, women and children) and to establish 6000 men selected from these on 6000 additional farms in the south-west. Few who embarked from Britain realised they were going out not as farmers but as destroyers of forest.

The area under attack included fine jarrah and karri forest, described by the Agricultural Commission as 'heavy to colossal' timber. Previous clearing methods involved steady and continuous burning after long periods of ringbarking and 'sucker-bashing'. Mitchell, impatient with the tentative and slowly cumulative action of private individuals, demanded immediate results—Western Australia's empire had to be built in a day. No one, however, had attempted rapid, large-scale clearing of heavily timbered country. Again, the war suggested models: the use of explosives and tree-pulling machines. Most settlers, however, were completely inexperienced with clearing land and few understood the use of explosives, tree-pullers and the hand tools with which they were expected to eradicate the forest. Removing the immense hardwood trees proved exceedingly difficult. At the rate of destroying one tree in four days, clearing ten hectares was going to take a very, very long time. Groups quickly abandoned complete clearing in favour of ringbarking the largest trees. But ringbarked trees took two or more years to die, and when cleared, much of the land proved extremely poor, deficient in minerals, water-logged in winter and sour where heavy timber had been uprooted by chains or explosives. Blocks were successively deserted and reoccupied by inexperienced newcomers. The state treasury continued sustenance payments, expenses mounted, and everybody complained. One settler, from Devon, described his situation:

> Some weeks we were working in water up to our knees slashing down Scrub, Mulocking Roots out best way we Could, Cold soaked into the Skin, go back at Night to our Old Shack, all water logged, cold, shivering. Well we would set to and light a fire and Boil our Billy for a Cup of Tea, then we have Tea and get to Bed. Sick to Death with the wet and cold. We woke up some mornings and the Water was as much as 6" from the Bottoms of our Beds. Boil up again Breakfast and away for the Day. Slushing about in the mud & water, till at Last one of the Settlers got up and said, I am having No More of these stunts, I'll be Dead.[9]

In June 1924, Mitchell's political successors suspended Group Settlement and appointed a Royal Commission to investigate the scheme. During hearings the Western Australian Conservator of Forests, S. K. Kessell, anxious to increase his own empire, suggested planting *Pinus pinaster* on the settlements on the coastal plains. Settlers rejected his advice; they wanted information, not on tree planting, but on 'how to kill a forest quickly.' Despite their criticism of Group Settlement, the new government men were no less enthusiastic about land development than James Mitchell. They continued to place settlers on the land, refinanced the scheme, and reduced the book value of the properties to give farmers some chance of paying off their debts. But costs consistently exceeded estimates. By 1936 over 80 percent of total Commonwealth, state and British Group Settlement loans had been written off. Less than half the number of farms planned were eventually established, although 40 000 hectares of virgin forest had been destroyed.

Elsewhere in Australia settlers regarded native animals an obstacle to development the equal of native trees. The morality of development sanctioned virtually unlimited increases in the quantity of humans and tolerated virtually any decrease in the populations of other life forms—except animals directly useful to humans, such as sheep and cattle. Settlers and professional hunters therefore shot anything that moved in the bush. Encouraged by an international demand for fur, hunters began, around the turn of the century, killing large numbers of koalas (*Phascolarctos cinereus*). In 1908,

58 000 koala pelts passed through the Sydney markets alone. In 1924 over two million were exported from the eastern states. By the end of the Great War the koala was extinct in South Australia. Other native animals survived, however, so in 1920 the state removed the brush-tailed possum (family *Phalangeridae*) from the protected list and declared an open season. Within four months hunters trapped more than 100 000. As a consequence of hunting and habitat destruction, over 70 percent of native land mammals in South Australia are now extinct, extremely rare or uncommon and endangered.

In 1927 the Queensland government declared an open season on possums and koalas. The eradication of wild animals, the government believed, promoted closer settlement. Despite widespread protest the government persisted in the slaughter, and within months 10 000 trappers disposed of over one million possums and 600 000 koalas—more than the total number of koalas which remain alive in the whole of Australia today. The slaughter caused the virtual elimination of koalas from Queensland. Four years later New South Wales declared an open season on possums and during June and July 1931, hunters and trappers brought over 800 000 possum skins to market. To avoid offending the sensibilities of city nature lovers, merchants marketed possum pelts as chinchilla and koala skins as wombat.[10]

Only a few Australians dissented from the aggressive boosterism of the post-war years. Geographer Griffith Taylor argued that contemporary margins of settlement already closely approximated the limits set by the nature of Australia's physical environment. The centre, he maintained, would always remain sparsely populated and northern development was a chimera, a 'white elephant'. But his challenge to the facile presumptions of Australia Unlimited thinking provoked a vigorous counter-response. Politicians publicly censured him in the Commonwealth Parliament, academic detractors called for his dismissal from the chair he occupied at the University of Sydney, and the Senate of the University of Western Australia proscribed his textbook. Taylor received greatest opprobrium when he claimed that intensive settlement would necessarily contravene

White Australia since it would require 'a small influx of Chinese labourers.' In a forthright rejoinder in a letter to the *Sydney Morning Herald*, Daisy Bates attacked Taylor's apostasy and predicted:

> The central portion and the north will be taken up in God's good time by British pioneers, and developed by them, for Australia is going to be for ever British, and whether red labour or yellow labour or green labour tries to hinder, it will be British sinew and British grit and British money that will win out in the end, as surely as it was British grit that won out in the beginning.[11]

Born in Ireland, Daisy O'Dwyer migrated to Australia in 1884, where she married Jack Bates, a cattleman, in 1885. Later, she bought a cattle station in the Kimberleys and thereafter devoted the rest of her life to studying the Aborigines. In 1910 she joined anthropologist A. G. Radcliffe-Brown on an expedition to the north-west, to investigate the remnants of Aboriginal tribes. She later accused Radcliffe-Brown of gross plagiarism. In 1912 she established the first of the isolated camps in the Nullarbor, where she spent most of the rest of her life. Convinced that the Aborigines were dying out, and of the necessity of communicating this fact, she wrote *The Passing of the Aborigines* (1938): 'The Australian native can withstand all the reverses of nature, fiendish droughts and sweeping floods, horrors of thirst and enforced starvation—but he cannot withstand civilisation.'[12]

Anthropologists agreed. Unable to progress or move forward, the hapless Aborigines had waited passively since creation for their own destruction at the hands of more creative and dynamic peoples. The conquest of Australia must necessarily lead to their complete extermination. The sooner Aborigines disappeared, the better they would serve Australian development. All that remained, Bates added, 'was to smooth the dying pillow'.

The barbarism of the Great War caused many in Europe to question which people on earth were savage and which civilised. In Australia, however, the categories remained inviolate. During the late nineteenth century, evolutionary biology gave the construction of human hierarchies a force and persuasiveness previously lacking. Ethnologists and natural scientists advanced the idea of recapitulation—among the most influential ideas of late nineteenth century science—to serve as a general theory of biological determinism.[13] Efforts to scientifically demonstrate innate differences in mental and moral capacity between various members of the human family grew into one of the central preoccupations of nineteenth century European and North American intellectuals. The notion of recapitulation provided an irresistible criterion for any scientists who wanted to rank human groups as higher and lower. The theory allegedly proved that primitive cultures represented an ancestral stage in the evolutionary development of more advanced cultures. By the early twentieth century few among educated Europeans continued to believe in the fundamental unity of humankind. In 1902, a member of the Australian Commonwealth Parliament, reflecting the era's confidence in scientific standards, stated, 'there is no scientific evidence that [the Aborigine] is a human being at all.'[14] The hierarchic categorisation of humans served as an ethic of conquest and provided the basic moral justification for dispossession—those best able to exploit the land have the best right to the land.[15]

Anthropologists did not doubt that Australian Aborigines represented primitive humanity, and Aboriginal culture but the inchoate, childlike stammerings of truths more clearly and more fully formulated by later rational thinkers—themselves. The scientific study of the Aborigines, claimed one academic, would help trace out the 'sequence of ideas by which mankind has advanced from the condition of the lower animals to that in which we find him at the present time, and by this means to provide really reliable materials for a philosophy of progress.'[16]

Unlike Daisy Bates, however, most anthropologists did not welcome the disappearance of their data and they found her extinction prediction disturbing. Fortunately for this science, the demise of the Aborigine also threatened the interests of the northern pastoral industry. By the 1920s the preservation of the Aborigines in the Kimberleys had became a matter of economic necessity, as they provided most of the pastoral labour. In 1920 the Western Australian Protector of Aborigines, A. O. Neville, argued, 'It is . . . economically sound to preserve the race as far as possible in order that it may continue to assist in the development of the Territory, in which it has materially helped in the past.'[17] One pastoralist, asked how he procured his labour, boasted, 'breed it myself'.[18]

The organisers of Australia's future, the boosters and the developers, excluded the possibility for any way of life beside the European. Accordingly, post-war state policies aimed at the complete destruction of Aboriginal culture: to break the social unit, drive Aborigines off their tribal lands and onto reserves, split groups into families and families into individuals, and force assimilation of the fragmented remnants.

In Western Australia the government segregated Aborigines in rural concentration camps. At Moore River, for example, regulations separated children from adults, boys from girls and prohibited exit or entry to the fenced compound without written permission. Despite pleas and protests from the Aborigines for equality under the law, the state moved toward greater segregation and stricter control. In 1927, the city of Perth banned Aborigines from the central district, and numerous other towns barred Aborigines from their streets. An amendment to the Western Australian Education Act in 1928 empowered teachers to exclude Aboriginal students on the basis of a complaint from a single European parent. The rule effectively prohibited all Aboriginal children from Education Department schools.

In the Northern Territory, Dr Cecil E. Cook became Chief Protector of Aborigines in 1927. Cook believed in the strictest superintendence of Aboriginal life, and even censored films which might tend to lower Aboriginal respect for the white man. He need not have bothered; celluloid buffoons were no competition for the deadly Europeans Aborigines encountered in their daily lives.

In response to the spearing of an East Kimberley settler in 1926, a posse of police and settlers from Wyndham rode out to the nearby Marndoc reserve and killed all the Aborigines they met, probably about 30 in number. To destroy the evidence, they burned all the bodies. Two policemen were tried for murder but were acquitted.[19] Two years later, in central Australia, Constable William Murray, under orders from the government resident, C. A. Cawood, led two punitive expeditions against the Walpiri, who had speared cattle and killed a dingo hunter in response to pastoral encroachment upon their traditional land. Seven men rode from camp to camp killing men and women as they encountered them, about 70 overall. Johny Martin Jumpijinpa, a small boy, saw his father killed, and later recalled, 'They just draftem out like cattle . . . shottem all the men.' A three-man commission of inquiry, which included C. A. Cawood, found the police action entirely justified.[20]

A national conference of government authorities in 1937 formally adopted a policy of assimilation: the separating of full-bloods on reserves as isolated as possible, and the granting of admission, via institutionalisation, to European society to those of mixed descent. Basically a breeding programme, the policy aimed at the complete disappearance of the Aborigines. Marriages between Aborigines and Europeans would lead to the dilution of offensive physical characteristics (chiefly skin complexion) in the offspring. The popular catch-phrase, 'black blood breeds out in three generations', received endorsement from eminent scientists, including Sir Raphael Cilento, the Director of Health in Queensland, Professor J. B. Cleland of the University of Adelaide and N. B. Tindale of the South Australian Museum. Tindale produced a scientifically based 'scale of absorbability' of the various types of cross-breeds, ranging from 'high' for the 1/8, 1/4, 3/8 and FI (first generation of half-caste) types to 'low' for the 3/4 and 7/8 types. The state should encourage 'high' breeds and discourage 'low'.[21]

No one in the European community questioned the need for strict control over Aboriginal life. The only debate concerned who should exercise that dominion: the government or the church. The National Missionary Council declared in 1926 in favour of apartheid and claimed, 'The only effective way of saving and developing the aboriginal natives of Australia is by a policy of strict segregation under religious influence.'[22]

But the policies of assimilation and segregation contained too many contradictions for them to ever succeed along the lines intended. Australians were simply unable to think clearly about the question of their relationship with Aborigines. For example, while they supported the breeding programme mandated by assimilation, most middle class Australians abhorred miscegenation. Indeed, in Queensland, the Aboriginal Act of 1934 expressly prohibited sexual intercourse between an Aboriginal woman and a non-Aboriginal man. Interestingly, the statute made no mention of intercourse between an Aboriginal man and a non-Aboriginal woman. Except in cases of rape, the legislators presumably could not even imagine the possibility of such an encounter. Without mixed marriages, however, the types of cross-breeds required for the dilution of Aboriginality could never be produced.[23]

'At the coming of civilisation, the aboriginal tribes dwindle like chaff before the wind,' Ernestine Hill told readers of her very popular *The Great Australian Loneliness* (1938), an account of extensive travels through Australia.[24] All Aborigines, Hill predicted, would be dead by the end of the century. Although she conceded the eugenicist logic of assimilation, Hill, like her friend Daisy Bates, found the intermediate forms terrible to behold. Born with a peculiar odour of their own, she thought, Bates attributed the paternity of half-caste children to low-class whites. Hill, in contrast, understood that all classes of men might find comfort in the company of Aboriginal women. The primary problem, she wrote, was lack of white women. White male pioneers needed white female companions, otherwise they forced their attentions on Aboriginal women. For the future of the north the consequence of these unions was 'a theme unthinkable.'[25] Part-Aboriginal workers were biologically incapable of performing the work necessary for northern development:

> As Saddlers, stockmen, teamsters, sailormen, blacksmiths and overseers of camping and droving plants, well-trained half-caste boys can always be assured of a good living where they are known. The girls make excellent cooks and domestic helps and first-class needlewomen. But in all cases other than those of unremitting watchfulness and personal direction, education proves quite worthless. Early adolescence finds a practically complete and inevitable reversion to the black.[26]

To reward soldiers' Great War sacrifices to Empire and civilisation every Australian state made provision to settle returnees on the land. Soldier settlement schemes, designed along the scientific lines advocated by Elwood Mead—comprehensive planning covering social, economic and technical aspects of landed settlement—represented the final phase of the great Australian project to populate the land with a sturdy, producing yeoman class. Soldiers who took advantage of the opportunity sought more immediate goals, chiefly independence: freedom from the necessity of selling their labour to others in order to live. Precedent opposed the realisation of these hopes. Previous government-sponsored intensive settlement had produced farmers who were usually neither independent, contented or settled. A few critics, cognizant of Australia's history, opposed soldier settlement from the beginning. William Clark, a Victorian politician, stressed, 'The settler's lot meant toil from daylight to dark; it meant wives working like slaves and children milking before dawn and after dark.'[27] Besides, most Crown lands available for settlement after the Great War represented surplusage, land rejected by generations of pioneers. Their descendants already occupied the most productive and most accessible land.

But the states discounted warnings of failure; the need to develop the land was too urgent. Australian politicians, intimidated by undeveloped spaces, saw land settlement as the best solution to the country's military vulnerability as the white man's outpost in the Pacific. Increasing urbanisation and a falling birth rate threatened Australia with race suicide. Only life on the land, because of the supposed greater vitality of rural Australians, could restore the country to vigour and health, increase the population and improve the race stock. Moreover, landed diggers would identify with property-owning conservative business interests, and farm families would provide social stability and a bulwark against socialism. Also, for the sake of future military enlistment, governments were concerned to show beneficence toward returnees.

Backed by Commonwealth loans, each state established Soldier Settlement Boards to superintend the schemes. The Boards selected settlers indiscriminately, including returnees who possessed little or no farming experience; indeed, many ex-soldiers were physically and mentally unfit for a life on the land. Few had survived the Great War unscathed. Of the 267 607 Australian men who returned, 155 422 were classified as casualties and by 1920 one-third were receiving invalid pensions. Injury, however, was no handicap to settler eligibility: cripples, amputees, the half-blind and the shell-shocked all obtained land. As a Royal Commission on

Repatriated Soldiers commented in 1923, 'many of the men were not normal after the war.'[28] In addition, most soldier settlers began farming with little or no capital. Their state overseers proved parsimonious in advancing credit to employ labour, erect fencing, eradicate vermin, provide for water supplies, clear the land or purchase machinery.

In Western Australia large-scale soldier settlement began in 1919. But the original intention of settling soldiers on virgin land proved untenable. Applicants preferred established farms rather than pioneer blocks, so the state began buying existing estates and selling the properties to soldier settlers. Depressed conditions before 1920 persuaded many established farmers to sell out, but in the early 1920s high prices for wool and wheat and the heavy demand for land encouraged the sale of existing farms at inflated prices, which in turn increased the financial burden of the final purchasers. Over 5 000 ex-servicemen attempted settlement in Western Australia but debt and inexperience caused a 60 percent failure rate.

Soldier Settlement Boards sought to overcome these problems through scientific management and an extensive system of surveillance of settlers and their activities. Farmers required approval for every transaction from local committees or district inspectors, who reported on every aspect of their lives, not only their farming endeavours, but also their personal behaviour and domestic arrangements. The paraphernalia of scrutiny reflected contemporary attitudes in favour of the rule of efficiency, the importance of which Prime Minister Bruce outlined in 1924:

> The future of Australia depends on efficiency. If to producers, primary and secondary, could be brought a realisation of the vital necessity for efficiency in management, control, finance and marketing; if to the workers could be brought an understanding that the standard of living and wages and of comfort they enjoyed depended on efficiency, Australia would be far towards the solution of its great problems, and could look forward with confidence to the great destiny that lay before it.[29]

Because the Boards discouraged the employment of outside labour, soldiers' wives worked double duty as housekeeper and farm worker: milking cows, feeding animals and working in the field. Women also bore the burden of procreation during the state's mobilisation of child producers to fill the underpopulated continent. Settlers' wives protested at being 'worked to death.' 'I have also milked with a baby in the pram', wrote 'Josephine' to the *Countryman* in 1926, 'and a toddler in a little wire-netting yard by the bail, and then bumped the pram home with the two in it, and a bucket in each hand.'[30] The strain imposed by excessive labour and the expectations of multiple conflicting roles proved too great and many wives left the farms and returned to the city. Their husbands followed later. Nearly 40 000 returned servicemen—and a few women—(over 100 000 men, women and children in total) were recruited as soldier settlers, but most did not succeed as farmers. Like their nineteenth century predecessors on the land, large numbers of soldier settlers, burdened by debt and overwork, abandoned their selections.

In the midst of soldier settlement failure, the Victorian Parliament passed a bill in 1932 to provide for the rule of business methods in the conduct of soldier settlement. A commission divided settlers between the inefficient and efficient and evicted the former. The state no longer believed in a yeomanry and henceforth reconstructed rural industry on an unashamedly capitalist basis. Future farmers would act primarily as businessmen, responsive to scientific progress and the imperatives of efficiency.

The publicists for Australia Unlimited, mesmerised by geographic bulk, dismissed the facts of the continent's aridity as erroneous. Artesian supplies were permanent and inexhaustible; irrigation and the conservation of water would solve the problems of interior settlement and provide for a population in excess of 100 million people. With proper management, the impounding of water behind dams and locks would transform eastern Australia and

> render permanently navigable three great rivers [the Murray, Darling and Murrumbidgee] for a distance of 3,000 miles inland . . . provide a plentiful and regular supply of water to vast territories sometimes smitten by drought . . . throw open fresh fields for home seekers . . .[31]

The promise of fresh fields to conquer proved irresistible; governments everywhere promoted irrigation, irrespective of whether the schemes made economic or social sense.

After a series of dry seasons in the New South Wales Riverina, culminating in the record drought of 1901, local landholders began lobbying for irrigation and stock water schemes. Their arguments proved persuasive. In 1912 the state government appointed a Commissioner for Water Conservation and Irrigation to oversee the development of Murrumbidgee Irrigation Areas (MIAs).[32] With authority to construct and operate railways, build roads, regulate road usage, control the transmission and sale of electric power and prescribe the prerogatives and duties of local government bodies, the commissioner possessed the powers of a hydraulic despot. He presided over a commission which regarded irrigation as essentially a technical task. Engineers assumed all the early planning but did not examine soils, nor investigate water tables, nor research suitable crops and trees. They ignored problems of waterlogging and salting, already manifest in earlier Victorian irrigation schemes. New South Wales planners were mainly concerned with social engineering. To ensure a well-regulated hierarchy of proprietors, planners parcelled the land into 0.8-, 4- and 20-hectare allotments, designating the 0.8-hectare subdivisions 'working men's blocks', whose occupiers were expected to provide labour for the owners of the larger blocks. The idea originated in South Australia where politician G. W. Cotton, mindful of the need to prevent labourers becoming landowners too soon, yet convinced of the necessity of giving the landless a stake in the system, proposed the blocks as a means of combatting what he saw as the coming working class revolution.

By June 1913, the commission had received 547 applications, mostly from people who lacked any agricultural experience, including miners from Broken Hill enticed by distorted claims as to their likely prospects as farmers. Many of the miners—suffering from silicosis and semi-invalid—unable to carry out the hard work necessary to develop a farm, died within a few years. To counter settler inexperience, the Commissioner extended special concessions to six practically minded Americans to take over strategically placed farms where they could demonstrate irrigation methods. Perhaps because of the American presence the commission continued to inflate claims concerning the possibilities and productivity of land under irrigation. The commission reminded the owners of the large blocks of the availability of labour from the owners of the workmen's blocks. To all settlers, the planners extended a vision of a secular utopia where technical control over the natural environment would provide all that was necessary for human happiness. But Murrumbidgee irrigation farmers discovered otherwise. In 1915, they accused high officials of corruption with respect to illegal land transactions and in 1916, dozens of farmers successfully sued for compensation on account of deception and misrepresentation concerning their prospects.

After the Great War, returned soldiers provided the commission with the chance to renew the Murrumbidgee irrigation empire. By 1923, soldier settlers held nearly half of the scheme's 2064 farms. But rising indebtedness and inexperience eventually forced many of them off the exhausted land. Practices introduced by the Chaffey brothers, where irrigation farmers ploughed deep and frequently, not only deprived the soil of humus but gradually broke down its structural units, leaving it compact, intractable and degraded.

During the inter-war period Australian foresters began propagating the necessity of extending their control over remaining Australian forests. New South Wales gazetted the first forestry reserves in Australia, in 1871, in the Murray and Clarence River districts. Later, Victoria, under the Forests Act of 1907, provided for the dedication of permanently reserved forest and the establishment of a Forests Department. By 1920 every Australian state had established a Forestry Commission. In addition, the University of Adelaide organised a School of Forestry in 1911 and Victoria opened a similar school in 1913. The students, the first professional Australian foresters, were trained in the utilitarian philosophy of their standard text, William Schlich's *Manual of Forestry* (1894), first published in England and in wide use in the United States. Schlich defined forestry as 'The human action directed to the production and utilization of forest produce,' an economic goal which led future Australian foresters to focus almost exclusively on wood production and ignore aspects of forest ecology not directly affecting yields.

Emboldened by the increase in their domain and by the growing recognition of their profession, foresters took the opportunity to publicise the significance of sustained yield—an idea of Gifford Pinchot's—and to promote conservation in the context of progress and efficiency. Modernisation and the support of a greatly augmented European population, they suggested, required reliable resource inventories. In an address to the University of Adelaide in 1925, conservationist and Antarctic explorer, Sir Douglas Mawson, warned of the imminent depletion of Australia's timber resources. He illustrated his argument with the aid of the fashionable business metaphor and contended that without conservation, and at present rates of natural resource exploitation, 'future generations of Australians are to be left with an overdraft arising from the payment of dividends from forests and other natural wealth; not from accrued surplus but from capital stock.'[33] Only conservation, afforestation and reforestation could ensure future supplies. Trees must be treated as a regular farm crop which 'differs . . . only in the period of harvesting, which is so far extended that forestry passes beyond the scope of the small farmer, though it may be a remunerative investment for the State, corporations or wealthy individuals.'[34]

Foresters also began to criticise agricultural development which ignored conservation. State ministers of lands, claimed C. E. Lanne-Poole in 1926, were selected only because of their ability to promote settlement:

> he is, as a rule, the type that is driven frantic by the sight of an un-subdivided region on the departmental maps . . . However poor the place, there will always be found sufficient areas of so-called first class land to warrant the subdivision of the area. When that is done, there comes the tragedy of putting immigrants on the blocks, which can never support them, for they are unsuitable for agriculture . . . Ten years usually sees the area abandoned . . . His electors are tickled by such phrases as 'we want men not trees' . . . To the Minister, all land is potentially agricultural . . .[35]

Neither sarcasm, nor the tenets of conservation, however, could dissuade state governments from continuing to regard lumbering and mining as synonymous; in the minds of politicians, forests were timbered obstacles. State forest status was reserved only for areas, generally rugged and infertile, which proved impractical for land survey and settlement. In 1931 the Queensland government appointed a Royal Commission to consider forest boundaries and development. The commissioners were determined for land clearance and settlement and concluded: 'Queensland needs no forestry science for present requirements . . . The productive wealth of the country at present suffers from the fact that there are too many, rather than too few trees.'[36] The commissioners' views reflected popular attitudes. E. J. Brady, for example, reminded his readers, as he surveyed the common Queensland sight of fields of stumps, that 'Regrets for the destruction of timber need not trouble us. Fields are worth more than trees.'[37]

Francis Ratcliffe, an English biologist who travelled widely through Queensland in the early 1930s, reluctantly agreed. 'Australians revel in felling trees', he concluded. On seeing the fine forest go down before the axe and the fire-stick, sealing the fate of all the queer creatures sheltered within, he admitted to a twinge of regret and anger but promptly judged his reaction as irrational; progress and development were necessary and inevitable, he reminded himself, and readers of *Flying Fox and Drifting Sand* (1938).[38] Elsewhere in his narrative—a popular account of aspects of Australian natural history and conservation—however, aesthetic principle triumphed over utilitarian expediency. When he came upon the man-made wilderness left by the logging of hoop pine (*Araucaria cunninghamii*), he no longer viewed nature as a stage set for the display of human activity; he found the scene ugly, wretched and empty and responded with forthright rage:

> Suddenly we found ourselves in the midst of horrible destruction. The axemen had made a clean sweep of the timber and the fire-stick had been applied to the remains. Nothing was left but naked soil and charred stumps. Here and there a tall scrub box had survived complete destruction, but its once delicately pink trunk was black and cracked and its beautiful foliage now a shiny brown.[39]

Australian author Frank Dalby Davison, who journeyed up the east coast in 1932, also noticed and condemned the desecration of the countryside. He abhorred the drab utilitarianism of Australian settlement and while he thought the battle against the bush heroic, he found the result unlovely. 'Dead trees, fire-blackened stumps and fallen logs—debris of the battle—litter the paddocks.'[40] Settlers had carried the devastation far beyond need and had produced 'a wealthy but parsimonious landscape' which 'revealed no pride in the means by which earth is brought to give her bounty.'[41] Australians, Davison thought, possessed an 'aptitude for vulgarizing a place of beauty ... there was scarcely any evidence of human presence [I] would not wish effaced' and he reflected that many generations would pass before people could call the land beautiful.[42]

Ten years before Davison's journey, D. H. Lawrence attempted to limn the nature of the relationship between Australians and the bush. Lawrence, however, spent little actual time in the bush and stayed most of his three months in Australia in two cities, Perth and Sydney. The novel which followed his Australian sojourn, *Kangaroo* (1923), vigorously expounded the man-against-the-land theme. Australia, said Lawrence, needed Real Men, possessed of limitless patience and perseverance, to fight the unlovable and hostile land, 'biding its time with a terrible ageless watchfulness'. Australians, he found, lived mainly in cities and towns and feared the bush. The supposed emptiness of Australia made people afraid, not necessarily for the real enough dangers of wild, untamed places, but of themselves. One character in *Kangaroo* says:

> Go into the middle of Australia and see how empty it is. You can't face emptiness long. You have to come back and do something to keep from being frightened of your own emptiness, and everything else's emptiness. It may be empty. But it's wicked, and it'll kill you if it can.[43]

Lawrence's characters, like most Australians, accepted the fundamental ideology of modern society, that pursuit of mastery over nature would bind the bitterly divided human species. The sources of inequality, injustice and tyranny lay not with individuals and societies in violent conflict among themselves, but in the incomplete domination of nature.

Although, as Lawrence discovered, few Australians actually lived in the bush—by 1891 two-thirds of the population lived in cities and towns—versifiers, writers and painters had begun in the 1880s to create a distinctive Australian culture based on an image of the bush: a sunlit landscape of faded blue hills, cloudless skies and noble gum trees. This contrived and facile countryside lacked tension and did not evoke any sense of relatedness between humans and the non-human world. Indeed, the subdued landscapes and the absence of conflict in the scenes of gum trees, sunny pastoral panoramas with winding rivers, green pastures and mountain backgrounds— vistas consistently evoked in the paintings of Arthur Streeton, Hans Heysen and their followers—suited the conservative patriotism of the post-war era, which sought to minimise dissension and impose a view of the colonisation of Australia as an unqualified success.

Opportunities for manufacturing a history which celebrated the triumph of industrial capitalism over nature arose several times during the inter-war years as Australians celebrated a number of foundation anniversaries. The Western Australian centenary in 1929, the Victorian centenary in 1934, the South Australian centenary in 1938 and the New South Wales sesquicentenary in the same year, required explanations of Australian history which glorified 'the memory of those gallant and resourceful men and women who . . . triumphantly conquered the land and bequeathed it to us.'[44] Australia's history became one of uninterrupted enterprise and progress which had led to the creation of a great new Dominion of the British Empire. These myths were paraded before large and willing audiences. At least 60 000 sightseers—over a quarter of Perth's population—watched Western Australia's centenary parade in 1929. More than 130 floats, celebrating the state's achievements in agriculture, pastoralism, gold and industry—three kilometres in length—passed by, including three truckloads of Aborigines to serve as 'a reminder of the dangers with which the pioneers were faced'.[45]

The showpiece of the New South Wales sesquicentennial of the British invasion on 26 January 1938 was a re-enactment of Governor Phillip's landing, including the putting to flight of a party of Aborigines. The staged fight served mainly for purposes of drama; no one actually believed the Aborigines had ever been more than a minor pest. Celebrants convinced themselves that their forebears had come to an empty continent; Australia, at the time of first

British settlement was, for all intents and purposes, unoccupied. Subsequently the Aborigines represented no more than a footnote, or codicil, to Australian history. 'The aborigines were negligible, both as an obstruction to settlement and as a source of labour,' concluded the academic authors of *The Peopling of Australia* in 1933.[46] In any case, judged historian W. K. Hancock in his *Australia* (1930), Aboriginal society proved 'pathetically helpless' when contacted by European civilisation.[47]

William Cooper, of the Australian Aborigines' League, viewed Australian history differently. Cooper and others organised a national day of mourning to commemorate the New South Wales sesquicentennial, called a meeting (for Aborigines only) and issued a manifesto which began, 'This festival of 150 years' so called 'progress' in Australia commemorates also 150 years of misery and degradation imposed upon the original native inhabitants by the white invaders of this country.'[48] The day of mourning marked the beginning of Aboriginal political activity which continues to the present day.

Despite the numerous post-war schemes to settle people on the land, more Australians began living around the major cities than ever before. Suburbanisation committed Australian governments to borrow huge sums for water and sewage services to facilitate urban sprawl, to build roads to accommodate the rising numbers of automobiles and to extend electrical grids to light and service homes. Most of the development capital came from overseas. Between 1925–28 the seven Australian governments secured 43 percent of new British overseas investment in government bonds. Australia planned to pay back these loans through the export of wool, wheat, hides and skins, dairy produce, meats and metals. Indeed, in the last two years of the 1920s, primary products generated 88 percent of Australia's export income. In the fervour for development and production, however, Australia's boosters overlooked the fact that increasing output was all to no avail without buyers. And without assured markets, without constant foreign demand for Australian products, overseas borrowing, in effect, mortgaged Australia's independence. In 1929, after the fall of stock prices on Wall Street,

Australia received two severe external shocks which highlighted the country's lack of sovereignty: the cessation of capital inflow as the London loan market ceased lending and a drastic fall in the prices for exports.

The Great Depression, the most generalised economic slump in history, affected all capitalist countries. Between 1929 and 1932 industrial production in the capitalist world fell by 35 percent, the volume of world trade in manufactured goods fell by over 40 percent, and by 1932 over 30 million people were unemployed in the four major capitalist economies alone. Australia rapidly joined in the worldwide economic collapse. By 1932 as many as one million people, out of a total workforce of a little over two million, lacked full-time employment. Domestic output fell and the prices of wheat and wool, Australia's principal exports, declined by more than 50 percent. Australian politicians, however, refused to accept the disappearance of markets. They resolved to increase production still further, and during the seeding and ploughing season of 1930, national and state politicians daily exhorted farmers to 'Grow More Wheat'. In response, farmers harvested a record crop—Western Australia's harvest was not bettered for 30 more years—and received a record low price.

The rural depression accentuated cumulative environmental destruction. In the pastoral Kimberleys, low prices, damage from the spread of natural pests, and increased erosion due to overgrazing undermined the viability of continued pastoralism. Pastoralists abandoned their homesteads, fences deteriorated, windmills became derelict and those who remained fell deeply into debt. Survivors managed only because they paid their Aboriginal employees no wages.[49]

South of the Kimberleys the pastoral industry had, during the first 30 years of the twentieth century, enjoyed a period of immense profitability. The area under lease almost trebled between 1900 and 1921, rising to 105 million hectares. But the average annual rainfall over the five years to 1939, on most stations south of the De Grey River, was less than 125 millimetres, less than two-thirds of the pre-drought average. Cattle and sheep numbers fell and pasture deteriorated. In the Murchison–Meekatharra area, 75 percent of the saltbush and 25 percent of the acacias had been destroyed by 1940. Some pastoralists reported losses of up to 90 percent of scrub and shrubs.[50]

Further south the huge expansion of wheat growing in the 1920s led to the sowing of crops in areas of very low and very unreliable rainfall. Drought, grasshopper plagues, and rabbit infestations devastated crops and reduced stock-carrying capacity by 50 percent. The short crop rotations adopted in the pioneering period rapidly depleted soils, and yields declined on average from 1.23 cubic metres per hectare in 1930 to 0.76 cubic metres per hectare in 1936. Low yields and falling prices brought about a contraction of the agricultural area as farmers abandoned marginal land. Indebtedness placed the surviving farmers under the strict supervision of their creditors, who forced on them such severe economies that many farmers reverted to using horses. 'Thrift and balance' replaced the earlier slogan of 'progress and development'.

Arid lands—areas of low, variable rainfall and high evaporation, where the vegetation and soils are extremely vulnerable to disturbance by grazing livestock, cover 60 percent of the Australian continent. By the early 1930s half of the arid lands grazed sheep and cattle. The remainder—sand plains, dunefields, rocky hills and highly saline areas—supported only indigenous, naturally adapted forms of life. Soil erosion spread over extensive areas of the arid grazing regions during the droughts of the inter-war years and became the concern of the CSIR. In 1938 Francis Ratcliffe, sent to investigate, noted of the pastoral inland:

> a marked general depletion of the vegetation, particularly of the bushes, shrubs and trees; the reversion of considerable areas to eroded and unprofitable wastes, which, if not abandoned, are held only because big sums are tied up in improvements ... One of the most extraordinary and ... discouraging aspects of the whole matter is the reluctance, amounting almost to stubborn refusal, on the part of the Australian people, to recognize the inevitability of drought. The tacit assumption that drought is an exceptional visitation to the island country has shaped and infected public thought and official policy alike.[51]

Ratcliffe insisted on lighter utilisation and a recognition by Australians as to the reality of the continent's environment—the fragility of inland ecosystems and the permanence of drought—but traditional pastoral practices continued and so did soil erosion.

In the midst of World War II, pastoralist Jock Pick issued an urgent warning. He named soil erosion a greater threat to Australia's existence than the enemy abroad. He attributed civilisation's greatest menace to ignorance and unwise expediency, but he diluted his warning with praise: 'A century of white settlement in Australia has converted a barren and poverty-stricken continent, sustaining only a very meagre population of barely human savages, into the home of a thriving, progressive nation.'[52] Pick did not question the motivations of conquest. On the contrary, he lauded self-interest as the mainspring of most worthwhile human endeavour.[53] Like most developers who couple their desire for profit with a sense of righteousness, Pick professed an unwavering faith in the efficacy of development, a belief that a new society could be ripped out of the Australian landscape. Soil conservation did not consist of acquiring a land ethic but could be accomplished through enlightened self-interest and efficient management.

Arable farmers also suffered the consequences of land degradation. The serious depletion of organic matter and loss of soil structure due to fallowing and continuous cropping led to severe wind and water erosion all over arable Australia. Rather than blame themselves, farmers sought scapegoats. Some Western Australians blamed their troubles on emus. Large flocks trampled wheatfields and knocked down fences, and in 1932 beleaguered farmers appealed to the federal government to declare war. The Minister for Defence, Sir George Pearce, ordered in the army. The offensive began at Champion on November 2 when an army unit, with two Lewis machines guns and 10 000 rounds of ammunition, took the field. Neighbouring farmers organised a 37-kilometre drive of emus to a predetermined killing ground. Gunners shot about twelve birds before the mob of about 40 scattered. The army decided successful extermination required greater stealth and accordingly set up an ambush where the birds came to drink. Two days later, as a mob of about 1000 emus approached a dam, a camouflaged army gunner opened fire. About a dozen birds fell, then the gun jammed; the army withdrew.[54]

189

As Australia's ability to meet interest payments on overseas debt became increasingly tenuous, the foreign holders of Australian securities grew concerned. To devise a scheme to protect the interests of British bondholders the Bank of England despatched an advisory team in 1930 headed by Sir Otto Niemeyer. Australia's living standards were too high, Niemeyer claimed; wages would have to fall. His advice corresponded with that of Australia's own economic experts, who, behind protestations of objective and apolitical analysis, mounted a highly politicised attack on the right of working people to maintain living standards. Economists agreed that Australia had to take measures which would make the country acceptable to the London loan market: budgets would have to balance, wages be reduced and assistance to the unemployed cut. For working people the Depression meant long periods without work, poverty, and in some cases, actual starvation. For economists, the crisis afforded a welcome opportunity to assert their importance. 'Just at the present moment it so happens that the economist is (or should be) king in this as in every other country', claimed the head of the University of Melbourne's School of Commerce.[55]

To complement the economists' keen scientific insight into the causes of, and appropriate measures for the relief of, the Depression, politicians developed their own perspicacious analyses. In 1930 Western Australia's Premier, James Mitchell, proclaimed:

> The position of the State is perfectly sound. In fact, if money were not tight the world over, our position would be considered magnificent, this notwithstanding that we have been going downhill at almost breakneck speed during the last three years. Having struck bottom we are now pulling ourselves together and feeling our pockets to find out where we stand . . .[56]

Mitchell feared Niemeyer's recommendations meant an end to extending human dominion over the earth—no more acres cleared and ploughed, no more railways and migration schemes and no more group settlements. In fact, Australia's total population actually declined by more than 10 000 during the Depression. Nevertheless, Mitchell managed to contrive a small amount of development in Western Australia. The unemployed had to be put to work, and for Mitchell, useful work encompassed only one activity—employing men against the bush. The state government directed many of the unemployed to the south-west to build dams and dig irrigation ditches. To maximise the use of labour, the projects refrained from using machines. In 1931, using little more than wheelbarrows and shovels, 2500 men dug a 26-kilometre diversion channel to divert the waters of the Harvey River towards the coast.

Worsening economic conditions encouraged extraordinary political mobilisation among the wealth-owning and managerial classes of Australia. Sydney Rotarians formed the All For Australia League in 1931 to promote national unity, balanced budgets and a return to the Anglo-Saxon virtues of thrift and self-reliance. Simultaneously, South Australian academics and businessmen formed the Citizens League, with similar aims, and in all states, The New Guard—a fascist, paramilitary organisation founded in the 1920s—became more active. The problem of the Depression, these groups claimed, was a problem of authority: whether parliamentary democracy could provide the administration necessary to protect the social and economic status quo. Since Australian political parties represented sectional interests, not national interests, someone above party must take power in order to put things right. 'What was needed', argued Mrs Herbert Brookes of the Australian Women's National League,

> was a combined party of honest politicians prepared to work for Australia and not for party, with an advisory board of business men, economic experts and a few experienced women to undertake scientific investigation of problems and to advise the Government.[57]

New leaders, in partnership with experts, must take charge and save the country from politicians, political parties and the working class. Advocacy of forceful executive action reflected contemporary fascist sentiments and derived from an earlier version of national efficiency which embodied a strongly technocratic approach to government. Victorian politician Robert G. Menzies, for example, stressed the necessity for the 'courage of brutality'. Under the new regime of national efficiency, technocrats—guided by science alone—would provide objectively valid solutions to social and political problems, quite independently of the wishes and beliefs of the governed.

Australian industrialists sympathised with the calls for strong, business-oriented government. Essington Lewis, chairman of Broken Hill Proprietary, Australia's largest company and monopoly steel maker, regarded the Depression as regrettable, but necessary to put the country on a proper economic basis, chiefly by lowering the cost of labour. The Depression was just punishment for reckless governments which had borrowed too much. Adversity would provide the discipline which the people and politicians had refused to accept.[58] Belief in technocracy united those who represented capital and those who struggled to promote the interests of the working class.

Even the Australian Communist Party believed in strong, centralised, technocratic government. Only a socialist state, managed by experts, could usefully redirect those human energies which the capitalist world wasted on the class struggle. In a socialist society, humankind would unite in the war against the natural environment. Ever since Marx, the socialist left had regarded domination over nature as a necessary condition of the post-revolutionary utopia—a state in which material needs were universally satisfied and social harmony prevailed.

In the last years before World War II, Australian conservatives, struggling to impose order after the challenge of the Depression, expressed considerable sympathy for the firm authority asserted by the European fascist dictators. The Premier of Victoria applauded Mussolini as 'the man whom Providence wanted to lead Italy'. When Commonwealth Attorney-General Menzies visited Germany in 1938 he found there 'a good deal of really spiritual quality in the willingness of young Germans to devote themselves to the service and wellbeing of the State . . . an enthusiasm [which] could well be emulated in Australia.'[59] Australian working people, however, were less enthusiastic about fascist regimes. In the summer of 1938–39 members of the Waterside Workers Federation at Port Kembla, south of Sydney, refused to load pig-iron for Japan, claiming the Japanese would use the pig-iron to manufacture armaments for the war on China and, at a future date, on Australia. Menzies, for whom the prospect of war with fascist countries seemed very remote, coerced the men back to work.[60]

On 3 September 1939, Neville Chamberlain announced that

Britain was at war with Germany. Within minutes, Menzies, who had become Australian Prime Minister five months earlier, and whose loyalty to the British Empire exceeded all other commitments during his long life, added, 'as a result, Australia is also at war.' The country now followed Britain into the new war as unquestioningly as it had joined the rush to participate in the Great War. Volunteers enlisted into a second Australian Imperial Force (AIF), air squadrons trained in Canada to fight in Britain, and Australian ships came under the command of the Royal Navy. In early 1940, despite misgivings about future Japanese action in South-East Asia, Australia sent troops to fight in the Middle East and North Africa. At home the government moved to suppress dissent, entrusted the army with censorship powers, and interned German- and Italian-born residents and even a shipload of Jewish refugees. But Menzies, unable to suppress dissent in his own conservative coalition, proved incapable of governing, and in August 1941, resigned. A Labor government, with new priorities, took office in October. Prime Minister John Curtin immediately concentrated on securing an American commitment to armed intervention if Japanese forces moved south.[61] The United States refused to commit until Japan's attack on Pearl Harbor on 8 December ensured American military involvement in the Pacific. Three weeks later, Curtin declared:

> Without any inhibitions of any kind, I make it quite clear that Australia looks to America, free of any pangs as to our traditional links or kinship with the United Kingdom ... and [we] shall exert all our energies towards the shaping of a plan, with the United States as its keystone, which will give to our country some confidence of being able to hold out until the tide of battle swings against the enemy.[62]

By the end of January 1942, Japanese forces occupied Guam, Wake Island, Hong Kong, British North Borneo, Rabaul in New Guinea, the Celebes and Moluccas in the Netherlands East Indies, Burma and the entire Malay peninsula. In February the Japanese began a massive bombardment of Singapore and on the 15th the British commander surrendered. Four days later Japanese aircraft bombed Darwin and shortly thereafter also Broome, Wyndham and other places on the northern mainland. The government now sought desperately to identify Australian interests with those of America and insisted on the centrality of Australia to America's own defence. Curtin appealed to the United States for aid and argued for Australia's strategic significance:

> Australia is the last bastion between the West Coast of America and the Japanese. If Australia goes the Americas are wide open . . . I say to you that the saving of Australia is the saving of America's West Coast. If you believe to the contrary then you delude yourselves.[63]

Short of actually abandoning the region, the United States had no real alternative but to develop Australia as the major base for Allied operations in the Pacific. Australia's freedom and security, however, were only incidental to America's long-term strategic objectives and interests. Economic aid, for example, was made available under a plan designed to promote the interests of American business. Lend-lease provisions reflected the United States' highly articulated war aims and committed signatories to free trade so as to permit penetration and domination by corporate America.

The needs of war hugely increased American industrial output. America's economic planners realised that peacetime domestic demand alone would never match the newly created capacity of the American industrial machine. Only a permanent war economy coupled with domination of all overseas markets would be sufficient to sustain the monster United States economy. As the Australian minister in Washington, Frederic W. Eggleston, observed in 1944:

> . . . history is repeating itself. When Great Britain secured complete industrial supremacy she went into free trade and thereby assisted in clamping her economic empire over the world in the Nineteenth Century. America is [now] in the same position . . . and the same urge is showing itself. It cannot be sufficiently realised that in a situation where one power is immensely superior to all others economically, free trade is the short way to economic imperialism.[64]

In March 1942 United States General Douglas MacArthur flew to Australia to establish a base from which to organise and mount a counter-attack on the Japanese. By the middle of the year, over 80 000 American troops had reached Australia, and by the end of the war, over two million troops had passed through the country.

Australian politicians rationalised the subjugation of Australian forces under United States command as the temporary surrender of Australia's 'sovereignty to another nation in order that the sovereignty may ultimately be preserved,'[65] while Curtin remained 'confident that encroachment or penetration by the U.S. will be limited to that invited by Australia.'[66]

8

WORLD QUARRY

WE CAN MAKE THIS COUNTRY INTO A
QUARRY TO SERVE THE WHOLE WORLD.

Henry Bolte, Victorian Premier, 1955–72

WORLD WAR II obliterated subtlety. Only heavy industry, abetted by engineering and science, could guarantee victory. What counted was heavy power: bulldozers, steam rollers, monster guns, huge bombers and ultimately, the atomic bomb. Both the Allies and the Axis strove to conduct the war with maximum efficiency and thoroughly up-to-date methods of destruction. In Australia the lesson of the war (the efficacy of heavy power) was applied to the renewed attack on the land.[1]

Bulldozers, for example, came into use in 1946 for tree-clearing. Crawler tractors hauling large logs cleared scrub and mallee. At Gnowangerup, in Western Australia, one crawler tractor hauled a huge log, about 50 centimetres in diameter and 7 metres long, to flatten the bush. Later, contractors used the 'hi-ball', where two large bulldozers dragged a 5-tonne steel ball attached by ships' anchor chains, for pulling down trees up to 10 metres high. Such 'tree-crushing machines' were easily able to demolish 5.5 hectares an hour. In clearing war service farms in the Western Australian wheatbelt in the mid-1950s, one contractor, by working his tractor drivers in 12-hour shifts, was able to flatten 400 hectares in a 24-hour period.

But few Australians were content to limit their new-found power to attacks on the bush. Post-war military alliances, progress in science and technology, the grossly increased demands the expanding world economy made on the earth's resources, and the inflated ambitions of Australia's leaders greatly enlarged the possibilities for peacetime conquest and its corollary, destruction.

The federation of Britain's Australian colonies in 1901 had not led to Australian independence. The importation of British ideas, capital and arms, all of which inhibited the growth of an Australian nation and undermined sovereign decision making, continued. But World War II enfeebled Britain's global reach and Australia sought another hegemonic, Anglo-Saxon guardian. Australian receptiveness to foreign domination coincided with the rising assertiveness of the United States. During the war the United States began a foreign policy directed towards creating and maintaining an international order favourable to the prosperity of United States-based business.

To ensure perpetual American attention, successive Australian governments offered their country as an indispensable piece of real estate—militarily and economically—to the United States. In 1947 Australia signed the UKUSA agreement, which bound the intelligence services of the member countries—the United Kingdom, Canada, Australia, New Zealand and the United States of America—into the largest transnational bureaucracy in the world. Eventually more than 1000 defence and security treaties between the UKUSA countries regulated secret service and military cooperation. Service personnel professed loyalty, not to particular democratically elected governments but to the west, in effect, the United States. As the dominant partner in UKUSA—technologically, militarily and economically—the United States ensured that the arrangement served its own interests first.[2]

As an adjunct to anti-communism, and to provide long-term immunity against self-determination in the countries emerging from colonial domination, the United States promoted development—the exploitation of human and natural resources by American corporations. Instead of independence, the United States proposed modernisation: the rational management of resources, the application of science to mass production, and the transfer of the principles of scientific investigation to the study of human behaviour. American wisdom and technology would enable new nations to accomplish in years what had taken the advanced countries decades to achieve. Science and technology would remake the world.[3]

In emulation of the American example, post-war Australian governments began selling The Australian Way of Life—a mental and physical fortification against communism. Despite the vagueness, imprecision and general meaninglessness of the term, the image closely conformed to that of the American way of life, and sought to impose a vision of Australia as a sophisticated, urban, industrialised society. For manufacturers and real estate speculators the most important feature of the Australian Way of Life was its identification with consumerism and suburbanisation. In 1951 an Australian government publication defined the Australian Way of Life:

> What the Australian cherishes most is a home of his own, a garden where he can potter, and a motor car . . . as soon as he can buy a house and a garden he . . . moves to the suburbs. This accounts for the enormous size of Australian cities—and also for the overwhelming middle-class outlook and way of life.[4]

The reconstruction of Australia as a consumer society, however, demanded more people. The greatest single need for future development and national greatness, argued the influential men of Australia, was more Australians. In December 1943, when Australia's population numbered 7 million, Prime Minister Curtin told the nation that only a population of 20 million could guarantee Australian security; several months later he increased the number to 30 million. Politicians of both parties adopted William Hughes' old slogan: 'Populate or Perish'. Because natural increase alone could never suffice to populate the country in accordance with the ambitions of the country's leaders, they called for massive immigration. In 1946, the Minister for Immigration, Arthur Calwell, arranged with the British government to provide free passages to Britons who wanted to migrate. When the numbers proved insufficient, Calwell and his successors made similar agreements with the governments of Holland, Italy, Greece, Yugoslavia and other European countries. Subsequently, Australia's post-war population grew at a rate of 2 percent per annum, a doubling every 35 years, a growth rate similar to those obtaining in undeveloped countries. In 1955 Australia received the one millionth post-war immigrant. Between 1947 and 1980 Australia gained nearly three million new settlers, representing over 58 percent of post-war population growth.

Besides their use as consumers, migrants also provided the labour force for large-scale economic expansion. The government required many immigrants, particularly those from European refugee camps, to work on development projects during the first two years of their Australian residence. The most spectacular development occurred in the Snowy Mountains of eastern Australia.

In 1949 the Commonwealth government commissioned the Snowy Mountains Hydro-Electric Authority to begin, in the alpine border area of New South Wales and Victoria, one of the largest engineering enterprises in the world. The scheme, unfolding over an area of more than 5000 square kilometres, involved the construction of more than 150 kilometres of tunnels, eleven large and many smaller dams, four hydro-electric power stations and the diversion of 922 500 megalitres of water a year to inland areas for irrigation.

In straightening the rivers—making them run as they should—the Snowy Mountains Scheme represented the rational, methodical development of Australia's natural resources. The Hydro-Electric Authority mobilised vast numbers of men and huge amounts of money against the rivers of the Snowy Mountains to give them direction and purpose. Just as the Tennessee Valley Authority (TVA) project in the United States acquired cultural implications, so did the Snowy. In 1958, at the Tumut dam site, Prime Minister Robert Menzies, now in his second prime ministership, said:

> In a period in which we in Australia are still . . . handicapped . . . by a slight distrust of big ideas and big people or of big enterprise . . . this scheme is teaching us . . . to think in a big way, to be thankful for big things, to be proud of big enterprises and . . . to be thankful for big men.[5]

The scheme became a symbol of the possibilities of development, of the potential control Australians could exercise over nature, and contributed to the exuberant self-confidence of the post-war development ethos. Although academics questioned the economics of the scheme, the spectacle of conquest overrode mere economic considerations. Engineers proclaimed the coming of a technological utopia:

> . . . hydro-power schemes such as [the Snowy Mountains] are the near-

est approach to the impossible human ideal of perpetual motion. The dams and tunnels will last for hundreds of years. The power stations are automated and require very little staff. The water turbines are so efficient that it is almost impossible for their design to become obsolete, and only the few moving parts will need replacement. The electric generators operate without replacement for three or more decades. After building such a system the Australian people can sit back and watch the sun's solar energy do the job of generating the power by causing rainfall.[6]

Even otherwise critical Australians were not immune to the allure of conquest. George Johnston, a novelist who despaired of ever finding anything inspiring in Australia, found the vision of conquest a revelation. In *Clean Straw for Nothing* (1969), Johnston's alter ego visits the Snowy Mountains and finds inspiration in a

scheme that was designed to drill great tunnels through the rocky hearts of mountains and to reverse the courses of five rivers ... The yellow tractors against the glaring drifts of snow, the beards and mackinaws, the polyglot babble of smoke-hazed mess huts, the tingling atmosphere of a collective excitement ... 'It's like coming to an oasis in a desert, when you've been thirsting for something of promise, something to believe in. It's magnificent, darling! It's exciting! It's the only *visionary* thing I've seen since I've been back in this bloody country ... It's the most fabulous theme. It's got everything. *Everything!*'[7]

As men and machines set about the transformation of the Snowy Mountains, there arose in the press, academe, government bureaucracies and Federal Parliament, a clamour to develop the Australian north. Development experts gathered at a Canberra conference in 1954 agreed that the discoveries of uranium and oil in the northern third of the continent

made it more than ever necessary to have a population to defend the North ... Australia could not justify her retention of it unless she exploited to the full its mineral resources and its capacity for food production.[8]

As a corollary of the defence argument, conferees also postulated a moral basis for development: Australia had an international obligation to develop the continent's resources for all mankind. These generous sentiments co-existed comfortably with arguments for development which excluded that portion of humanity closest to Australia. As Governor-General Slim warned the delegates: 'if twelve hundred million pairs of [Asian] eyes looking hungrily for land see to the south of them a million square miles occupied by only 100 000 Australians, sooner or later they may not be content with looking.'[9]

Conference participants further agreed, in the words of Professor McDonald Holmes, that the north then constituted a vast 'no man's land', entirely empty. But, of course, the north was not empty.[10] As the last region of the continent to suffer the British invasion, large numbers of the original inhabitants had survived, retained many of the features of their traditional society and, by the 1930s, began increasing in numbers.

Although they still clung to the necessary myth of an empty continent, post-war European Australians realised they were going to have to live with Aborigines, and not only because Aborigines were not dying out. Prior to the war, Australian governments kept Aborigines segregated on remote reserves. But when valuable minerals began to be discovered on northern Aboriginal land, governments devised a new policy to dispossess Aborigines and to move them to the cities and townships, where they would be unable to interfere with the usurpers' plans. Previously, efforts at assimilation had been directed only at people of mixed Aboriginal/European descent; those of full Aboriginal descent had remained on the reserves. But in 1951, Paul Hasluck, Minister for Northern Development, redefined assimilation to include *all* persons of Aboriginal descent:

> Assimilation means, in practical terms that, in the course of time, it is expected that all persons of Aboriginal birth or mixed blood in Australia will live like white Australians do. We recognize now that the noble savage can benefit from measures taken to lead him in civilised ways of life.[11]

The alternative policy of leaving Aborigines alone, of letting them follow their own lives on their own (now highly valuable) land, would

> create a series of minority groups living on little bits of territory on

their own ... it would result in the very situation in Australia that we have always sought to avoid, namely the existence of a separate minority group living on its own.[12]

In 1957 the Queensland government officially adopted the policy of assimilation, and began the destruction of northern reserves a few months later when the state awarded Comalco (a consortium of Conzinc Rio Australia [CRA], a subsidiary of Rio Tinto Zinc [RTZ] of London, and British Aluminum, and later, the United States-based Kaiser Aluminum) mining rights for bauxite over 5800 square kilometres of land on the Aboriginal reserves of Weipa, Mapoon and Aurukun on Cape York Peninsula—the largest reserves of Aboriginal land in eastern Australia. Comalco obtained an 84-year lease over the area at royalties of five to ten cents a ton—the cheapest in the world. To remove the bauxite, Comalco planned to bulldoze 230 centimetres of topsoil, then rip out the six or so metres of ore-bearing clay from the land over hundreds of square kilometres.

The people of Mapoon lived much by the traditional ways. They hunted and fished and spoke their own language. They refused to make way for the miners. Mining, nonetheless, pushed on around their settlement. In November 1963, the state government, unable to tolerate Aboriginal independence, and under cover of night, sent in an armed party of police to arrest and evict the community and torch the settlement.[13]

Although Comalco claimed a policy 'which has Aboriginal advancement as its central aim,'[14] the company actually employed few Aborigines and these few in menial jobs which, the company claimed, required 'detailed and constant supervision'.[15] In contrast, to reward those leading Australians most sympathetic to the company's aspirations, Comalco later invited politicians, public servants and journalists to buy corporate shares at a nominal price. Victorian Premier Sir Henry Bolte, Western Australian Premier Sir David Brand and New South Wales Governor Sir Roden Cutler accepted. In Queensland, six cabinet members and the Premier's wife availed themselves of the special offer. Comalco, however, refused cash compensation to the Aborigines, claiming money was 'socially destructive' to Aboriginal communities. Money, however, acquired more constructive qualities once distributed among the foreign shareholders and managers of Kaiser and RTZ, who were the principal beneficiaries of Aboriginal dispossession and of the mutilation of hundreds of square kilometres of Cape York.[16] As a result of Mission and Queensland state government complicity, Comalco received Aboriginal land containing A$60 billion worth of bauxite, converted by 1980 into A$340 million net profit. Weipa became the biggest bauxite exporting port in the world.

At the end of World War II, Queensland's politicians and bureaucrats did not anticipate the prominent role mineral exploitation would come to occupy in the state's development. On the necessity of development, however, they harboured no doubts. In 1950, Queensland economist Colin Clarke estimated that Australia faced a military challenge within twenty years: 'If we do not quickly settle all the available land in Queensland to its fullest capacity, somebody will come and do it for us.'[17] The most influential men in Queensland believed that rural settlement was the best way to fill empty spaces. Accordingly, the state gave priority to the provision of rural infrastructure—roads, dams and irrigation schemes—which would encourage agriculture and pastoralism. Government devoted particular attention to the undeveloped fertile soils of the brigalow country.

Brigalow, the popular name given to woodland containing brigalow (*Acacia harpophylla*), a leguminous tree of the wattle family, belah (*Casuarina cristata*) and associated eucalyptus species, once dominated the 500- to 750-millimetres rainfall belt, stretching from northern New South Wales to northern Queensland, and probably covered 9.3 million hectares.[18] By 1953 approximately one-third of the area had been cleared, but with only partial success. Brigalow demonstrated an extraordinary tenacity to survive limb loss; regrowth was rapid and clearing proved very expensive. By 1960 the brigalow lands—home to a great number of birds, wallabies, kangaroos, echidnas and a host of other animals—still constituted the largest area of undeveloped forest country in moderate-rainfall Australia, a circumstance Queensland found intolerable. The government determined on eradication and offered farmers willing to clear brigalow land generous leases, loans and tax concessions. The financial incentives made possible the use of large D8 tractors dragging a ball and chain and capable of flattening ten to fourteen hectares of thick brigalow an hour. Clearing, in conjunction with the use of defoliants applied from aircraft, proceeded rapidly. Millions upon millions of hectares fell before the bulldozers; today only trivial amounts of brigalow forest remain standing.

The attitude towards the land which underlay the destruction of the Queensland brigalow predisposed politicians to viewing the state as a vast storehouse of riches and every feature upon the land as a potential quarry. Indeed, besides the massive bauxite deposits on Cape York Peninsula, Queensland contained uranium, mineral sands and immense deposits of coal. Foreign mining interests began investing in Queensland's mineral industry, particularly coal, in the mid-1960s, to provide cheap, high-quality fuel to Japanese steelmakers.

But perhaps the most attractive site for development lay on and under the Great Barrier Reef, the world's largest and oldest living structure. The Reef—actually not one, but a complex of more than 2500 reefs—began life around eighteen million years ago, and stretches for some 2300 kilometres from Torres Strait, between Papua New Guinea and Australia, continues parallel and close to the eastern shores of the Cape York Peninsula to gradually swing away from the Australian coast until latitude 21°, where the coral terminates at Swain Reefs, 280 kilometres out to sea from the Queensland coast. The seaward fringe, a jagged knife-edged mass of broken coral rocks pounded by Pacific breakers, falls away rapidly to deep waters, while the landward side forms sand-smoothed beaches fringing quiet lagoons, dotted with hundreds of islands. The conglomerate of drowned hills, coastlines, various coral formations, sea water and all the associated plants and animals of the Great Barrier Reef covers an area of 260 000 square kilometres.

Ever since European settlement in Queensland, there had been individuals who loved the Reef and disparaged development. They almost always acted alone, however, and their protests were ineffective. But in the 1960s, nature lovers banded together and formed organisations to campaign for the Reef's preservation. In 1963 a few dozen private citizens, alarmed at what developers and the state planned for the Reef, formed the Wildlife Preservation Society of Queensland and began agitating in favour of protection. They needed to act quickly to counter the many threats to the Reef's biological integrity.

By the mid-1960s, a flood of pollution from the rivers which flowed out to reef waters from the adjacent populated mainland—silt from deforested land, agricultural fertilisers, mining wastes, industrial discharges, cane mill wastes, garbage and sewerage—was smothering and killing the living coral. In 1967 a local contractor applied for a permit to mine Ellison Reef, off Innisfail, for lime to use as canefield fertiliser. Fearful lest the mine establish a precedent allowing commercial exploitation of the Reef, the Wildlife Preservation Society and other concerned groups lodged objections and thwarted the application. John Busst, president of the Innisfail branch of the Wildlife Preservation Society, summed up the attitude of the protesters: 'Anything, no matter how profitable for commerce that in any way destroys the Great Barrier Reef . . . is an act of vandalism.'[19] Busst's declaration ranks among the first public challenges to the Australian development ethos in the country's history. His appeal left the state's rulers unimpressed.

Politicians never doubted the primacy of exploitation, and by the late 1960s, government-granted oil exploration leases covered almost the entire Reef. The first off-shore drilling began in 1967. Companies holding leases included five of the seven largest oil companies in the world—Shell, Mobil, Socal, British Petroleum and Esso. International capital received significant Australian support. Most of the scientists who conducted research on the Reef, and mainstream conservation organisations, including the Australian Conservation Foundation (ACF), regarded utilisation of resources as an aspect of conservation. Development was inevitable, they argued. It required only scientific supervision. In 1967, scientists on the Great Barrier Reef Committee, an organisation devoted to scientific research, called for 'the formulation of an overall plan for the controlled exploitation of mineral resources on the Great Barrier Reefs.'[20] Busst, who championed no compromise in defence of the Reef, objected to the term 'controlled exploitation' and responded:

This I regard not as a scientific contribution to the argument but as a half-hearted sop to the exploiters, a not very courageous attempt to save some meagre portions of the whole reef from exploitation. I will have none of it ... The control of exploitation, once it has begun, exists only as a myth in the minds of those who advocate it.[21]

In early 1968, pollution from the wreck of the oil-tanker *Torrey Canyon*, off England's south coast, alerted people in Australia to the dangers of oil spills and undercut oil company assurances of the safety of oil exploration. Coincidentally, another conservation organisation, the Queensland Littoral Society, began campaigning in favour of conservation, and soon iridescent red bumper stickers with 'Save the Barrier Reef' embossed in black block letters appeared on cars throughout the state. In mid-1968 the Society presented a Save the Barrier Reef petition, containing over 10 000 signatures, to the Queensland Parliament. Premier Johannes Bjelke-Petersen ignored the public outcry.

By the end of January 1969, 40 groups of oil search companies had applied for exploration permits, an event a spokesman for the Queensland Mines Department described as 'history making.'[22] The Reef appeared about to share the fate of other Australian natural resources. But the catastrophic blow-out at Santa Barbara, California, the following month, further heightened awareness of the dangers of off-shore oil drilling, and when the government began granting exploration permits, citizens formed a 'Save the Barrier Reef Campaign Committee' to publicise their opposition around Australia. The federal government, as well as prominent Australians from the sciences, arts and academe, voiced disapproval of the Queensland actions. Sir John Barry, Chief Justice of the Supreme Court of Victoria, observed that if things kept going the way they were, Queensland would soon be just a huge quarry surrounded by an oil slick.[23] The prospect did not concern Queensland's rulers and in August 1969, the state government gave final approval to Japex, a Japanese oil exploration company, to begin drilling. The decision provoked a public furore. All over Australia, newspapers, radio and television ran articles and comment on the proposal. Five months later, as Japex's ship *Navigator* began approaching reef waters, unions representing transport workers, waterside workers, storemen and packers, announced a ban on all goods and services for the oil rig. A few days later Japex suspended the drilling operation. Bjelke-Petersen insisted the drilling proceed, but Prime Minister John Gorton pressed for a committee of inquiry. A Royal Commission commenced hearings late in 1970 but did not issue a recommendation for four years. In the meantime, oil companies suspended operations on the Reef.

As in Queensland, the borders of Western Australia enclose vast areas north of the Tropic of Capricorn, relatively unsettled by Anglo-Australians by the end of World War II. Unlike Queensland politicians, however, the leaders of Western Australia emerged from the experience of depression and war dissuaded of the view that agriculture alone was sufficient to sustain civilisation; only industrial development, based on the extraction and processing of raw materials, guaranteed true progress. Soon after the war, the state government began promoting large-scale mining and assisted the Colonial Sugar Refinery (CSR) in opening a blue asbestos mine at Wittenoom, in the north-west. The virtues of developing a remote area and populating the north silenced any doubts as to the likely economic viability of the industry.

Then, in the early 1950s, the state arranged for the first large-scale industrial development in Western Australia at Kwinana, south of Perth. The Anglo-Iranian Oil Company (later British Petroleum) built an oil refinery, another British firm undertook construction of a large cement works, and BHP built a steel rolling mill on Kwinana's coastal heathland, necessarily condemned by politicians as 'waste land'. The state's success at attracting transnational capital captured the imagination of even those politicians who claimed allegiance to the operations of the free market. Charles Court, Minister for Industrial Development in the conservative government of David Brand, elected in 1959, said:

> Capital will not come here of its own volition. We have to go out after it and convince them that we not only have some natural resources that are worth having but that we have the stability and determination to develop and exploit those resources.[24]

The existence of huge deposits of iron ore in the north had been known for some time. In 1889 the Western Australian Department of Mines noted that the Pilbara 'is essentially an iron country. There is enough to supply the whole world should the present sources be worked out.'[25] Until the 1960s, however, when the expanding Japanese economy and steel-making industry required massive supplies of raw material, no one wanted the ore. But with assured Japanese demand, transnational capital opened up major iron ore fields in the Pilbara[26] and began mining nickel, salt, mineral sands, bauxite, oil and gas elsewhere in the state. Thus the actual invasion of northern Australia came not by surprise but by invitation, the result of a combination of Japanese demand and Court's salesmanship.

The prospect of conquest, of exerting human dominion in regions hitherto inhabited only by Aborigines, pastoralists and sheep, overwhelmed any other consideration. The state, however, did not regard the creation of employment as a priority; on the contrary, development should be capital intensive, designed to make people obsolete. As Court explained in 1966: 'We must ask firms which approach us, not how many men can you employ but how few? How efficient can you be, how much can you mechanize and automate?'[27] Court's concerns to exclude labour from wealth-creation reflected the worldwide ambitions of transnational capital to eliminate as many wage workers as possible. The state and transnational corporations viewed labour as an expense. Some labour, of course, was essential, but highlighting the importance of labour—of the actual people who laid the railway tracks, drove the trucks, operated the mining machines, and constructed buildings and plant—interfered with the priorities of propaganda. The task of public relations was to emphasise the pre-eminent role of capital. In partnership with the state, transnational capital was building an empire, extending dominion over the earth and of some people over others. 'We are only at the beginning,' Court declared in 1968:

> We are a handful of people privileged to develop a great continent . . . In our north west and Kimberleys we have half a million square miles—an area as big as the whole of the Republic of South Africa . . . Just imagine if somebody said to you—'go and develop South Africa'

... To say the least, you would think that it was a fairly tall order. But this is the sort of thing we are trying to do.[28]

The state viewed the north as wild and uncivilised, and the region's Aborigines as invisible and irrelevant. The north, the politicians agreed, was a 'no man's land.' In an echo of the British view of early Australia, modern developers justified their designs for the north by picturing the region as a cultural wilderness, standing in need of redemption, of civilisation and of settlement. Only development and exploitation conferred these benefits. According to the state, exploitation led always to improvement, advance and progress, never to disadvantages or negative consequences. But since development enriched only a relatively few people (and most of those lived overseas), the state needed to justify exploitation on more than strictly material terms. Development was an intrinsic part of the civilising mission, Court claimed in 1969. 'A modern community stripped of minerals is virtually stripped of civilisation ...' Nations have 'an inescapable responsibility' to continue the legacy of the past and protect that of the future through development.[29]

The experts in Canberra in 1954 had argued that 'the development of Northern Australia requires above all an intense propaganda campaign.'[30] All Australian governments concerned with development agreed. In Western Australia, pro-development propaganda, generated by the Premier's department, revealed a preoccupation with size and numbers. Publicity brochures, videos, films and press releases always described ore deposits as vast—Premier Brand, for example, described iron ore as existing in 'uncounted cubic miles'. The statistics of development—so many million tonnes of ore extracted, requiring the construction of so many kilometres of roads and railways and the provision of so many ports and harbours—received constant reiteration. Pilbara trains could be up to a kilometre and a half long and each train hauled enough ore to make 13 000 Toyotas. The privately owned Hamersley track alone in 1975 carried more freight than the combined Victorian and New South Wales government railway system. But most of the lauded benefits of development, such as an increase in power supply and expansion of infrastructure, benefited the resource extraction industry, not people. The apologists of development never specified the exact nature of the benefits supposedly accruing to citizens. According to Court, the opening of mines, the export of minerals and the expansion of industry aimed at

> the full development of the dignity, the personality and true satisfaction of the individual within society. [The willingness to] unlock some of our natural resources and put them to work [released] substantial sums for things like a concert hall.[31]

Apart from the concert hall, most of the domestic benefits of development remained in the realm of an abstract, oblique political discourse. Politicians proved unable to connect development with the concrete, short term, immediate goals of identifiable living individuals. The opportunities resource development offered 'to our young people', for example, were never made clear. Instead, status and statistics became the only legitimate gauge of human worth. The successful integration of Western Australia as world quarry into the international capitalist economy became the necessary and sufficient justification for the massive invasion of the state by foreign capital. By 1981, proclaimed Peter Jones, the state Minister for Resources Development, Western Australia was the world's biggest exporter of iron ore, and in addition supplied 'one tonne in eight of the Western world's aluminum, one tonne in 12 of the world's nickel, and one tonne in five of the world's heavy mineral sands.'[32]

In previous decades Australian governments justified development, principally land development, as a means to an end (however imperfectly realised): to settle on the land a class of yeoman farmers who would build a nation of independent, self-sufficient families. But in the 1960s politicians abandoned all pretence to some higher goal. Development became a necessary good in and of itself; development required no further justification. The means had become the ends. Human life on the Australian continent aimed at nothing beyond economic development. Conquest lost any immediate rationale and became an end in itself.

Although the establishment of huge processing plants and the opening of vast mines captured most of the attention of Western

Australian politicians, the state did not entirely neglect land development. In 1956 the government invited an American syndicate, headed by Alan Chase, and including the entertainer Art Linkletter, to develop 600 000 hectares of land in the south, at Esperance. In exchange for clearing and capital improvement, the state promised freehold title to the syndicate, which in turn intended to sub-divide and sell off the land. Chase Associates, however, overestimated the area's potential and within a few years withdrew from the scheme. But the state, which now trusted corporate enterprise more than individual initiative, invited Chase back in 1960 and development began again. Nevertheless, the social goal of a stable, happy community, which the state and Chase claimed would accompany development, was never realised. Although sheep and cattle numbers increased in the area, speculation, frequent amalgamation, absentee ownership and high turnover of occupancy marked the human settlement of the area.

But Western Australia's showcase of agricultural development lay in the far north. In 1945 the CSIRO established a research station on the Ord River to investigate the area's agricultural and irrigation potential. Thereafter, politicians never missed a chance to denounce the waters of the Ord for running to waste in the sea. What was needed, they claimed, was a dam and a vast irrigation scheme. Although the state government never planned any particular use for the water once prevented from going to waste, the project's glamour suited electoral purposes. The construction of an irrigation scheme, regardless of what crops might or might not grow in the area, would constitute proof of northern conquest. Purpose could wait until after the dam was built. Only a dam could turn the waters to public good and private profit.

In 1968, the state awarded the Ord River Scheme's prime construction contract to Dravo Corporation of Pittsburgh. The contract described the dam as part of a flood control programme, although, since the government officially proclaimed the north empty, the Ord's annual flood never actually inconvenienced anyone. The Commonwealth government, which provided the $100 million necessary for construction, predicted the scheme 'will, in the long run, contribute far more to the development of northern Australia than any of the major mineral developments.'[33]

When the main Ord dam, which held back Lake Argyle—at 725 square kilometres, Australia's largest reservoir—opened in 1972 the state recommended farmers grow cotton. But severe caterpillar infestations killed most of the crop. Attempts at cultivating sorghum, rice and other tropical products, all aided with subsidies, tax concessions and massive amounts of insecticide, proved equally unsuccessful. By the end of the decade farmers had largely abandoned the Ord. Water sat unused in the artificial reservoir of Lake Argyle, a giant fishing and breeding ground for myriads of Asian water birds, DDT-resistant insects, and disease-carrying mosquitoes. A Commonwealth review of the Ord Scheme in 1979 concluded, 'In terms of contributing to net increase in national output, the project has been of no benefit.'[34] Finally, even the state government accepted the economic futility of the scheme, and in 1985 the Premier pronounced the project unviable.[35]

The outcome of one of the greatest scientific achievements of the twentieth century—the splitting of the atom—was the more efficient killing of people. The conquest of nature had resulted in a frightful new means for the exercise of domination in human affairs. As they began constructing their post-war political and economic order, the leaders of the United States kept their monopoly on the science of nuclear explosions. The United Kingdom, denied access to these atomic secrets, but convinced that possession of the bomb provided the best means of retaining international authority, decided to build and test its own bomb. The British Foreign Secretary, Ernest Bevin, said that without nuclear weapons to support his arguments, he felt he would be going naked into the negotiating chamber. The Australian Prime Minister, Robert Menzies, anxious lest Britain suffer embarrassment, unhesitatingly offered Australia as a test site.

To simulate a nuclear attack on a coastal city (the site of Britain's major cities), Britain decided to explode a bomb among the Montebello Islands off the north-west coast of Western Australia. Britain exploded the first bomb there in 1952 and followed with two more in 1956. Meanwhile, British reconnaissance parties searched Australia for a suitable inland site and settled first on Emu Field, in the South Australian desert, where they exploded two bombs in 1953, then moved to the nearby but less remote site of Maralinga. The construction here of a permanent British atomic bomb testing site received enthusiastic government support. Howard Beale, the Minister for Supply, described Maralinga as

> a challenge to Australian men to show that the pioneering spirit of their forefathers who developed our country is still the driving force of achievement . . . [Together with Britain] we shall build the defence of the free world, and make historic advances in harnessing the forces of nature.[36]

In the course of conquering nature, Britain detonated seven bombs at Maralinga. Throughout the tests, Australian newspapers carried exuberant reports of the activities and applauded every explosion with undisguised glee. The Melbourne *Argus*, of 27 September 1956, headlined its story 'Bombs Away!' and continued:

> The atom bomb's gone up at last . . . Minutes after the explosion, Government members cheered and Labor MPs shouted: 'Thank goodness,' and 'At last, at last,' as Mr Beale, Supply Minister, announced in the House of Representatives the test had been successful . . . As the [radioactive] cloud faded, convoys of trucks and jeeps brought back the servicemen who'd faced the blast at close range. AND EVERY FACE WORE A SMILE [original emphasis]. They could have been coming back from a picnic.[37]

The smiles faded in later years. Although the British military issued the usual bland assurances about the absolute safety of the tests, radioactive contamination spread over wide areas of Australia. In the vicinity of the Maralinga and Emu Field tests, hundreds of nomadic Aborigines, oblivious to the English language warning signs, walked through the blast area. Many died within a few hours or weeks, others became blind and many, many more contracted cancer. Some had camped in the bomb craters and servicemen later reported finding the bodies of Aborigines lying in one crater. In addition, dozens of servicemen, sent into the area immediately after the blasts, suffered in later years from abnormal cancers. Although Britain exploded the last bomb at Maralinga in 1957, tests involving minor explosions and the burning of quantities of highly toxic plutonium continued until 1963. These tests rendered the sites permanently contaminated and today they remain fenced off and guarded. Britain, with the connivance of the Australian government, had, for the sake of sartorial respectability at the negotiating table, put the lives of thousands of Australians at risk.[38]

Although few people in Australia protested at the time, people elsewhere, especially in Britain, began campaigning for nuclear test bans, marched in 'Ban the Bomb' demonstrations and participated in other forms of protest. As dissension spread, the United States became anxious to demonstrate and propagandise the peaceful use of nuclear energy. Besides nuclear power stations, the American Atomic Energy Commission (AEC) pressed for the engineering use of atomic bombs. In 1958 the AEC announced the inauguration of 'Project Plowshares', an attempt to transform the nuclear sword into a peacetime tool by using thermonuclear bombs to excavate harbours, canals and mountain passes, to extract petroleum from low-grade deposits, and fracture ore bodies to facilitate mining. Edward Teller, a Commission physicist, dreamed of engaging in the 'great art of geographical engineering, to reshape the earth to your pleasure'—with nuclear explosives. But the AEC's first project, Project Chariot, planned as a prelude to a new sea-level Panama Canal, and designed to create an instant harbour on the coast of Alaska, was thwarted by protests from the Innuit and young environmentalists.[39]

Teller and the AEC did not abandon their nuclear dreams, however, and sought opportunities elsewhere. In 1967, an Australian member of parliament suggested, at Teller's urging, the use of nuclear explosives to clear channels through the Great Barrier Reef and Torres Strait, where the shallow, coral-strewn waterways block entrance to supertankers. Unfortunately for commerce, but fortunately for the Reef, the idea attracted only limited support. But two years later, American-owned Sentinel Mining, faced with the problem of creating an instant harbour at Cape Karaudren on the northwest coast of Australia, from where it planned to export iron ore, enlisted the AEC's help. Nuclear scientists suggested burying five

200-kiloton nuclear bombs in a row, spaced 330 metres apart. Simultaneous detonation would blow out a ditch over a mile long, with the earth heaped high on the sides. A month later, however, because of the low-grade nature of their ore deposit, Sentinel Mining decided to forgo mining in the area. The United States had hoped the harbour project would provide a demonstration of the peaceful use of atomic bombs and a technological rehearsal for digging a canal across the Central American isthmus.[40] Such giant, earth-remaking projects became an intrinsic part of the United States' post-war Imperial policies.

In the late 1940s the United States began supporting France's effort to reconquer its Indochina colonies—occupied during the war by the Japanese army, and subsequently taken over by indigenous nationalist groups. Following France's military defeat by the Viet Minh, and facing political defeat itself, the United States overturned a settlement arranged in Geneva in 1954. Unable to prevail politically, the Americans shifted the struggle from the political to the military arena. In this province of violence, the United States and its terrorist client regime in South Vietnam, maintained an unchallenged supremacy.

In 1964 Australia sent military advisors to Vietnam and introduced military conscription. When, in early 1965, the United States commenced an outright invasion of Indochina, with massive deployment of American combat troops, regular bombing of North Vietnam and unrestricted bombing of South Vietnam, Australia was ready. In April, Prime Minister Menzies, who, during the Great War had elected not to serve in the army because, as he reflected in a poem, his own life was too valuable to be used for cannon-fodder,[41] announced his decision to commit Australian troops to the war.

The next year a new Prime Minister, Harold Holt, increased Australia's military commitment, including the use of conscripts. Later in 1966 Holt visited Washington, where at a state dinner he promised President Johnson that Australia would go 'all the way with L.B.J.' and invited him to visit. When Johnson came, huge crowds turned out. But not all were welcoming. Thousands of anti-war demonstrators jeered the cavalcade in Sydney and Melbourne. Protestors splattered his car with red paint and lay down in the road to block his procession. The Premier of New South Wales, Robin Askin, ordered his chauffeur to 'drive over the bastards!'

The nation's newspapers, business leaders, the academic elite and most politicians supported the war and argued in favour of the nobility of United States war aims. The United States, they told Australians, was making a selfless sacrifice in the service of generous ideals. Their goal was to defend South Vietnam from aggression and terrorism in the interests of democracy and self-determination. Proponents of the war argued that Australia's commitment was a vital aspect of Australian–American friendship. But unions, sections of the Labor Party, students and others who participated in the Moratorium Movement, marches, teach-ins and sit-ins, questioned the very righteousness of the United States cause. Opponents maintained that the invasion served only to defend the right of the United States to impose its will by violence. Australia's contribution amounted to a defence of the American Empire. Australia's leaders, however, entertained none of these doubts. In 1969, when Holt's successor, John Gorton, journeyed to Washington, he told President Nixon that Australia was prepared to 'go a-Waltzing Matilda' with the United States.

Gorton's proclamation was consistent with post-war Australian governments' invariable policy of placating United States government opinion. One day, a grateful United States might protect Australia from a possible Asian invasion. But Australia's unstinting efforts to demonstrate its faithfulness have never secured any reciprocal commitment from the United States.

Political subservience reflected Australia's economic subordination. Willingness to commit the country to the needs of foreign heads corresponded to the belief that Australian resources—land, minerals, forests, rivers and wildlife—existed only for the time when developers, preferably foreign, demanded them. Australia's leaders repeatedly expressed their allegiance, not to the land, not to the country of their birth, but to overseas imperial interests. Robert Menzies, for example, upon his retirement in 1966 after sixteen years as Australian Prime Minister, described himself as 'British to my boot-heels.'

Menzies' profession of Imperial loyalty was not unique. Throughout Australia's history politicians have identified Australian development with the interests of overseas empires. State intervention in economic life largely meant intervention for the purpose of helping foreign capitalists; the most important function of the state has been to provide a constantly expanding resource base upon which private enterprise can build.

To complement attempts to integrate Australia into the United States global strategic network, the federal government, from 1949–72, opened Australia to virtually unrestricted foreign investment, increasingly American. With remarkable speed, American interests during the 1950s entered the most influential sectors of the economy. American advertising firms like J. Walter Thompson persuaded Australians that every home needed cars, washing machines, refrigerators, telephones and television sets. In 1963, for the first time, American investment in Australia exceeded British investment. Foreign control (chiefly American) of the mineral sector increased from 37 percent in 1963 to 59 percent in 1975, and in manufacturing industry, from 24 percent in 1963 to 34 percent in 1973. By 1971 Australia had become the fourth largest recipient of American capital in the world and hosted some 500 subsidiaries of American companies. American investment had accounted for nearly 60 percent of the total inflow since 1948. Indeed, the prosperity Australia enjoyed during the 1950s and 1960s depended on the nation's capacity to import capital and to export resources to the expanding world capitalist economy.

Ever since the nineteenth-century Land Acts, Australian governments promoted clearing the forest for settlement. But after the bulldozed extinction of the Queensland brigalow, Australian state forest services—charged with conservation—replaced agriculture as the main destroyers of the continent's remaining natural forests.[42]

In the 1960s South Korea and Japan enriched themselves through their participation in the destruction of Indochina. War demands stimulated the Japanese economy and led to a huge growth in Japanese exports. To satisfy the needs of their burgeoning pulp and paper and packaging industry, Japanese corporations approached Australian states about acquiring Australian eucalyptus fibre in the form of woodchips—produced by chipping the timber obtained from large clear-cuts. Since states competed to offer their forests for exploitation, the forests of Australia became, for the Japanese, a very cheap resource. To Australian forest services, who viewed forests as essentially, and most importantly, cellulose producers, woodchipping promised maximum wood production. Foresters welcomed the opportunity to convert Australia's unproductive forests into productive ones. A. C. Harris, Conservator of Forests in Western Australia (later President of the Australian Institute of Foresters), said of woodchipping in 1968, 'through the medium of this industry we can see ourselves realizing the dream of all foresters—complete utilization.'[43] By the early 1970s, plans for woodchipping covered one-quarter of Australia's total real forest area and one half of all the publicly owned coastal forests.[44] The application of the total-use doctrine demonstrated that Australian forest services were actually opposed to forest preservation.

Australian forests depend on a constant cycling of nutrients between the trees and the soil. Cycling allows a large forest biomass to develop on inherently poor soils. Tree removal, however, terminates cycling and a new forest must depend entirely on remaining soil nutrient reserves. The disruption is especially catastrophic in the case of clearfelling. Total destruction prevents regeneration of native bush and leads to erosion and a massive loss of biological diversity. Woodchip projects destroyed wilderness, consumed large areas of bushland—usually 200 000 to 400 000 hectares or more— and attacked substantial areas of land previously untouched because of unsuitability for farming or sawnwood logging. Blinded by their commitment to the utilitarian notion of total use, foresters minimised the fact or even denied that woodchipping produced environmental penalties. On the contrary, they maintained, intensive wood production actually benefited wildlife, augmented soils, enhanced watershed protection and supplemented aesthetic values; woodchipping only improved the environment.

In every state, forest services operated their woodchip projects on the principle of socialising the losses while keeping the profitable parts firmly in a few private hands. While the revenue from woodchips generated a good return on investment for the Japanese—especially because the price they paid for chips equalled that for firewood and was far lower than that paid for sawnlogs— few Australians benefited. Woodchip royalties were so trivial they did not even cover the cost of regeneration. The states not only gave the forests away but, by providing roads and wharfs, actually paid for foreign companies to take them away.

When Australians began protesting the destruction and selling off of native forests, foresters urged the forest industry to join with them to save the forests from conservation. Public dissatisfaction and disquiet about intensive forestry, foresters argued, resulted from misunderstanding and ignorance of forestry operations, easily dispelled by a proper education campaign:

> We must improve our public relations and explain to the public, who are also deeply concerned, what we are doing, why we are doing it . . . [We must] recognize public concern and public misunderstanding and overcome it by properly informing the public of our methods and the reasons behind our planning.[45]

Thus sensitivity to public opinion did not take the form of sensitivity to actual wishes. Foresters saw the solution to conflict in propaganda, rather than in reform of destructive forestry practices. Accordingly, forest services began presenting woodchip devastation as 'apparent devastation'. The Victorian Forests Commission, for example, described clearcutting as 'the full sunlight method of regeneration.'[46] Foresters denigrated old forests as 'decadent and damaged', stagnant, and so full of ugly, defective old trees, as to form a 'standing cemetery'. Nature cannot be left unmanaged, the foresters explained; forest destruction actually produced a better forest, and '. . . only through the periodic stimulation of forest use [can a forest be] maintained in a dynamic and healthy state.'[47]

Woodchip plans for New South Wales sprawled over the Eden forests, the wildest and least spoilt coastal area in south-eastern Australia. A large range of animals—five species of gliders, pygmy

possums, tree-dwelling bats, the tiger quoll and the tuan—
depended upon and complemented the forest ecosystem. Resident
birds included owls, nightjars, cockatoos, parrots, kookaburras and
kingfishers. Although woodchipping eradicated vast areas of habitat, forestry experts could imagine: 'On past experience it is likely
that the resulting increased silvicultural operations [clear-cutting]
will result in a build-up of the native animal population.'[48]

In 1973 the Western Australian government announced the
Manjimup woodchip scheme, covering 485 000 hectares of forest,
more than a quarter of the state's remaining forest area. The state
forestry department claimed that long periods of selective logging
had run down the forests; their total destruction, through
woodchipping, would lead to their rejuvenation. Woodchipping,
explained the foresters, was 'essential for . . . maximization of the
future product resource.'[49]

Even without the lure of Japanese woodchip contracts, Australian
forest services proved efficient at destroying Australian forests.
During the early 1960s the Australian Forestry Council advocated
the planting of vast plantations of exotic conifers. In 1966 the
Commonwealth government inaugurated a scheme to provide
long-term loans to the states to encourage coniferous forest plantations. The plan called for the razing of existing natural woodlands
and forests to make way for monocultural plantations of *Pinus
radiata*, *Pinus elliottii* and *Pinus caribaea*. The states agreed to plant
1.2 million hectares of coniferous exotics by the year 2000. Foresters justified the eradication of native forests as 'a positive contribution to man's search for a better environment.'[50] Forester
M. R. Jacobs cited historical precedent in support of the project.
Australians had long endeavoured, he said, 'to make the Australian
forest resource better suited to European civilisation.' Since 'European type industries need at least 50 percent of coniferous wood,'
native trees—almost entirely non-coniferous—would have to give
way to superior foreign species.[51]

In destroying the forests for monoculture, the forest services also
destroyed the many birds and animals which depend crucially on
the eucalypt environment. In New South Wales, for example, the

planting programme aimed to eliminate practically all wet mountain sclerophyll forests of the southern or cooler type, between altitude ranges of 600 and 1200 metres. These montane tracts contained a rich variety of fauna, including several species of gliders, possums, koalas, wombats, lyre birds, kangaroos, wallabies, platypus, the native cat and tiger cat.

Undaunted by the loss of biological diversity, and responsive only to wood production as the ultimate aesthetic value, Australian forest services celebrated the planting of the millionth acre in exotics in 1970. Foresters failed to note that also by 1970, 80 to 90 percent of Australian forests had been clearfelled or so thinned as to entirely change their nature; an equivalent percentage of indigenous woodlands had been similarly affected. Additionally, clearing, cultivation and grazing had resulted in radical modification of 50 to 90 percent of the areas of mixed grassland, woodland and shrubland combined.[52]

Unlike mainland Australia, Tasmania, the smallest state, enjoys a high average rainfall, and the mountainous, forested west contains many lakes and fast-flowing rivers. The region had long attracted bushwalkers and dam builders. Bushwalkers began journeying through the south-west after the Great War. Walking for pleasure, independent of any formal objective, they viewed the region differently from the dam builders. As more and more people scrambled through the bush, climbed the mountains and forded the streams, they came away impressed by the beauty of the region and especially of the remote, unique, alpine Lake Pedder.[53] The lake's whisky-brown-coloured water, encircled by an unusual beach of shimmering, pink-tinted quartz sand, mirrored surrounding mountains. Lake and shore regions supported a higher degree of endemicity than any other Australian lake. In 1955 bushwalkers and climbers convinced the government to declare Lake Pedder a scenic reserve. Five years later the Tasmanian Hydro-Electric Commission (HEC) began investigating possible hydro-development in the area. In 1962, bushwalkers, conservationists and naturalists formed the South West Committee to lobby for a rational land use plan for the south-west. But in 1963 the HEC built a 100-kilometre road from Maydena to a potential dam site on the Middle Gordon, just below

Lake Pedder. Premier Gordon Reece dismissed public concern over what damage the road might do to scenery as 'a matter of opinion.' His own opinion was unequivocal: 'Our engineers have changed contours, with the aesthetic achievement of landscape gardeners.' Contrary opinions were inadmissible and Reece accused the South West Committee, which advocated habitat protection, of interfering in public affairs.

Meanwhile, the HEC began making secret plans to build a dam and hydro-electric power station on the Middle Gordon and flood Lake Pedder. Early in 1967 conservationists exposed the HEC plans and formed a more militant organisation. The Save Lake Pedder Committee began a campaign to enlist the aid of mainland and overseas conservationists. The government then appointed a committee, composed of engineers and HEC representatives, to consider the future development of the south-west. The committee, which viewed the matter purely as one of resource management, recommended the flooding of Lake Pedder. The government immediately revoked the area's scenic reserve status; the HEC claimed the new reservoir, which would flood Lake Pedder to a depth of fifteen metres, would far exceed the old lake in beauty. A huge outpouring of protest followed and split Tasmanian society between development and anti-development factions.

Conservationists formed a political party, the United Tasmania Group (UTG), to contest the 1972 state elections. The two main parties (Liberal and Labor), however, united on the need to narrow political debate and refused representation in the public forum to any people critical of development. A strong political motive now existed to drown Lake Pedder. The politicians who clamoured for the lake's destruction allowed the HEC to intercede in the political process and to use public money to campaign against the UTG. HEC bureaucrats and engineers had been educated to believe that the world was a set of problems awaiting technically refined solutions. They warned voters that the conservationists' proposals were irresponsible and would lead to higher electricity charges. The HEC's plans for major modifications of the wild valleys, rivers and lakes of Tasmania, on the other hand, were justifiable costs of a higher standard of living; a generous supply of cheap power would do for Tasmania what oil had done for the sheikdoms of the Middle East. Despite the propaganda against them, the UTG missed winning a seat by just 150 votes. But dam construction continued and in 1974 the rising waters of the new reservoir drowned Lake Pedder. UNESCO described the inundation as 'the greatest ecological tragedy since European settlement in Tasmania.'

Change brings absolute losses as well as gains. Some forms of valuable experience may vanish forever, irreplaceable by similar forms of equal value. As technology advances, a world of artificial structures replaces the world of complex structures given in nature, and people no longer live in anything remotely resembling a natural setting. During the struggle for Lake Pedder, Australians began to appreciate the ways development deprived them. Opposition to destruction mounted. Tens of thousands of Australians deeply regretted the destruction of Lake Pedder and determined that such a catastrophe would not happen again.

Nature lovers fought an equally protracted, but ultimately successful battle in Victoria. The wheat farmers who invaded the mallee country along the South Australia/Victoria border early in the century settled around, but had never actually occupied, an area known as the Little Desert. The varied soils of the Little Desert's 120 000 hectares supported an extensive cover of yellow gum forest, mallee broombrush and open heaths, a mixed habitat for a wide range of wildlife. In the early 1950s local authorities and farming associations, unable to co-exist with an undeveloped area, began to pressure the state to develop the Little Desert for agriculture. In 1957 the Victorian Department of Agriculture opened up eleven new farms in the area. But, for the first time in Australian history, bush destruction faced organised opposition. A few individuals and local groups began arguing for the preservation of areas within the Little Desert for the protection of native flora and fauna and the maintenance of soil and water resources. The state government ignored the agitation. Premier Bolte believed life was a jungle, a constant war against nature, a struggle, moreover, which uplifted the people involved: 'Fire, flood, tempest, drought, pestilence, and other things mould one's character.'[54] In 1963 the Australian Mutual Provident Society (AMP), an insurance and development company, approached the government with a scheme to develop a third of the Little Desert as a new farming region. Bushwalkers, nature groups, apiarists and ornithologists again asked, in vain, that the government declare at least some of the area a nature reserve. The protestors kept their demands moderate; most people accepted the need for at least some development. A few years later the government made the AMP responsible for access roads; with the loss of a guaranteed state subsidy the company abandoned the project.

In 1967 new Minister of Lands, Sir William J. F. McDonald, brought fresh resolve to the issue. 'In this day and age,' he stated, 'the country could not afford not to develop land.'[55] He offered a simple choice for the Little Desert: development by the government or by private bodies. Despite negative departmental evaluations of the area's agricultural potential, McDonald pressed ahead, and in 1969 introduced legislation providing for the sub-division of the Little Desert. His unabashed pro-developmentalism only served to increase the determination of the opposition. McDonald's electorate stretched over parts of the Little Desert and local conservationists, including his neighbours, started organising against him. In Melbourne, eco-activists[56] formed the Save Our Bushlands Action Committee (SOBAC) and began questioning the very basis of the development ideology. A. G. Lloyd, of the University of Melbourne's Faculty of Agriculture, pointed out:

> From the idea that hard work is an end in itself, having divine approval, it is a small step to regard the holding of unused resources such as virgin land as being wasteful, perhaps even a little sinful. To justify possession, such land should be 'developed'.[57]

Protesters now rejected all settlement plans for the Little Desert and demanded complete preservation. In 1970, after the loss of a seat in a by-election over the issue of the environment, a government committee recommended the abandonment of the scheme and the declaration of the entire area as a protected reserve. In the following state election, McDonald was the only government minister to lose his seat.

In response to the Little Desert controversy, the government appointed a nominally independent body of experts—the Land Conservation Council (LCC)—to take responsibility for land use decisions and to defuse conservation issues. In future the LCC would function to remove the government from areas of controversy, to promote traditional exploitative activities and to protect the interests of timber concerns, mining companies, skiing concessions and grazing rights.[58] Nonetheless, the final resolution of the Little Desert conflict, in favour of conservation, marked the first time in Australia's history when, in a direct confrontation between developers and nature lovers, the latter prevailed.

By the end of the 1960s personal experience had acquainted Australians with their deteriorating surroundings and with the environmentally degrading consequences of development. The level of air pollution in Sydney, for instance, ranked among the worst in the world. Town planning duplicated the failures apparent in nineteenth-century land legislation; zoning laws failed to prevent land speculation, and, in a culture committed to speculation and monopoly, property owners consistently manipulated the planning process for private profit. Groups who profited from property objected to controls over sub-division.

The long post-war boom corresponded with a massive shift to a car-based system of transport and living. Motor manufacturing, servicing and fuel industries became the country's major industrial complex. Those who planned the growth of Australian cities assumed—for self-interested and ideological reasons—the inevitability of a motorised society. Speculation and complacency resulted in a vast expansion of single-house suburban living. Automobiles demanded highways and roads, which in turn encouraged further suburbanisation. Sub-dividers bulldozed the land flat, eliminating every tree, every bush. The new occupiers planted exotics in place of the natives and few doubted that what they had contrived was superior to what had been destroyed. Suburbanisation necessitated a more expensive way of life than people had known in modest urban apartments. The suburbs, developed at minimum cost to private builders or housing commissions, lacked community services and facilities. The cost of cars, washing machines, vacuum cleaners, television sets and refrigerators went into household budgets and onto hire-purchase bills. Television told people what they needed and buying became a way of life. Towns became smothered in advertising and consumer culture began to crowd out all other cultural possibilities. Commercial, industrial and mixed-use buildings spread along main highways—factories, junkyards, shops, houses, used-car lots, service stations and take-away food outlets— and noise, fumes, dirt and visual ugliness intruded on a vast scale.

In the late 1960s Australian cities began formally planning for roads. In 1968, Adelaide's Highway Department compiled the Metropolitan Adelaide Transportation Study (MATS). The planning committee, mostly engineers who regarded environmental impact as a peripheral matter, called for a massive expansion of highways and 125 kilometres of freeway. Those with a vested interest in the automobile industry, or who stood to gain from increased road expenditures, supported the plan. People whose houses and lives stood in the way of redevelopment, as well as people who disliked the aesthetics of freeways, opposed it. Sir Arthur Rymill, chairman of the Bank of Adelaide, and a large rural and urban property owner, argued that the MATS plan expressed

> the attitude that no one counted except the traffic engineer . . . sweeping geometrical curves have been drawn over the plans of the metropolitan area and no part of the plan has sought to avoid things that might be in the way of these geometrical curves.[59]

Meanwhile, in Melbourne, the Metropolitan Transportation Plan (MTP) called for 568 kilometres of metropolitan freeways. As in Adelaide, engineers, automobile clubs and contractors supported the proposals; community groups in the affected areas opposed the plans. By 1972, 93 kilometres of freeway had been built in accordance with the MTP, but in the following year, under public pressure, the government announced cuts to the original plan amounting to 278 kilometres. The opposition's success reflected increasing public opposition to freeways, high-rise public housing, terrace demolition, overbuilding of the central business district and environmental pollution. Throughout Australia's sprawling cities, as neighbourhoods came under threat from expressways and redevelopment, residents began to feel that cities were growing too fast, becoming too large, too congested, too dependent on the automobile, and that houses were becoming too expensive. By 1970 Sydney, for example, covered 1300 square kilometres—a city one-third the population of London covered an equal area.

In December 1970 the Town Council of Hunters Hill, an upper-class Sydney suburb, voted to allow the A. V. Jennings Company to build in an area known as Kelly's Bush—three hectares of the last patch of native bushland on the Parramatta River. Three local women—Kath Lehany, Betty James and Chris Dawson—formed a committee, Battlers for Kelly's Bush, to oppose the plans to raze the bush, mounted protests and called public meetings. Citizens resolved to ask the Builders Labourers' Federation (BLF) to with-hold their labour from any construction on the site. During the late 1960s the BLF had acquired a reputation for militancy in pushing claims for better wages and improved safety conditions on building sites. The union also endorsed the radical notion of social responsi-bility. Union accountability was described by secretary Jack Mundey, as part of a movement in which 'a growing number of workers are demanding a greater say, a greater control over their working lives, and are insisting that the work performed should be socially beneficial to the community as a whole'.[60] The BLF banned work at Kelly's Bush and extended their protest to other Jennings company projects. Thousands of people throughout Aus-tralia joined in a campaign in support of the Battlers and the BLF. Author Kylie Tennant summed up the significance of the struggle:

> Kelly's Bush is a symbol of our lost land. Take away Kelly's Bush and you take away more assurance that in man is left a possibility for the future. The unborn Australian will ask for his birthright and be handed a piece of concrete.[61]

Jennings, conceding the pressure, agreed to swap Kelly's Bush for another piece of land suitable for development but the state government refused to allow the company to compromise. Politi-cians did not want local groups and working people deciding on matters concerning the environment in which they lived. The ban, however, remains in place and negotiations over Kelly's Bush continue to the present day.

Originally, the term 'black ban' described workers' refusal to handle materials deemed unsafe or perform work contrary to their interests, either immediate or political. 'Green ban' seemed more appropriate to describe actions on behalf of the environment—'an environment to live in instead of a concrete and glass jungle.'[62] The idea and the term quickly spread from Kelly's Bush.

Undeterred by official hostility, other Resident Action Groups (RAGS) approached the BLF for assistance in opposing destructive development. In response, the BLF imposed green bans on a state government plan to excavate a car park for the Sydney Opera House under the adjacent Botanical Gardens, and on a plan to build a sports complex in Centennial Park, the largest non-foreshore park in Sydney. Opposition from residents and the BLF thwarted both plans. Residents and the BLF also joined together to stop freeway development through inner city areas and the redevelopment plans of private developers. In Woolloomooloo, developer Frank Theeman planned to turn Victoria Street, an old mixed neighbourhood, into two massive 45-storey tower blocks. With the support of the BLF, residents squatted in buildings marked for demolition and defied mysterious fires and police raids. The green ban cost Theeman millions of dollars in interest payments and eventually he agreed to a compromise which kept most of the street intact.

Perhaps the most famous and most symbolic confrontation occurred in the inner city area known as The Rocks, the oldest European-inhabited part of Australia, containing some of Australia's oldest buildings, and housing residents whose families had lived in the area for generations. The state-appointed Sydney Cove Redevelopment Authority (SCRA), under the directorship of Colonel Owen Magee, who had overseen the construction of the Snowy Mountains Scheme, controlled 21 hectares of The Rocks. SCRA planned a massive redevelopment for the area: erection of high-rises, shops and commercial establishments. Plans called for extensive demolition and excluded any participation by local residents, who no longer endorsed every piece of construction as a sign of progress. Long-term Rocks resident and organiser, Nita McRae, together with other residents, formed a Resident Action Group and asked the BLF for help. Unprepared to compromise, or negotiate on any terms other than its own, SCRA sent in non-union labour to demolish buildings and recruited the police against defiant occupiers. BLF members helped residents form human barricades against evictions and demolitions. In the face of widespread support for the green ban, SCRA agreed to discuss development plans with the people affected. But in the intervening years the development authority has continued to encroach on The Rocks and to construct high-rises.

All over Sydney, building workers and residents claimed moral rights against the legal rights and privileges enjoyed by developers. Within three years of the first green ban, the BLF in conjunction with local groups had imposed 50 bans covering $4 billion worth of construction. Green bans spread across Australia and helped save the old Palace Hotel in Perth and prevented urban sprawl into the Adelaide Hills in South Australia. Building workers also placed bans on demolition and construction in Melbourne and Hobart.

In 1974 the New South Wales Builders Association successfully moved for the deregistration of the New South Wales BLF. The federal building workers' union immediately took over the local body, ended green bans and expelled those members most prominent in the struggle.

The citizen environmental revolt alarmed Australian politicians, who continued to avow faith in development. 'We care about water pollution, but it isn't as important as a $100 million industry . . . Pollution of minds is a more important problem than air or water pollution,' Victorian Premier Henry Bolte declared in 1970.[63] The men in charge of Australia's development agreed with Bolte. In defence of their utilitarian philosophies and profit-making ventures, they vowed to fight the increasing numbers of Australians who looked upon Australia as home, a home they did not want conscripted for war, sold off, dug up, cut down, dammed and paved over. In 1969, Charles Court, Western Australian Minister for Development, told American industrialists in New York he would not tolerate threats to progress and development. His government would not let ratbag conservationists and anti-pollutionists stand in the way of even more massive overseas investment in his state.

The challenge to utilitarianism implicit in much of the Australia-wide eco-activity also challenged the monopoly of science. Traditional, scientifically motivated conservation felt no need to re-examine inherited theories that define human relationship to natural creation—a relationship involving possession, transformation and domination. Industrial development had habituated society, or at least decision makers, to the idea of all things as potential commodities to be mined, developed, processed, packaged, marketed, used and discarded. And, overwhelmingly, scientists continued to view nature as a stock of economic goods in need of careful management. This conception of nature harmonised with an urban, industrial, utilitarian, capitalist understanding of human life. When green bans and environmental protest made conservation a political issue, scientists with a vested interest in the established way of reaching decisions attacked environmentalists for their extreme views and emotionalism. In 1973, Dr R. G. Downes, Director of Conservation in Victoria, dismissed the 'crooked thinking' of environmentalists and added, 'Achieving conservation is a hard-headed, unemotional business of using and managing our resources as the basis of rational decisions.'[64] Only scientists were capable of such rationality, an opinion seconded in an editorial in *Search*, the official journal of the Australian and New Zealand Association for the Advancement of Science. 'There is no time for the luxury of revolution', declared the editors:

> The application of science is essential to solve the problems of environmental quality and population control. But the wise application of science depends upon Governments which are thoroughly professional and well-informed.[65]

Politics—and by implication, morality—had no place in deciding environmental questions; political activity meant democracy and the subversion of elite power.

9

NOT BY CONQUEST

*IT IS FUNDAMENTAL TO OUR LEGAL
SYSTEM THAT THE AUSTRALIAN COLONIES
BECAME BRITISH POSSESSIONS BY SETTLE-
MENT AND NOT BY CONQUEST.*

Opinion of the Australian High Court, 1979

*THE NUMBER ONE ENEMY OF CIVILISA-
TION, AND HENCE AUSTRALIA ... RESIDES
IN THE ENVIRONMENTAL MOVEMENT
[AMONG] SUBVERSIVES WHO, FOR PER-
SONAL GAIN OR A LUST FOR POWER, ARE
DESIROUS OF BREAKING DOWN WHAT IS
LEFT OF OUR 'FREE ENTERPRISE' SYSTEM
ENTIRELY; THESE PEOPLE, WHOSE NUM-
BERS ARE SWELLED BY A GREAT MASS OF
UNWASHED, UNSPANKED, DOLE-BLUDGING
DROPOUTS, ARE THREATENING THE LIVES
AND FORTUNES OF THE AUSTRALIAN COM-
MUNITY AS IT HAS NEVER BEEN THREAT-
ENED BEFORE.*

Mining magnate Lang Hancock, 1978

I N THE YEARS after World War II the business conducted by foreign-owned firms in Australia created a substantial domestic interest in defending transnational capital. As Prime Minister Gorton said in 1969, 'the importance to Australia of a strong and continuing inflow of overseas capital has never been questioned by my Government'.[1] Questioned or not, Australia's role in the international division of labour as supplier of raw materials and site of foreign investment seriously exposed the economy to changes in commodity export prices, movements in foreign capital and fluctuations in exchange rates.

In 1969–70, transnational corporations began a speculative mining boom. Although the period saw few actual mines dug, many firms announced fabulous discoveries which fueled furious stock market activity. The collapse of the boom in 1970–71, and the accompanying general depression of stock market prices, attracted a wave of foreign takeovers. In 1971–72, $3 billion of foreign currency entered Australia to speculate against the Australian currency. Speculatively induced price rises in land and housing, and the subsequent general inflation, followed by stagflation—a combination of low economic growth, increasing unemployment and accelerating inflation—exposed Australia's lack of political capacity to benefit from the country's mineral and human riches.

In November 1972 the Australian people elected the first federal Labor government since 1949. Under the leadership of Gough Whitlam, Labor promised to promote Australian control over development, oppose pollution and protect the natural landscape. Two months after the election, the federal Labor cabinet made environmental impact statements mandatory for all developmental projects which involved the Commonwealth of Australia. The first test of the new policy occurred in the nation's capital.

During the 1960s the Australian Post Office began secret planning for a new communications tower on Canberra's Black Mountain, the city's most conspicuous natural object, rich in native flora. In October 1972 Federal Parliament had approved the construction on Black Mountain of a massive 195-metre concrete and steel tower—almost as high again as the height of the mountain from the surrounding plains. Canberra residents immediately objected to the proposed development's disturbance of bushland and to the future tower's visual monopoly of the city skyline. Opponents hoped the Post Office's now mandatory environmental impact statement would grant fair hearing to their protest. The Post Office, however, did not welcome public attempts to review decisions reached by experts. Bureaucrats countered objections by reiterating old arguments in favour and by releasing clever composite photographs contrived so as to minimise the tower's visual impact and to reduce its appearance in bulk and height. Unconvinced by bureaucratic sophistry, citizens formed a protest committee and appealed to the responsible government minister, the Postmaster General. He refused to cancel or modify the project, continued to zealously advance the cause inherited from the outgoing conservative government, and eventually persuaded his cabinet colleagues to go ahead with the scheme. Demonstrations, protests, petitions and a court injunction against construction failed to prevent the erection of the tower on Black Mountain.[2]

Despite the record of obeisant behaviour and unceasing attempts at ingratiation from Australia's leaders, the United States never accepted formal responsibility for the country's defence. But due to geographic location, diametrically opposite the globe, Australia figured prominently in post-war American strategic planning. By 1970 Australia hosted over 20 American defence, scientific and intelligence facilities, involving Pentagon agencies, the CIA and the NSA (National Security Agency). The presence of the bases obviously constrained any independent Australian policy.

The Labor government proved as protective of American interests as its predecessors. Shortly after the 1972 election Prime Minister Whitlam told the country he would not disclose information about the bases 'because they are not our secrets. We never told the people at the election that we would disclose other people's secrets.'[3]

Such reassurances did not satisfy the Nixon administration, however, which neither welcomed not expected a Labor victory. American concern over Australian loyalty increased when, within a month of taking office, three senior Labor ministers publicly condemned Nixon's Christmas 1972 bombing of Hanoi as barbaric. Australia's novel unwillingness to be wholly supportive of American actions caused the CIA to react as if communists had taken charge in Canberra. William Colby, CIA chief, Theodore Shackley, in charge of clandestine activity, and James Angleton, chief of counter-intelligence, all expressed misgivings at Australian assertions of independence. CIA alarm increased when the Australian government voiced suspicions that ASIO (Australian Security Intelligence Organisation) was a renegade agency, unresponsive to the elected government. Australia's establishment of diplomatic relations with China and North Vietnam, withdrawal of security operatives working to undermine the Allende government in Chile, and shutdown of an intelligence listening post in Singapore caused further consternation. Fortunately for the CIA, the Labor government's agenda provided numerous opportunities for dirty tricks.

In response to widespread unease over the economic penetration of the country by transnational capital, the Labor Party came to power determined to 'buy back the farm'—i.e., establish Australian control over Australian natural resources. Accordingly, ministers sought to raise billion dollar loans on the international market in order to finance large-scale petroleum and mining developments and buy-backs. Unfortunately for the government, the financiers who offered their services as middlemen in loan negotiations maintained links—undetected at the time—with organised crime, international arms dealing, drug smuggling and the CIA. Few of the businessmen approached actively pursued the securing of loans. Most appeared intent on mischief making, dissemination of misinformation and amassing sufficient documentation to embarrass the government. Although no loan was ever raised, the tales of loan dealing and huge fees to be earned received widespread coverage in the Australian media—largely hostile to Labor—and created a crisis atmosphere in Australian political life. Provocateurs frequently materialised, accused government ministers of receiving kick-backs, then disappeared. Perhaps the most obviously bogus loan proposal appeared on 8 July 1975, when the Australian media reported that the Mercantile Bank and Trust Company, based in Freeport, Bahamas, claimed to be seeking, for a monster fee of $267 million, over $4.2 billion on behalf of the government of Australia. The Bank, one of a number of Caribbean banks the CIA used to launder money,[4] never produced documentation proving their authority to act on behalf of the Australian government.

Later in the year, Whitlam publicly disclosed that Richard Stallings, formerly in charge at Pine Gap, worked for the CIA. He also accused the right-wing opposition of accepting CIA funds. Whitlam's revelations heightened United States alarm. The lease for Pine Gap, one of the CIA's most valuable signals intelligence spy bases, expired on 9 December 1975, and the Agency feared Labor might refuse to renew or might demand changes in the operation of the base. On 8 November 1975, Theodore Shackley sent an urgent message to ASIO warning that 'if this problem cannot be solved they [the CIA] do not see how our mutually beneficial relationships are going to continue.'[5] Three days later the Governor-General, John Kerr, dismissed the Whitlam government. Malcolm Fraser, the replacement Prime Minister, recommended Kerr for a knighthood.[6]

The Whitlam government retained power for less than three years and its conservative successors thwarted much of Labor's original programme. Whitlam, however, had viewed political power as an instrument for social change and the expectations raised by his government's activist intentions endured. People who had taken Labor's promises seriously continued to believe that the exercise of public power might halt and reverse environmental destruction. Thereafter the men who ruled and benefited from domination were unable to return Australians to a state of unquestioning obeisance to the imperatives of conquest. Future Australian governments had to contend with an increasingly vocal and disputatious environmental movement.

One contentious environmental dispute unresolved at the time of the *coup d'état* against the Whitlam government concerned sand mining on Fraser Island, off the coast of Queensland at Maryborough.

Australia holds a virtual monopoly on the world's supply of mineral sands—essential ingredients for the production of titanium steel and paint pigments. The beach sands along Australia's coast contain more than 98 percent of known reserves of rutile, 80 percent of zircon and 25 percent of ilmenite. Fraser Island, the world's largest vegetated sand island, contains particularly heavy mineral sand concentrations. The almost pure silica sand extends from a depth of 61 metres below sea level to sand hill heights exceeding 240 metres above. Vegetation covers most of the island's 163 000 hectares—rainforest, eucalyptus forest, pine forest, heathland, marsh and mangroves. More than 40 fresh water perched lakes lie among the dunes.

During sand mining, bulldozers remove all beach and coastal dune vegetation and topsoil and push the leftover sand into ponds, where dredges suck up the mixture and extract the minerals. Most of the mining companies operating in Australia by 1970 were American owned. During the 1960s one of the largest, Dillingham-Murphyores, negotiated in secret with the Queensland government for vast leases over Fraser Island. In 1971 the company applied, publicly, for more leases. Local eco-activists immediately began campaigning for the island's preservation and the Fraser Island Defense Organisation (FIDO) challenged the granting of leases to Dillingham-Murphyores in the local Mining Warden's Court. The warden, however, overruled the more than 1300 objections lodged with the court and granted the company's application. FIDO appealed the decision through the state courts to the High Court, which ruled that the Maryborough mining warden had failed to perform his duty in looking after the public interest.

Despite the adverse ruling, Dillingham-Murphyores continued mining. The controversy, however, prompted the Whitlam government to convene the first Australian environmental impact inquiry.

The inquiry's report recommended strongly against mining Fraser Island. After considerable delay, new Prime Minister Fraser accepted the report and declined export licences for the minerals mined from Fraser Island. The export refusal effectively left Dillingham-Murphyores without a market and mining ceased.[7]

Fraser's decision coincided with a worldwide slump in the market for mineral sands. Nevertheless, the effective exclusion of mining from Fraser Island represented the most significant conservation victory in Australia's history. For the first time in a confrontation between the defenders of the Australian environment and foreign capital, nature preservation won—a part of Australia had been reclaimed from foreign interests. The federal government, however, had not retreated from its pro-development ideology or abandoned its embrace of foreign capital. For Malcom Fraser, the decision represented only a tactical concession in a much larger battle of conquest.

During the boom in mining shares in 1970 the London-based Rio Tinto announced the discovery, by their Australian uranium subsidiary, of a huge uranium deposit at Nabarlek, an Aboriginal reserve to the east of Darwin. Rio Tinto represented the find as constituting the richest uranium deposit in the world. Huge speculation in Nabarlek-linked shares followed, especially by trading companies whose only purpose was to buy and sell shares, not to mine. The frenzy of trading contributed to the stock market crash later in the year. In the meantime the uranium remained in the ground. By the mid-1970s, confirmed Australian reserves constituted about 20 percent of the uranium available in western-world countries. Many Australians, however, opposed the mining and export of uranium.

In response to public concern, the Whitlam government had appointed a committee in 1974, headed by Justice R. W. Fox, to inquire into the environmental impact of mining the Ranger uranium deposit in the area of a proposed national park, Kakadu, and adjacent to an Aboriginal reserve. Before the committee released its first report, the Liberal Party assumed federal office. Under pressure from overseas governments and mining companies, who saw in Australia a dependable source of large amounts of low-cost uranium, the Liberals had long made clear their determination to proceed with large-scale uranium mining. They especially did not want a public debate. Far more than minerals from Fraser Island, the federal government and transnational capital desired unimpeded (and Australia-wide) uranium mining. Accordingly, Fraser had calculated that a low-cost concession to conservation on Fraser Island sand mining would lessen opposition to uranium mining. He was wrong.

Until the Fox Commission reports were tabled in Parliament, the Fraser government was obliged to wait before announcing uranium mining policy. The delay enabled discussion, debate and controversy to flourish, and more and more people became opposed. The Australian Conservation Foundation (ACF), Friends of the Earth and other groups began a campaign against the export of uranium. In 1975 the Australian Council of Trade Unions (ACTU) congress voted to ban uranium mining altogether, but later reversed this decision.

The first Fox report, released in October 1976, recommended public discussion of all aspects of uranium mining. A few months later, to preclude further debate, federal government declared its intention to proceed with uranium mining. Fraser claimed Australian uranium would contribute 'to the application of effective nuclear safeguards and to the avoidance of the misuse of nuclear materials.'[8] Moreover, he added, the countries buying Australian ore promised to use uranium responsibly. But precisely how the supply of uranium for fueling nuclear reactors reduced the risk of nuclear proliferation the government left unanswered. Those who favoured mining preferred to ignore the issue. Transnational corporations and their domestic spokespersons focused instead on the pecuniary benefits Australians would gain from uranium mining. Pro-uranium groups—the Uranium Producers Forum, the Australian Mining Industry Council (AMIC), Esso and Utah Development Corporation—advertised widely on radio and television and spent millions of dollars on a public relations campaign in favour of mining. Full page newspaper advertisements and television commercials showed scientists harmlessly fondling uranium ore samples. In Western Australia and Queensland, the two states most penetrated by transnational capital, politicians raised the possibility of secession from the Australian federation if the Commonwealth government prohibited uranium mining. Secession, they argued, would permit mining by overseas developers to proceed without interference from Big Government. But appeals to provincialism and utilitarian self-interest, and slick and empty assurances of safety could never convince on their own.

Pro-uranium interests also invoked the wider ideology of development and appended a moral argument for mining: Australia had an international obligation to provide energy to an energy-deficient world. On behalf of his constituents—all humankind apparently—Liberal member W. C. Wentworth warned Federal Parliament in 1977:

> There is a dreadful responsibility on those who . . . have campaigned . . . against the growth of nuclear energy. Let them remember that in the coming decades millions of people will starve to death because of what they have done. Let them try to bear on their consciences the guilt of those deaths which are now, I am afraid, irrevocable . . . A delay of four or five years has already cost the world dearly enough.[9]

In 1979 Australian mining magnate Lang Hancock flew American physicist and hydrogen bomb pioneer (and future proponent of Star Wars) Edward Teller, and a public relations crew, around Australia, 'to wake up Australians to the need to develop their own country.'[10] Australia, claimed Hancock, had 'a birthright' to enter 'the technological nuclear age,' and must use nuclear power to '. . . mine our vast mineral deposits . . . create dams to save the water which is now running uselessly to the sea . . . desalinate the ocean . . . quarry rock and blast tunnels . . . [and] excavate channels at our sea coast. . .'[11]

Opponents of Australia's participation in the international nuclear trade—scientists, as well as environmentalists—never accepted the promises of experts that nuclear power was cheap, safe and inevitable. Despite the most strenuous counter-efforts of pro-nuclear propagandists, opponents insisted on an indissoluble link between uranium mining and the atomic bomb. They dismissed the promises of 'atoms for peace' propaganda as bogus, and rejected the ambitious 'high-tech' future planned for them by transnational capital. Environmental groups organised seminars, petitions, bicycle-rides-against-uranium, letters to editors, public demonstrations and street theatre. Public debates gave rise to the spectacle of eminent scientists vigorously disagreeing with each other. The scientist and expert now appeared as biased promoters of particular values and interests and the uranium debates disabused many people of the objectivity and omnipotence of science. In 1980, in a characteristically hyperbolic defence of uranium mining, Sir Ernest Titterton, professor of physics at the Australian National University, official observer of the British atomic bomb test at the Montebello Islands in 1952, and former chairman of the oxymoronic Maralinga Safety Committee, informed a university audience:

> Unless we harness nuclear power national economies will fail, there will be no commerce, trade or employment, nations will fight to obtain the remaining, dwindling energy supplies, standards of living will collapse, and man will return to the Dark Ages.[12]

The splitting of the atom and the harnessing of nuclear energy represented the fulfillment of the longest held and most cherished of scientific and Enlightenment ambitions: in the words of Francis Bacon, to 'penetrate the innermost secrets of nature and conquer and subdue her'. Thus the nuclear debate—between those who profited from enacting the Enlightenment promise of domination and those sceptical of the benefits from the conquest of nature— assumed an unprecedented prominence in Australian public life. Not since the schism over conscription during the Great War and the war in Vietnam had Australian society been so polarised. The controversy involved more than a dispute over policy: two fundamentally irreconcilable world views conflicted.

The uranium debate brought questions of technology and progress onto the public agenda in a new and problematic way. But on an issue so fundamental, the ruling powers could not concede. Confronted by a vigorous assertion of democracy, of widespread questioning of the very legitimacy of capitalist development, the Fraser government adopted a policy which aimed at overcoming and subverting protest rather than acknowledging the concerns of the protestors. In 1978, in order to deny people the facts about transnational domination of the Australian economy, the government announced that official data about the level of foreign ownership and control of Australian industry would no longer be kept. In future, Australians would no longer be able to find out how much of their country had been annexed by transnational corporations. To facilitate further the intrusion of transnational capital, the government also liberalised local equity requirements. In the following year the United States company, Esso, acquired a large stake in the Western Mining Corporation uranium project at Yeelirrie in Western Australia, the British company, British Petroleum, acquired half share in the South Australian Roxby Downs uranium deposit, and the United States company, Phelps Dodge, acquired half of the Beverley uranium deposit, also in South Australia.

Troubles in the United States nuclear industry, falling demand for nuclear power generation, continuously downward revised projections of future nuclear energy needs, and the Three Mile Island accident in March 1979 raised grave questions about the future of nuclear energy generation. Despite international concern, the Australian government, the mining companies and the Australian Atomic Energy Commission continued to deny the seriousness of the problems affecting the nuclear industry and to overestimate the future demand for Australian uranium. Furthermore, in the name of competitiveness, the government and leading entrepreneurs supported a domestic nuclear industrial complex, and pushed ahead with plans to establish a commercial uranium enrichment project.

In 1984, after assuming national office and despite clamorous opposition, the new Labor government of Bob Hawke agreed to the opening of a third Australian uranium mine at Roxby Downs. In national elections a few months later, half a million Australians voted for the hastily formed Nuclear Disarmament Party (NDP) in protest. The NDP's success, including the election of a senator, Jo Vallentine, destroyed the Australian Labor Party's monopoly on progressive politics. But NDP and rank and file protest did not

242

alter government support for uranium mining. In 1986 the Labor government announced the resumption of uranium sales to France, which continued to ignore all protests, including those from the Australian and New Zealand governments, and to detonate atomic bombs in the Pacific. The Prime Minister claimed the sale would save public revenue $66 million.

Throughout the uranium debate, proponents sought to assure the public of the safety of nuclear waste and the credibility of governments which handle nuclear matters. Such assurances appeared untrustworthy when organisations representing veterans, who served at the Montebello, Emu Field and Maralinga atomic bomb sites, began pressing the Commonwealth government to hold an inquiry into the safety procedures surrounding the British tests and to survey the health records of the people involved. Dozens of veterans reported entering the contaminated area without protective clothing. They also attested to the prevailing cavalier attitude towards the handling of radioactive wastes. Reports of catastrophic health problems among hundreds of area Aborigines and the premature death of dozens of men who served at Maralinga left the government unmoved. Spokespersons denied the tests compromised anyone's health and attributed cancer deaths to natural causes. The government opposed an investigation, not only to protect the British government from scrutiny, but also because pro-uranium mining officials feared an inquiry would expose state dishonesty and negligence in dealing with nuclear technology. But eventual exposure came in 1985. A Royal Commission established that military personnel, scientists and politicians involved with the tests had concealed, fabricated and withheld important information. Safety experts had blandly and untruthfully guaranteed that no harm would come to test participants or to the Australian public.[13]

Australia's successful development as a quarry required that the people who lived on the continent believed their cooperation in the nation's collective conquest of nature would benefit themselves; that their freedom, prosperity and happiness would be ensured. Aboriginal Australians, however, withheld assent, resisted domination and assimilation, and insisted on the right to be themselves—a right best secured, they believed, by moral and legal recognition of their ownership of traditional lands.

In March 1969 the Yirrkala Aborigines applied to the Northern Territory Supreme Court for an interim injunction restraining the Commonwealth and the mining company, Nabalco, from continuing with allegedly wrongful acts within the Gove region of the Arnhem Land Aboriginal Reserve. The Yirrkala objected to the Commonwealth's unilateral appropriation of Aboriginal land for the purposes of bauxite mining. Nabalco and the government viewed the Yirrkala action as a remarkable, misconceived and disruptive attack on the laws of property; the law simply could not recognise tribal and traditional rights to the land. Nabalco and the Crown told the Court that 'to accede to the aboriginal propositions would be to unsettle the property law of the continent.'[14] The Court agreed, dismissed prior Aboriginal occupation of the land as legally irrelevant, and ruled that the law did not require the Commonwealth to consult the Yirrkala.

In *Milirrpum v. Nabalco Pty Ltd and Commonwealth of Australia* (1971), the Yirrkala tried again to assert traditional rights to the land. Justice Blackburn, however, decided the doctrine of communal native land title did not form and never had formed part of the law of Australia. Moreover, since Australia became a colony by discovery and settlement, not by conquest or cession, political sovereignty over, and ultimate title to, the land became vested in the Crown by reason of Governor Phillip's landing at Sydney Cove in 1788. Prior to 1788 the continent had been devoid of property-owning inhabitants.[15]

Ever since the British invasion, the state and courts upheld the self-beneficial view of Australia as having been discovered and annexed *terra nullius*. The tenacity of this fiction created a reality, based on a necessary illusion, which became immune to factual refutation. Land rights claimants realised that only political action could change this reality and win recognition of traditional rights in land.

On 26 January 1972 Aboriginal activists erected a tent embassy on the lawn in front of Parliament House, Canberra to symbolise the foreign status of Aborigines within Australia. From all over the country Aborigines came to help staff the Embassy and to claim extensive areas of reserve and Crown land as homeland. They also demanded financial compensation for land appropriated. An acute embarrassment to the Australian government, the Aboriginal Embassy stood for seven months and attracted international media coverage. In July Prime Minister William McMahon ordered police to tear down the tents. Conflict continued for three weeks as Aborigines re-established the Embassy after each police raid. The publicity the Embassy generated for the Aboriginal cause gave the question of the basic right to occupy the continent more attention and clarity than any other time since the nineteenth century squatting invasion.

In 1973 Prime Minister Whitlam appointed a Commission, headed by Justice A. E. Woodward, to advise the government on 'the most appropriate means' of recognising traditional Aboriginal interests in land. Woodward's reports detailed procedures for Aboriginal land claims and conditions of tenure and in 1976 the Commonwealth passed the *Land Rights Act*, which enabled Aborigines, under certain strict conditions, to make claims to unoccupied and unalienated Crown land in the Northern Territory. Territorian pastoralists determinedly opposed Aboriginal land rights, and subsequent legislative amendments successively restricted the rights of groups to lay claim to ancestral land. By 1990, 250 pastoral leases, controlled by 150 bodies—only a handful of which were Aboriginal—covered over half of the Northern Territory's 1 346 200 square kilometres. The great bulk of Aboriginal land obtained under the 1976 Act lay in the most arid and least commercially valuable country.[16]

Elsewhere in Australia the political power of mining and grazing interests ensured Aborigines did not obtain rights over even the most arid country. Transnational mining companies believed, and encouraged the public to believe, that Aboriginal land rights were fraudulent and that the only legitimate interest in the land was in its development as a commodity. In 1980, Bernard Wheelahu, a Dutch citizen and manager of Billiton Metals in Australia, a wholly owned subsidiary of Dutch Shell and an investor in the York Peninsula bauxite mines, said:

> I prefer not to give land rights to the Aborigines. It is a complex issue. When we give land rights to the Aboriginal people it means that they will be in the same position as the other white Australians. I don't like it. It is a very big problem and it is dangerous to the mining industries.[17]

The developers of Australia viewed the domination of some human beings over others as a necessary precondition for human progress. The prospect of Aboriginal equality, which so worried Dutch Shell, also concerned Conzinc Rio Australia (CRA), Australia's largest mining conglomerate, which claimed:

> Minerals in Australia are owned by the 'Crown', that is by the whole Australian people through their respective state governments . . . Giving mineral rights, in effect to Aboriginals and not to other land-holders is divisive. CRA believes that Aboriginal title to land should be held on the same basis as that of any other Australian.[18]

But as CRA already knew, other Australians who held freehold title did own the minerals on their land. In 1979 a majority of the judges of the High Court affirmed the superior freehold rights of Bernard Wheelahu's 'other Australians' with respect to Aboriginal Australians. In *Coe v. Commonwealth* (1979), the justices ruled that Australia, possessed of no civilised inhabitants or settled law prior to 1788, belonged to the select and unique class of countries acquired by peaceful settlement and therefore the Crown owed no legal obligation to the continent's indigenes. Justice Lionel Murphy dissented and remarked that the view that the English annexation of no-man's-land Australia had been peaceful was either 'made in ignorance or [was] a convenient falsehood to justify the taking of Aborigines' land.'

Emboldened by the Court's ruling, mining companies, who regarded Aboriginal Australians as obstacles to the extraction of minerals and the flow of profit, continued to campaign against Aboriginal claims. In 1981 the Australian Mining Industry Council (AMIC) warned that Aboriginal land rights threatened Australia's 'special responsibility to make its resources available to the world community on equitable terms.'[19] Australia's moral obligation to supply the world with minerals required the violation of the independence and rights in land the Aborigines had enjoyed for tens of thousands of years prior to the British invasion.

The assumption that the coming of European civilisation had uplifted the Aborigines informed much of the anti-land rights propaganda. Men of the Enlightenment refused to believe that Aborigines did not want what Europeans had forced on them. Queensland Premier Bjelke-Petersen suggested Aborigines be raised up to the level of Europeans; 'Don't we want to bring them into modern society? You want to leave them out in the bush believing in the Spirit of the Goanna and all this other stuff? Don't you want to make them a bit more equal with yourself?'[20] A bit more equality might take some time, however. In 1981, when asked why freehold title should not be granted to Aboriginal people, the Queensland Minister for Aboriginal Affairs, Ken Tomkins, said, 'I'm not satisfied at this point in time that Aborigines can handle mortgage documents ... perhaps with fifty or so years of evolution they could learn how.'[21]

A similar belief in European superiority has informed all the rationalisations which, throughout Australian history, upheld the appropriation of Aboriginal land. 'How are these unlettered savages ever to arrive at a knowledge of the glorious Gospel of Christ unless someone will carry it to them?', asked a settler in the Perth *Inquirer* in 1849.[22] One hundred and thirty-five years later, in 1984, Hugh Morgan, managing director of Western Mining Corporation, claimed land rights for Aborigines were fundamentally anti-Christian, a regression into an uncivilised state, 'a symbolic step back to the world of paganism, superstition, fears and darkness'.[23]

But the chief concern of foreign-dominated mining interests lay in the possible loss of royalty-free access to mineral wealth under Aboriginal-claimed land. By means of eulogies to progress and development, miners succeeded in pressuring all Australian governments into opposing Aboriginal land rights. Transnational capital found the task of mobilising people against land rights easy. Propaganda depicted Aboriginal claims as hostile to property itself. Since most Australians desire ownership of land, those born here, as well as migrants, saw their interests served by joining the anti-land rights campaign. By 1990 deep antagonism to Aboriginal demands

distinguished all governments and major political parties throughout Australia.

During the 1970s and 1980s, reaction to the democratic protests of
the 1960s mounted. Western governments and intellectuals began
reasserting the authority of the marketplace. In the United States
after the Vietnam war, elites began reconstructing an ideology of
domination. Many Americans had become disillusioned about the
nobility of intent and the integrity of their rulers. In response,
United States President Ronald Reagan and British Prime Minister
Margaret Thatcher denounced the hedonistic anarchy of the 1960s
as a moral wasteland responsible for economic and political disaster.
They simultaneously celebrated the untrammelled self-
aggrandisement of the market as a personal quest for autonomy,
self-realisation and adventure. Reagan, Thatcher and those who
gathered around them were determined to give modern capitalism
the power to impose an exclusive path to human fulfilment—a
path considered universally valid. Their arguments declared industrial capitalism to be a transcendent force and, ultimately, the measure of all things.

Popular criticism and oppositional politics made the task of elab-
orating an ideology of development urgent in Australia as well.
Uranium mining advocates defended the institution of property
and vigorously reasserted the virtues of the market and of free
enterprise. Prime Minister Fraser, for example, had found the lesson
of history 'self-evident . . . life has not been easy for people or for
nations [and in] the future . . . that condition will not alter . . . I
would add that life is not meant to be easy.'[24] Accordingly, the state
need not provide for people who lost out in the competitive race
which development entailed. Political and social objectives must
wait while entrepreneurs ran the economy, unfettered by the state.
The state existed primarily to condition people to the economic
'facts of life'—a formula which business propagandists never tired
of reiterating. The facts cited, not surprisingly, affirmed those
social arrangements which benefited business.

In a 1977 address entitled 'To convince our Children', Roderick
Carnegie, chairman of CRA, listed the 'five facts of life': private

enterprise, management, profit, individualism and small government.[25] But the propaganda in favour of the market and free and private enterprise actually corresponded very little with either freedom or individual effort. In reality, public money and legislation were used to support the greater growth and profit of capitalist corporations.

The engineers of development never conceded that the interests of Australia might conflict with those of foreign-owned enterprise, or that foreign interests might even eclipse the interests of people who actually lived in Australia. But increasing numbers of Australians disputed their leaders' claims about the benefits of development. Fewer and fewer prepared to wait on government to act on their behalf. People began mobilising in their own defence. The examples of green bans, of people sitting in front of bulldozers, of the effectiveness of direct action and confrontation, provided an inspiration for many. Oppositional politics also sounded a warning to those who profited from and managed Australia's continued exploitation.

In the late 1970s the two states most exploited by foreign-owned miners—Western Australia and Queensland—took action to ensure that the freedom of transnational capital to mine and export (and to pollute and destroy) took precedence over the civil liberties and political freedoms of Australians. Both states adopted repressive legislation designed to silence critics of development, increase police powers and prevent public meetings.

In 1979 the Western Australian Premier's department began promoting the state as 'The Land of Movable Mountains'. To Premier Court, topography constituted no obstacle to development and the conquest of nature, nor did people. Two years previously, the Western Australian Police Commissioner, Owen Leitch, had warned Parliament against 'militants within unions and radical groups' who 'foment unrest.' Leitch assured the state's politicians, however, that 'the Police Service accepts the challenge presented by these social events, and it does so in full confidence of being impartial to the issue and mindful of its oath of office to uphold the law.'[26] As a demonstration of impartiality, the police acquired anti-riot equipment, including two armoured cars, and trained with the Army's

Special Air Services regiment. This regiment had been specially constituted to fight civil, not foreign, wars. In addition, Leitch obtained the power to require written application for union meetings and marches. Protest, however, continued and demonstrations against bauxite mining in the jarrah forests of the Darling Range, south of Perth, led to the passing of a *Government Agreements Act*, which gave police special powers to arrest people who occupied land designated in any development legislation (or who hindered any activity pursuant to development legislation). Essential services legislation outlawed strikes in those industries most essential to the operations of transnational capital—fuel, energy and power. To remove the environment as an obstacle to growth, the government granted development ministries power of veto over environmental legislation. Political leaders, obsessed with remaking the nature of Western Australia, restricted personal and public freedoms without hesitation.

Similar developments unfolded in Queensland. In the name of greater economic opportunity and progress, the state increased police powers and restricted civil liberties. To create a favourable climate for transnational investment, the state not only subsidised the costs of doing business in Queensland, but also controlled opposition.

In 1977 the Queensland government banned street marches. Premier Bjelke-Petersen announced the end of protest:

> The day of the political street march is over. Anyone who holds a street march spontaneously or otherwise will know they're acting illegally ... Don't bother applying for a permit. You won't get one. That's government policy now.[27]

This measure, a reaction to the growing anti-uranium movement, sought to ensure the continued, unchallenged export of Mary Kathleen uranium oxide (yellowcake). The cost of enforcing the ban, however, proved excessive. With only a few police required at lawful marches, but thousands needed to prevent illegal ones, the ban was not worth the trouble and lasted only two years. Nevertheless, the period led to other, longer-lasting repressive developments.

During the street struggles against the ban, the Queensland

police force became a political machine, an arm of the executive, vested with the unfettered power of the state.[28] Developers and the state had found a corrupt police force amenable to political work. Journalists and opposition politicians made repeated allegations of widespread police corruption—involving organised crime, extensive bribery, drug running, prostitution, operation of brothels, illegal gambling, tax evasion, money laundering, protection rackets and election rigging. The police, backed by the Premier, consistently denied the evidence of crime and corruption. Confirmation of malfeasance at the highest levels of government threatened to undermine the state's commitment to development.

Bjelke-Petersen grew up in rural Queensland and became rich from clearing land, as one of the first contractors to deploy large bulldozers against the brigalow. The destroyers of the bush worked without knowledge of or concern for the effects of their machinations on the land. Destroying forest was progress; fewer trees meant more grazing, more crops and, most importantly, more personal wealth. Christian fundamentalist beliefs often reinforced devotion to development at any cost. Man's goal on earth was to progress materially through production and trade; the earth existed only as a means to compile riches in this life while waiting for the next.

During Bjelke-Petersen's long reign as Premier, his commitment to development and authoritarian government attracted large amounts of overseas money, especially from Asian countries under anti-democratic regimes. By 1980 transnational capital owned almost 90 percent of Queensland's mineral resources. But the 1987 Fitzgerald Royal Commission into the Queensland police uncovered high-level official misconduct and corruption of the rule of law. These disclosures finally forced Bjelke-Petersen's resignation, after a reign of nineteen years.

The engineers and scientists who implemented the human control of nature in Australia viewed the continent as a sphere of pure externality, a stage-set for the display of human activity. 'It is clear', summarised C. H. Munro, Emeritus Professor of Civil Engineering at the University of New South Wales in 1974, 'that in Australia, Nature has set a very poorly-furnished stage for man to act upon, at least as far as water resources are concerned.'[29] Accordingly, engineering, particularly water engineering, must 'overcome the curses invoked by Nature.'[30]

Few engineering authorities in Australia tried harder to fulfil this mandate than the Tasmanian Hydro-Electric Commission (HEC). Established by an act of state Parliament in 1930, the HEC gained the sole right to generate, distribute and sell electricity throughout Tasmania and began vigorously promoting 'hydro-industrialisation'—a strategy of attracting heavy industries with the promise of cheap power. Over the years the monopolistic HEC came to dominate Tasmanian politics and functioned as the state's pre-eminent economic planning authority, coordinating the state's investments, and granting extensive forest concessions to sawmillers and pulp and paper manufacturers. By the mid-1980s the HEC had undertaken 25 hydro-electric schemes—or one for every 4362 electors on the state rolls—and built 39 dams.[31] In the 30 years to 1975, Tasmania's available electric power grew by more than 1000 percent. The subsidised power induced nineteen, mainly foreign, energy-intensive industries to establish processing operations on the island. But cheap electricity encouraged firms to depend on equipment rather than on humans, and manufacturing employment grew hardly at all. The highly capitalised metal processing and paper manufacturing projects employed less than 6 percent of Tasmania's workforce. The promise of hydro-industrialisation—that employment and economic growth would follow the installation of electrical capacity—was not realised. Tasmanian unemployment remained the highest in Australia and per capita income the lowest. For the engineers at the HEC the solution lay in more hydro-industrialisation, and in the late 1970s they proposed another giant dam, to be known as Gordon-below-Franklin, for the south-west, in one of the few intact wet temperate wilderness regions in the world.

Years before the HEC planned to pour the first bucket of concrete at the Franklin dam, however, the people who had fought and lost the campaign to save Lake Pedder from drowning began organising against further dams in the south-west. In 1976 they formed the Tasmanian Wilderness Society and started campaigning. Film nights, public meetings and publications captivated thousands and they walked the streets in protest. In 1980, following huge street protests, the Premier, Doug Lowe, rejected the Gordon-below-Franklin proposal in favour of a marginally less destructive scheme, known as Gordon-above-Olga.

The HEC, a champion of technocratic expertise and a foe of public participation, lobbied politicians to reverse the decision. HEC Commissioner Russell Ashton warned national television viewers that 'If the Parliament tries to work through popular decisions we're doomed in this state and doomed everywhere.'[32] Thus cautioned, the Tasmanian Parliament rejected the compromise scheme, insisted the wilderness should drown, and forced Lowe to put the two dam sites to a referendum in December 1981. The referendum, the first in Australian history without the provision to say no, did not give people the option of voting for neither of the two projects; the choice lay between either a lot more, or very much more hydro-industrialisation. In the event, 55 percent voted for one or other of the hydro-schemes (47 percent for Gordon-below-Franklin and 8 percent for Gordon-above-Olga), but, in an unprecedented display of civil disobedience, 45 percent of the voters chose to vote informal and most endorsed their ballots with the words 'No dams'. The government interpreted the vote as a sanction for development and withdrew the areas to be affected from the Wild Rivers National Park—the seventeenth revocation of national park status to facilitate development in recent Tasmanian history.

Tasmania's politicians saw damming the Franklin as a political imperative, not because they necessarily believed in the need for another dam, because many did not. The real impulse behind the determination to build the dam was cultural. The undammed Gordon River constituted a challenge and provided an opportunity for the display of technical virtuosity on the part of HEC engineers. The HEC could not afford to let the opportunity pass. Over the decades the HEC had cultivated an overwhelming pro-growth ethos. Most politicians felt powerless to question their role in the HEC script. Paradoxically, the very rigidity of Tasmanian political institutions, the inability of politicians to decide, to present alternatives, proved the downfall of the Franklin scheme. When politicians unanimously accepted development as inevitable, effective democratic decision making passed to a new extra-parliamentary opposition.

After the referendum the Tasmanian Wilderness Society began a national 'No Dams' campaign. Dam opponents held rallies, marches, poster campaigns and debates. Conservationist pressure forced the Commonwealth government to nominate south-west Tasmania for inclusion on the United Nations World Heritage list. In August 1982 when the Tasmanian HEC began road clearing on the Gordon-below-Franklin site, huge demonstrations followed. Later the HEC despatched barges, laden with bulldozers, from the tiny west coast community of Strathan for the Gordon River. On 14 December, a blockade, coordinated by the Tasmanian Wilderness Society, but joined by people from all over Australia, began. Protestors confronted bulldozers, interrupted construction work, and occupied the dam site. HEC employees assaulted and harassed demonstrators and the police eventually arrested nearly 1500 peaceful blockaders. Environmentalists appealed to the Commonwealth government to halt the project but Prime Minister Fraser claimed he lacked the power to intervene. Instead he offered Tasmania $500 million in compensation to desist but the state refused the money. HEC technocrats viewed the Franklin Dam as only a small part of the untapped potential of south-west Tasmania; their plans included five additional hydro sites and the development of significant timber and mineral resources.

Although the obstruction at the dam site probably did little to delay construction, the vivid media images of the three-month blockade against the backdrop of the Tasmanian wilderness flashed across Australia made a profound political impact. The leader of the federal Labor opposition, Bob Hawke, saw the dispute as a potential election-winning issue and he promised federal intervention if elected. The dam issue engaged the Australian electorate as nothing else in living memory, and in March 1983 the Labor Party won national office. On election night the new Prime Minister said, 'The dam will not be built.' The federal government then demanded a halt to construction work. The Tasmanian government appealed to the courts; in July the High Court rejected Tasmania's arguments and confirmed the Commonwealth's power to preserve the south-west Tasmanian wilderness.

Bob Brown, of the Tasmanian Wilderness Society, hailed the Court's judgement as an acknowledgement 'that there is a limit to the technological destruction we can allow in the name of progress . . .'[33] Brown, euphoric in victory, read too much into the decision. The political structures that produce dam-building proposals remained intact. Within weeks of the decision stopping work, the Tasmanian Parliament approved the construction of seven more dams in the highlands and river gorges of south-west Tasmania.

The Gordon River flows through forest representative of the flora which covered Australia when it was still joined to Antarctica but which, in modern times, survived only in remnants in a narrow broken band from the Kimberleys to Cape York Peninsula and down the east coast to Tasmania. These rainforest types range from wet and dry tropical in the north, through sub-tropical to wet, cool temperate in the south. In less than 200 years, settlers and loggers had cleared about three-quarters of Australia's rainforests. Only a few stands, mostly in the least accessible areas, survived into the late twentieth century.

In the 1970s the New South Wales Forestry Commission mapped the previously untouched rainforest in the Terania Valley in northern New South Wales preparatory to roading, clearfelling, burning and replacement with a homogenous eucalypt forest. In 1975, when the logging plans became known, local people formed a group to oppose the destruction of Australia's most diverse rainforest—a combination of sub-tropical, warm temperate and wet sclerophyll rainforest. As a result of appeals, the Commission post-poned the logging but did not abandon its plans and by 1979 logging again became imminent. In early August, 100 or so people, determined to prevent destruction, set up camp at the edge of the forest at Terania Creek. Protestors posted lookouts to maintain a 24-hour watch on all roads into the area, and formed a radio network and a telephone tree to relay news of any developments out of the valley to supporters ready to come quickly. At the approach of bulldozers and chain saws, people climbed trees and flitted in and out of the undergrowth near where trees were to be felled. But with the aid of the police, loggers forced their way into the forest. Lin Gordon, the New South Wales Minister for Forests and Conservation, described the protestors as 'filthy hippies' and declared that logging must continue. 'It's a matter of principle', he said.[34] The loggers pushed on, felling the ancient trees and ripping the forest apart. Lying in front of bulldozers did not prevent destruction. One night, late in the month, two young protestors slipped into the forest with a climbing belt, chain saw, hammer and 300-millimetre nails. They drove the nails into the trees marked for cutting the next day and with the chain saw cut deep gashes in the already sawn logs on the ground, rendering the timber unusable. A few days later the government halted logging activities pending an inquiry.

Although the inquiry was designed to approve logging, its two-year duration allowed conservation organisations to mount an intense campaign to preserve all the remaining rainforests in New South Wales. Public lobbying changed the terms of debate about rainforest destruction and most people now favoured preservation. Nevertheless, in October 1982, logging of rainforest began in the Nightcap Range, in northern New South Wales. Protestors again blocked bulldozers, climbed trees and placed obstacles on the road. Police reinforcements pushed the protestors into the bush. But late in the month, under notice of a Court injunction requiring an Environmental Impact Study and in response to conservationist pressure, the government announced that most of the state's remaining rainforests would be preserved. The Premier, Neville Wran, said:

> I know it was not everyone who thought it was a great thing to save the rainforests, but I make this prediction here today: when we are all dead and buried and our children's children are reflecting on what was the best thing the Labor Government in New South Wales did in the 20th century, they will come up with the answer that we saved the rainforests.[35]

Wran's sentiments reflected an uncommon generosity of spirit and

imagination. The triumph of market ideologies and the enshrine-
ment of profit, efficiency and the bottom line as the sole judge of
human worth had effectively banished the subject of posterity from
public discourse in Australia. Bound by an ideology of pragmatism,
Wran's fellow political leaders did not share his liberality towards
people yet unborn. They preferred ignorance to the knowledge that
present actions connect us to the future as surely as the deeds of our
ancestors connect us to the past. The capacity to imagine, to feel
empathy for concerns beyond market imperatives, did not appear
anywhere else in contemporary Australia, especially in Queensland.

In 1983 all the resources of the state, backed by editorials in
Queensland's newspapers, succeeded in crushing popular discontent
with plans to push a road through the Daintree rainforest at Cape
Tribulation. In December, eco-activists occupied the proposed
route, dug themselves into the ground in front of bulldozers, and
sat in trees to prevent their destruction. By the end of the month,
protestors had succeeded in postponing construction until the end
of the wet season. The Queensland Minister for the Environment,
Martin Tenni, vowed the road would be built and told a national
television audience:

> We will bring 'dozers in, we will cut the tops of the ranges if it's
> necessary, and it will be necessary. And no hippie, no greenie, no
> environmentalists will stop that from happening, they can go their
> hardest, they won't win.[36]

The Minister's determination proved equal to his prediction. Massive police reinforcements, police violence and police dogs defeated
the second blockade and the road broke through the forest. Every
wet season, the rains erode the road and roadside edges onto the
coral of the Great Barrier Reef.

Following the report of the commission of inquiry into oil drilling in Great Barrier Reef waters, the Whitlam government had
passed the *Great Barrier Reef Marine Park Act 1975*. Park status,
however, did not mean protection from development; economic
values remained paramount. The Act aimed 'to ensure a level of
usage which is consistent with maintenance of the ecological
system and which will be accepted as reasonable by society.'

Graeme Kelleher, Chairman of the Great Barrier Reef Marine Park Authority, later wrote that the Act, and the establishment of the Authority as facilitator of development, demonstrated Australian maturity; the public had reached the incontestable 'realization that both conservation and development are necessary, and must be made compatible each with the other.'[37]

The Queensland government agreed and throughout the 1970s kept up pressure for Great Barrier Reef oil drilling. In 1980 Premier Bjelke-Petersen intimated that drilling the Reef was only a matter of time and told a press conference, 'I think before long you, and you, and every one of us will be saying, "Please get on with the job because I'm sick and tired of walking and things are coming to a halt." '[38]

Meanwhile the state government continued to encourage tourist development at an unprecedented rate. Resort developers offered buyers and visitors a paradise never imagined on heaven or earth, where sun and blue skies vied with palm trees and ocean breezes to drive all troubles away. In pursuit of this utopia, the state provided public assistance to private entrepreneurs.

In 1986 Queensland passed legislation permitting Great Barrier Reef tourist developers to convert leasehold land on Queensland's islands to freehold title. The new rules encouraged large-scale residential sub-division on Great Barrier Reef islands.

Reef development attracted huge numbers of tourists. One and a half million people visited the Reef in 1989—a number increasing by 30 percent each year. By 1989 developers had applied for more than 250 new tourist resorts along Queensland's coast—including 50 marinas, 20 golf courses, 2 monorails, a floating hotel and a space base. The concrete coastline extended south to northern New South Wales where Paul Rubie, of the New South Wales Tourism Commission, said, 'we want no perception that it is harder to develop a site in New South Wales than in Queensland.'[39]

In 1990 a state government report warned that tonnes of coral-killing chemicals from mainland rivers and tourist resort sewerage were killing the Reef and that a dead reef would destroy the state's multi-billion dollar tourist industry. The warning reflected the state's exclusive concern with the Reef's economic potential. Three months after the state report, the federal government announced new plans for reef oil exploration. In 1979 Prime Minister Fraser had promised that 'The Government will not permit any drilling on the Great Barrier Reef, or any drilling or mining which could damage the Reef. That is a categoric and absolute guarantee'.[40] Australians might have expected Fraser's commitment to preserve the Reef to endure. Progress, however, demanded a different conclusion. The imperative of development proved more abiding than political promises and Fraser's successors did not feel bound by his pledge. At the annual conference of the Australian Petroleum Exploration Association in Darwin in June 1990, the Federal Minister for Resources, Alan Griffiths, released what he described as 'a comprehensive program for the release of offshore areas for exploration by companies.' The association's director, Keith Orchison, immediately predicted the resumption of drilling off the coast of Queensland within ten years.[41]

While rich in non-renewable resources such as sand minerals, lead, silver, bauxite, zinc, iron ore and fossil fuels, Australia is poor in renewable resources—forests, water and arable land. Yet by 1990 the least wooded of continents next to Antarctica—in area only 6 percent forest—was the world's largest woodchip exporter. Constant and uncritical repetition, by the forestry industry and government, of the view of forests as a sustainable resource had evolved into a view which equated renewable resource with infinite resource.

Australia's first woodchipping project began in 1970 when Harris-Daishowa, a subsidiary of the large Japanese paper manufacturer, Daishowa Paper Manufacturing, started chipping operations at Eden on the south-east coast of New South Wales. Harris-Daishowa claimed woodchipping would improve the forests 'after centuries of neglect'. In 1977 the Australian government extended Harris-Daishowa's woodchip licence for twelve years, despite protest. A few years later the government increased Harris-Daishowa's annual export quota from 350 000 to 850 000 tonnes. With the decline and steady destruction of Australian forests, governments became more and more accommodating to the needs of forest exploiters. In 1989, again over conservationist protest, and after the arrest of hundreds of forest blockaders, the federal government extended Harris-Daishowa's woodchip licence another seventeen years. In October 1990 the federal government reversed a pre-election promise to protect the south-east forests and agreed to open significant areas to logging.

State endorsement of the view of forest as potential profit encouraged further private speculation. In 1988 North Broken Hill, in partnership with Canadian corporation Noranda Forests Inc., announced plans for a giant pulp mill at Wesley Vale on the north-west coast of Tasmania. Noranda executive Adam Zimmerman told Tasmanians that a tree is of no use unless it can be turned into profit. Prime Minister Hawke acclaimed the mill as Australia's biggest-ever manufacturing project. Opponents, however, charged the mill would pollute the skies and beaches and Bass Strait with toxic wastes, alienate some of Australia's best agricultural land and accelerate destruction of native forests. The mill consortium never denied the plant would pollute but claimed progress demanded people accept pollution. Wesley Vale resident, Christine Milne, and Concerned Residents Opposing the Pulp Mill Site (CROPS) refused to concede the inevitability of destruction and began organising against the project. Milne particularly objected to the overbearing attitude of the partners who, she said, had told the people of Wesley Vale: 'You have to have this development. We're not going to justify it on planning grounds or on environmental grounds. We say it's good for you, therefore you'll have it.'[42] When Tasmanians lodged dozens of objections to the mill, the Tasmanian government passed legislation enabling the joint venturers to bypass normal planning approval procedures. In March 1989, however, the federal government insisted on tougher guidelines. Noranda and North Broken Hill declined to meet the anti-pollution standards and terminated the project.

State determination to subjugate and utilise the forests did not end with the Noranda and North Broken Hill withdrawal. In October 1990, four years after the federal government increased Tasmanian woodchip quotas to higher levels than ever before, the Tasmanian government enlarged the area of native forest subject to logging. Across Bass Strait the logging industry continued to assert superior claims to the timber in Australian forests.

In February 1984 the Nomadic Action Group had mounted a blockade on the Errinundra Plateau of East Gippsland. The largest area of temperate rainforest in Victoria, the Errinundra Plateau contained old growth eucalyptus, stands of errinundra shining gum (an undescribed species awaiting a formal Latin name) and ancient mountain plum pine (*Podocarpus lawrencei*). Although police and bulldozers broke through the blockade, the action focused attention on logging in East Gippsland. At a subsequent inquiry, sawmillers denied clearcutting decimated wildlife. On the contrary, argued Ray Richards, co-owner of a major East Gippsland sawmilling company:

> ... immediately you start to chop down useless timber ... the birds for 50 and 100 miles move there ... There is a fresh supply of grubs and all the things that come out of the rotten wood, and before you know where you are, birds ... are that fat and heavy they can hardly fly off the ground ... Coupe logging ... can not harm the birds and animals ... [they] ... just move out and sit on the side ... They are quite intelligent really, they stand and watch what you are doing.[43]

Consequent upon the inquiry, the Victorian government increased national park areas in East Gippsland. Park boundaries, however, perhaps because of Richard's affirmation of life after clearcutting, excluded large areas of old growth forests, and logging for sawlogs and, most significantly, woodchips, continued.

Over the summer of 1989–90, eco-activists mounted another blockade of East Gippsland forests. After police arrested over 800 blockaders, the Commonwealth and Victorian governments imposed a logging moratorium in East Gippsland National Estate forests subject to finding alternative logging sites. The moratorium preceded a promise to the logging industry and timber unions by Prime Minister Hawke to maintain 'resource supply and industry activity in East Gippsland.'[44] In October 1990 the state government fulfilled Hawke's promise and decided to keep National Estate forests open to logging.

Only in Western Australia, where woodchipping commenced in 1976, did the government eventually acknowledge limits to the state's forests. In 1983, after a campaign by environmentalists, the government reserved the Shannon River Basin from logging. In 1989 the government undertook to phase out woodchipping in state forests within ten years. The following year, Premier Carmen Lawrence announced that a previously proposed pulp mill would not proceed until the wood required could be obtained from plantations. In the meantime, Lawrence said, 'The resource is simply not available.'

Arable soils, another resource suffering catastrophic decline, were never widely distributed over Australia. While a big country, Australia farms about the same amount of land as France. The soil is of much lower quality, however, and subsequently Australia grows less cereal than does the United Kingdom on one-third the area. Good soils—those easiest to cultivate and containing sufficient inherent plant nutrients to sustain plant growth for several years without fertilisers, in temperate, moist areas—originally covered only about 8 percent of the continent. Elsewhere, Australians partly made good the deficiency through irrigation and dryfarming.

Irrigation in Australia expanded from only about 50 000 hectares at the turn of the century to around 1.5 million by 1979. Most of the increase occurred in the arid and semi-arid Murray River basin, which, by the 1980s, produced one-third of Australia's agricultural output. But intensification of production invariably produced environmental degradation.

All agriculture based on irrigation, particularly in arid regions, faces problems of long-term sustainability due to the poisoning of water and soil alike by salt build-up. In the past, experts took the view that high watertables and salinity were unlikely on the Murray and Murrumbidgee plains. But what took nature geological eons to achieve, the leaching of salts from the root zone of plants, the engineer and the irrigator reversed in a matter of decades—sometimes far less. The artificial wetting of irrigation builds up excess water in the soil, which raises salts from underlying sediments to the surface. By 1985 salinity affected nearly 60 000 square kilometres of irrigated land—a figure expected to double by the year 2015. In the Kerang region of Northern Victoria, salting visibly affects 25 percent of the irrigated area. Where Thomas

Mitchell once looked over the Tragowel Plains and saw a vast grassland, today salt-encrusted mud stains the ground; where once productive pastures flourished, only salt-tolerant saltbush survives. Although the most concentrated problem occurs on land under irrigation, salinity affects dryland farming to an even greater extent.

No other comparably sized area in the world has suffered as much destruction of natural vegetation in such a short period of time as the Western Australian wheatbelt. The replacement of indigenous species with fields and exotic crops increased the amount of water moving over and beneath the surface. The water, which the original vegetation intercepted, retained and transpired, now transports salt to the surface. The amount of once-productive wheatbelt land rendered useless through salinity increased from 72 219 hectares in 1955 to 256 314 in 1979—an increase of 255 percent in only 24 years. Every year salt poisoning relentlessly renders another 250 square kilometres of land unproductive. In addition, major Western Australian rivers, with headwaters in cleared agricultural land—the Blackwood, Avon and Murray—cannot now be used because high salinity has made their water unfit for both human consumption and irrigation.

Ameliorating salinity requires lowering watertables and reducing the amount of water flowing through the soil. Not surprisingly, the majority of salinity mitigation measures proffered by hydraulic engineers involve engineering—plumbing the landscape. Sub-surface drains, designed to reduce watertables, only create problems of disposal. This arrangement, the most common solution in the Murray River basin, daily pours highly saline water into streams and rivers, all of which flow back into the Murray. Engineering has turned the Murray into an irrigation channel and drainage conduit for the increasingly salt-laden discharge from irrigated areas, and has destroyed Australia's major river.

Plumbing the landscape conforms to the tradition of technocratic control over nature in Australia. To the engineered mind, the grander the scheme, the more perfect the solution. In fact, to engineers, reshaping the earth to their own pleasure appears the *only* solution. The most audacious proposal to deal with Murray basin salinity requires a pipeline to the sea to carry away saline groundwater. Such a project, involving hundreds of kilometres of pipeline or open trench and dozens of enormous pumping stations, would rival the scale of the Snowy Mountains Scheme.

Despite Labor's commitment to stopping the Franklin dam and to conservation and protection of the environment, the 1983 Hawke government came to power dedicated to economic growth. Dominant factions in the party subscribed to a monomaniacal belief in the market as the pivot of economic and social life. Economic rationalism had persuaded most senior Labor government figures that the play of market forces determined the best use of the country's resources. Pragmatism required massive foreign investment in Australian industries and resources. Under Labor, Australia remained a partner in its own dismemberment. That most growth can occur only at the expense of the natural world, by pushing back 'the last walls of nature',[45] did not concern the Party's chief ideologues.

But economic rationalism, even by its own standards, failed to solve the problems associated with high interest rates, the balance of payments current account deficit and inadequate levels of productive investment. In every year of the 1980s the balance of payments on current account was in substantial deficit. Payments due for foreign ownership of assets in Australia, such as interest and dividends, together with payment for services, such as shipping and insurance, contributed most to the deficit. Unemployment increased and inflation continued.[46]

Efficiency, argued the economic rationalists, demanded governments abandon the provision of public services. Previously, the state maintained responsibility for constructing infrastructure—tunnels, railways, roads, harbours—but in the 1980s, Australian governments began ceding this prerogative to transnational, private capital.

In 1984 Dr Paul Wild and others at the CSIRO developed a Very Fast Train (VFT) proposal to link Melbourne and Sydney via Canberra. The Federal Ministry of Transport rejected the idea but in June 1986, the corporate giants, Elders IXL, transport firm

Thomas Nationwide Transport (TNT), and the Japanese construction firm Kumagai, formed a VFT Joint Venture to build the railway and to lobby Australian governments. The next year BHP joined the consortium. Based on the high speed trains which operate in France and Japan, the VFT would involve one of the largest and most extensive construction projects ever attempted in Australia.

For the venture partners, the train existed chiefly as a vehicle for inducing land development—simultaneously the means to offset the initial huge capital expenditure and the source of real profits. Sir Peter Abeles, chair of Ansett/TNT, described the project as

> the catalyst for the major redevelopment of Australia ... It would be more appropriate if one would call this project the restructuring of our sociological and economic structure of the east coast ... The train is only a by-product.[47]

The proposed route, around Australia's south-east coast, would cut a wide swath through the largest continuous area of forest left in Australia, through valleys, river flats and prime development sites. As the project's dimensions became clear, conservationists and people living in the train's path began protesting. Gippsland residents vowed to disrupt any construction and individuals removed orange plastic tags placed along the route to expedite aerial surveys. Letters to the editor, the formation of action groups in most of the towns and localities to be affected, coupled with the absence of any substantial public opinion in favour, convinced the New South Wales and Victorian governments of possible electoral liability in endorsing the project. But because of their disdain for Australia's landscape, politicians and their technocratic advisors have been unable to resist the compelling attractions of really big projects which promise to remake the continent. In August 1989, just as public pressure began to build against the VFT, Prime Minister Hawke gave the scheme his full public endorsement.

Although requiring state and federal government cooperation, the VFT involves the novel idea of a basic public service constructed and operated by private enterprise. Implementation necessitates the abandonment of responsibility for development by government, to which the people have recourse by the political process, to private enterprise, to which the people have no recourse.[48] In 1989 Alan Castleman, Chief Executive Officer of the VFT consortium, clarified his employer's intentions with respect to public participation: 'It's not appropriate to have some form of public enquiry to make the decisions that we should be making.'[49]

The fear that open, democratic discussion would lead to community rejection lay behind the elaboration, in secret, of another giant project for Australia—the Multifunction Polis (MFP). In 1987 the Japanese Ministry of International Trade and Industry (MITI) proposed the building of a high-tech city of 100 000 to 200 000 people in Australia which would recreate the conditions necessary for innovative technology research and production. Although vague and often contradictory—simultaneously a centre for tourism, retirement, education, medical treatment, communications, conventions, development of raw materials and biotechnology—the MFP's lack of definition did not prevent the Australian states from vigorously competing for site selection. All states held conventions and seminars—designed to exclude the public and include only business interests—which issued reports heavily biased in favour of the MFP. While the Japanese stressed tourism and real estate, the MFP's Australian publicists emphasised high-technology manufacture. Australian propaganda justified the project in terms of a new order of Asia–Pacific cooperation and of a high-tech utopia. The MFP accommodated a vision of the world to come and represented a new direction for humanity which would enable the highest realisation of human scientific ingenuity.

MITI had especially coveted a continent 'blessed with nature and open spaces', and relished investment opportunities where 'Acquisition of extensive land is relatively easy due to the scarcity of regulations on development projects ... and extremely low prices.'[50] The Japanese depiction of Australia as an undifferentiated and empty space needing to be developed and filled up with projects received influential Australian endorsement. One Victorian government official lauded the beauty of the MFP as lying in the absence of a need for a sense of place.[51] This view of Australia as an entirely fungible commodity, devoid of intrinsic beauty or worth, suited economic rationalists who advocated Australia's transformation into a sector of the international market. Australia thus became, not a home, not a land loved, but a field of investment, the profitability of which increased in proportion to the continent's tethers to the rest of the world.

Although bereft of a sense of place, the MFP, unavoidably, required a geographic location. In June 1990, the MFP Steering Committee selected a site near Queensland's Gold Coast—the first choice of the Japanese, who saw the MFP primarily in terms of tourism and resort development. Five hundred residents of the small town of Coomera, in the area chosen, immediately demonstrated against the proposal and the Queensland government refused to spend the 320 million dollars necessary to buy the required 4700 hectares of land.[52] The Steering Committee then recommended a site near the capital of South Australia. The South Australian Premier, John Bannon, welcomed the decision as marking the beginning of an exciting new era in Adelaide's development.[53]

The enthusiastic government and business reception accorded the Japanese-inspired MFP reflected Australia's increasing dependence on Japanese capital. Indeed, politicians welcomed the colonisation of Australia by Japanese interests as inevitable. 'What are the alternatives to the MFP in terms of Australia's future?', John Button, Minister for Industry, Technology and Commerce, asked in July 1990. He dismissed opposition to the MFP as short-sighted.[54]

Japan's takeover of the Australian economy, however (evident throughout the 1980s), did not result from inexorable economic logic. Japanese penetration arose as a product of Japanese strategy directed towards securing long-term interests in the Pacific region. The absence of any intention for greater economic independence in Australia made the Japanese objective an easy one to obtain. Australia's politicians and entrepreneurs identified more with the spectacle of Japanese economic success than with the sovereign needs of their own country. Mindlessly loyal to orthodox economic theory, Australia's leaders ignored the costs of Japan's success: long working hours, rigid education, severe gender inequality, tyrannical conformity. These costs resulted from the predatory conduct of

Japanese corporations towards the planet's natural reserves of wealth.

When finally located, fixed to a specific place on a finite earth, the reality of the visionary utopia embodied in the MFP appeared profoundly banal: diversity and creativity equalled a wider choice of consumer goods and services and expanded opportunities for corporate profit. The future looked remarkably like the present.[55]

In 1987, the World Commission on Environment and Development, chaired by Norwegian Prime Minister Gro Harlem Brundtland, recommended that, to counter pollution and restore deteriorating environments, countries pursue economic growth which sustained and expanded the resource base. Sustainable development should 'meet the needs of the present without compromising the ability of future generations to meet their own needs.' In June 1990 the Australian government approved sustainable development as the goal for the future use of Australian resources. The market, the government believed, best achieved those objectives.

Business naturally favoured a market-led approach to the environment. Sustainable development, the journal *Australian Mining* assured readers in June 1990, does not mean economic activity should decline or cease.[56] On the contrary, sustainable development heralds no fundamental change in the way miners quarry Australia. The utilitarian view of the earth as a stock of economic goods, owned and exploited by transnational capital, endures.

In 1989 the Hawke government established the Resources Assessment Commission to adjudicate between competing development and conservation interests. The Commission head, Justice Donald Stewart, claimed to be appalled at the extent of environmental destruction in Australia, but said, 'I don't wish to point the finger or lay the blame on anybody or any government.'[57] Stewart's legalism reflected official preference to view pollution and environmental destruction as accidental activities, the fault of no one. The Commission's policy, to proceed by consensus between developers and environmentalists, undermined the democratic necessity of identifying and holding accountable the makers of decisions responsible for destructive development and growth. Environmental mediation aims to deny the reality that conflict stems from exploitation and domination in favour of the fiction that all interests can and will be brought into harmony. Thus the Hawke government established the Resources Assessment Commission to diffuse environmental issues, and to depoliticise questions of development, while retaining Australia's unqualified commitment to growth.

In Australia, sustainable development and the Resources Assessment Commission must conform to the imperatives of economic rationality and the belief that competitiveness, efficiency, profit and growth are entirely valid, rational and enlightened goals of human life. Economic rationalism promotes these categories as all-embracing and self-justifying. The creed of economic growth reduces the whole of political, social, economic and spiritual life to a set of economic maxims. Economic rationalism imposes a utilitarian understanding of society as a trading company held together by contractual obligations incurred in the market place. Utilitarianism denies the possibility of any association of human beings held together by something more than a quest for mutual advantage. Moreover, utilitarianism denies the possibility of community based on mutual love, loyalty, common history, emotion, outlook and a shared identification with the land.

In the late 1980s the physical architecture of economic rationality appeared most visibly in the crane-crowded skylines of the central business districts of Australia's cities. Politicians applauded the construction boom in office blocks, luxury apartments and shopping centres as evidence of stability, affluence and progress. But the construction frenzy really signified that, by 1990, speculators, developers and property owners were as powerful, and remained as much in possession of Australia's destiny, as they had ever been in the country's history. The environmental movement had not significantly affected the political context within which decision makers work. For every development Australian greens fought (whether they won or lost), developers proposed two more.

The owners[58] and managers of Australia, those who looked on the country as a quarry, and whose paramount interest lay in profit and speculation, accused those who fought for nature of deceit and malignancy. Empire building had so constricted the mental universe of the empire builders that they could only impute motives of self-aggrandisement and power hunger to their environmental adversaries—mirror images of their own intent. Imaginatively incapable of understanding people who acted from motives other than those which animated their own behaviour, the demagogues of development attributed the foulest of ambitions to eco-activists.[59] Australia's rulers, heirs to the ideological frameworks inherited from the Enlightenment, found inaccessible the full dimensions of the havoc wrought on the living world by their projects. Intellectually and emotionally fully devoted to developmentalism, the servants of growth and progress found impossible any way of living besides the one prescribed by the logic of their own self-glory. The need to ensure that people identify their hopes and prospects with mass consumption required the suppression of all evidence of any human motives and aspirations other than those encompassed by the vision of progress. 'Capitalism means life—Environmentalism means death', the propaganda thundered.[60]

Commercial expansion and the pursuit of profit entail an exploitative cast of mind which has proven impossible to eradicate and which tolerates no interference in the conquest of nature in Australia.

EPILOGUE

ALUMINA, MANGANESE, IRON, COPPER,
CALCIUM, PLATINUM, MOLYBDENUM,
URANIUM—NAME IT, AND ALL YOU HAD TO
DO WAS PULL DOWN A HILL, DRAIN A
BILLABONG, LEVEL A FOREST, TEAR UP A
BEACH, TO BECOME A MILLIONAIRE! WHAT
MATTER IF YOU LEFT A DESERT BEHIND,
WHEN YOU DIDN'T HAVE TO LIVE THERE?

Xavier Herbert, Poor Fellow My Country,
1975

FOR OVER 200 YEARS a class of men with terribly simple purposes and equally simple conceptions of the ends of life, highly organised and wielding great powers, have imposed their impoverished outlook on the people and nature of Australia. The heirs to the Enlightenment told Australians they must adopt science and technology and embrace the free market to harness fully the forces of nature to human ends. But the conquest of nature has always involved power relations among humans. And the prescriptions about how people ought to construct their lives on planet Earth never survived undisputed.

In Australia, as in every other country invaded by enlightened Europeans, the conquest of nature generated conflict. Although the narrow, dogmatic ideology of conquest claimed absolute allegiance, the rulers of Australia never actually secured absolute allegiance. Complete implementation of the programme of conquest was never possible. The struggle to remake the face of the country left winners and losers. The hegemony of the dominant classes has always been constrained by the defiance of those whom they presume to rule—Aborigines, convicts, working people, women and middle class dissenters. But, with the significant exception of the Aborigines, most of these rebels shared the basic ideology of their rulers. To some extent, all believed that progress, growth and development would bring an improvement in human life commensurate with the advance in human control over nature.

Belief in progress implies the assumption that the losers of history failed to grasp the evolving truth. Nevertheless, losers existed and they left a legacy. Moreover, now that we can see the kind of society and world the winners made, we might profitably examine what the losers said, hoped and feared. Opposition to the central ideas of the Enlightenment is as old as the Enlightenment itself. The most formidable challenge came from the relativist and sceptical tradition rooted in the ancient world. Critics opposed the assumption that the methods employed by Newtonian physics, which achieved such triumphs in the realm of inanimate nature, could be applied with equal success to the fields of ethics, politics and human relationships. Montaigne, Giambattista Vico, William Blake, William Wordsworth, Mary Shelley, the German Romantics and others refused to regard humans as mere objects. For these dissenters, human beings were ultimately and irredeemably creative subjects—beings who thought and made choices, who were free and who *acted*. The counter-Enlightenment did not discount science. But the men and women of the counter-Enlightenment viewed science as an achievement of the creative imagination, not as an accurate reproduction of the structure of reality. The dissenters revolted against a conception of the world as a mechanical system to be manipulated for utilitarian ends by teams of rational experts. Philosophers, poets, bohemians and anarchists held that reason and science's construction of an all-embracing system constricted and obstructed their own vision of the world, a world which did not exist separately from human consciousness but in interaction with it.[1]

Ever since Georgiana Molloy walked into the bush at Augusta and opened herself to the beauty of her surroundings, a minority of immigrants and their descendants have loved Australia as it was—unreconstructed. They felt no need to impose a rational, profit-making order on the land; they did not consider themselves as exiles, tourists or interlopers whose first loyalty lay overseas. For the most part, however, these bushwalkers and naturalists remained individualistic and unorganised; they did not engage in collective action. Some formed social clubs and pressured politicians to grant nature reserve and national park status to special areas, but very few openly challenged the Australian obsession with development.

In the social ferment of the 1960s, however, in the protest against the war in Vietnam and in resistance to conscription, many Australians discovered that the destruction of the earth did not improve human life. On the contrary, they discovered that the unrestrained use of resources did not so much benefit humankind as corporations, transnational enterprises and military establishments. The demonic element in capitalist accumulation, the limitless and uninterrupted pursuit of more, beyond the calculations of rationality or purpose, appeared morally bankrupt. Abundance produced neither human happiness, nor led to equality and freedom. So when Australia withdrew from the war in Vietnam in 1972, social and political protest continued. After all, the kind of order the United States sought to impose by violence on Vietnam was exactly the kind of order developers and leading politicians wanted to impose on Australia. Marketeers, entrepreneurs and investors promised a future based on the premise that all humans want more or less the same things—which turn out to be precisely those things marketeers, entrepreneurs and investors happen to find profitable to market, produce and destroy.

The environmental rebels of the 1970s and 1980s—those who struggled against uranium mining, for Aboriginal land rights and for preservation of wilderness—managed to make some developments a matter of public debate. The days of unquestioning acceptance seemed at an end.[2] But the dissidents remained a small minority. The Australia-wide commitment to growth remained as strongly entrenched as ever. Here, as elsewhere, most decisions—in parliaments, cabinets or corporate board rooms—are still made on the assumption that science, technology and development yield only progress and profit. The dream of domination remains powerfully compelling, despite the loose logic of its promise: control is freedom, profit is fulfilment, development is security, minerals are civilisation. The reality is less appealing.

For the sake of efficiency, industrial societies have simplified the biological world, shortened food chains, reduced their number, substituted new ones for old, eliminated other species competition and lessened biological diversity. Science aims to maintain the truncated food chains in equilibrium, a difficult, but not an impossible management task. Because we live on a very resilient planet, the environment can adjust to pollution and biological disruption. Tens, hundreds of thousands of species may die, the rainforests disappear and the oceans turn to sludge, but some species—adaptable, stubborn, resourceful and opportunistic—*will* survive. Humans *can* live in a world without wilderness, reproduce in a biosphere restricted to food crops and domestic animals, and procure advantage in an environment of extreme artificiality. Providing at least some life survives the present worldwide flora and fauna convulsions, applied science can ensure the continuance of capitalism, exploitation and profit.

In 1989 a special issue of *Scientific American*, 'Managing Planet Earth', argued the case for maintaining scientific sovereignty over the planet.[3] In between eleven pages of advertising for General Motors, and full-page ads for Saab, BMW, Audi, Goodyear, Arco, Amoco, the American Petroleum Institute, McDonnell Douglas, Boeing, the Hughes Aircraft Company, International Paper, Union Carbide, and the Du Pont Chemical Company,[4] scientists confronted the grim catalogue of impending ecological disaster.

The groups who contrived the notion of progress and who, ever since the Enlightenment, have continually pressed for increased growth and development—capitalists, politicians, engineers, scientists and technicians—claim cleaning up the environment will cost money and can be paid for only through more economic growth— a dismal but highly profitable circularity. As *Scientific American* sought to affirm, the world's environmental problems do not amount to a crisis for capitalism but rather an opportunity. The magazine's editors felt no need to re-examine inherited theories that define industrial society's proprietary and predatory relationship to natural creation. Contributors unquestioningly viewed nature as a stock of economic goods in need of a careful management regime of exploitation. In response to environmental degradation, the state, science and transnational capital intend to maintain the earth as a field of exploitation.

For example, by engineering plants that prefer saline soils and others that can grow in drought conditions or resist low temperatures, biotechnology can extend the number of natural environments able to sustain agriculture. Biotechnologists and their employers claim our capacity to alleviate starvation depends on further technological conquest. But the poor, the hungry and the landless will not benefit from these technologies. Almost all biotechnological research is carried out in the laboratories of, or under the auspices of, transnational corporations who favour science which contributes to profit and enhanced social control. Thus the market-led technological extension of farmland actually aims to sustain the landscape of capitalism and concomitant social relations, not to relieve social and environmental distress.

Additional reassurance that capitalism's industrial tableau can be maintained in the face of environmental degradation came from *Time* magazine. In their 2 January 1989 issue the editors wrote, '[We] decided the growing concern about the planet's future had become the year's most important story'. In the diverting pages of *Time*, pollution and destruction became activities without human authors: 'Smokestacks have disgorged . . . factories have dumped . . . automobiles have guzzled . . . forests have been denuded . . . lakes poisoned, underground aquifers pumped dry'. The cause lay in 'recklessness', 'carelessness', 'sloppy handling' and 'profligacy'. *Time*'s partiality for the passive voice and the remote cause absolved the magazine and its readers from dealing directly with the destruction of tangibles. The abstract notion of the planet's future substituted for the very real and concrete devastation of neighbourhoods, rivers, forests, soils, air, people, flora and fauna. Anonymous human sins of omission and commission replaced those decision-making corporations, run by educated, well-paid people, which consciously choose to manufacture products in ways that disgorge, guzzle, denude, poison and pump dry. *Time*'s editors excluded from their story the names and addresses of those doing the destroying—the US, USSR, UK, German and Japanese governments, oil companies, mining companies—and the names and addresses of the economists, government officials and scientists who propagandise in favour of progress, growth, jobs and national security. Nor did *Time* mention the people around the world, who are resisting the poisoners and destroyers. On the premise that there is no problem that capitalism and the state cannot overcome, *Time* called for 'mobilization of political will, international cooperation and sacrifice unknown except in wartime'. The problems of the environment can be dealt with by established institutions and within prevailing power structures. The status quo, the power of the polluters over the polluted, must remain intact.[5]

The world's leaders, of course, find *Time*'s reaffirmation of orthodoxy enormously comforting. Both the President of the United States, George Bush, and the former Prime Minister of the United Kingdom, Margaret Thatcher, prescribe free-market solutions to pollution problems. Thatcher, for example, planned a price tag for environmental resources so that consumers would be charged and producers taxed for a better quality of life. Every environmental asset, from rivers and soil to butterfly species, would have a hard cash value so that damage to them could be fairly assessed. If the market decides the extinction of butterflies is worth the price, then society must accept the market's judgement.

In Australia, the Business Council maintains that the country is not facing an environmental emergency requiring radical change. Instead, market-based measures such as assigning private ownership rights to natural assets like air, water and forests will ensure Australia competes successfully in the global marketplace. Technology and social reorganisation to favour greater private profit will sustain the environment indefinitely. [6]

The real choice, however, lies not between different market mechanisms but between industrial capitalism and collective social action, between continued destruction and a more sensitively and democractically planned, non-exploitative future. This is also the choice for freedom and, not incidentally, social justice. To the extent environmental organisations refrain from challenging existing political relationships and omit social justice from their agenda, they are a sham; they fight against something they do not really wish to defeat.[7] Rich people, rich countries, profitable corporations and wealthy environmental organisations all live by robbing nature; their standard of living demands that the robbery continue. In contrast, eco-activists must pursue a counter-hegemonic strategy, and oppose technical fixes and regulatory controls which aim at keeping environmentally destructive industry working. Strategy which honestly seeks to prevent and eliminate pollution and environmental destruction must aim to halt, reverse and terminate the industrial machine. To affirm freedom means saying no to economic growth and development.

Leading progressive interpreters of Australian culture and history—authors, critics and historians such as Patrick White, Alan Moorehead and Manning Clark—subscribe to a mythic geographical determinism. The spiritual darkness they detect at the heart of Australian civilisation they claim emanates from the land itself—a continent of primeval cruelty sustained by omnipotent sunlight and a dry interior. Australian indifference to human suffering reflects the apathy of land and sky to all human striving and travail.

According to Moorehead, primeval Australia presented 'an appearance of exhaustion and weariness . . . A kind of trance was in the air, a sense of awakening infinitely delayed [until an] awakening did occur in the south-eastern corner of the continent when the first white settlers arrived in 1788'.[8] But Australia was never asleep. Long before the arrival of the First Fleet, the Australian continent supported a life of fecundity, exuberance, drama, continuity and change. To Australia's pre-Enlightenment inhabitants, who for 2000 generations or more, lived, moved and had their being under the Australian sun, the landscape possessed everything necessary to construct a life. Out of the elements of Australian nature, Aborigines found both the source and locus of existence and fashioned their own sense of belonging. If European Australians, as the learned critics maintain, turned out an obdurate, alienated people, it was because of the nature of the society they constructed in Australia, not because of the landscape. The natural world imparts no moral qualities or lessons; the world of organisms, of replication, reproduction, life, death and decay is neither good nor bad, just nor unjust. The Australian landscape is neither harsh nor gentle, indifferent nor compassionate, primevally cruel nor humanely forgiving, male nor female. Cruelty and forgiveness, injustice and compassion are human inventions. The British Empire and Australia's tethers to the post-Enlightened industrial world—human constructions all—not nature, created modern Australia. Science, technology and the pursuit of profit transformed the face of the continent and determined the manner of life the invaders lived upon it.

The environmental history of Australia is essentially a political history and bears the stamp of human will, ideals and purposes. The environmental future of Australia will be no different. But only new purposes and new ideals, no longer predicated on dreams of conquest, can reverse the destructive habits outlined in preceding chapters.

This book has attempted to trace how the ideas of the Enlightenment contributed to Australia's human-made landscape, how the promise of conquest was reconstructed on Australian soil and converted to fact: a continent robbed, people and animals exterminated, land pauperised, air and water poisoned, forests eliminated. But in examining the ways European society in Australia so quickly and radically transformed the natural environment and built Australian society, I have also sought to show that while constrained by circumstances inherited from their past, people always made choices; no development was preordained, no decision inevitable. The biological transformation of Australia was possible only on the basis of a strong and pervasive social agreement, on a shared conviction that science, technology and economic growth contained the capacity to provide permanent solutions to all genuine problems of life or thought, to all questions of human worth. All history reveals an essential tension between the power of predictable forces and the influence of individuals. What social justice, liberty, economic equality and unbound nature Australians currently enjoy came about because individual people, in opposition to established doctrines, consciously pursued goals which seemed to them intrinsically valuable and not necessarily socially or historically prescribed. The realisation of those goals depended upon dedicated private and collective effort and not upon inexorable impersonal forces of history.

Without an acquaintance with the past, one remains complicit in the orthodoxy of the present. Only when Australians reclaim their own history, a history they made, can they succeed not only in fighting *for* nature but also *against* an historical trend of which a poorer and uglier world is the result.

ENDNOTES

Abbreviations used in endnotes and bibliography

ABC	Australian Broadcasting Commission
ABS	Australasian Book Society
ACF	Australian Conservation Foundation
AGPS	Australian Government Printing Service
ANU	Australian National University
ANZ	Australian and New Zealand Book Company
APCOL	Alternative Publishing Cooperative Limited
CUP	Cambridge University Press
HUP	Harvard University Press
LBC	Left Book Club
MIT	Massachussetts Institute of Technology
MUP	Melbourne University Press
OUP	Oxford University Press
SUP	Sydney University Press
UCP	University of Chicago Press
UNC	University of North Carolina
UQP	University of Queensland Press
UWA	University of Western Australia

1   A continent adrift

1 J. Tuzo Wilson (ed.), *Continents Adrift and Continents Aground: Readings From Scientific American*, W. H. Freeman, San Francisco, 1976.

2 See Francis Jacob, *The Logic of Life*, New York, 1982.

3 Part of the natural landscape in Australia, *Casuarinae* (*C. equisetifolia* and *C. lepodophloia*) have become a noxious pest in Florida. Originally introduced to adorn the streets of Palm Beach and Miami in the late 1890s, *Casuarinae* preferred canal banks and inland areas and grew into forests which shaded out all other vegetation, creating a monotonous and unproductive biological community. On Key Biscayne and other Miami-area beaches, the trees completely replaced the native sand pine scrub. On Cape Sable *Casuarinae* ruined one of the rare green turtle's few remaining nesting grounds. See Mark Derr, *Some Kind of Paradise*, William Morrow, New York, 1989, p. 57.

4 Based on Francis Laseron, *The Face of Australia*, Angus & Robertson, Sydney, 1954, pp. 2–37.
5 See Josephine Flood, *Archaeology of the Dreamtime*, University of Hawaii Press, Honolulu, 1983.
6 Aboriginal story from J. W. Gregory, *The Dead Heart of Australia*, John Murray, London, 1906, p. 3.
7 For the number of Aborigines in Australia at the time of the first European settlement I have used the figure of Jack Davies, 'The first 150 years', in Ronald M. and Catherine H. Berndt (eds), *Aborigines of the West*, UWA Press, Nedlands, Western Australia, 1980. The accounts of early settlers and explorers make clear that Aborigines occupied *every* part of Australia. Journals and diaries record constant contact with large numbers of Aborigines and note the evidence of their ubiquitous presence: camps, large villages, trails, even engineering works, and the smoke signals which followed and preceded explorers everywhere. Few explorers were probably ever out of sight of Aborigines, even of earshot, when they imagined themselves alone in an unpopulated wilderness. A long-standing preference for the low figure of 300 000 as the number of original inhabitants has enabled historians and anthropologists to perpetuate the basic conquest myth that Australia was a virgin land, or wilderness, and to ignore the bloody consequences of the European invasion of Australia—a necessary illusion. See also N. G. Butlin, *Our Original Aggression*, Allen & Unwin, Sydney, 1983.

2 Terra Incognita

1 W. W. Hyde, *Ancient Greek Mariners*, New York, 1947, p. 308.
2 Science describes those endeavours aimed at gaining knowledge of the natural environment, while technology represents those efforts to exercise control over the environment.
3 Almost all the scientists of the seventeenth and eighteenth centuries were men. The period saw a new faith in male initiative and an increase in male self-confidence; for the publicists of the Enlightenment, mankind chiefly meant men. I have retained the term to convey that meaning. Similarly, I employ the terms 'mastery', 'influential men' and 'lords of the earth' precisely because they are gender-specific. When Enlightenment thinkers promulgated the ideology of conquest they imagined men at the front exercising dominion. Mastery is exactly what they aspired to.
4 See William Leiss, *The Domination of Nature*, G. Braziller, New York, 1972; Evelyn Fox Keller, *Reflections on Gender and Science*, Yale University Press, New Haven, 1985; and Carolyn Merchant, *The Death of Nature*, Sierra Club Books, San Francisco, 1980.
5 See Isaiah Berlin, *Against the Current*, New York, 1980.
6 Based on Neil McKendrick, 'Josiah Wedgwood and Factory Discipline', *Historical Journal*, vol. 4, no. 1, 1961, pp. 30–55.
7 See Albert Borgmann, *Technology and the Character of Contemporary Life*, UCP, Chicago, 1987, p. 63.
8 J. C. Beaglehole, *The Life of Captain James Cook*, Stanford University Press, Stanford, California, 1974, p. 148.

9 J. C. Beaglehole (ed.), *The Endeavour Journal of Joseph Banks, 1768–1771*, Angus & Robertson, Sydney, 1962, in two volumes, vol. II, p. 50.

10 ibid., p. 55.

11 Beaglehole, *Cook*, op. cit., p. 230.

12 Beaglehole, *Banks*, op. cit., p. 100.

13 Beaglehole, *Cook*, op. cit., p. 228.

14 Beaglehole, *Banks*, op. cit., pp. 112–13.

15 ibid., pp. 122–3. Banks and Cook viewed the Aborigines differently. While the unabashed nudity of the natives fascinated both—they returned to the subject time and time again in their journals—Cook displayed none of Banks' impetuous initial judgements about negroid characteristics, poisoned weapons and treacherous behaviour. Banks' antagonistic judgements ultimately achieved greater influence. See Glyndwr Williams, *Historical Studies*, vol. 19, no. 77, October 1981, pp. 499–512.

16 Among historians, considerable controversy attends the reasons behind the establishment of penal settlements in Australia. See Alan Frost, *Convicts and Empire: A Naval Question, 1776–1811*, OUP, Melbourne, 1980.

17 See Michael Ignatieff, *A Just Measure of Pain*, New York, 1978, p. xiii.

18 Bentham proposed a cheaper alternative, a 'total penitentiary' of his own design, the Panopticon. Under Bentham's scheme, prisoners remained in separate cells arranged in circular tiers around a central observation lodge from which they could be readily and economically observed. By a careful arrangement of light and blinds, the prisoners would not be able to tell when they were being watched and would have to assume they were under constant surveillance. Bentham described his Panopticon as 'a new mode of obtaining power of mind over mind'. Transportation, he believed, would only inefficiently effect this outcome. Although the Panopticon was never built, the law reformers who carried the abolitionist campaign through to the end of transportation relied heavily on Bentham's arguments. See J. B. Hirst, *Convict Society and its Enemies*, Allen & Unwin, Sydney, 1983.

19 Frost, op. cit., p. 181.

3 No Eden

1 Lieutenant-Colonel David Collins, *An Account of the English Colony in New South Wales*, Cadell & Davies, London, 1804, p. 11.

2 ibid., p. 231.

3 Edouard A. Stackpole, *The Sea Hunters: the New England whalemen during two centuries*, Lippincott, New York, 1953, pp. 190–2.

4 J. S. Cumpston, *First Visitors to Bass Strait*, Roebuck Society, Canberra, 1973, p. 4.

5 ibid., p. 7.

6 ibid., p. 9.

7 ibid., p. 11.

8 D. R. Hainsworth, *The Sydney Traders*, Sydney, 1972, p. 130.

9 Translated by Helen Mary Micco, *King Island and the Sealing Trade, 1802*, Roebuck Publications, Canberra, 1971, p. 30.

10 Based on Robert Hughes, *The Fatal Shore*, Knopf, New York, 1986, p. 332.

11 Figure estimated from numbers given for various Bass Strait voyages in Cumpston, op. cit.

12 Hainsworth, op. cit., p. 90.

13 From the diary of Robert Knopwood in John J. Shillinglaw (ed.), *Historical Records of Port Phillip*, Government Printer, Melbourne, 1879, p. 123.

14 William John Dakin, *Whalemen Adventurers*, revised edition, Angus & Robertson, Sydney, 1963, pp. 31–2.

15 Derek Whitelock, *Conquest to Conservation*, Wakefield Press, Adelaide, 1985, p. 61.

16 See Sir Sydney Frost, *The Inquiry into Whales and Whaling*, Canberra, 1978.

17 P. Cunningham, *Two Years in New South Wales*, London, 1827, in two volumes, vol. II, p. 102.

18 L. G. Churchward, *Australia & America, 1788–1972*, APCOL, Sydney, 1979, p. 24.

19 J. Lort Stokes, *Discoveries in Australia*, T. & W. Boone, London, 1846, in two volumes, vol. II, p. 131.

20 J. S. Battye, *Western Australia*, OUP, Oxford, 1924, p. 471.

21 See Dorothy Shineberg, *They Came for Sandalwood*, MUP, Melbourne, 1967.

22 Collins, op. cit., p. 321.

23 ibid., p. 336.

24 Stephen Nicholas (ed.), *Convict Workers*, CUP, Sydney, 1988, p. 24.

25 Alexander Harris, *Settlers and Convicts or Recollections of Sixteen Years' Labour in the Australian Backwoods*, (ed.) Manning Clark, MUP, Melbourne, 1953, p. 151.

26 ibid., p. 109, original emphasis.

27 Alan J. Marshall (ed.), *The Great Extermination*, Heinemann, Melbourne,, 1966, p. 166.

28 Harris, op. cit., p. 87.

29 ibid., p. 89.

30 Members of the First Fleet knew, from North and South American example, of the use of smallpox as a depopulating agent. Smallpox requires a population nucleus of a quarter of a million persons—the probable indigenous population of south-eastern Australia in 1788—with reasonably continuous contact to become epidemic. Assuming, conservatively, a mortality rate of 50 percent among a highly vulnerable people, the disease must have caused at least 125 000 deaths. See N. G. Butlin, *Our Original Aggression*, Allen & Unwin, Sydney, 1983, especially pp. 16–24.

31 Collins, op. cit., p. 336.

32 ibid., p. 410.

33 Keith Willey, *When the Sky Fell Down*, Collins, Sydney, 1979, p. 189.

34 The estimate of 40 dead from C. D. Rowley, *The Destruction of Aboriginal Society*, ANU Press, Canberra, 1970, p. 45. Official papers relating to the massacre were destroyed.

35 Shillinglaw, op. cit., p. 118.

36 Henry Melville, *The History of Van Diemen's Land*, Hobart, 1839, reprint, Sydney, 1965, p. 31, original emphasis.

37 Lloyd Robson, *A History of Tasmania*, OUP, Melbourne, 1983, p. 50.

38 ibid., p. 211.

39 ibid., p. 232.

40 ibid., pp. 245–6.

41 ibid., p. 231.
42 ibid., p. 212.
43 Hughes, op. cit., p. 416.
44 Lyndall Ryan, *The Aboriginal Tasmanians*, University of British Columbia Press, Vancouver, 1981, p. 151.
45 James Backhouse, *A Narrative of a Visit to the Australian Colonies*, Hamilton Adams, London, 1843, p. 84.
46 ibid., p. 174.
47 Barron Field (ed.), *Geographical Memoirs of New South Wales*, John Murray, London, 1825, p. 443.
48 ibid., p. 424.
49 ibid., p. 179.
50 ibid., p. 156.
51 ibid., pp. 223–4.
52 ibid., p. 409.
53 ibid., p. 254.
54 ibid., p. 305.
55 See Paul Carter, *The Road to Botany Bay*, Knopf, New York, 1988, p. 58.
56 Mitchell's contribution based on ibid., chapter 4, passim.

4   A camping ground for profit

1 Thomas Carlyle, cited in Michael Adas, *Machines as the Measure of Men*, Cornell University Press, Ithaca, New York, 1989, pp. 138–9.
2 See E. P. Thompson, *The Making of the English Working Class*, New York, 1964, chapter 11, passim.
3 Stephen Nicholas (ed.), *Convict Workers*, CUP, Cambridge, 1988, p. 74.
4 An account of the trial of the Scottish Martyrs in Thompson, op. cit., p. 125.
5 For political prisoners in Australia see Robert Hughes, *The Fatal Shore*, Knopf, New York, 1987, chapter 6.
6 Alexandra Hasluck, *Thomas Peel of Swan River*, OUP, Melbourne, 1965, p. 61.
7 The view of Edward Gibbon Wakefield quoted in J. S. Battye, *Western Australia*, OUP, Oxford, 1924, p. 93.
8 Pamela Statham (ed.), *The Tanner Letters*, UWA Press, Nedlands, Western Australia, 1981, pp. 23, 55.
9 Ken Buckley and Ted Wheelwright, *No Paradise for Workers*, OUP, Melbourne, 1988, p. 67.
10 See J. M. R. Cameron, 'Patterns on the Land, 1829–1850', in J. Gentilli (ed.), *Western Landscapes*, UWA Press, Nedlands, Western Australia, 1979, pp. 203–19.
11 R. T. Appleyard and Toby Manford, *The Beginning*, UWA Press, Nedlands, Western Australia, 1980, pp. 185–6.
12 Neville Green, *Broken Spears*, Focus Education Services, Cottesloe, Western Australia, 1984, p. 97.
13 Nearly 100 years later, Western Australia's pre-eminent historian judged the massacre a 'salutary lesson, which ought to have been given two years earlier'. Battye, op. cit., p. 133.

14 The facts of Georgiana Molloy's life are based on Alexandra Hasluck, *Portrait with Background*, OUP, Melbourne, 1955. The interpretation is mine.

15 ibid., p. 73.

16 ibid., p. 81.

17 ibid., p. 157.

18 ibid., p. 194.

19 Karl Marx, *Capital*, New York, 1967, p. 717.

20 A. Grenfell Price, *The Foundation and Settlement of South Australia, 1829–1845*, F. W. Preece, Adelaide, 1924, p. 12.

21 ibid., p. 118.

22 Douglas Pike, *Paradise of Dissent*, second edition, MUP, Melbourne, 1967, p. 113.

23 Price, op. cit., p. 94.

24 C. M. H. Clark, *A History of Australia*, vol. III, MUP, Melbourne, 1973, p. 55.

25 John Wrathall Bull, *Early Experiences of Life in South Australia*, E. S. Wigg & Son, Adelaide, 1884, p. 76.

26 Diary entries from Graham Jenkin, *Conquest of the Ngarrindjeri*, Rigby, Adelaide, 1979, p. 283.

27 Bull, op. cit., p. 194.

28 Michael Williams, *The Making of the South Australian Landscape*, New York, 1974, p. 15.

29 ibid., p. 129.

30 Stephen H. Roberts, *History of Australian Land Settlement, 1788–1920*, Macmillan, Melbourne, 1924, p. 96.

31 Edward Gibbon Wakefield, *A Letter From Sydney and Other Writings*, London, 1929, p. 47.

32 See Frederick Turner, *Beyond Geography*, Viking, New York, 1980, p. 239.

33 R. L. Heathcote, *Back of Bourke*, MUP, Melbourne, 1965, p. 35.

34 Brian Fitzpatrick, *The British Empire in Australia, 1834–1939*, MUP, Melbourne, 1941, p. 19.

35 Major T. L. Mitchell, *Three Expeditions into the Interior of Eastern Australia*, second edition, T. & W. Boone, London, 1839, vol. II, pp. 171, 195.

36 ibid., vol. I, Preface, and vol. II, p. 159.

37 Charles Sturt, *Two Expeditions into the Interior of Southern Australia*, second edition, Smith Elder & Co., London, 1834, in two volumes, vol. 2, pp. 74, 126.

38 Lloyd Robson, *A History of Tasmania*, OUP, Melbourne, 1983, pp. 212–13.

39 F. J. Meyrick, *Life in the Bush, 1840–1847*, Nelson, London, 1939, p. 95.

40 Margaret Kiddle, *Men of Yesterday*, MUP, Melbourne, 1961, p. 46.

41 Based on the argument presented in R. Therry, *Reminiscences of Thirty Years' Residence in New South Wales and Victoria*, second edition, Sampson Low, Son & Co., London, 1863, p. 302.

42 Francis Jennings, *The Invasion of America*, UNC Press, Chapel Hill, North Carolina, 1975, p. 82.

43 C. M. H. Clark, *Select Documents in Australian History, 1788–1850*, Angus & Roberston, Melbourne, 1950, p. 93.

44 Clark, *A History of Australia*, op. cit., p. 250.

45 Anne Allingham, *Taming the Wilderness*, second edition, James Cook University, Queensland, 1978, p. 33.

46 P. L. Brown (ed.), *The Narrative of George Russell*, OUP, London, 1935, p. 366.
47 Stephen H. Roberts, *The Squatting Age in Australia, 1835–1847*, second edition, MUP, Melbourne, 1964, p. 175.
48 ibid., p. 156.
49 Thomas Francis Bride (ed.), *Letters From Victorian Pioneers*, Government Printer, Melbourne, 1898, p. 175.
50 Mitchell, op. cit., p. 290.
51 M. F. Christie, *Aborigines in Colonial Victoria, 1835–86*, SUP, Sydney, 1979, p. 55.
52 Bridge, op. cit., p. 152.
53 Edward M. Curr, *Recollections of Squatting in Victoria*, second edition, Melbourne, 1965, p. 52. Another 100 years would pass before more than a handful of European-Australians shared Curr's judgement.
54 Based on the witness account reprinted in Therry, op. cit., pp. 272–4.
55 ibid., p. 282.
56 Clark, op. cit., p. 145.
57 Therry, op. cit., p. 283.
58 Historians remember Myall Creek because it was the best documented of all the massacres.
59 Alexander Harris, *Settlers and Convicts*, MUP, Melbourne, 1953, p. 206.
60 Christie, op. cit., p. 44.
61 Bride, op. cit., p. 31.
62 Therry, op. cit., p. 277.
63 For example, in 1965 historian Alexandra Hasluck in her introduction to *Thomas Peel of Swan River* (Melbourne, 1965), seriously wondered 'if they [the wild black men] could be called human.'
64 Therry, op. cit., p. 299.
65 William Howitt, *Land, Labour and Gold*, Boston, 1855, in two volumes, vol. II, p. 416.
66 Bride, op. cit., p. 34.
67 Mitchell, op. cit., p. 329.
68 Samuel Sidney, *The Three Colonies of Australia*, Ingram, Cooke & Co., London, 1853, p. 147.
69 ibid., p. 152.
70 ibid., p. 154.
71 William Westgarth, *Victoria*, Oliver & Boyd, Edinburgh, 1853, p. 243.
72 Coral Lansbury, *Arcady in Australia*, MUP, Melbourne, 1970, p. 108.

5 Dark deeds in a sunny land

1 Alexander Harris, *The Secrets of Alexander Harris*, Angus & Robertson, Sydney, 1961, p. 111.
2 Geoffrey Blainey, *The Rush That Never Ended*, third edition, MUP, Melbourne, 1978, p. 20.
3 ibid., p. 32.
4 G. L. Buxton, *The Riverina, 1861–1891*, MUP, Melbourne, 1976, p. 20.
5 William Howitt, *Land, Labour and Gold*, Boston, 1855, in two volumes, vol. 1, p. 17.
6 ibid., p. 189.

7 Michael Williams, *The Making of the South Australian Landscape*, New York, 1974, p. 135.

8 Anthony Trollope, *Australia and New Zealand*, Leipzig, 1873, in three volumes, vol. 3, p. 83.

9 Alexander Harris, *Settlers and Convicts*, (1847), (ed.) Manning Clark, MUP, Melbourne, 1953, p. 403.

10 R. Therry, *Reminiscences of Thirty Years' Residence in New South Wales and Victoria*, Sampson Low, Son & Co., London, 1863, p. 459.

11 The advent of self-government partly based on J. B. Hirst, *The Strange Birth of Colonial Democracy*, Allen & Unwin, Sydney, 1988, especially pp. 1–45.

12 Trollope, op. cit., vol. 2, p. 301.

13 Howitt, op. cit., vol. 1, p. 246. Howitt's opinion has not become entirely obsolete. Modern Australian foresters describe remaining Australian forests as 'decadent and damaged', 'stagnant' and 'standing cemeteries', and ceaselessly propagate their preference for 'young, vigorous, healthy new forest'. See R. Routley and V. Routley, *The Fight For The Forests*, second edition, Canberra, 1974, p. 15.

14 A person who selected land under the Land Acts was known as a selector.

15 Margaret Kiddle, *Men of Yesterday*, MUP, Melbourne, 1961, p. 231.

16 Edgars Dunsdorfs, *The Australian Wheat-Growing Industry, 1788–1948*, MUP, Melbourne, 1956, p. 126.

17 J. M. Powell, *The Public Lands of Australia Felix*, OUP, Melbourne, 1970, p. 199, quoting Pember Reeves, *Economic Journal*, vol. XXI, December 1911.

18 Stephen H. Roberts, *History of Australian Land Settlement*, Macmillan, Melbourne, 1924, p. 224.

19 Attrition figures from Geoffrey Serle, *The Rush To Be Rich*, MUP, Melbourne, 1971, p. 51.

20 W. K. Hancock, *Discovering Monaro*, CUP, Cambridge, 1972, p. 107.

21 Foregoing partly based on D. W. Meinig, *On The Margins of the Good Earth*, UCP, Chicago, 1962, p. 120.

22 Williams, op. cit., p. 33.

23 Meinig, op. cit., p. 43.

24 Williams, op. cit., p. 138.

25 See Meinig, op. cit., p. 118.

26 See Marc Reisner, *Cadillac Desert*, Viking, New York, 1986, p. 37.

27 The claim of George Ranken, quoted in R. L. Heathcote, *Back of Bourke*, MUP, Melbourne, 1965, p. 26.

28 See Meinig, op. cit., p. 87.

29 Arnold Guyot Cameron, *The Torrens System*, New York, 1915, pp. 41, 102.

30 Alan Powell, *Far Country*, MUP, Melbourne, 1982, p. 126.

31 Quoted in ibid., p. 132.

32 Williams, op. cit., p. 11.

33 ibid., p. 147.

34 See A. S. Kenyon, 'The Story of the Mallee', *The Victorian Historical Magazine*, vol. IV, no. 1, September 1914 and vol. IV, no. 3, March 1915.

35 For the history of the mallee district in Victoria see ibid.

36 Dunsdorfs, op. cit., p. 152.

37 Robert Hughes, *The Fatal Shore*, Knopf, New York, 1987, p. 571.

38 ibid., p. 577.

39 C. M. H. Clark, *A History of Australia*, vol. IV, MUP, Melbourne, 1978, p. 194.
40 See Peter Biskup, *Not Slaves Not Citizens*, UQP, St Lucia, Queensland, 1973.
41 Reverend J. B. Gribble, *Dark Deeds in a Sunny Land*, Perth, 1905, reprint UWA Press, Nedlands, Western Australia, 1987.
42 Henry Taunton, *Australind*, Arnold, London, 1903, p. 172.
43 G. C. Bolton, *A Thousand Miles Away*, ANU Press, Canberra, 1970, p. 19.
44 Thomas Major, *Leaves from a Squatter's Note Book*, Sands & Company, London, 1900, p. 30.
45 David Adams (ed.), *The Letters of Rachel Henning*, London, 1985, p. 150.
46 Gordon Reid, *A Nest of Hornets*, OUP, Melbourne, 1982, p. 85.
47 ibid., pp. 102–4.
48 Thomas Francis Bride (ed.), *Letters From Victorian Pioneers*, Government Printer, Melbourne, 1898, p. 267.
49 Harold Finch-Hatton, *Advance Australia*, W. H. Allen & Co., London, 1885, p. 147.
50 ibid., pp. 148–9.
51 ibid., p. 148.
52 See Donald Worster, *Nature's Economy*, Sierra Club Books, San Francisco, 1977, pp. 170–3; and Michael Adas, *Machines as the Measure of Men*, Cornell University Press, Ithaca, New York, 1989, p. 222.
53 Quoted in Ann Moyal, *A Bright and Savage Land*, Collins, Sydney, 1986, p. 37.
54 For details of this collecting zeal see Moyal, *A Bright and Savage Land*.
55 Thomas H. Huxley, *Evolution and Ethics*, New York, 1896, Prolegomena.
56 Howitt, op. cit., vol. 1, p. 34.
57 ibid., p. 62.
58 ibid., p. 274.
59 Henry Reynolds, *The Other Side of The Frontier*, Penguin, Ringwood, Victoria, 1982, p. 151.
60 God's monochromatism hypothesised by Trollope, op. cit., p. 149.
61 C. D. Rowley, *The Destruction of Aboriginal Society*, ANU Press, Canberra, 1970, pp. 104–5.
62 Reynolds, op. cit., p. 126.
63 Trollope, op. cit., vol. II, pp. 151, 256.
64 See Chapter 3, p. 50–1.
65 J. M. Powell, *Environmental Management in Australia, 1788–1914*, MUP, Melbourne, 1976, p. 71.
66 Linden Gillbank, 'The Origins of the Acclimatisation Society of Victoria: Practical Science in the Wake of the Gold Rush', *Historical Records of Australian Science*, vol. 6, no. 3, December 1986.
67 M. E. Hoare, 'Learned Societies in Australia: The Foundation Years in Victoria, 1850–1860', *Records of the Australian Academy of Science*, vol. 1, no. 2, December 1967, pp. 6–29.
68 Trollope, op. cit., vol. 2, p. 247.
69 The story of the rabbits based on Eric C. Rolls, *They All Ran Wild*, Sydney, 1969, pp. 7–185, and Geoffrey Bolton, *Spoils and Spoilers*, Allen & Unwin, Sydney, 1981, pp. 89–93.
70 Kenyon, op. cit.
71 H. M. Tolcher, *Drought or Deluge*, MUP, Melbourne, 1986, p. 194.

72 Sean Glynn, *Government Policy and Agricultural Development*, UWA Press, Nedlands, Western Australia, 1975, pp. 104–5.
73 For marsupial extinction see Derrick Ovington, *Australian Endangered Species*, Cassell, Sydney, 1978, pp. 60–78.
74 Serle, op. cit., p. 61.
75 ibid., p. 62.
76 See George Seddon and Mari Davis (eds), *Man and Landscape in Australia*, AGPS, Canberra, 1976, pp. 14, 43.
77 Joseph Jenkins, *Diary of a Welsh Swagman, 1869–1894*, (ed.) William Evans, Macmillan, South Melbourne, 1975, p. 23.
78 J. W. Eisdell, *Back Country, or the Cheerful Adventures of a Bush Parson in the Eighties*, OUP, London, 1936, p. 50.
79 Dr. Moorhouse, 'Victoria', *The Journal of the Manchester Geographical Society*, vol. IV, 1888, pp. 38–57.
80 Paul Carter, *The Road to Botany Bay*, Knopf, New York, 1988, pp. 168–9.
81 Marcus Clarke, from the Preface to *Poems (Sea Spray and Smoke Drift)*, by Adam Lindsay Gordon, London, 1904.
82 A. B. Paterson, 'Clancy of the Overflow'.
83 Quoted in J. A. Alexander, *The Life of George Chaffey*, Macmillan, Melbourne, 1928, p. 88.

6 To the firing line

1 Based on Geoffrey Blainey, *A Land Half Won*, revised edition, Sun Books, Melbourne, 1982, p. 290.
2 Geoffrey Serle, *The Rush To Be Rich*, MUP, Melbourne, 1971, p. 255.
3 Francis Adams, *The Australians*, T. Fisher Unwin, London, 1892, p. 191.
4 Serle, op. cit., p. 280.
5 F. H. Bauer, 'Significant features in the white settlement of Australia', *Australian Geographical Studies*, vol. 1, 1962.
6 Samuel Dixon, 'The effects of settlement and pastoral occupation in Australia upon the indigenous vegetation', *Transactions and Proceedings, Royal Society of South Australia*, vol. 15, 1892, pp. 195–206, and W. Woolls, 'The Destruction of Eucalypts', *The Victorian Naturalist*, vol. VIII, 1891, pp. 75–80.
7 John Muir to Louise Muir, 28 December 1903, *John Muir Correspondence*, reel no.13, Bancroft Library, University of California, Berkeley.
8 Journal, 3 January 1904, *John Muir Papers*, reel no. 29, Bancroft Library, University of California, Berkeley.
9 Alfred Deakin, *Irrigated India*, W. Tacket & Co., London, 1893, p. 10.
10 ibid., p. 20.
11 J. A. Alexander, *The Life of George Chaffey*, Macmillan, Melbourne, 1928, p. 76.
12 Bernhard Ringrose Wise, *The Making of the Australian Commonwealth*, Longmans, London, 1913, p. 52.
13 ibid., p. 222.
14 John Quick and Robert Randolph Garran, *The Annotated Constitution of the Australian Commonwealth*, Angus & Robertson, Sydney, 1901, p. 235.

15 Roger C. Thompson, *Australian Imperialism in the Pacific*, MUP, Melbourne, 1980, p. 2.
16 Partly based on E. J. Hobsbawm, *The Age of Empire*, Random House, New York, 1987, pp. 143–8.
17 See C. N. Connolly, 'Manufacturing "spontaneity": The Australian offer of troops for the Boer War', *Historical Studies*, vol. 18, no. 70, April 1978, pp. 106–17.
18 C. M. H. Clark, *A History of Australia*, vol. V, MUP, Melbourne, 1981, p. 169.
19 Barbara Penny, 'Australia's Reactions to the Boer War: a study in colonial imperialism', *Journal of British Studies*, vol. 7, pp. 97–130.
20 R. L. Wallace, *The Australians at the Boer War*, Canberra, 1976, p. 35.
21 May Vivienne, *Travels in Western Australia*, London, 1902, p. 80.
22 Clark, op. cit., p. 169.
23 Russel Ward, *The History of Australia*, New York, 1977, p. 35.
24 ibid., p. 36.
25 John Mildred Creed, *My Recollections of Australia & Elsewhere, 1842–1914*, Herbert Jenkins Ltd, London, 1914, p. 206.
26 W. H. Traill, *A Queenly Colony*, Edmund Gregory, Government Printer, Brisbane, 1901, p. 72.
27 ibid., p. 38.
28 ibid.
29 ibid., p. 95.
30 Harold Finch-Hatton, *Advance Australia!*, W. H. Allen & Co., London, 1885, p. 159.
31 Thompson, op. cit., p. 55.
32 G. C. Bolton, *A Thousand Miles Away*, ANU Press, Canberra, 1970, p. 251.
33 Australian Institute of Political Science, *Northern Australia*, Sydney, 1954, p. 185.
34 Peter Corris, *Passage, Port and Plantation*, MUP, Melbourne, 1973, p. 1.
35 *Western Australia and its Resources*, Government publication, Perth, 1901, p. 3.
36 J. R. Robertson, 'The Western Australian Timber Industry', *University Studies in Western Australian History*, vol. III, no. 1, September 1957.
37 Vivienne, op. cit., p. 214.
38 *Western Australia and its Resources*, op. cit., p. 109.
39 ibid.
40 Edgars Dunsdorfs, *The Australian Wheat-Growing Industry, 1788–1948*, MUP, Melbourne, 1956, p. 211.
41 *Western Australia and its Resources*, op. cit., p. 19.
42 An English paddock was a small enclosure in a field but in Australia, the term paddock denotes any enclosed area, irrespective of size, from half a hectare to 40 000 hectares.
43 See Samuel P. Hays, *Conservation and the Gospel of Efficiency*, HUP, Cambridge, Massachusetts, 1959, and Donald Worster, *Nature's Economy*, San Francisco, 1977, p. 266.
44 Elwood Mead, 'Irrigation in Victoria', in A. M. Laughton and T. S. Hall (eds), *Handbook To Victoria*, Government Printer, Melbourne, 1914, pp. 255–68.
45 Elwood Mead, *Helping Men Own Farms*, New York, 1920, p. 89.

46 A. S. Kenyon, 'The Story of the Mallee', *The Victorian Historical Magazine*, vol. IV, no. 3, March 1915, pp. 121–50.
47 See Raymond Evans, Kay Saunders and Kathryn Cronin, *Race Relations in Colonial Queensland*, UQP, St Lucia, Queensland, 1988.
48 Cited in Neville Green, 'Aborigines and White Settlers in the Nineteenth Century', in C. T. Stannage (ed.), *A New History of Western Australia*, UWA Press, Nedlands, Western Australia, 1981, pp. 72–123.
49 Peter Biskup, *Not Slaves Not Citizens*, UQP, St Lucia, Queensland, 1973, p. 142.
50 Anna Haebich, *For Their Own Good*, UWA Press, Nedlands, Western Australia, 1988, p. 67.
51 *Western Australia and its Resources*, op. cit., p. 44.
52 Haebich, op. cit., 'Aborigines and Agricultural Development', pp. 1–46.
53 *Nature*, vol. 76, 2 May 1907.
54 Ian Turner, *Sydney's Burning*, Alpha Books, Sydney, 1969, p. 5.
55 Michael McKernan, *The Australian People and the Great War*, Collins, Sydney, 1984, p. 3.
56 McKernan, op. cit., pp. 7, 23.
57 Marilyn Lake, *A Divided Society*, MUP, Melbourne, 1975, p. 66.
58 C. M. H. Clark, *A History of Australia*, vol. VI, MUP, Melbourne, 1987, p. 32.
59 Ian Turner, 'Chapter 8, 1914–19', in F. K. Crowley (ed.), *A New History of Australia*, Heinemann, Melbourne, 1974.
60 ibid.
61 Based on Geoffrey Blainey, *The Peaks of Lyell*, MUP, Melbourne, 1954, pp. 57, 93. In 1976 Blainey, supported by a number of scientists, urged that the natural regeneration of the mountains around Mt Lyell be prevented so as to preserve the barren slopes in their 'delicate beauty' and for their possibilities as tourist attractions. See Geoffrey Blainey, 'History of a Pummelled Landscape', in M. R. Banks and J. B. Kirkpatrick, *Landscape and Man*, Royal Society of Tasmania, Hobart, 1977, pp. 1–6.
62 Union pamphlet, cited in R. W. Connell and T. H. Irving, *Class Structure in Australian History*, Longman Cheshire, Melbourne, 1980, p. 244.
63 Based on D. Coward, 'Crime and Punishment: The Great Strike in New South Wales', in J. Iremonger *et al.* (eds), *Strikes*, Angus & Robertson, Sydney, 1973.

7 An undeveloped enterprise

1 Quoted in Robert Murray, *The Confident Years*, Penguin, Ringwood, Victoria, 1978, p. 1.
2 George Currie and John Graham, *The Origins of CSIRO*, CSIRO, Melbourne, 1966, p. 15.
3 ibid., p. 43.
4 Ross Fitzgerald, *From 1915 to the Early 1980s*, UQP, St Lucia, Queensland, 1984, p. 77.
5 Edwin J. Brady, *Australia Unlimited*, Robertson, Melbourne, 1918, p. 447.
6 ibid., p. 636.
7 ibid., p. 689.

8 Edward Shann, 'Group Settlement of Migrants in Western Australia', *The Economic Record*, vol. 1, no. 1, November 1925.

9 G. C. Bolton, *A Fine Country to Starve In*, UWA Press, Nedlands, Western Australia, 1972, p. 41.

10 See Ellis Troughton, *Furred Animals of Australia*, Angus & Robertson, Sydney, 1941, pp. 116–37.

11 J. M. Powell, *An Historical Geography of Modern Australia*, CUP, Cambridge, 1988, p. 136.

12 Daisy Bates, *The Passing of the Aborigines*, Pocket Books, New York, 1973, p. 57.

13 Stephen Jay Gould, *The Mismeasure of Man*, Norton, New York, 1981, chapter 4, passim.

14 W. E. H. Stanner, *White Man Got no Dreaming*, ANU Press, Canberra, 1979, p. 322.

15 A belief still widely held. The moral prerogative of a superior race is the theme of Geoffrey Blainey's *A Land Half Won* (Sun Books, Melbourne, 1980, 1983), in which he argues that because Aborigines failed to make full use of the land in Australia, they forfeited their right to existence and had to make way for people who could more fully exploit the land.

16 Peter Biskup, *Not Slaves Not Citizens*, UQP, St Lucia, Queensland, 1973, p. 90.

17 ibid., p. 96.

18 ibid., p. 97.

19 ibid., p. 84.

20 Alan Powell, *Far Country*, MUP, Melbourne, 1982, p. 180.

21 Biskup, op. cit., p. 187.

22 ibid., p. 89.

23 The fundamental cause of the confusion lay in the slavish adherence to the fabricated nineteenth century notion of race. For while the findings of anthropologists and ethnologists reinforced popular Australian prejudice, they did not reflect biological reality. So-called human races are not separate species, are not even true races. All humans are but recent, poorly differentiated sub-populations of our modern species, *Homo sapiens*, separated at most by tens of thousands of years and distinguished by remarkably small genetic differences. Nowhere on earth does there exist a human community combining a distinctive genetic make-up with a degree of reproductive isolation sufficient to sustain it. Evolution has not given rise to any racial difference between people. So-called racial differences are literally no more than skin deep. See P. B. and J. S. Medawar, *Aristotle to Zoos*, HUP, Cambridge, Massachusetts, 1983, entry under 'Taxon', and Stephen Jay Gould, *The Flamingo's Smile*, Norton, New York, 1985, chapter 12, 'Human Equality Is a Contingent Fact of History'.

Similarly, the terms 'black' and 'white' gratuitously draw attention to skin colour as of overriding significance. Except when quoting or paraphrasing, I have refrained from employing the description. 'Black' and 'white' evoke an image of opposites, of irreconcilables, and validate the idea of categorising people according to skin complexion, a fact of no more gravity than eye colour. Differences between people derive from cultural and social circumstances, not pigmentation.

24 Ernestine Hill, *The Great Australian Loneliness*, Robertson & Mullins, Melbourne, 1956, p. 35.

25 ibid., p. 150.

26 ibid., p. 228.

27 Marilyn Lake, *The Limits of Hope*, MUP, Melbourne, 1987, p. 10.

28 Sean Glynn, *Government Policy and Agricultural Development*, UWA Press, Nedlands, Western Australia, 1975, p. 122.

29 Lake, op. cit., p. 89.

30 ibid., p. 185.

31 David J. Gordon, *The "Nile" of Australia*, Government Printer, Adelaide, 1906, Preface.

32 The story of the MIAs based on Trevor Langford-Smith and John Rutherford, *Water and Land*, ANU Press, Canberra, 1966.

33 Douglas Mawson, *Some Aspects of Forestry in South Australia*, Commemoration Address, University of Adelaide, Adelaide, 1925.

34 ibid.

35 Leonard Webb, 'The Rape of the Forests', in A. J. Marshall (ed.), *The Great Extermination*, Heinemann, Melbourne, 1966.

36 L. T. Carron, *A History of Forestry in Australia*, ANU Press, Canberra, 1985, p. 108.

37 Brady, op. cit., p. 768.

38 Francis Ratcliffe, *Flying Fox and Drifting Sand*, Chatto & Windus, London, 1938, p. 65.

39 ibid., p. 99.

40 Frank Dalby Davison and Brooke Nicholls, *Blue Coast Caravan*, Angus & Robertson, Sydney, 1935, p. 42.

41 ibid., p. 53.

42 ibid., p. 75.

43 D. H. Lawrence, *Kangaroo*, Penguin, New York, 1985, p. 227.

44 Flora S. Eldershaw (ed.), *The Peaceful Army*, Women's Executive Committee and Advisory Council of Australia's 150th Anniversary Celebration Council, Sydney, 1938. From the Foreword by Lady Zara Gowrie.

45 Bolton, op. cit., p. 8.

46 P. D. Phillips (ed.), *The Peopling of Australia*, Macmillan/MUP, Melbourne, 1933, p. 237.

47 W. K. Hancock, *Australia*, Brisbane, 1961, p. 20.

48 Richard Broome, *Aboriginal Australians*, Allen & Unwin, Sydney, 1982, p. 166.

49 See F. K. Crowley, *Australia's Western Third*, Macmillan, London, 1960.

50 G. H. Burvill (ed.), *Agriculture in Western Australia*, UWA Press, Nedlands, Western Australia, 1979, p. 258.

51 Ratcliffe, op. cit., pp. 332, 338.

52 Jock H. Pick, *Australia's Dying Heart*, MUP, Melbourne, 1944, Preface.

53 ibid., p. 64.

54 Army against the emus from Vincent Serventy, *A Continent in Danger*, Ure Smith, Sydney, 1966, pp. 108–9.

55 Stuart Macintyre, *The Oxford History of Australia*, vol. 4, 1901–1942, OUP, Melbourne, 1986, p. 240.

56 Bolton, op. cit., p. 111.

57 Robert Cooksey (ed.), *The Great Depression in Australia*, no. 17 of *Labour History*, Sydney, 1970.
58 Geoffrey Blainey, *The Steel Master*, Macmillan, South Melbourne, 1972, p. 105.
59 Cameron Hazlehurst, *Menzies Observed*, Allen & Unwin, Sydney, 1979, pp. 138–40.
60 To facilitate its occupation of cold Manchuria, Japan became a major buyer of Australian wool—second only to that of the United Kingdom by the late 1930s—and simultaneously created a strong Japanese appeasement lobby in Australia, especially among the conservative establishment: bankers, importers and exporters, wool organisations and shippers. Notwithstanding Australia's White Australia policy, most of the press became pro fascist Japan. See Rupert Lockwood, *War on the Waterfront*, Allen & Unwin, Sydney, 1989.
61 Below based on Roger J. Bell, *Unequal Allies*, MUP, Melbourne, 1977.
62 ibid., p. 47.
63 ibid., p. 60.
64 ibid., p. 112.
65 The opinion of Percy Spender, Opposition Spokesman for Foreign Affairs, in ibid., p. 103.
66 ibid.

8 World quarry

1 See Paul Fussell, *Wartime*, OUP, New York, 1989, p. 9.
2 For the story of UKUSA see Jeffrey T. Richelson and Desmond Ball, *The Ties That Bind*, Allen & Unwin, Sydney, 1985.
3 See Michael Adas, *Machines As The Measure of Men*, Cornell University Press, Ithaca, New York, 1989, Epilogue, 'Modernization Theory and the Revival of the Technological Standard'.
4 Richard White, *Inventing Australia*, Allen & Unwin, Sydney, 1981, p. 163.
5 Lionel Wigmore, *Struggle for the Snowy*, OUP, Melbourne, 1968, p. 194.
6 C. H. Munro (Emeritus Professor of Civil Engineering, University of New South Wales), *Australian Water Resources and Their Development*, Angus & Robertson, Sydney, 1974, p. 143.
7 George Johnston, *Clean Straw for Nothing*, Collins, London–Sydney, 1969, p. 99.
8 Australian Institute of Political Science, *Northern Australia*, Angus and Robertson, Sydney, 1954, Introduction.
9 ibid., Preface.
10 ibid., p. 45.
11 Jan Roberts, *Massacres to Mining*, Dove Communications, Blackburn, Victoria, 1981, p. 73.
12 ibid.
13 At their new settlement of Weipa South, the people of Mapoon found themselves living amongst people from diverse geographical regions of the state, most of whom spoke languages different from their own. Disoriented and lacking occupation, people fell to drinking, gambling and fighting. In 1980 police charged a young Mapoon man, Alwyn Peter, with the murder

of his girlfriend, Deidre. The defence argued that Peter's criminal act was at least partly related to the devastation inflicted on Aboriginal society by European conquest. The judge accepted the defence and sentenced Peter to 21 months' imprisonment. See Paul Wilson, *Black Death White Hands*, Allen & Unwin, Sydney, 1982.

14 Statement of Comalco chairman Sir Don Hibberd at the 1980 Annual General Meeting, Roberts, op. cit., p. 108.

15 ibid.

16 ibid., p. 107.

17 Ross Fitzgerald, *From 1915 to the Early 1980s*, UQP, St Lucia, Queensland, p. 187.

18 For estimates of brigalow coverage see A. J. Marshall, *The Great Extermination*, Heinemann, Melbourne, 1966, p. 188.

19 Fitzgerald, op. cit., p. 365.

20 Patricia Clare, *The Struggle for the Great Barrier Reef*, Collins, Sydney, 1971, p. 213.

21 Judith Wright, *The Coral Battleground*, Thomas Nelson, Melbourne, 1977, p. 189.

22 D. W. Connell, 'The Barrier Reef Conservation Issue', *Search*, vol. 2, no. 6, June 1971, pp. 188–92.

23 Fitzgerald, op. cit., p. 366.

24 Elizabeth J. Harman and Brian W. Head, *State, Capital and Resources in the north and west of Australia*, UWA Press, Nedlands, Western Australia, 1982, p. 158.

25 Humphrey McQueen, *Gone Tomorrow*, Angus & Robertson, Sydney, 1982, p. 78.

26 The major iron-ore miners were Hamersley Holdings (controlled by RTZ of London), Mt Newman Mining Co. (owned by Australian, American and Japanese interests), Goldsworthy (American and British) and Robe River (Australian and Japanese).

27 Harman & Head, op. cit., p. 171.

28 ibid., pp. 179, 158–9.

29 ibid., p. 179.

30 *Northern Australia*, op. cit., Introduction.

31 C. T. Stannage (ed.), *A New History of Western Australia*, UWA Press, Nedlands, Western Australia, 1981, pp. 748–9.

32 See Peter V. Jones (Western Australian Minister for Industrial Development), 'Resources Development Policies in Western Australia', chapter 5, in Harman and Head, op. cit., pp. 103–32.

33 McQueen, op. cit., p. 89.

34 E. M. O'Loughlin (ed.), *Irrigation and Water Use in Australia*, Australian Academy of Science, Canberra, 1980, p. 65.

35 Brian Head (ed.), *The Politics of Development in Australia*, Allen & Unwin, Sydney, 1986, p. 172.

36 Denys Blakeway and Sue Lloyd-Roberts, *Fields of Thunder*, Unwin Paperbacks, London, 1985, p. 124.

37 Adrian Tame and F. P. J. Robotham, *Maralinga*, Fontana/Collins, Melbourne, 1982, p. 10.

38 See Blakeway, op. cit., and Tame and Robotham, op. cit.

39 Dan O'Neill, 'Project Chariot: How Alaska Escaped Nuclear Excavation',

Bulletin of The Atomic Scientists, vol. 45, no. 10, December 1989, pp. 28–37.

40 *Wall Street Journal*, 10 February and 31 March 1969.

41 Russel Ward, *The History of Australia*, Harper & Row, New York, 1977, p. 215.

42 The story of the fate of Australia's forests largely based on R. and V. Routley, *The Fight For The Forests*, second edition, Canberra, 1974.

43 ibid., p. 18.

44 ibid., p. 92.

45 ibid., p. 11.

46 Robert Birrell, Doug Hill and John Stanley (eds), *Quarry Australia?*, OUP, Melbourne, 1982, p. 220.

47 Routley and Routley, op. cit., p. 15.

48 ibid., p. 105.

49 ibid., p. 154.

50 ibid., p. 21.

51 ibid., p. 22.

52 R. L. Heathcote, *Australia*, New York, 1975, p. 195.

53 Named after the early Tasmanian Chief Justice, John Lewes Pedder, who opposed the plans of Governor George Arthur and Aboriginal conciliator G. A. Robinson to confine the Tasmanian Aborigines to Flinders Island. See Chapter 3.

54 Peter Blazey, *Bolte*, Milton, Queensland, 1972, p. 80.

55 J. M. Powell, *An Historical Geography of Modern Australia*, CUP, Cambridge, 1988, p. 238.

56 I prefer the term eco-activist to conservationist or environmentalist, as both are open to too wide an interpretation. Conservation originally denoted a system of rational exploitation and is clearly compatible with the elimination of everything natural. Environmentalist formerly denoted someone with an active concern for nature but now, since George Bush and Margaret Thatcher describe themselves as environmentalists, the term is wedged somewhere between *family values* and *free market*. Developers even claim environmentalist consciences. The term is fraudulent and meaningless. Nature lover is a far more honest description of people genuinely concerned with the natural world. I shall, however, continue to use conservationist and environmentalist in cases where the subjects explicitly identified themselves as such.

57 Powell, op. cit., p. 240.

58 See Community Research Action Centre, *Wilderness to Waste*, Monash University, Melbourne, 1981.

59 Leonie Sandercock, *Cities for Sale*, MUP, Melbourne, 1975, p. 131.

60 Richard J. Roddewig, *Green Bans*, New York, 1978, p. 66.

61 ibid., p. 14.

62 Jack Mundey, *Green Bans and Beyond*, Angus & Robertson, Sydney, 1981, p. 107.

63 Sandercock, op. cit., p. 147.

64 Alan Gilpin, *The Australian Environment*, Sun Books, Melbourne, 1980, p. vi.

65 *Search*, vol. 2, no. 4, April 1971.

9 Not by conquest

1 R. W. Connell, *Ruling Class Ruling Culture*, CUP, Cambridge, 1977, p. 94.
2 See W. K. Hancock, *The Battle of Black Mountain*, Canberra, 1974.
3 Desmond Ball, *A Suitable Piece of Real Estate*, Hale & Iremonger, Sydney, 1980, p. 22.
4 *Wall Street Journal*, 17 February 1981.
5 Jonathan Kwitny, *The Crimes of Patriots*, Norton, New York, 1987, p. 138.
6 For the CIA in Australia and the events surrounding the dismissal of the Whitlam government see Denis Freney, *CIA's Australian Connections*, Sydney, 1977, *Get Gough!*, Sydney, 1985 (both self-published) , and Kwitny, op. cit.
7 After the ban, exploitation—subsidised by the state—shifted to what the sand grew. In 1990, over blockades and protest, the Queensland government insisted that the logging of Fraser Island's ancient rainforests continue. See *Habitat Australia*, vol. 18, no. 5, October 1990.
8 Joseph A. Camilleri, *Australian–American Relations*, Macmillan, Melbourne, 1980, p. 108.
9 Alan Gilpin, *The Australian Environment*, Sun Books, Melbourne, 1980, p. 115.
10 Lang Hancock, *Wake up Australia*, E. J. Dwyer, Sydney, 1979, p. 5.
11 ibid., pp. 60, 56.
12 Adrian Tame and F. P. J. Robotham, *Maralinga*, Fontana/Collins, Melbourne, 1982, p. 169.
13 See Tame and Robotham, *Maralinga* and Denys Blakeway and Sue Lloyd-Roberts, *Fields of Thunder*, Unwin Paperbacks, London, 1985.
14 W. E. H. Stanner, *White Man Got no Dreaming*, ANU Press, Canberra, 1979, p. 282.
15 Since at least the eighteenth century all western nations have accepted the principle that conquest—even achieved in the course of a just war—did not give the victor the right to confiscate property. Hence, there exists a powerful motive for the Australian state to deny the continent was acquired through conquest and to believe, instead, that the British occupation of a few hectares at Sydney Cove in 1788 extinguished *all* native title in Australia. Thus, by means of peaceful settlement, the colonists gained legal title to land which no conqueror could legitimately claim. Henry Reynolds calls this subterfuge 'the ultimate confidence trick—vast in scope, breathtaking in ambition. The settlers embraced all the advantages of acquisition by settlement while avoiding most of the attendant obligations towards the dispossessed.' Henry Reynolds, *Frontier*, Allen & Unwin, Sydney, 1987, pp. 176–80.
16 Pamela Lyon and Michael Parsons, *We Are Staying*, IAD Press, Alice Springs, Northern Territory, 1989, p. ii.
17 Jan Roberts, *Massacres to Mining*, Dove Communications, Blackburn, Victoria, 1981, p. 124.
18 ibid., p. 91.
19 Scott Bennett, *Aborigines and Political Power*, Allen & Unwin, Sydney, 1989, p. 55.
20 ibid., p. 60.
21 Ross Fitzgerald, *From 1915 to the Early 1980s*, UQP, St Lucia, Queensland, 1984, p. 543.

22 Neville Green, *Broken Spears*, Focus Education Services, Cottesloe, Western Australia, 1984, p. 148.
23 *The Age*, 3 May 1984, quoted in Bennett, op. cit., p. 56.
24 Humphrey McQueen, *Gone Tomorrow*, Angus & Robertson, Sydney, 1982, p. 188.
25 ibid., p. 74.
26 ibid., p. 94.
27 Fitzgerald, op. cit., p. 572.
28 See Evan Whitton, *The Hillbilly Dictator*, ABC Books, Crows Nest, New South Wales, 1989.
29 C. H. Munro, *Australian Water Resources and Their Development,* Angus & Robertson, Sydney, 1974, p. 119.
30 ibid., p. x.
31 James McQueen, *The Franklin*, Penguin, Ringwood, Victoria, 1983, p. 65.
32 M. Sornarajah (ed.), *The South West Dam Dispute*, University of Tasmania, Law School, Hobart, 1983, p. 16.
33 Peter Thompson, *Bob Brown of the Franklin River*, Allen & Unwin, Sydney, 1984, p. 3.
34 Jeni Kendell and Eddie Buivids, *Earth First*, ABC Books, Sydney, 1987, p. 50.
35 ibid., p. 71.
36 ibid., p. 135.
37 Graeme Kelleher, 'Australia's Great Barrier Reef Marine Park: Making Development Compatible with Conservation,' *AMBIO*, vol. XI, no. 5, 1982, pp. 262–7.
38 *National Times*, 10 May 1980.
39 *Sydney Morning Herald*, 5 November 1988.
40 Wayne Hanley and Malcolm Cooper (eds), *Man and the Australian Environment*, McGraw-Hill, Sydney, 1982, p. 150.
41 *The Age*, 17 July 1990.
42 *The Age*, 17 January 1989.
43 Evidence given by Ray Richards to the Timber Industry Inquiry (Victoria), 3 September 1984 (transcript pp. 788–9).
44 *The Age*, 24 July 1990.
45 Edwin J. Brady, *Australia Unlimited*, Robertson, Melbourne, 1918, p. 447.
46 Abe David and Ted Wheelwright, *The Third Wave*, LBC, Sydney, 1989, p. 94.
47 *Canberra Times*, 8 December 1988.
48 See *The Social Implications of the Very Fast Train*, Fast Train Polis Action Group (Melbourne, 1990), reprint of submission to the VFT Review Panel by Harold P. Carter, 1 March 1990.
49 Public meeting, Bairnsdale, 23 February 1989. Quoted in *VFT: Need or Greed?*, VFT Awareness Groups Coalition, Melbourne, 1990.
50 *A Multifunction Polis Scheme for the 21st Century: Basic Concept* (1987), by the Japanese Ministry of International Trade and Industry (MITI), reprinted in *A Tale of New Cities, Japan's Plans for Australia*, Melbourne, 1990.
51 *Four Corners*, ABC Television, 15 May 1990.
52 *The Age*, 19 June 1990.
53 *The Age*, 20 June 1990.
54 *The Age*, 6 July 1990.

55 See Gavan McCormack, 'And Shall the Multifunction Polis yet be Built?', in Paul James (ed.), *Technocratic Dreaming*, Melbourne, 1990, pp. 129–37, and Joseph Wayne Smith, *The Australia That Can Say 'No!'*, Flinders University, Bedford Park, South Australia, 1990. Smith describes the MFP as 'perhaps the most outrageous example of the de-democratization of Australian society ... the project is a messianic drive to build a twenty-first century society ... [which] ... will set society upon a specific course, a course which has been decided *for* the Australian people, not freely chosen by them' (pp. 144–5).

56 Victor Bivoltsis, 'Environmental technology—a world of opportunity', *Australian Mining*, vol. 82, no. 6, June 1990, pp. 14–16.

57 *The Age*, 17 June 1990.

58 By 1986, World Bank statistics suggested that Australia had the most unequal distribution of wealth of any western nation. The richest 10 percent of Australians hold more than half the country's personal wealth and the poorest 30 percent hold none. *The Age*, 4 July 1990.

59 Although accusing greens of 'insufferable arrogance' and 'pseudo-intellectual imperialism', the critics are not without presumption of their own. See Michael Barnard, 'Scoop! Lost lake is safe', *The Age*, 19 June 1990, p. 13. Other examples of the attempt to reimpose economic growth as the only valid measure of human life in the face of heightened eco-activity are G. Sheridan, 'Green Menace Threatens to Destroy the Economy', *The Weekend Australian*, 14–15 October 1989, p. 22, and 'Labor Can't See the Wood for the Trees', *The Weekend Australian*, 11–12 November 1989, p. 26, D. Keegan, 'Greenies are Lineal Descendants of Luddites', *The Australian*, 24 October 1989, p. 17, and G. Hendersen, 'Greenies: Off Course and Off Their Tree', *The Australian*, 6 November 1989, p. 13.

60 Hancock, op. cit., p. 35.

Epilogue

1 See Isaiah Berlin, *Against the Current*, New York, 1980.

2 See the optimistic essays in Robert Birrell, Doug Hill and John Stanley (eds), *Quarry Australia?*, OUP, Melbourne, 1982.

3 *Scientific American*, 'Managing Planet Earth', September 1989.

4 Each of these associations and corporations sponsor or manufacture environmentally obnoxious products and engage in environmentally destructive procedures in so doing.

General Motors, along with other automobile manufacturers, is a vigorous opponent of government regulations designed to improve fuel efficiency and lower automobile exhaust emissions which contribute to air pollution, add to greenhouse gases and deplete the ozone level. GM's lack of concern for the wider environment reflects the company's indifference to its immediate neighbours. In the early 1980s, despite community opposition, GM and the city of Detroit destroyed 1500 homes and displaced 3400 people in the old neighbourhood of Poletown to build new manufacturing plants.

ARCO has given money to the Nature Conservancy, the Environmental Law Institute, the Conservation Foundation and the Peregrine Fund while investing heavily in oil exploration in the fragile Alaskan environment. In

1989 ARCO's Carson refineries were charged with and convicted of major pollution violations.

AMOCO has made large monetary contributions to right-wing think-tanks, such as the American Enterprise Institute and the Heritage Foundation, preoccupied with diminishing societal concern about threats to the environment. In 1978 the company tanker, Amoco Cadiz, ran aground off the coast of Brittany. Eleven years later damage is still evident, particularly with respect to the loss of diversity among the region's wildlife. Amoco has since been responsible for oil spills in the Gulf of Mexico and pipeline breaks in Colorado.

McDonnell Douglas is one of the world's major war contractors, whose professed concerns on behalf of the environment cannot be taken seriously, considering the company's whole reason for being lies in the manufacture and development of means to destroy life.

Workers at Boeing's Seattle plant recently sued the company due to excessively high rates of leukemia among production staff. Boeing carried out tests on unsuspecting workers by exposing them to electromagnetic fields (EMF), which promote miscarriages, foetal deformities, learning disabilities, depression and cancer. Boeing workers have also organised against the use of toxic chemicals on aircraft assembly lines.

Hughes Aircraft, a subsidiary of General Motors, manufactures missiles and other war materials. The company's business demonstrates major indifference to life on earth.

International Paper's Maine plants cause major air and water pollution in that state. The company's South Carolina plant is responsible for the worst case of dioxin pollution in the United States.

An explosion at Union Carbide's chemical plant in Bhopal, India, in 1984 killed 3600 people and injured 20 000. In the United States, Union Carbide maintains an abysmal environmental record and throughout the 1970s, operated the most polluting factory in the country. The company has consistently and wilfully violated health and safety regulations. Union Carbide is also the subject of a consumer and environmental boycott as a result of its refusal to tell residents near its Henderson, Kentucky PCB plant the nature of and the impact on health and the environment of a secret chemical emitted into the atmosphere and simply referred to as 'TF-1'.

In 1974, when scientists first calculated that chlorofluorocarbons (CFCs) used in aerosol sprays and other products would deplete the earth's ozone layer, the world's largest CFC manufacturer, Du Pont, dismissed the findings as 'speculative' and successfully fought proposed legislation to restrict the chemicals. In 1988 the company still maintained there was no reason to cease manufacturing CFCs; public pressure later forced the company to change its mind. In the meantime, the long resistance by Du Pont and others caused fifteen years of dangerous additional damage to the ozone layer. Du Pont, a major nuclear warfare contractor, has been named as California's chief releaser of CFCs and was recently cited for putting excess lead in the gasoline at its New Jersey refinery.

Above information from the respective company files at *The Data Center*, Oakland, California.

5 Analysis of *Time* based on Richard Grossman, 'Of TIME and Tide', *Earth Island Journal*, San Francisco, Spring 1989.

6 *The Age*, 13 July 1990.
7 Many of the major United States environmental organisations (the World Wildlife Fund/Conservation Foundation, the National Audubon Society, the Nature Conservancy and the National Wildlife Federation) accept corporate donations. In addition, the governing boards of some groups include the chair of the New York Stock Exchange, as well as executives from major polluters and earth destroyers such as Exxon, Philip Morris and the giant paper and pulp maker, Union Camp Corporation. See *Mother Jones*, April/May 1990.
8 Alan Moorehead, *Cooper's Creek*, Harper & Row, New York, 1963, p. 2.

BIBLIOGRAPHY

Australian history

Adams, Francis, *The Australians: A Social Sketch*, T. Fisher Unwin, London, 1892.

Alexander, Fred, *Australia Since Federation: A Narrative and Critical Analysis*, Nelson, Melbourne, 1967.

Alexander, J. A., *The Life of George Chaffey: A Story of Irrigation Beginnings in California and Australia*, Macmillan, Melbourne, 1928.

Allingham, Anne, *Taming the Wilderness: The First Decade of Pastoral Settlement in the Kennedy District*, 2nd ed., James Cook University, Townsville, Queensland, 1978.

Appleyard, R. T. and Toby Manford, *The Beginning: European Discovery and Settlement of Swan River, Western Australia*, UWA Press, Nedlands, 1980.

Australian Institute of Political Science, *Northern Australia: Task for a Nation*, Angus & Robertson, Sydney, 1954.

Backhouse, James, *A Narrative of a Visit to the Australian Colonies*, Hamilton Adams, London, 1843.

Ball, Desmond, *A Suitable Piece of Real Estate: American Installations in Australia*, Hale & Iremonger, Sydney, 1980.

Banks, M. R. and J. B. Kirkpatrick, *Landscape and Man: The Interaction Between Man and Environment in Western Tasmania*, Royal Society of Tasmania, Hobart, 1977.

Barnard, A., *The Simple Fleece*, MUP, Melbourne, 1962.

Barrett, Sir James (ed.), *Save Australia: A Plea for the Right Use of Our Flora and Fauna*, Melbourne, 1925.

Bassett, Marnie, *The Hentys: An Australian Colonial Tapestry*, OUP, London, 1954.

Bates, Daisy, *The Passing of the Aborigines*, Pocket Books, New York, 1973.

Bateson, Charles, *Dire Strait: A History of Bass Strait*, Reed, Sydney, 1973.

Battye, J. S., *Western Australia: A History from its Discovery to the Inauguration of the Commonwealth*, OUP, Oxford, 1924.

Beaglehole, J. C. (ed.), *The Endeavor Journal of Joseph Banks, 1768–1771*, Angus & Robertson, Sydney, 1962.

——, *The Life of Captain Cook*, Stanford University Press, Stanford, California, 1974.

Bean, C. E. W., *On the Wool Track*, Alston Rivers, London, 1910.

Bell, Roger J., *Unequal Allies: Australian–American Relations and the Pacific War*, MUP, Melbourne, 1977.

Bennett, Scott, *Aborigines and Political Power*, Allen & Unwin, Sydney, 1989.

Berndt, Ronald M. and Catherine H. Berndt (eds), *Aborigines of the West: Their Past and Their Present*, UWA Press, Nedlands, 1980.

Birrell, Robert, Doug Hill and John Stanley (eds), *Quarry Australia? Social and Environmental Perspectives on Managing the Nation's Resources*, OUP, Melbourne, 1982.

Birrell, Robert, Douglas Hill and Jon Nevill (eds), *Populate and Perish? The Stresses of Population Growth in Australia*, Fontana/ACF, Sydney, 1984.

Biskup, Peter, *Not Slaves Not Citizens: The Aboriginal Problem in Western Australia, 1898–1954*, UQP, St Lucia, Queensland, 1973.

Blainey, Geoffrey, *A Land Half Won*, revised ed., Sun Books, Melbourne, 1983.

——, *The Peaks of Lyell*, MUP, Melbourne, 1954.

——, *The Rush That Never Ended*, 3rd ed., MUP, Melbourne, 1978.

——, *The Steel Master: A Life of Essington Lewis*, Macmillan, Melbourne, 1972.

——, *The Triumph of the Nomads: A History of Ancient Australia*, Macmillan, Melbourne, 1975.

Blakeway, Denys and Sue Lloyd-Roberts, *Fields of Thunder: Testing Britain's Bomb*, Unwin Paperbacks, London, 1985.

Blazey, Peter, *Bolte: A Political Biography*, Milton, Queensland, 1972.

Boehm, E. A., *Prosperity and Depression in Australia, 1887–1897*, OUP, Oxford, 1971.

Bolton, G. C., *A Fine Country to Starve In*, UWA Press, Nedlands, 1972.

——, *Spoils and Spoilers: Australians Make Their Environment 1788–1980*, Allen & Unwin, Sydney, 1981.

——, *A Thousand Miles Away: A History of North Queensland to 1920*, ANU Press, Canberra, 1970.

Boyd, Robin, *The Australian Ugliness*, revised ed., Penguin, Ringwood, 1980.

Brady, Edwin J., *Australia Unlimited*, Robertson, Melbourne, c. 1918.

Bride, Thomas Francis (ed.), *Letters From Victorian Pioneers*, Government Printer, Melbourne, 1898.

Broome, Richard, *Aboriginal Australians*, George Allen & Unwin, Sydney, 1982.

Brown, Max, *The Black Eureka*, ABS, Sydney, 1976.

Brown, P. L. (ed.), *The Narrative of George Russell*, OUP, London, 1935.

Buckley, Ken and Ted Wheelwright, *No Paradise for Workers: Capitalism and the Common People in Australia, 1788–1914*, OUP, Melbourne, 1988.

Bull, John Wrathall, *Early Experiences of Life in South Australia*, E. S. Wigg & Son, Adelaide, 1884.

Burroughs, P., *Britain and Australia, 1831–1855: A Study in Imperial Relations and Crown Lands Administration*, OUP, Oxford, 1967.

Burvill, G. H. (ed.), *Agriculture in Western Australia: 150 Years of Development and Achievement, 1829–1979*, UWA Press, Nedlands, 1979.

Butlin, N. G., *Our Original Aggression: Aboriginal Populations of Southeastern Australia, 1788–1850*, George Allen & Unwin, Sydney, 1983.

Buxton, G. L., *The Riverina, 1861–1891: An Australian Regional Study*, MUP, Melbourne, 1976.

Cameron, Arnold Guyot, *The Torrens System: Its Simplicity, Serviceability and Success*, New York, 1915.

Camilleri, Joseph A., *Australian–American Relations: The Web of Dependence*, Macmillan, Melbourne, 1980.

Campbell, Elizabeth, *The Journal of Mrs Fenton: A Narrative of her Life in India, the Isle of France (Mauritius) and Tasmania during the years 1826–1830*, London, 1901.

Cannon, Michael, *The Land Boomers*, MUP, Melbourne, 1966.

Carron, L. T., *A History of Forestry in Australia*, ANU Press, Canberra, 1985.

Carter, Harold B., *Sir Joseph Banks, 1743–1820*, British Museum, London, 1988.

Charlesworth, Max, *The Aboriginal Land Rights Movement*, Deakin University, Victoria, 1983.

Christie, M. F., *Aborigines in Colonial Victoria, 1835–86*, SUP, Sydney, 1979.

Churchward, L. G., *Australia & America, 1788–1972*, APCOL, Sydney, 1979.

Cilento, Sir Raphael and Clem Lack, *Triumph in the Tropics: An Historical Sketch of Queensland*, Smith & Peterson, Brisbane, 1959.

Clare, Patricia, *The Struggle for the Great Barrier Reef*, Collins, Sydney, 1971.

Clark, C. M. H., *A History of Australia*, vol. 1, *From the Earliest Times to the Age of Macquarie*, MUP, Melbourne, 1962.

——, *A History of Australia*, vol. 2, *New South Wales and Van Diemen's Land, 1822–1838*, MUP, Melbourne, 1968.

——, *A History of Australia*, vol. 3, *The Beginning of an Australian Civilization, 1824–1851*, MUP, Melbourne, 1973.

——, *A History of Australia*, vol. 4, *The Earth Abideth For Ever, 1851–1888*, MUP, Melbourne, 1978.

——, *A History of Australia*, vol. 5, *The People Make the Laws, 1888–1915*, MUP, Melbourne, 1981.

——, *A History of Australia*, vol. 6, *The Old Dead Tree and the Young Tree Green, 1916–1935*, MUP, Melbourne, 1987.

——(ed.), *Select Documents in Australian History, 1788–1850*, Angus & Robertson, Melbourne, 1950.

——(ed.), *Select Documents in Australian History, 1851–1900*, Angus & Robertson, Melbourne, 1955.

Collins, David, *An Account of the English Colony in New South Wales*, Cadell & Davies, London, 1804.

Colwell, Max, *Whaling Around Australia*, Rigby, Adelaide, 1969.

Community Research Action Centre, *Wilderness to Waste*, Monash University, Melbourne, 1981.

Connell, R. W., *Ruling Class Ruling Culture*, CUP, Cambridge, 1977.

Connell, R. W. and T. H. Irving, *Class Structure in Australian History: Documents, Narrative and Argument*, Longman Cheshire, Melbourne, 1980.

Cooksey, Robert (ed.), *The Great Depression in Australia*, no. 17 of *Labour History*, Sydney, 1970.

Corris, Peter, *Passage, Port and Plantation: A History of Solomon Islands Labour Migration, 1870–1914*, MUP, Melbourne, 1973.

Creed, John Mildred, *My Recollections of Australia & Elsewhere, 1842–1914*, Herbert Jenkins Limited, London, 1916.

Crowley, F. K., *Australia's Western Third*, Macmillan, London, 1960.

——(ed.), *A New History of Australia*, Heinemann, Melbourne, 1974.

Cumpston, J. S., *First Visitors to Bass Strait*, Roebuck Society, Canberra, 1973.

Cunningham, P., *Two Years in New South Wales*, 2 vols, London, 1827.

Curr, Edward M., *Recollections of Squatting in Victoria*, 2nd ed., Melbourne, 1965.

Currie, George and John Graham, *The Origins of CSIRO: Science and the Commonwealth Government, 1901–1926*, CSIRO, Melbourne, 1966.

Dakin, William John, *Whalemen Adventurers*, revised ed., Angus & Robertson, Sydney, 1963.

Daly, Mrs Dominic D., *Digging, Squatting, and Pioneering Life in the Northern Territory of South Australia*, London, 1887.

David, Abe and Ted Wheelwright, *The Third Wave: Australia and Asian Capitalism*, LBC, Sydney, 1989.
Davison, Frank Dalby and Brooke Nicholls, *Blue Coast Caravan*, Angus & Robertson, Sydney, 1935.
Deakin, Alfred, *Irrigated India*, W. Tacker and Co., London, 1893.
———, *Irrigation in Western America*, Melbourne, 1885.
Dempsey, Robert J., *The Politics of Finding Out: Environmental Problems in Australia*, Cheshire, Melbourne, 1974.
Drummond, Ian M., *Imperial Economic Policy, 1917–1939: Studies in Expansion and Protection*, OUP, London, 1974.
Dunderdale, George, *The Book of the Bush*, originally published, London, c. 1870, facsimile, Ringwood, Victoria, 1973.
Dunn, Michael, *Australia and the Empire: From 1788 to the Present*, Fontana/Collins, Sydney, 1984.
Dunsdorfs, Edgars, *The Australian Wheat Growing Industry, 1788–1948*, MUP, Melbourne, 1956.
Dunstan, Keith, *Wowsers: Being an Account of the Prudery Exhibited by Certain Outstanding Men and Women in such Matters as Drinking, Smoking, Prostitution, Censorship, and Gambling*, Cassell, Melbourne, 1968.
Easterby, Harry T., *The Queensland Sugar Industry: An Historical Review*, Brisbane, (n.d.).
Eisdell, J. W., *Back Country or The Cheerful Adventures of a Bush Parson in the Eighties*, OUP, London, 1936.
Eldershaw, Flora S. (ed.), *The Peaceful Army: A Memorial to the Pioneer Women of Australia, 1788–1938*, Women's Executive Committee and Advisory Council of Australia's 150th Anniversary Celebration Council, Sydney, 1938.
Epps, William, *The Land Systems of Australasia*, Swan Sonnenschein, London, 1893.
Evans, Howard Ensign, *Australia, a Natural History*, Smithsonian Institution Press, Washington, D.C., 1983.
Evans, Raymond, Kay Saunders and Kathryn Cronin, *Race Relations in Colonial Queensland: A History of Exclusion, Exploitation and Extermination*, UQP, St Lucia, 1988, originally published as *Exclusion, Exploitation and Extermination*, Sydney, 1975.
Ewers, J. K., *Men Against the Earth*, Georgian House, Melbourne, 1946.
Facey, Albert, *A Fortunate Life*, Fremantle Arts Centre Press, Fremantle, 1981.
Fast Train Polis Action Group, *The Social Implications of the Very Fast Train*, Melbourne, 1990.
Field, Barron (ed.), *Geographical Memoirs of New South Wales*, John Murray, London, 1825.
Finch-Hatton, Harold, *Advance Australia!: an account of eight years' work, wandering and amusement in Queensland, New South Wales and Victoria*, W. H. Allen & Co., London, 1885.
Firkins, P., *A History of Commerce and Industry in Western Australia*, UWA Press, Nedlands, 1979.
Fitzgerald, Ross, *From the Dreaming to 1915: A History of Queensland*, UQP, St Lucia, Queensland, 1982.
———, *From 1915 to the Early 1980s: A History of Queensland*, UQP, St Lucia, Queensland, 1984.
Fitzpatrick, Brian, *The British Empire in Australia, 1834–1939*, MUP, Melbourne, 1941.

———, *British Imperialism and Australia, 1788–1832*, George Allen & Unwin, London, 1939.

Flood, Josephine, *Archaeology of the Dreamtime*, University of Hawaii Press, Honolulu, 1983.

Fox, Len, *Multinationals Take Over Australia*, APCOL, Sydney, 1981.

Freney, Denis, *CIA's Australian Connections*, Sydney, 1977.

———, *Get Gough!*, Sydney, 1985.

Frith, H. J. and G. Sawer (eds), *The Murray Waters: Man, Nature and a River System*, Angus & Robertson, Sydney, 1974.

Frost, Alan, *Convicts and Empire: A Naval Question, 1776–1811*, OUP, Melbourne, 1980.

Frost, Sir Sydney, *The Whaling Question: The Inquiry by Sir Sydney Frost of Australia*, Friends of the Earth, San Francisco, c. 1979.

Gammage, Bill and Andrew Markus (eds), *All That Dirt: Aborigines 1938*, ANU Press, Canberra, 1982.

Gee, Helen and Janet Fenton, *The South West Book*, ACF, Hawthorn, Victoria, 1978.

Gentilli, J. (ed), *Western Landscapes*, UWA Press, Nedlands, 1979.

Giles, Ernest, *Australia Twice Traversed: The Romance of Exploration, being A Narrative Compiled from the Journals of Five Exploring Expeditions into and Through Central South Australia, and Western Australia, from 1872 to 1876*, 2 vols , Sampson Law, Marston, Searle and Rivington, London, 1889.

Gilpin, Alan, *The Australian Environment: 12 Controversial Issues*, Sun Books, Melbourne, 1980.

Glynn, Sean, *Government Policy and Agricultural Development: a study in the role of government in the development of the Western Australian Wheatbelt, 1900–1930*, UWA Press, Nedlands, 1975.

Gollan, Anne (ed.), *Questions for the Nineties*, LBC, Sydney, 1990.

Gordon, Adam Lindsay, *Poems (Sea Spray and Smoke Drift)*, London, 1904.

Gordon, David J., *The 'Nile' of Australia: Nature's Gateway to the Interior*, Adelaide, 1906.

Green, Neville, *Broken Spears: Aborigines and Europeans in the Southwest of Australia*, Focus Education Services, Cottesloe, Western Australia, 1984.

Green, Roger (ed.), *Battle for the Franklin*, Fontana/ACF, Sydney, 1981.

Gregory, J. W., *The Dead Heart of Australia*, John Murray, London, 1906.

Gribble, Reverend J. B., *Dark Deeds in a Sunny Land*, originally published, Perth, 1905, reprint, UWA Press, Nedlands, 1987.

Groves, R. H. and W. D. L. Ride (eds), *Species at Risk: Research in Australia*, Australian Academy of Science, Canberra, 1980.

Haebich, Anna, *For Their Own Good: Aborigines and Government in the Southwest of Western Australia, 1900–1940*, UWA Press, Nedlands, 1988.

Hainsworth, D. R., *Builders and Adventurers: The Traders and the Emergence of the Colony, 1788–1821*, Cassell, Melbourne, 1968.

Hallam, Sylvia J., *Fire and Hearth: A Study of Aboriginal Usage and European Usurpation in south-western Australia*, Australian Institute of Aboriginal Studies, Canberra, 1979.

Hancock, Lang, *Wake up Australia*, E. J. Dwyer, Sydney, 1979.

Hancock, W. K., *Australia*, originally published by Jacaranda Press, 1930, Brisbane, 1961.

———, *The Battle of Black Mountain*, Canberra, 1974.

———, *Discovering Monaro: A Study of Man's Impact on his Environment*, CUP, Cambridge, 1972.

Handbook to Victoria, Government publication, Melbourne, 1877.

Hanley, Wayne and Malcolm Cooper (eds), *Man and the Australian Environment*, McGraw-Hill, Sydney, 1982.

Harcus, William (ed.), *South Australia: Its History, Resources, and Productions*, Adelaide, 1876.

Hardman, Marion and Peter Manning, *Green Bans: The Story of an Australian Phenomenon*, ACF, Melbourne, 1975. `

Harman, Elizabeth J. and Brian W. Head, *State, Capital and Resources in the North and West of Australia*, UWA Press, Nedlands, 1982.

Harris, Alexander, *Secrets of Alexander Harris*, (ed.) A. H. Chisholm, Angus & Robertson, Sydney, 1961.

———, *Settlers and Convicts or Recollections of Sixteen Years' Labour in the Australian Backwards* (1847), (ed.) Manning Clark, MUP, Melbourne, 1953.

Hasluck, Alexandra, *Portrait with Background: A Life of Georgiana Molloy*, OUP, Melbourne, 1955.

———, *Thomas Peel of Swan River*, OUP, Melbourne, 1965.

Hawke, Steve and Michael Gallagher, *Noonkanbah: Whose Land, Whose Law*, Fremantle Arts Press, Fremantle, 1989.

Hay, J. G., *The Visit of Charles Fraser (Botanist) to the Swan River in 1827*, Perth, 1906.

Haydon, G. H., *Five Years' Experience in Australia Felix*, Hamilton, Adams, London, 1846.

Hazlehurst, Cameron, *Menzies Observed*, George Allen & Unwin, Sydney, 1979.

Head, Brian (ed.), *The Politics of Development in Australia*, Allen & Unwin, Sydney, 1986.

———(ed.), *State and Economy in Australia*, OUP, Melbourne, 1983.

Heathcote, R. L., *Australia*, New York, 1975.

———, *Back of Bourke: A Study of Land Appraisal and Settlement in Semi-Arid Australia*, MUP, Melbourne, 1965.

Henning, Rachel, *The Letters of Rachel Henning*, (ed.) David Adams, Penguin, Ringwood, Victoria, 1969.

Hicks, Neville, *'This Sin and Scandal': Australia's Population Debate, 1891–1911*, ANU Press, Canberra, 1978.

Hill, Ernestine, *The Great Australian Loneliness*, Robertson and Mullins, Melbourne, 1956.

Hirst, J. B., *Convict Society and its Enemies*, George Allen & Unwin, Sydney, 1983.

———, *The Strange Birth of Colonial Democracy: New South Wales 1848–1884*, Allen & Unwin, Sydney, 1988.

Howitt, William, *Land, Labour and Gold: Two Years in Victoria with Visits to Sydney and Van Diemen's Land*, 2 vols, Boston, 1855.

Hughes, Robert, *The Fatal Shore: The Epic of Australia's Founding*, Knopf, New York, 1986.

Hurley, P. J., *Red Cedar: The Story of the North Coast*, Dymock's Book Arcade, Sydney, 1948.

Hutton, Drew (ed.), *Green Politics in Australia*, North Ryde, New South Wales, 1987.

Iremonger, John (ed.), *Strikes: Studies in Twentieth Century Australian Social History*, Angus & Robertson, Sydney, 1973.

Jaensch, Dean, *The Hawke–Keating Hijack: The ALP in Transition*, Allen & Unwin, Sydney, 1989.

James, Paul (ed.), *Technocratic Dreaming: Of Very Fast Trains and Japanese Designer Cities*, LBC, Sydney, 1990.

Jenkin, Graham, *Conquest of the Ngarrindjeri*, Rigby, Adelaide, 1979.

Jenkins, Joseph, *Diary of a Welsh Swagman, 1869–1894*, (ed.) William Evans, Macmillan, South Melbourne, 1975.

Johnston, George, *Clean Straw For Nothing*, Collins, London–Sydney, 1969.

Jones, Richard (ed.), *Damania: The Hydro–Electric Commission, The Environment & Government in Tasmania*, Fullers Bookshop, Hobart, 1972.

Kendell, Jeni and Eddie Buivids, *Earth First*, ABC Books, Sydney, 1987.

Kiddle, Margaret, *Caroline Chisholm*, MUP, Melbourne, 1957.

———, *Men of Yesterday: A Social History of the Western District of Victoria*, MUP, Melbourne, 1961.

Lake, Marilyn, *A Divided Society: Tasmania During World War 1*, MUP, Melbourne, 1975.

———, *The Limits of Hope: Soldier Settlement in Victoria, 1915–38*, MUP, Melbourne, 1987.

Langford-Smith, Trevor and John Rutherford, *Water and Land: Two Case Studies in Irrigation*, ANU Press, Canberra, 1966.

Lansbury, Coral, *Arcady in Australia: The Evocation of Australia in Nineteenth Century English Literature*, MUP, Melbourne, 1970.

Laseron, Francis, *The Face of Australia*, Angus & Robertson, Sydney, 1954.

Laughton, A. M. and T. S. Hall (eds), *Handbook To Victoria*, Melbourne, 1914.

Lawrence, D. H., *Kangaroo*, Penguin, New York, 1980.

Lloyd, Clem J., *The National Estate: Australia's Heritage*, Cassell, Stanmore, New South Wales, 1977.

Lockwood, Rupert, *War on the Waterfront*, Allen & Unwin, Sydney, 1987.

Lunn, Hugh, *Johannes Bjelke-Petersen: A Political Biography*, UQP, St Lucia, Queensland, 1984.

Lyon, Pamela and Michael Parsons, *We Are Staying: The Alyawarre Struggle for Land at Lake Nash*, IAD Press, Alice Springs, Northern Territory, 1989.

MacDonald, Donald, *Gum Boughs and Wattle Blooms gathered on Australian hills and plains*, Cassell, London, 1887.

Macintyre, Stuart, *The Oxford History of Australia*, vol. 4, *1901–1942, The Succeeding Age*, OUP, Melbourne, 1986.

Mackaness, G., *Sir Joseph Banks, Bart*, Sydney, 1962.

———, *Sir Joseph Banks: His Relations with Australia*, Angus & Robertson, Sydney, 1936.

Mackay, David, *In the Wake of Cook: Exploration, Science and Empire, 1780–1801*, Victoria University Press, Wellington, 1985.

Mackinolty, Judy (ed.), *The Wasted Years? Australia's Great Depression*, George Allen & Unwin, Sydney, 1981.

Maddox, Graham, *The Hawke Government and Labor Tradition*, Penguin, Ringwood, Victoria, 1989.

Maiden, J. H., *Manual of the Grasses of New South Wales*, Government Printer, Sydney, 1898.

———, *Sir Joseph Banks: the 'Father of Australia'*, Government Printer, Sydney, 1909.

Major, Thomas, *Leaves from a Squatter's Note Book*, Sands and Company, London, 1900.

Manning, Peter and Marion Hardman, *Green Bans*, ACF, Melbourne, 1975.

Marshall, Alan J. (ed.), *The Great Extermination: A Guide to Anglo–Australian Cupidity Wickedness & Waste*, Heinemann, Melbourne, 1966.

Mawson, Douglas, *Some Aspects of Forestry in South Australia*, Commemoration Address, University of Adelaide, 1925.

McDonald, G. and W. S. Cooper, *The Gosnells Story*, Gosnells, Western Australia, 1988.

McKernan, Michael, *The Australian People and the Great War*, Collins, Sydney, 1984.

McLaren, John, *A Nation Apart: Essays in Honour of Andrew Fabinyi: Personal Views of Australia in the Eighties*, Longman Cheshire, Melbourne, 1989.

McQueen, Humphrey, *Gallipoli to Petrov: Arguing with Australian History*, Allen & Unwin, Sydney, 1984.

——, *Gone Tomorrow: Australia in the 80s*, Angus & Robertson, Sydney, 1982.

McQueen, James, *The Franklin: Not Just a River*, Ringwood, Victoria, 1983.

Mead, Elwood, *Helping Men Own Farms*, New York, 1920.

Meinig, D. W., *On The Margins of the Good Earth*, UCP, Chicago, 1962.

Melville, Henry, *The History of Van Diemen's Land: From the Year 1824 to 1835, Inclusive*, originally published, Hobart, 1839, reprint, Sydney, 1965.

Meyrick, F. J. (ed.), *Life in the Bush, 1840–1847: A Memoir of Henry Howard Meyrick*, Nelson, London, 1939.

Micco, Helen Mary, *King Island and the Sealing Trade, 1802*, Roebuck Publications, Canberra, 1971.

Milliken, Robert, *No Conceivable Injury*, Penguin, Ringwood, Victoria, 1986.

Mitchell, Major T. L., *Three Expeditions into the Interior of Eastern Australia*, 2 vols, 2nd ed., T. & W. Boone, London, 1839.

Moore, R. E. (ed.), *Australian Grasslands*, Canberra, 1973.

Moorehead, Alan, *Cooper's Creek*, Harper & Row, New York, 1963.

Moyal, Ann, *A Bright & Savage Land: Scientists in Colonial Australia*, Collins, Sydney, 1986.

Muir, John, *Correspondence*, microfilm reel no. 13, Bancroft Library, Berkeley.

——, *Papers*, microfilm reel no. 29, Bancroft Library, Berkeley.

Mulvaney, D. G. *The Prehistory of Australia*, revised ed., Penguin, Melbourne, 1975.

Mundey, Jack, *Green Bans & Beyond*, Angus & Robertson, Sydney, 1981.

Munro, C. H., *Australian Water Resources and Their Development*, Angus & Robertson, Sydney, 1974.

Murray, Robert, *The Confident Years: Australia in the Twenties*, Penguin, Ringwood, Victoria, 1978.

Nicholas, Stephen (ed.), *Convict Workers: Reinterpreting Australia's Past*, CUP, Sydney, 1988.

O'Brien, Brian J. O. (ed.), *Environment and Science*, UWA Press, Nedlands, 1979.

The Official Guide to Western Australia, Government publication, third edition, E. S. Wigg & Son, Perth, 1909.

O'Loughlin, E. M. (ed), *Irrigation and Water Use in Australia*, Australian Academy of Science, Canberra, 1980.

Osborne, G. and W. F. Mandle (eds), *New History: Studying Australia Today*, George Allen & Unwin, Sydney, 1982.

Ovington, Derrick, *Australian Endangered Species: Mammals, Birds and Reptiles*, Cassell, Sydney, 1978.

Parv, Valerie, *The Changing Face of Australia: The Impact of 200 Years of Change on Our Environment*, Bay Books, Sydney, 1984.

Pascoe, F. R., *The Manufacture of Australian History*, OUP, Melbourne, 1979.

Perry, T. M., *Australia's First Frontier: The Spread of Settlement in New South Wales, 1788-1829*, MUP, Melbourne, 1963.

Phillips, P. D. (ed.), *The Peopling of Australia*, (Further Studies), Melbourne, 1933.

Phillips, P. D. and G. L. Wood (eds), *The Peopling of Australia*, Macmillan/MUP, Melbourne, 1928.

Pick, Jock H. and V. R. Alldis, *Australia's Dying Heart: Soil Erosion and Station Management in the Inland*, MUP, Melbourne, 1944.

Pike, Douglas, *Paradise of Dissent: South Australia 1829-1857*, 2nd ed., MUP, Melbourne, 1967.

Powell, Alan, *Far Country: A Short History of the Northern Territory*, MUP, Melbourne, 1982.

Powell, J. M., *Environmental Management in Australia, 1788-1914: Guardians, Improvers and Profit*, OUP, Melbourne, 1976.

——, *An Historical Geography of Modern Australia: The restive fringe*, CUP, Cambridge, 1988.

——, *Mirrors of the New World: Images and Image-makers in the Settlement of the New World*, ANU Press, Canberra, 1978.

——, *The Public Lands of Australia Felix*, Melbourne, OUP, 1970.

Powell, J. M. and M. Williams (eds), *Australian Space, Australian Time*, OUP, Melbourne, 1975.

Praed, Mrs Campbell, *My Australian Girlhood*, T. Fisher Unwin, London, 1904.

Price, A. Grenfell, *The Foundation and Settlement of South Australia, 1829-1845*, F. W. Preece, Adelaide, 1924.

Quick, John and Randolph Garran, *The Annotated Constitution of the Australian Commonwealth*, Angus & Robertson, Sydney, 1901.

Ratcliffe, Francis, *Flying Fox and Drifting Sand: The Adventures of a Biologist in Australia*, Chatto & Windus, London, 1938.

Reid, Gordon, *A Nest of Hornets*, OUP, Melbourne, 1982.

Reynolds, Henry, *Frontier: Aborigines, Settlers and Land*, Allen & Unwin, Sydney, 1987.

——, *The Other Side of the Frontier: Aboriginal Resistance to the European Invasion of Australia*, Penguin, Ringwood, Victoria, 1982.

Richelson, Jeffrey and Desmond Ball, *The Ties That Bind: intelligence cooperation between the UKUSA countries—the United Kingdom, the United States of America, Canada, Australia and New Zealand*, George Allen & Unwin, Sydney, 1985.

Roberts, Jan, *Massacres to Mining: The Colonisation of Aboriginal Australia*, Dove Communications, Blackburn, Victoria, 1981.

Roberts, Stephen H., *History of Australian Land Settlement, 1788-1920*, Macmillan, Melbourne, 1924.

——, *The Squatting Age in Australia, 1835-1847*, 2nd ed., MUP, Melbourne, 1964.

Robinson, W. S., *If I Remember Rightly: The Memoirs of W. S. Robinson 1876-1963*, (ed.) Geoffrey Blainey, Cheshire, Melbourne, 1967.

Robson, Lloyd, *A History of Tasmania*, vol. I, *Van Diemen's Land from the Earliest Times to 1855*, OUP, Melbourne, 1983.

Roddewig, Richard J., *Green Bans: The Birth of Australian Environmental Politics*, New York, 1978.

Rolls, Eric, *A Million Wild Acres: 200 Years of Man and an Australian Forest*, Melbourne, 1981.

———, *They All Ran Wild: The Story of Pests on the Land in Australia*, Sydney, 1969.
Routley, R. and V. Routley, *The Fight for the Forests: The takeover of Australian forests for pines, wood chips, and intensive forestry*, 2nd ed., Canberra, 1974.
Rowley, C. D., *The Destruction of Aboriginal Society*, ANU Press, Canberra, 1970.
Rude, George, *Protest and Punishment: The Story of the Social and Political Protesters Transported to Australia, 1788–1868*, OUP, Oxford, 1978.
Russell, Archer, *Bushways: a Bush-lover's Wanderings on Plain and Range*, Australasian Publishing Co. Pty. Ltd., Sydney, 1944.
Russell, H. S., *Genesis of Queensland*, 1888.
Russell, J. S. and R. F. Isbell (eds), *Australian Soils: The Human Impact*, UQP, St Lucia, Queensland, 1986.
Ryan, Lyndall, *The Aboriginal Tasmanians*, Vancouver, 1981.
Sandercock, Leonie, *Cities for Sale: Property, politics and urban planning in Australia*, MUP, Melbourne, 1975.
Sanders, Norm, Bob Brown and Chris Bell, *A Time to Care: Tasmania's Endangered Wilderness*, Hobart, 1980.
Scholes, Alex G., *Education for Empire Settlement*, Royal Empire Society, London, 1932.
Searle, G. R., *The Quest for National Efficiency: A Study in British Politics and Political Thought, 1899–1914*, University of California Press, Berkeley, 1971.
Seddon, George and Mari Davis (eds), *Man and Landscape in Australia*, AGPS, Canberra, 1976.
Serle, Geoffrey, *From Deserts the Prophets Come: The Creative Spirit in Australia, 1788–1972*, MUP, Melbourne, 1973.
———, *The Rush to be Rich: A History of the Colony of Victoria, 1883–1889*, MUP, Melbourne, 1971.
Serventy, Vincent, *A Continent in Danger*, Ure Smith, Sydney, 1966.
Sherrington, Geoffrey, *Australia's Immigrants, 1788–1978*, George Allen & Unwin, Sydney, 1980.
Shillinglaw, John J., *Historical Records of Port Phillip*, Government Printer, Melbourne, 1879.
Shineberg, Dorothy, *They Came for Sandalwood*, MUP, Melbourne, 1967.
Sidney, Samuel, *The Three Colonies of Australia: New South Wales, Victoria, South Australia: Their Pastures, Copper Mines and Gold Fields*, 2nd ed., Ingram, Cooke and Co., London, 1853.
Skemp, J. R., *Memories of Myrtle Bank*, MUP, Melbourne, 1952.
Skinner, L. E., *Police of the Pastoral Frontier: Native Police, 1849–59*, UQP, St Lucia, Queensland, 1975.
Smith, Bernard, *The Spectre of Truganini*, 1980 Boyer Lectures, ABC Books, Sydney, 1980.
Smith, Joseph Wayne, *The Australia That Can Say 'No!': The Multifunction Polis Project, Asia-Pacific Millenarianism and the Tyranny of Technocracy*, Flinders University, Bedford Park, South Australia, 1990.
Sornarajah, M. (ed.), *The South West Dam Dispute: The legal and political issues*, University of Tasmania, Law School, Hobart, 1983.
Stackpole, Edouard A., *The Sea Hunters: the New England whalemen during two centuries*, Lippincott, New York, 1953.
Stannage, C. T. (ed.), *A New History of Western Australia*, UWA Press, Nedlands, 1981.
Stanner, W. E. H., *White Man Got No Dreaming*, ANU Press, Canberra, 1979.

State of the Environment in Australia, AGPS, Canberra, 1985.

Statham, Pamela (ed.), *The Tanner Letters: A Pioneer Saga of Swan River & Tasmania, 1831–1845*, UWA Press, Perth, 1981.

Stokes, J. Lort, *Discoveries in Australia*, 2 vols , T. and W. Boone, London, 1846.

Stuart, E. J., *A Land of Opportunities: Being an Account of the Author's Recent Expedition to Explore the Northern Territories of Australia*, J. Lane, the Bodley Head, London, 1923.

Sturt, Charles, *Narrative of an Expedition into Central Australia*, 2 vols, T. and W. Boone, London, 1849.

——, *Two Expeditions into the Interior of Southern Australia*, 2 vols, Smith, Elder and Co., London, 2nd ed., 1834.

Sydney Labour History Group, *What Rough Beast? The State and Social Order in Australian History*, Sydney, 1982.

Sykes, Roberta B., *Black Majority*, Hudson, Hawthorn, Victoria, 1989.

Tame, Adrian and F. P. J. Robotham, *Maralinga: British A-Bomb Australian Legacy*, Fontana/Collins, Melbourne, 1982.

Taunton, Henry, *Australind: Wanderings in Western Australia and the Malay East*, Arnold, London, 1903.

Therry, R., *Reminiscences of Thirty Years' Residence in New South Wales and Victoria*, 2nd ed., Sampson Low, Son and Co., London, 1863.

Thompson, Peter, *Bob Brown of the Franklin River*, George Allen & Unwin, Sydney, 1984.

Thompson, Roger C., *Australian Imperialism in the Pacific: The Expansionist Era, 1820–1920*, MUP, Melbourne, 1980.

Tolcher, H. M., *Drought or Deluge: Man in the Cooper's Creek Region*, MUP, Melbourne, 1986.

Tonkinson, Robert, *The Jigalong Mob: Aboriginal Victors of the Desert Crusade*, Menlo Park, California, 1974.

Traill, W. H., *A Queenly Colony: Pen Sketches and Camera Glimpses*, Edmund Gregory, Government Printer, Brisbane, 1901.

Trezise, Percy, *Last Days of a Wilderness*, Collins, Sydney, 1973.

Trollope, Anthony, *Australia and New Zealand*, 3 vols, Leipzig, 1873.

Troughton, Ellis, *Furred Animals of Australia*, Angus & Robertson, Sydney, 1941.

Turner, Ian, *Sydney's Burning*, revised ed., Alpha Books, Sydney, 1969.

VFT Awareness Groups Coalition, *VFT: Need or Greed?*, Melbourne, 1990.

Vivienne, May, *Travels in Western Australia*, London, 1902.

Wadham, Sir Samuel, R. Kent Wilson and Joyce Wood, *Land Utilization in Australia*, MUP, Melbourne, 1957.

Wakefield, Edward Gibbon, *A Letter From Sydney and Other Writings*, London, 1929.

Wallace, R. L., *The Australians at the Boer War*, Canberra, 1976.

Ward, Russel, *The History of Australia: The Twentieth Century*, New York, 1977. Published in Australia under the title *A Nation For a Continent: The History of Australia 1901–1975*.

Watson, Don, *Caledonia Australis: Scottish Highlanders on the Frontier of Australia*, Collins, Sydney, 1984.

Wearne, Heather, *A Clash of Cultures: Queensland Aboriginal Policy, 1824–1980*, Uniting Church in Australia, Brisbane, 1980.

West, Richard, *River of Tears*, Earth Island Ltd., London, 1972.

Westgarth, William, *Victoria: Late Australia Felix*, Oliver & Boyd, Edinburgh, 1853.

White, Richard, *Inventing Australia: Images and Identity*, Allen & Unwin, Sydney, 1981.

Whitelock, Derek, *Conquest to Conservation: History of Human Impact on the South Australian Environment*, Wakefield Press, Adelaide, 1985.

———, *A Dirty Story: Pollution in Australia*, Sun Books, Melbourne, 1971.

Whitton, Evan, *The Hillbilly Dictator: Australia's Police State*, ABC Books, Crows Nest, New South Wales, 1989.

Wigmore, Lionel, *Struggle for the Snowy: The Background of the Snowy Mountains Scheme*, OUP, Melbourne, 1968.

Willey, Keith, *When The Sky Fell Down*, Collins, Sydney, 1979.

Williams, Michael, *The Making of the South Australian Landscape*, New York, 1974.

Wilson, J. Tuzo (ed.), *Continents Adrift and Continents Aground: Readings From Scientific American*, W. H. Freeman, San Francisco, 1976.

Wilson, Paul R., *Black Death White Hands*, George Allen & Unwin, Sydney, 1982.

Wise, Bernhard Ringrose, *The Making of the Australian Commonwealth, 1889–1900: A Stage in the Growth of the Empire*, Longmans, London, 1913.

Woods, L. E., *Land Degradation in Australia*, AGPS, Canberra, 1984.

Wright, Judith, *The Coral Battleground*, Thomas Nelson, Melbourne, 1977.

Articles

Bauer, F. H., 'Significant features in the white settlement of Australia', *Australian Geographical Studies*, vol. 1, 1962.

Butcher, B. W., 'Science and the imperial vision: the imperial geophysical experimental survey, 1928–1930', *Historical Records of Australian Science*, 1984.

Cameron, J. M. R., 'Information Distortion in Colonial Promotion: The Case of Swan River Colony', *Australian Geographical Studies*, vol. 12, no. 1, 1974, pp. 57–76.

Carter, H. J., 'Australia's dwindling wild life', *Australian Quarterly*, no. 17, March 14, 1933, pp. 114–20.

Cole, D., 'The Crimson Thread of Kinship: Ethnic Ideas in Australia, 1870–1914', *Historical Studies*, vol. 14, no. 56, April 1971, pp. 511–25.

Conkin, Paul, 'The Vision of Elwood Mead', *Agricultural History*, no. 34, 1960, pp. 88–9.

Connell, D. W., 'The Barrier Reef Conservation Issue', *Search*, vol. 2, no. 6, June 1971, pp. 188–92.

Connolly, C. N., 'Manufacturing "spontaneity": The Australian offer of troops for the Boer War', *Historical Studies*, vol. 18, no. 70, April 1978, pp. 106–17.

Corris, Peter, '"Blackbirding" in New Guinea Waters, 1883–84: an episode in the Queensland labour trade', *The Journal of Pacific History*, vol. 3, 1968, pp. 85–105.

Deakin, Alfred, 'Science and Empire', *Nature*, vol. 76, May 9, 1907, pp. 37–8.

Dixon, S., 'The effects of settlement and pastoral occupation in Australia upon the indigenous vegetation', *Transactions and Proceedings, Royal Society of South Australia*, vol. 15, 1892, pp. 195–206.

Gillbank, Linden, 'The Origins of the Acclimatisation Society of Victoria: Practical Science in the Wake of the Gold Rush', *Historical Records of Australian Science*, vol. 6, no. 3, December 1986.

Hainsworth, D. R., 'Exploiting the Pacific Frontier: The New South Wales Sealing Industry, 1800–1821', *The Journal of Pacific History*, vol. 2, 1967, pp. 59–75.

Hamilton, A. G., 'On the Effect which Settlement in Australia has produced upon

Indigenous Vegetation', *Journal and Proceedings of the Royal Society of New South Wales*, vol. XXVI, 1892, pp. 178–239.

Hoare, M. E., 'Learned Societies in Australia: The Foundation Years in Victoria, 1850–1860', *Records of the Australian Academy of Science*, vol. 1, no. 2, December 1967.

Hunt, I. L., 'Group settlement in Western Australia: a criticism', *University Studies in Western Australian History*, Fremantle, 1958.

Jacobs, M. R., 'History of the use and abuse of wooded lands in Australia', *Australian Journal of Science*, vol. 19, 1957, pp. 132–9.

Janson, Susan and Stuart Macintyre (eds), 'Making the Bicentenary', *Australian Historical Studies*, vol. 23, no. 91, October 1988.

Kelleher, Graeme, 'Australia's Great Barrier Reef Marine Park: Making Development Compatible with Conservation,' *AMBIO*, vol. XI, no. 5, 1982, pp. 262–7.

Kenyon, A. S., 'The Story of the Mallee', *The Victorian Historical Magazine*, vol. IV, no. 1, September 1914, pp. 23–56 and vol. IV, no. 3, March 1915, pp. 121–50.

Kidson, E., 'Australian origin of red rain in New Zealand', *Nature*, vol. 125, 1930.

Little, Barbara, 'Sealing and Whaling in Australia before 1850,' *Australian Economic History Review*. vol. IX, no. 2, September 1969, pp. 109–27.

Lunney, Danniel and Chris Moon, 'The Eden Woodchip Debate, 1969–86', *Search*, vol. 18, no. 1, January/February 1987.

Macleod, Roy, 'On Visiting the "Moving Metropolis": Reflections on the architecture of Imperial Science', *Historical Records of Australian Science*, vol. 5, no. 3, 1982, pp. 1–16.

Marshall, P., 'Dust storms in New Zealand', *Nature*, vol. 68, July 9, 1903, p. 223.

McKendrick, Neil, 'Josiah Wedgwood and Factory Discipline', *Historical Journal*, vol. 4, no 1, 1961, pp. 30–55.

Megaw, R., 'Australia and the Great White Fleet, 1908', *Royal Australian Historical Society Journal*, vol. 56, no. 2, June 1970.

Mercer, David, 'Australia's Constitution, federalism and the "Tasmanian Dam Case" ', *Political Geography Quarterly*, vol. 4, no. 2, April 1985, pp. 91–110.

Mercer, David and Jim Petersen, 'Battle for a wild river', *The Geographical Magazine*, vol. LV, no. 3, March 1983, pp. 122–8.

Moorhouse, Dr., 'Victoria', *The Journal of the Manchester Geographical Society*, vol. IV, 1888, pp. 38–57.

Nance, Beverly, 'The Level of Violence: Europeans and Aborigines in Port Phillip', *Historical Studies*, October 1981, pp. 532–52.

O'Neill, Dan, 'Project Chariot: How Alaska Escaped Nuclear Excavation', *Bulletin of The Atomic Scientists*, vol. 45, no. 10, December 1989, pp. 28–37.

Penny, Barbara, 'Australia's Reactions to the Boer War: a study in colonial imperialism', *Journal of British Studies*, vol. 7, pp. 97–130.

Perry, T. M., 'The Lower Shoalhaven District, 1797–1822', *Australian Geographer*, vol. VI, no. iii, May 1954, pp. 26–34.

Powell, J. M., 'Elwood Mead and California's state colonies: An episode in Australian–American contacts, 1915–31', *Royal Australian Historical Society Journal*, no. 67, 1982, pp. 328–53.

Robertson, J. R., 'The Western Australian Timber Industry', *University Studies in Western Australian History*, vol. III, no. 1, September 1957.

Rutherford, J., 'The Interplay of American and Australian Ideas for the Development of Water Projects in Northern Victoria', *Annals of the Association of American Geographers*, no. 54, 1964, pp. 88–106.

Scientific American, 'Managing Planet Earth', New York, September 1989.

Shann, E., 'Group Settlement of Migrants in Western Australia', *The Economic Record*, vol. 1, no. 1, November 1925.

Smith, Thomas, 'Forming a uranium policy: why the controversy?', *The Australian Quarterly*, vol. 51, no. 4, December 1979, pp. 32–50.

Stearn, William T., 'Sir Joseph Banks and Australian Botany', *Records Australian Academy of Science*, vol. 2, no. 4, 1974.

Taylor, G., 'Development of Group Settlement in Western Australia', *The Economic Record*, vol. 1, no. 10, May 1930.

Woolls, W., 'The Destruction of Eucalypts', *The Victorian Naturalist*, vol. VIII, 1891, pp. 75–80.

Background reading

Abbey, Edward, *The Monkey Wrench Gang*, Avon, New York, 1976.

Adas, Michael, *Machines as the Measure of Men: Science, Technology, and Ideologies of Western Dominance*, Cornell University Press, Ithaca, New York, 1989.

Adorno, Theodore and Max Horkheimer, *The Dialectic of Enlightenment*, trans. J. Cumming, Herder & Herder, New York, 1972.

Berlin, Isaiah, *Against the Current: Essays in the History of Ideas*, New York, 1980.

Borgmann, Albert, *Technology and the Character of Contemporary Life: A Philosophical Inquiry*, UCP, Chicago, 1987.

Carter, Paul, *The Road to Botany Bay: An Exploration of Landscape and History*, Knopf, New York, 1988.

Childe, V. Gordon, *Man Makes Himself*, OUP, New York, 1963.

Cragg, G. R., *From Puritanism to the Age of Reason*, CUP, Cambridge, 1950.

Crosby, Alfred W., *Ecological Imperialism: The Biological Expansion of Europe, 900–1900*, CUP, New York, 1986.

Derr, Mark, *Some Kind of Paradise: A Chronicle of Man and the Land in Florida*, William Morrow, New York, 1989.

Devall, Bill and George Sessions (eds), *Deep Ecology: Living as if Nature Mattered*, G. M. Smith, Salt Lake City, Utah, 1985.

Ellul, Jacques, *The Technological Society*, Jonathan Cape, London, 1965.

Foreman, Dave and Bill Haywood (eds), *EcoDefense: A Field Guide to Monkeywrenching*, 2nd ed., Ned Ludd Books, Tucson, Arizona, 1987.

Fussell, Paul, *Wartime: Understanding and Behavior in the Second World War*, OUP, New York, 1989.

George, Susan, *Ill Fares the Land*, Penguin, London, 1990.

Gould, Stephen Jay, *Ever Since Darwin: Reflections in Natural History*, Norton, New York, 1977.

——, *The Flamingo's Smile: Reflections in Natural History*, Norton, New York, 1985.

——, *Hen's Teeth and Horse's Toes: Further Reflections in Natural History*, Norton, New York, 1983.

——, *The Mismeasure of Man*, Norton, New York, 1981.

——, *The Panda's Thumb: More Reflections in Natural History*, Norton, New York, 1983.

——, *Time's Arrow, Time's Cycle: Myth and Metaphor in the Discovery of Geological Time*, HUP, Cambridge, Massachusetts, 1987.

————, *An Urchin in the Storm: Essays About Books and Ideas*, Norton, New York, 1987.

Grant, George, *Technology and Empire: Perspectives on North America*, House of Anansi, Toronto, 1969.

Hays, Samuel P., *Conservation and the Gospel of Efficiency: The Progressive Conservation Movement, 1890–1920*, HUP, Cambridge, Massachusetts, 1959.

Heilbroner, Robert L., *The Worldly Philosophers: The Lives, Times and Ideas of the Great Economic Thinkers*, Simon and Schuster, New York, 1972.

Herman, Edward S. and Noam Chomsky, *Manufacturing Consent: The Political Economy of the Mass Media*, Pantheon Books, New York, 1988.

Hobsbawm, E. J., *The Age of Empire, 1875–1914*, Random House, New York, 1987.

————, *The Age of Revolution: Europe 1789–1848*, Weidenfeld and Nicolson, London, 1962.

Horkheimer, Max, *Critique of Instrumental Reason: Lectures and Essays Since the End of World War II*, trans. Matthew O'Connell *et al.*, Continuum, New York, 1974.

Huxley, Thomas H., *Evolution and Ethics*, New York, 1896.

Hyde, W. W., *Ancient Greek Mariners*, New York, 1947.

Ignatieff, M., *A Just Measure of Pain: The Penitentiary in the Industrial Revolution, 1750–1850*, London, 1978.

Jacob, Francois, *The Possible and the Actual*, Pantheon Books, New York, 1982.

Jay, Martin, *The Dialectical Imagination: A History of the Frankfurt School and the Institute of Social Research, 1923–1950*, Little Brown & Co., Boston, 1973.

Jennings, Francis, *The Invasion of America: Indians, Colonialism and the Cant of Conquest*, UNC Press, Chapel Hill, 1975.

Keller, Evelyn Fox, *Reflections on Gender and Science*, Yale University Press, New Haven, Connecticut, 1985.

Koyre, A., *From the Closed World to the Infinite Universe*, New York, 1958.

Kwitny, Jonathan, *The Crimes of Patriots: A True Tale of Dope, Dirty Money, and the CIA*, Norton, New York, 1987.

Le Goff, Jacques, *The Medieval Imagination*, UCP, Chicago, 1988.

Leiss, William, *The Domination of Nature*, G. Braziller, New York, 1972.

Leopold, Aldo, *A Sand Country Almanac: And Sketches Here and There*, OUP, New York, 1987.

Lewis, C. S., *The Abolition of Man*, London, 1946.

Limerick, Patricia Nelson, *The Legacy of Conquest: The Unbroken Past of the American West*, Norton, New York, 1988.

Lovejoy, A. O., *The Great Chain of Being: A Study in the History of an Idea*, HUP, Cambridge, Massachusetts, 1936.

Marcus, Greil, *Lipstick Traces: A Secret History of the Twentieth Century*, HUP, Cambridge, Massachusetts, 1989.

Marx, Karl, *Capital*, New York, 1967.

Marx, Leo, *The Machine in the Garden: Technology and the Pastoral Ideal in America*, OUP, New York, 1964.

Matthiessen, Peter, *Wildlife in America*, Viking, New York, 1959.

Medawar, P. B., *The Limits of Science*, Harper & Row, New York, 1984.

————, *Pluto's Republic: Incorporating 'The Art of the Soluble' and 'Induction and Intuition in Scientific Thought'*, OUP, New York, 1982.

Medawar, P. B. and J. S. Medawar, *Aristotle to Zoos: A Philosophical Dictionary of Biology*, HUP, Cambridge, Massachusetts, 1983.

317

Merchant, Carolyn, *The Death of Nature: Women, Ecology, and the Scientific Revolution*, Sierra Club Books, San Francisco, 1980.

——, *Ecological Revolutions: Nature, Gender and Science in New England*, UNC Press, Chapel Hill, 1989.

Montgomery, David, *The Fall of the House of Labor: The Workplace, the State and American Labor Activism, 1865–1925*, CUP, New York, 1987.

Passmore, J., *Man's Responsibility for Nature*, Duckworth, London, 1974.

Purver, Margery, *The Royal Society: Concept and Creation*, Routledge & Kegan Paul, London, 1967.

Reisner, Marc, *Cadillac Desert: The American West and Its Disappearing Water*, Viking, New York, 1986.

Shepard, Paul, *Man in the Landscape: A Historic View of the Esthetics of Nature*, New York, 1972.

Smith, Bernard, *European Vision and the South Pacific, 1768–1850*, OUP, Oxford, 1960.

Thompson, E. P., *The Making of the English Working Class*, New York, 1964.

Thomson, J. O., *History of Ancient Geography*, CUP, Cambridge, 1948.

Turner, Frederick, *Beyond Geography: The Western Spirit Against the Wilderness*, Viking, New York, 1980.

——, *Rediscovering America: John Muir in his Time and Ours*, Sierra Club Books, San Francisco, 1987.

White, Lyn, *Medieval Technology and Social Change*, OUP, Oxford, 1962.

Winner, Langdon, *Autonomous Technology: Technics out of Control As a Theme in Political Thought*, MIT Press, Cambridge, Massachusetts, 1977.

——, *The Whale and the Reactor: A Search for Limits in an Age of High Technology*, UCP, Chicago, 1986.

Wolfe, Tom, *The Right Stuff*, Farrar, Strauss and Giroux, New York, 1979.

Worster, Donald, *Nature's Economy: The Roots of Ecology*, Sierra Club Books, San Francisco, 1977.

——, *Rivers of Empire: Water, Aridity and the Growth of the American West*, Pantheon, New York, 1985.

ILLUSTRATION CREDITS

1 Aboriginal language map (approximate only). Reproduced (with modifications) from *Koorie Boogaja*, with permission of the Aborigines Advancement League of Victoria.

2 Marysville, Victoria. Edwin Carton Booth, *Australia Illustrated*, vol. 1, p. 73, The University of Melbourne Library.

3 Mount Laura, Camperdown. Edwin Carton Booth, *Australia Illustrated*, vol. 1, p. 72, The University of Melbourne Library.

4 Concordia Gold Mine. Edwin Carton Booth, *Australia Illustrated*, vol. 1, p. 42, The University of Melbourne Library.

5 The Land Boom—A Saturday's Sale. Australian National University, Archives of Business & Labour, *The Australasian*, 20 October 1888, p. 860.

6 Forest cover changes in Victoria, 1869–1987. Reproduced by permission Department of Conservation and Environment from Woodgate and Black (1988) *Forest Cover Changes in Victoria 1969–1987*.

7 A mallee roller at rest. Australian National University, Archives of Business & Labour, *The Australasian*, 11 June 1910, p. 1473.

8 Subdivision of Stroud, NSW. Australian National University, Archives of Business & Labour. Australian Agricultural Company, 1/Map A53, Negative # 1336.

9 Reclaiming the mallee. From the *Illustrated Australian News*, 1 July 1892. National Library of Australia.

10 Ringbarked trees, King Island, c. 1909. Australian National University, Archives of Business & Labour, *The Australasian*, 26 February 1910, p. 534.

11 Clearing in the Strzelecki Ranges, c. 1900. Courtesy Shire of Alberton, Victoria.

12 Two men in neck chains. Australian Archives (ACT): CRS A1, Item # 1928/10743 (pt).

13 Spread of the rabbit over mainland Australia. From E. Stodart and I. Parer, *Colonisation of Australia by the Rabbit*, CSIRO, 1988.

14 Adaminaby Dam, December 1956. Published with kind permission of the Snowy Mountains Hydro Electric Authority. Negative # 9366.

15 The 'Hi-Ball'. Australian Archives (ACT): CRS A1200/3, Item # L30616.
16 'Men, Money and Markets' immigration poster. Permission of the Department of Immigration, Local Government and Ethnic Affairs and the Australian Archives (ACT): CRS A434, Item # 49/3/21685 (pt).
17 Australia, land of tomorrow. Permission of the Department of Immigration, Local Government and Ethnic Affairs and the Australian Archives (ACT): CRS A434, Item # 49/3/21685 (pt).
18 Rail systems of Australia, 1953. Australian Archives (ACT): CRS A1200/1, Item # L19466.
19 Bulldozer constructing road to Guthega Bridge site, November 1951. Published with kind permission of the Snowy Mountains Hydro Electric Authority. Negative # 1372.
20 Dead forest in salty marshland, WA. Australian Foreign Affairs and Trade Department photograph K7/5/82/23.
21 Opening Ceremony—Tumut Pond Dam, 9 September 1958. Published with kind permission of the Snowy Mountains Hydro Electric Authority. Negative # 12395.
22 Gully erosion. Australian Archives (ACT): CRS A1200/6, Item # L59989.
23 W. H. Spooner at Weipa. Australian Archives (ACT): CRS A1200/1, Item # L26753.
24 Denuded mountains surrounding Queenstown, Tasmania. Australian Foreign Affairs and Trade Department photograph 14/3/72/21.
25–36 British nuclear tests in Australia 1952–57. Various sources cited below:
25 *Hurricane*, 3 October 1952, Monte Bello Islands. Atomic Ex-Servicemen's Association.
26 *Totem One*, 14 October 1953, Emu Field. Atomic Ex-Servicemen's Association.
27 *Totem Two*, 26 October 1953, Emu Field. Atomic Ex-Servicemen's Association.
28 *G1*, 16 May 1956, Monte Bello Islands. Author's collection.
29 *G2*, 19 June 1956, Monte Bello Islands. Australian Archives (ACT): CRS 6456/3, File # R120/95, Photo # P843.
30 *One Tree*, 27 September 1956, Maralinga. Australian Archives (ACT): CRS A6456/3, File # R75.4, Photo # P747.
31 *Marcoo*, 4 October 1956, Maralinga. Australian Archives (ACT): CRS A6456/3, File # R75.4, Photo # P748.
32 *Kite*, 11 October 1956, Maralinga. Australian Archives (ACT): CRS A6456/3, File # R29/239, Photo # P648.
33 *Breakaway*, 22 October 1956, Maralinga. Australian Archives (ACT): CRS A6456/3, File # R75.4, Photo # P750.
34 *Tadje*, 14 September 1957, Maralinga. Atomic Ex-Servicemen's Association.

35 *Biak*, 25 September 1957, Maralinga. Atomic Ex-Servicemen's Association.
36 *Taranaki*, 9 October 1957, Maralinga. Atomic Ex-Servicemen's Association.
37 Say *No* to Uranium Development. Reproduced with permission of the Australian Conservation Foundation from a poster lent by the Canberra and South-East Region Environment Centre.
38 The Federation Tree, August 1990. Author's collection.

Poetry credits

Extract from 'Song of the Future' and 'Clancy of the Overflow' by A.B. Paterson from *The Collected Verse of A.B. Paterson*, Copyright Retusa Pty. Limited, 1921. Reprinted with permission from Collins/Angus & Robertson Publishers.

INDEX